The Research Process

*What's your ne~~xt step?~~ ...
guide to help y~~...~~*

g the Conversation

II Working with Sources

III Collecting Information

IV Writing Your Document

V Documenting Sources

The Bedford
RESEARCHER

THIRD EDITION

The Bedford
RESEARCHER

Mike Palmquist

Colorado State University

Bedford/St. Martin's   Boston ◆ New York

For Bedford/St. Martin's
Developmental Editor: Rachel Goldberg
Production Editor: Kerri A. Cardone
Senior Production Supervisor: Joe Ford
Marketing Manager: Casey Carroll
Editorial Assistant: Sarah Guariglia
Copyeditor: Steven M. Patterson
Text Design: Claire Seng-Niemoeller
Cover Design and Art: Billy Boardman
Composition: TexTech International
Printing and Binding: RR Donnelley and Sons

President: Joan E. Feinberg
Editorial Director: Denise B. Wydra
Editor in Chief: Karen S. Henry
Director of Marketing: Karen R. Soeltz
Director of Editing, Design, and Production: Marcia Cohen
Assistant Director of Editing, Design and Production: Elise S. Kaiser
Managing Editor: Elizabeth M. Schaaf

Library of Congress Control Number: 2008932704

Manufactured in the United States of America.

3   2   1   0

f   e   d   c   b

For information, write: Bedford/St. Martin's, 75 Arlington Street, Boston, MA 02116 (617-399-4000)

ISBN-10:   0–312–66775–2
ISBN-13:   978–0–312–66775–7

Acknowledgments

Figure 1.3: Google College Admissions Advance Search Database. © 2008 Google.
Figure 2.1: Colorado State University Libraries catalog screenshot. © 2008 Colorado State University Library. Reprinted with the permission of Colorado State University Libraries.
Figure 2.3: EBSCOHost Research Databases. © EBSCO Publishing, Inc. Reprinted with the permission of EBSCO Industries, Inc. All rights reserved.
Figure 2.4: ASK.com screen site. © 2008 Ask.com. Used with permission of IAC/Search & Media. All Rights Reserved.
Figure 2.5: DMOZ "Open directory project" screenshot. Copyright © 1998–2008 Netscape. Used with permission. All Rights Reserved.

Acknowledgments and copyrights are continued at the back of the book on pages 399–400, which constitute an extension of the copyright page. It is a violation of the law to reproduce these selections by any means whatsoever without the written permission of the copyright holder.

Preface for Instructors

Since the first edition of *The Bedford Researcher* was published, the amount of information available online has grown rapidly. *Google* has become a verb. Blogs have emerged as important players in shaping public opinion and disseminating information. Podcasts of lectures are available at iTunes U and at many major universities' Web sites. Databases have become more comprehensive and, increasingly, are offering access to the complete text of the articles they reference. Libraries have responded to these changes by making significant investments in online information resources, including online access to scholarly journals and books.

Research writers, understandably, have struggled to keep up with the rapid pace of change. They recognize that blogs can be relevant sources, but they're uncertain how to find the blogs that best meet their needs. They're familiar with news search sites, such as Google News or Yahoo! News, but they wonder about the credibility of the content they deliver. They use YouTube, instant messaging, and social networking Web sites for personal communication, but they are unsure of the role these tools might play in their research.

With this situation in mind, I began the third edition of *The Bedford Researcher* by revisiting the question that guided my work on the first and second editions: *What significant new challenges face today's research writers?* As before, I found the answers by turning to the work I've done with students in my own classes:

- In today's information-rich environment, learning when and how to locate and use information is vital. Gaining "information literacy" goes far beyond learning simple tips for conducting electronic searches. It means developing a thorough and nuanced understanding of how to identify, obtain, evaluate, and work with information from a variety of sources.

- Choosing the most relevant sources for a research writing project continues to challenge less experienced writers. They are often overwhelmed by the large number of sources produced by their initial searches of library catalogs, databases, and Web sites, and they are unsure of the distinctions among those resources. Helping students develop strategies for refining research questions and identifying relevant search terms is critical to their success. Teaching them to differentiate among resources ensures that they will consider which source types are most relevant to their particular research writing project.

- Managing the sources collected during a research project—whether print, electronic, or field sources—and making sure that each source is cited appropriately remains of central importance.

- The misuse of electronic sources and digital media continues to be a growing concern. Understanding plagiarism and fair use—not just of text but also of images, audio, and video—continues to rank among the most significant challenges facing research writers.

- Finally, the range of documents created by research writers continues to expand. Multimodal documents, for example, allow writers to take advantage of new opportunities for conveying information by incorporating audio, video, and other digital media. Understanding how to choose and work within an appropriate genre to present information, ideas, and arguments clearly and effectively is crucial for today's research writers.

These challenges strongly shaped my work on this new edition of *The Bedford Researcher*. But, as in the previous editions, I continued to focus on the enduring challenges that face writers who work with sources: considering purpose and audience, taking notes carefully and accurately, developing clear and appropriate thesis statements, integrating information from sources into a draft, and revising and editing efficiently and effectively. This book addresses the rapidly changing conditions under which research writers work without sacrificing its strong foundation of proven strategies for conducting research, working with sources, and drafting, revising, and editing.

Like the previous editions, this edition of *The Bedford Researcher* offers writers and teachers a rich set of instructional technology resources on its companion Web site, bedfordresearcher.com. These tools are relevant, easy to use, and focused on the needs of research writers.

FEATURES

The Bedford Researcher is based on the premise that the decisions good research writers make are shaped primarily by rhetorical concerns—the writer's purposes and interests, the readers' needs, interests, values, and beliefs, the setting in which a document is written and read, and the requirements and limitations associated with an assignment. To illustrate this premise, the book presents research writing as a process of choosing, learning about, and contributing to a conversation among readers and writers.

Complete Coverage of the Research Writing Process   As in the previous editions, the text is divided into five parts. The first four parts correspond to the stages of an idealized research writing process, although the book stresses the recursive nature of research writing. The fifth part focuses on documentation systems. Part One, Joining the Conversation, introduces the concept of research writing as a social act. It helps students understand that research writing involves exploring conversations among writers and readers, narrowing their focus to a single conversation, and developing a research question to guide their inquiry into that conversation. Part Two, Working with Sources, establishes the importance of critical reading strategies, source evaluation, note taking, and avoiding plagiarism. Part Three, Collecting Information, helps students create a research plan and search for information using print resources, electronic resources, and field research methods. Part Four, Writing Your Document, guides students as they develop their thesis, organize their information and ideas, frame their argument, develop an outline, draft their document, integrate source material, revise and edit their drafts, and design their document. Finally, Part Five, Documenting Sources, provides comprehensive and up-to-date chapters on MLA, APA, *Chicago*, and CSE styles.

Engaging and Useful Apparatus   The book is designed so that students can find information easily and work competently through each stage of their projects. Each chapter is structured around a set of *Key Questions* that enables students to find information quickly and ends with *Quick Reference* boxes to stress the chapter's main points. The *What's My Purpose?* boxes throughout the text remind students to constantly reflect upon—and reconsider—their writing situation. The design employs clear and accessible illustrations, annotations, checklists, activities, and documentation guidelines—the parts of the text students will return to again and again as they write.

A Conversational, Student-Friendly Tone   *The Bedford Researcher* is written in an accessible, easy-to-follow style that treats students with respect. It helps students gain confidence in their ability to write well, conduct research effectively, and think critically. Clear, relevant examples address students' questions about research writing by concretely illustrating writing, research, and critical reading strategies.

Detailed Case Studies of Real Student Researchers   Six featured writers, real students who undertook a variety of research writing projects, including traditional research essays, Web sites, and multimodal documents, provide accessible models for your students as they conduct their own research and draft their own documents.

Emphasis on Project Management   Our surveys of teachers about parts of the research process students find most difficult tell us that managing a research project ranks first. To that end, numerous prompts throughout the text help keep research writers on track. In Chapter 1, for example, students learn how to create and use a research log and a project timeline to plan and manage their work. Throughout the book, *My Research Project* activities provide comprehensive support for project management.

A Cross-curricular Companion   Because students need a research text suitable for a variety of academic purposes, *The Bedford Researcher* and its companion Web site feature examples and models that span the disciplines, providing research writing help for composition courses and beyond. Part Five provides guidelines for writing papers and detailed citation models for a multitude of source types in MLA style, APA style, *Chicago* style, and CSE style. Each style is further illustrated on *The Bedford Researcher* Web site through sample documents created by the featured writers.

NEW TO THIS EDITION

This edition of *The Bedford Researcher* features the following updates:

Stronger Attention to Developing Arguments   The *Framing My Argument* feature throughout the book illustrates how to construct an argument one step at a time and how to use evidence skillfully. A new argumentative student essay on a provocative topic, U.S. responses to coca farming in South America, shows how to put these argumentation strategies to work.

New Focus on Information Literacy   Information literacy sidebars in each chapter provide more than just tips for carrying out electronic searches. These features help students learn to navigate the complexities of finding, evaluating, and integrating information from print, electronic, and field sources.

New Writing with Style Chapter   This edition devotes an entire chapter to concrete strategies for drafting, revising, and developing a clear and effective style — a perennial concern for instructors and students.

A Revised Organization Reflects the Way Instructors Actually Use this Book   Recognizing the way you teach your courses, I've reorganized the text and moved the Working with Sources section earlier. Students now learn how to read critically, take notes, and evaluate sources *before* they begin to collect information, so they don't waste time on sources that won't be useful to their argument.

Expanded Discussion of Avoiding Plagiarism   In the revised chapter on avoiding plagiarism, I've debunked students' top reasons for plagiarizing and illustrate how they don't make sense in the long run. Covering plagiarism earlier helps students avoid it right from the start.

Extensive and Up-To-Date Coverage of Electronic Sources and Tools   The text offers relevant, hands-on advice for searching for and evaluating audio, video, and other digital sources; saving and organizing sources with personal and social bookmarking sites and Web capture tools; integrating images, audio, and video into multimodal documents; and revising and editing with electronic tools.

VALUABLE ONLINE RESOURCES

The Bedford Researcher **Web site** (**bedfordresearcher.com**) provides an extensive collection of free and premium materials, including tools and content designed specifically for the needs of research writers:

Free Resources:

New Interactive Research and Writing Exercises   These exercises extend the tutorials in the book with step-by-step prompts for the toughest research writing tasks in each chapter.

Research Project Activities   Each *My Research Project* activity in the text can be downloaded or printed from the companion Web site, for individual or class work.

Featured Student Writer Portfolios   Readers can view notes, outlines, completed activities, rough drafts, and final research documents of the six student writers featured in the book. They can also view edited transcripts of interviews in which the featured writers discuss their research writing processes.

Research Writing "How-To" Guides   These guides offer specific advice for using online library catalogs, databases, Web search sites and directories, and other electronic resources. They also offer up-to-date support for designing documents and creating Web sites.

Annotated Links for Research Writing   The companion Web site gives students access to a wealth of Web-based resources for research writing and document design. Diana Hacker's *Research and Documentation Online* offers an extensive list of databases and indexes, Web resources, and reference books for more than thirty disciplines.

Bibliography Tools   Straightforward, easy-to-use bibliography tools help students evaluate and keep track of sources, and create an annotated bibliography in MLA, APA, *Chicago,* or CSE style.

Teaching with THE BEDFORD RESEARCHER   The instructor's manual can be downloaded from **bedfordresearcher.com**. In addition to chapter overviews and teaching goals and tips, the manual directs you to specific resources for each skill that you'll teach (for example, refining a thesis statement or integrating sources) and illustrates how the book's content aligns with content on the companion Web site.

Premium Resources:

The Bedford Researcher e-Book   With this premium e-Book, students can navigate quickly through the research process and find the help they need right away. They can customize their books by highlighting key sections, bookmarking the pages they refer to most, adding notes, and more.

CompClass with THE BEDFORD RESEARCHER *e-Book*   An online course space designed specifically for composition courses, *CompClass* is innovative and easy to use. You can customize the site and add your own course material, tailoring it to the needs of your students.

New Premium Video Research Tutorials   These engaging video tutorials illustrate each research task and guide students through a hands-on activity, from refining a research question to performing an electronic search.

Other Premium Resources for Teaching Research

i·cite visualizing sources   Do your students need help working with sources? This research and documentation CD-ROM brings research to life with an animated introduction and four interactive tutorials that explore fundamental concepts about working with sources. Students get concrete practice recognizing, evaluating, incorporating, and citing a wide range of real-life sources from across the disciplines.

i·claim visualizing argument   Do your students need help writing persuasively or supporting their arguments? With six tutorials on the fundamental qualities good arguments share, this student-friendly CD-ROM also provides an illustrated glossary defining 50 key terms from argument theory and classical rhetoric and includes a visual index providing access to more than 70 multimedia arguments.

Bedford/St. Martin's Research Pack   This collection includes the *i·cite visualizing sources* CD-ROM, two laminated quick-reference cards for using MLA and APA style, with brief checklists and model citations, and a comprehensive suite of online research resources.

Re:Writing Plus   All of Bedford/St. Martin's premium digital content for composition, including our new premium video research tutorials, hundreds of model documents, and the first ever peer review game, gathered into one online library.

To order any of these ancillaries, please contact your Bedford/St. Martin's sales representative, email sales support (sales_support@bfwpub.com), or visit our Web site at **bedfordstmartins.com**. Activation codes are required for the e-book, *CompClass,* and *Re:Writing Plus.* Codes can be purchases separately or packaged with the print book at a significant discount.

The Bedford Researcher e-Book   To order *The Bedford Researcher* packaged free with e-book, use ISBN-10: 0-312-55537-7 or ISBN-13: 978-0-312-55537-5.

i·cite visualizing sources   To order *The Bedford Researcher* packaged free with *i·cite,* use ISBN-10: 0-312-55525-3 or ISBN-13: 978-0-312-55525-2.

i·claim visualizing argument   To order *The Bedford Researcher* packaged free with *i·claim,* use ISBN-10: 0-312-55526-1 or ISBN-13: 978-0-312-55526-9.

Bedford/St. Martin's Research Pack   To order *The Bedford Researcher* packaged free with the Research Pack, use ISBN-10: 0-312-55527-X or ISBN-13: 978-0-312-55527-6.

CompClass with THE BEDFORD RESEARCHER e-Book To order an access card for *CompClass with* THE BEDFORD RESEARCHER *e-Book*, use ISBN-10: 0-312-55541-5 or ISBN-13: 978-0-312-55541-2.

Re:Writing Plus To order *The Bedford Researcher* with an access card for *Re:Writing Plus,* use ISBN-10: 0-312-55628-4 or ISBN-13: 978-0-312-55628-0.

ACKNOWLEDGMENTS

Once again, I offer my thanks to my family—my wife Jessica, my daughter Ellen, and my son Reid—for their support as I worked on this edition of *The Bedford Researcher.* I continue to be grateful for the guidance and support I received from David Kaufer, Chris Neuwirth, and Richard Young, who have helped me, in graduate school and in the many years since, to think critically and carefully about the relationships among rhetoric, pedagogy, and technology. I offer my thanks as well to my colleagues Kate Kiefer, Jill Salahub, Stephen Reid, Will Hochman, Lynda Haas, Carrie Lamanna, and Nick Carbone for their willingness to share ideas and offer support as I worked on this book. I also thank Barbara D'Angelo for her insights into information literacy, and Myleah Kerns, who updated the instructor's manual.

I am also grateful for the opportunity to work with reviewers who provided thoughtful advice and suggestions for revising this book: Cora Agatucci, Central Oregon Community College; James Allen, College of DuPage; Gillian F. Andersen, Eastern New Mexico University; [Anonymous], Emerson College; Gwen S. Argersinger, Mesa Community College at Red Mountain; Susan Ariew, University of South Florida; Abdallah Boumarate, Valencia Community College; Amy Braziller, Red Rocks Community College; Shelley Brulotte, College of Southern Idaho; Robin Casady, Eastern New Mexico University; Teri Ferguson, Oklahoma State University-Oklahoma City; Amy Goodloe, University of Colorado-Boulder; Kevin D. Hunt, Goldey–Beacom College; Jennifer Jett, Bakersfield College; John Kivari, Erie Community College; Robert Jeremy Lespi, University of Alabama; S. E. Lewis, Sienna Heights University; Karen Powers Liebhaber, Black River Technical College; Vickie C. Machen, Texas A&M University–Corpus Christi; Danielle Melvin, East Carolina University; Kathleen Mollick, Tarleton State University; Louise Levine Montalvo, The College of Staten Island; Elizabeth J. Nesbitt, Ball State University; Larry Silverman, Seattle Central Community College; Kimberly Skeen, College of Southern Idaho; Michael Sohan, University of Louisville; Richard Urdiales, Metropolitan Community College–Blue River; Amy Vidali, University of Colorado at Denver; and Robbin Zeff, George Washington University. Their reactions, observations, and suggestions led to many of the improvements in this edition.

I have once again been impressed by the extraordinary support offered by the editors at Bedford/St. Martin's. Development editor Rachel Goldberg's insightful advice and careful edits kept me grounded as we wrestled with how best to address the challenges of supporting research writers in a rapidly changing technological environment. Nick Carbone's able leadership of the new media group—along with his good humor, patience, and generosity of spirit—made the revisions of the Web site pleasant and rewarding. Dan Schwartz's ideas about how to support students as they used the site and his hard work to put those ideas into practice significantly enhanced its quality. I am indebted to Kerri Cardone, who has done a superb job directing the production of the book, and Steven M. Patterson, who copyedited the manuscript. I am grateful, once again, for the extraordinary design work of Claire Seng-Niemoeller, and for the meticulous care with which Sara Eaton Gaunt and Barbara Flanagan updated the documentation models. My thanks are offered as well to editor in chief Karen Henry for her good advice and able leadership of the editorial team. And I am grateful for the contributions and good ideas of editorial assistant Sarah Guariglia.

I offer my thanks once again to Rory Baruth, regional sales manager for Bedford, Freeman, and Worth Publishers, who introduced me to the editors at Bedford/St. Martin's many years ago and who has continued to support and offer suggestions for improving *The Bedford Researcher*. I am grateful as well to Joan Feinberg, Denise Wydra, and Leasa Burton for their support of *The Bedford Researcher* and for their thoughtful suggestions about the directions this new edition might take.

Finally, I offer my thanks to the six student writers who shared their work, their time, and their insights into their research writing processes with the readers of this book: Alexis Alvarez, Patrick Crossland, Kevin Fahey, Pete Jacquez, Elizabeth Leontiev, and Chris Norris. As I worked on this edition, their work served as a constant reminder that research writing is a process of continuous discovery and reflection.

Mike Palmquist
Colorado State University

Introduction for Writers

You live in the information age. You surf the Web, text your friends, download videos and mp3s, use email, send instant messages, carry a mobile phone, watch television, read magazines and newspapers, listen to podcasts, view advertisements, attend public events, and meet and talk with others. Understanding how to work with information is among the most important writing skills you can have. In fact, most of the writing that you'll do in your lifetime—in college courses or for a career or community project—requires this skill. Take as examples the following types of documents—all of which require a writer to use information from sources:

- college research essays
- informative Web sites
- feature articles in a newspaper or magazine
- product brochures or promotional literature
- market research analysis to help start a new business or launch a new product
- proposals to a school board or community group
- PowerPoint presentations at business meetings
- letters of complaint about a product or service
- restaurant reviews or travel guides

Because such a wide range of documents relies heavily on a writer's ability to work with information, *The Bedford Researcher* is not so much about research papers as about research writing. What I hope you'll take from this text is a way of thinking about how to conduct research and write a document based on the sources of information you find.

The primary goals of *The Bedford Researcher* are to help you learn how to:

- choose and learn about a topic
- read critically, evaluate, and take notes
- develop a research question and thesis statement
- collect and manage information
- develop, write, revise, and design an effective document
- document sources of information

Meeting these goals requires thinking about research writing in a new way. Research writing is more than simply searching for and reporting information;

it is a process of inquiry—of asking and responding to key questions. Instead of thinking of research writing as an isolated activity, think of it as a social act—a conversation in which writers and readers exchange information and ideas about a topic.

The research writing process you'll follow in this book consists of five main activities, which correspond to the five parts of this book:

Part I: Joining the Conversation ▶	Chapters 1, 2, and 3 focus on getting started, exploring and narrowing your topic, and developing your research question and proposal.
Part II: Working with Sources ▶	Chapters 4 through 7 address reading critically, evaluating sources, taking notes, and avoiding plagiarism
Part III: Collecting Information ▶	Chapters 8 through 12 discuss planning your search for information; searching with electronic resources, print resources, and field research methods; and managing the information you collect.
Part IV: Writing Your Document ▶	Chapters 13 through 18 focus on developing, supporting, and organizing your ideas; drafting; integrating sources; writing with style; and revising, editing, and designing your document.
Part V: Documenting Sources ▶	Chapters 19 through 23 discuss the reasons for documenting sources and provide detailed guidance on four of the most commonly used documentation systems—MLA, APA, *Chicago*, and CSE.

As you read about these activities and carry them out in your own research project, keep in mind that they reflect a typical writing process—not a step-by-step recipe. Also keep in mind that the writing process seldom follows a straight line from choosing a topic to producing a polished document; most writers move back and forth among writing processes, rethinking their steps and revising their ideas as they work on their writing projects. Whatever your process turns out to be, remember that the order you follow is far less important than adapting these processes to the needs of your particular project.

SUPPORT THROUGHOUT YOUR RESEARCH WRITING PROCESS

The Bedford Researcher offers a wealth of support—in the book and on the companion Web site—to help you complete a research project.

In the Text

The textbook you are holding provides step-by-step guidance for writing research documents. It includes clear descriptions of research writing strategies, examples, activities, documentation guidelines, and model citations.

Color-coded tabs help you find information quickly.

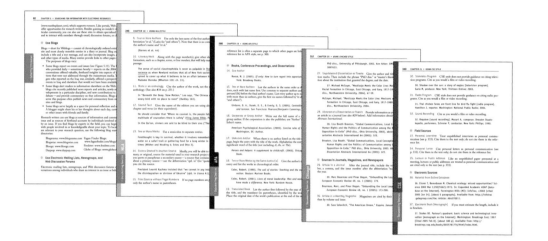

Key Questions begin each chapter and enable you to match your research writing needs to the material in the chapter.

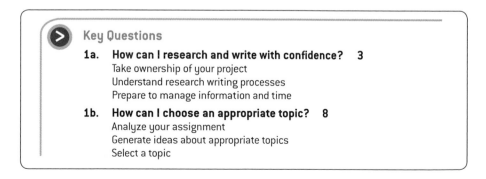

> **Key Questions**
>
> **1a.   How can I research and write with confidence?   3**
> Take ownership of your project
> Understand research writing processes
> Prepare to manage information and time
>
> **1b.   How can I choose an appropriate topic?   8**
> Analyze your assignment
> Generate ideas about appropriate topics
> Select a topic

Checklists offer at-a-glance views of a specific research or writing process.

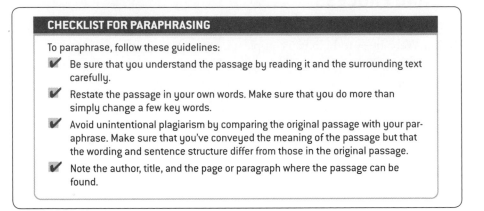

CHECKLIST FOR PARAPHRASING

To paraphrase, follow these guidelines:

- ✔ Be sure that you understand the passage by reading it and the surrounding text carefully.
- ✔ Restate the passage in your own words. Make sure that you do more than simply change a few key words.
- ✔ Avoid unintentional plagiarism by comparing the original passage with your paraphrase. Make sure that you've conveyed the meaning of the passage but that the wording and sentence structure differ from those in the original passage.
- ✔ Note the author, title, and the page or paragraph where the passage can be found.

What's My Purpose? **Boxes** help you consider — and reconsider — your purpose at every stage of the research writing process.

? WHAT'S MY PURPOSE?

Make sure your preliminary thesis statement still fits the purpose of your research writing project and the role (or roles) you've adopted as a research writer. Kevin Fahey, for example, wanted to analyze Ernest Hemingway's characterization of Nick Adams. His preliminary thesis statement, "Nick Adams is a flawed character with whom readers can identify," answered the research question, "How is Nick Adams characterized by Ernest Hemingway?" Nick decided that his preliminary thesis statement was consistent with his purpose (to conduct a literary analysis) and his role (interpreter).

Framing My Argument **Boxes** help you construct your argument one step at a time and use evidence skillfully.

[**FRAMING MY ARGUMENT**]

Refer to Shared Assumptions and Existing Conditions   You can refine your research question by using qualifying words and phrases to narrow its scope, by calling attention to assumptions that have been made by the community of writers and readers who are addressing your issue, or by referring to existing conditions relevant to your issue. Note the difference between these three versions of featured writer Alexis Alvarez's research question:

Original Question:

What should be done about steroid use by adolescent girls involved in competitive sports?

Alternative 1:

Even though we know that widespread drug testing of all athletes, younger and older, is impossible, what should be done about steroid use by adolescent girls involved in competitive sports?

Alternative 2:

Given the lack of knowledge about the health consequence of steroid use among athletes and their parents, what should be done about steroid use by adolescent girls involved in competitive sports?

Information Literacy **Sidebars** offer suggestions and identify opportunities as you find, evaluate, and integrate information from print, electronic, and field sources.

Identify Relevant Databases

To identify databases that might be relevant to the issue you are addressing in your research writing project, review your library's list of databases or consult a reference librarian. Ask yourself the following questions:

Am I Focusing on an Issue that is Likely to Have Been Addressed in Recent News Coverage?   If so, consider searching databases that focus on newspapers and weekly magazines, such as:

- LexisNexis Academic
- ProQuest Newspapers
- Alternative Press Index
- Newspaper Source

Information Literacy

A growing number of databases — often called "full–text" databases — allow you to view the complete text of a source. In some full-text databases, sources are provided in the form of a fully formatted PDF file (a type of file that can be viewed in Adobe's Acrobat Reader). These files provide exact copies of the source as it appeared when it was originally published. In other cases, the text of the source is provided, but the document is formatted in a way that differs from its original publication format, usually either in HTML format or as plain text.

Annotated Examples make it easier for you to learn from the many illustrations and screen shots throughout the text.

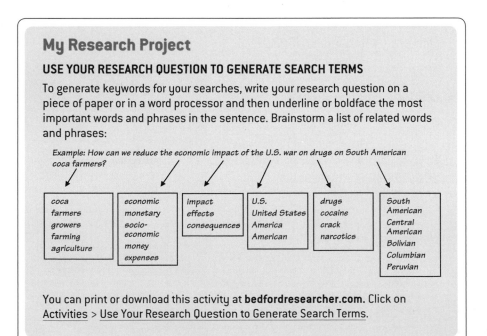

Available search types

Searches can be limited (see p. 119).

Patrick's keyword search

Search tips open in a new window.

My Research Project **Activities** connect what's in the text with your own research writing.

My Research Project

USE YOUR RESEARCH QUESTION TO GENERATE SEARCH TERMS

To generate keywords for your searches, write your research question on a piece of paper or in a word processor and then underline or boldface the most important words and phrases in the sentence. Brainstorm a list of related words and phrases:

Example: How can we reduce the economic impact of the U.S. war on drugs on South American coca farmers?

| coca
farmers
growers
farming
agriculture | economic
monetary
socio-
economic
money
expenses | impact
effects
consequences | U.S.
United States
America
American | drugs
cocaine
crack
narcotics | South
American
Central
American
Bolivian
Columbian
Peruvian |

You can print or download this activity at **bedfordresearcher.com.** Click on Activities > Use Your Research Question to Generate Search Terms.

Tutorials in the book provide you with extra help for important research writing issues, such as developing a research question, evaluating Web sites, and integrating quotations.

TUTORIAL

How do I refine my research question?

The first draft of your research question might be too broad, which can make it difficult for you to focus your research efforts. Refine your initial research question so that you can collect information efficiently.

In this example, Pete Jacquez refines his research question about the use of wind-generated electrical power. He used his research question as he collected and worked with sources, and later, he developed his thesis statement to answer his question.

Preliminary Research Question:
How can we increase our reliance on alternative energy?

1 Refer to shared assumptions and existing conditions by using phrases such as *although it is clear that ..., because we cannot ...,* and *given that studies have shown....*

In light of consumer demand for low-cost electricity, how can we increase our reliance on alternative energy?

2 Identify vague words and phrases, such as *alternative* and *reliance on*, and replace them with more specific words.

In light of consumer demand for low-cost electricity, what steps can U.S. citizens take to encourage local, state, and federal governments to support increased use of wind-generated electrical energy?

3 Using these specific terms, conduct preliminary searches in your library catalog, databases, and on the Web. If you get too many results, narrow your focus even further. (Here, Pete narrows his target audience from *U.S. citizens* to *Colorado citizens* and focuses on passing a statewide referendum.)

In light of consumer demand for low-cost electricity, what steps can Colorado citizens take to pass a statewide referendum requiring increased use of reliance on wind-generated electrical energy?

Review another example and work on narrowing your own research question at **bedfordresearcher.com**. Click on Interactive Exercises.

Quick Reference **Boxes** at the end of every chapter give you a brief overview of steps to take before you move on.

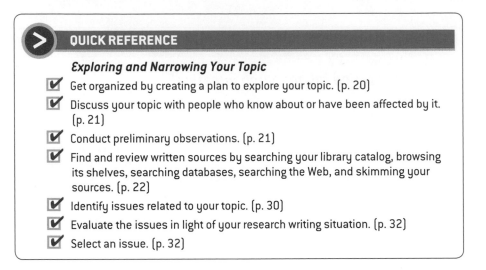

> **QUICK REFERENCE**
>
> ***Exploring and Narrowing Your Topic***
> ☑ Get organized by creating a plan to explore your topic. (p. 20)
> ☑ Discuss your topic with people who know about or have been affected by it. (p. 21)
> ☑ Conduct preliminary observations. (p. 21)
> ☑ Find and review written sources by searching your library catalog, browsing its shelves, searching databases, searching the Web, and skimming your sources. (p. 22)
> ☑ Identify issues related to your topic. (p. 30)
> ☑ Evaluate the issues in light of your research writing situation. (p. 32)
> ☑ Select an issue. (p. 32)

Cross-references to the companion Web site help you extend your knowledge online at **bedfordresearcher.com**.

Online library catalogs give information on the print publications in a library collection. They can also provide information about publications in other media. Online catalogs typically help you locate

> Find other sites that list online library catalogs at bedfordresearcher.com. Click on Links > Resources for Conducting Electronic Searches.

- books
- journals owned by the library (although not individual articles)

On the Web Site

The Bedford Researcher Web site at **bedfordresearcher.com** offers tools and resources to aid you with the most challenging parts of the research writing process.

Bibliography Tools   Use the online tools to evaluate your sources and generate an annotated bibliography in MLA, APA, *Chicago*, or CSE style.

Interactive Exercises   The tutorials in each chapter are expanded online, breaking down the most pressing research-related challenges into manageable steps.

Activities   *My Research Project* activities throughout the text allow you to make progress on your own projects. The activities can be downloaded or printed from the Web site.

Featured Writer Portfolios   Take a tour of the research writing process by following six students featured in the text. View their notes and drafts, and read interviews with the students explaining how they tackled their research writing projects.

Research Writing "How-To" Guides   You'll find advice for electronic searching, designing documents, and using other digital research and writing tools in our easy-to-follow guides.

Annotated Links for Research Writing   Access Web-based resources for research writing and document design, along with an extensive list of specialized research sources for more than thirty disciplines.

Brief Contents

Contents

The Bedford Researcher

I	Joining the Conversation
II	Working with Sources
III	Collecting Information
IV	Writing Your Document
V	Documenting Sources

PART I

Joining the Conversation

1 Getting Started 3

2 Exploring and Narrowing Your Topic 19

3 Developing Your Research Question and Proposal 35

Working on a research writing project is similar to joining a conversation. Before you contribute to the conversation, listen carefully to what others are saying. By reading widely, talking with knowledgeable people, and making firsthand observations, you can gain the knowledge you need to add your voice to the discussion.

In Part I you'll read about how to get started, how to choose an appropriate topic, how to explore and narrow that topic, and how to develop a clearly stated research question and a proposal.

Part I
Joining the Conversation

> | **1** | **Getting Started** |
> | 2 | Exploring and Narrowing Your Topic |
> | 3 | Developing Your Research Question and Proposal |

1

Getting Started

> ## Key Questions
>

Getting started can be the hardest part of a research writing project. You'll likely find yourself staring at a blank computer screen or twirling a pen in your fingers as you ask, "Is this project really necessary?" or "What in the world should I write about?"

This chapter helps you get started. It provides an overview of research writing processes and project management strategies and discusses how to select an appropriate topic.

1a

How can I research and write with confidence?

Even writers who are new to research writing can approach it confidently. All that's needed is a personal investment in your writing project, an understanding of the processes involved in research writing, and a willingness to learn how to work with sources. You can also enhance your confidence about undertaking a research writing project by learning about genre and design, paying attention to changes brought about by new information technologies, and learning how to manage your time.

Take Ownership of Your Project

Confident research writers have a strong personal investment in their research writing project. Sometimes this investment comes naturally. You might be interested in your topic, committed to achieving your purposes as a writer, intrigued by the demands of writing for a particular audience, or looking forward to the challenges of writing a new type of document, such as a Web site or a magazine article. At times, however, you need to create a sense of personal investment by looking for connections between your interests and your writing project. This can be a challenge, particularly when you've been assigned a project that wouldn't normally interest you.

The key to investing yourself in a project you wouldn't normally care about is taking ownership of the project. To take ownership, ask yourself how your project might help you pursue your personal, professional, or academic interests. Think about how the project might help you meet new people or learn new writing or research strategies. Or look for unique challenges associated with a project, such as learning how to develop arguments or use document design techniques more effectively. Your goal is to feel that you have a stake in your research writing project by finding something that appeals to your interests and helps you grow as a researcher and writer.

Understand Research Writing Processes

Research writing involves learning about a topic, drawing conclusions about that topic, and sharing your conclusions with your readers. Many factors affect how you will accomplish your goals. If you are writing an argument, your overall process will be somewhat different than it would be if you are writing to inform your readers. If you are writing about a topic that is new to you, you'll search for and work with sources in a way that differs from how you'd work with information about a topic you know well. Understanding the research writing processes you can draw on will help you accomplish your purposes as a writer and consider the needs, interests, values, and beliefs of your readers. You'll find a description of these processes in Figure 1.1.

Learn How to Work with Sources

Almost every writing project you'll encounter in college and the workplace involves working with information. To bring these projects to a successful conclusion, you'll need to learn how to identify and locate promising sources, and then how to read, evaluate, take notes on, and decide how to use the information, ideas, and arguments you encounter in them. From your initial exploration of a topic to your decisions about how to use quotations to make a point, you'll be engaged with sources—the work of other writers who share your interest in an issue.

Working with sources also includes managing them so that you can easily locate information when you need it. If you've ever forgotten a phone number or misplaced tickets to a concert, you know how frustrating it can be to lose something. It can be just as frustrating to lose your interview notes or forget

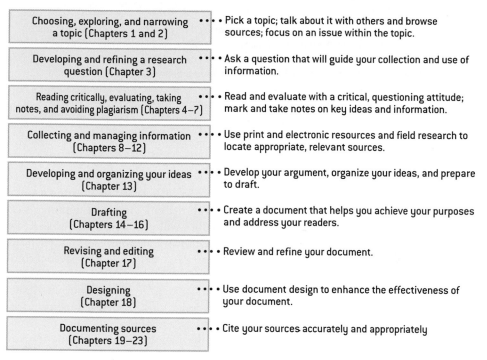

Choosing, exploring, and narrowing a topic (Chapters 1 and 2)	• Pick a topic; talk about it with others and browse sources; focus on an issue within the topic.
Developing and refining a research question (Chapter 3)	• Ask a question that will guide your collection and use of information.
Reading critically, evaluating, taking notes, and avoiding plagiarism (Chapters 4–7)	• Read and evaluate with a critical, questioning attitude; mark and take notes on key ideas and information.
Collecting and managing information (Chapters 8–12)	• Use print and electronic resources and field research to locate appropriate, relevant sources.
Developing and organizing your ideas (Chapter 13)	• Develop your argument, organize your ideas, and prepare to draft.
Drafting (Chapters 14–16)	• Create a document that helps you achieve your purposes and address your readers.
Revising and editing (Chapter 17)	• Review and refine your document.
Designing (Chapter 18)	• Use document design to enhance the effectiveness of your document.
Documenting sources (Chapters 19–23)	• Cite your sources accurately and appropriately

FIGURE 1.1 Research Writing Processes   As you learn about your topic and reflect on your progress, you'll move back and forth among these processes.

where you found a quotation or fact. As you begin your research writing project, decide how you'll keep track of what you'll learn. You might want to start a research log — a place where you can keep the sources you collect and record your thoughts and progress. A research log can take many forms.

- a notebook
- a word processing file or a folder on your computer
- a folder or binder
- a set of note cards
- notes taken on a smart phone or a personal digital assistant (such as a Palm handheld or a Pocket PC)
- a tape recorder or voice recorder

Although it might seem like extra work now, creating a research log as you begin your project will save time in the long run.

My Research Project

CREATE A RESEARCH LOG

Create your research log now so you'll be prepared to face the challenges of planning and carrying out your project.

↓

The *Bedford Researcher* Web site at **bedfordresearcher.com** can help you create your research log. You'll find electronic versions of the "My Research Project" activities in this book and Interactive Exercises, which extend the book's tutorials. You'll also find bibliography tools that allow you to save bibliographic information and brief annotations for your sources as you work on your project. You can use these Web resources to make progress on your research writing project, keep track of sources, and decide how to use sources to develop and present your argument.

Understand Genre and Design

Understanding how information is used in particular types of documents—or *genres*—will improve your ability to present information, ideas, and arguments effectively to your readers. An awareness of genre will affect your decisions about the type of sources you collect and how you use them to accomplish your purposes as a writer. It can help you determine, for example, whether you can best accomplish your goals by writing a letter to the editor, building a Web site, or creating a brochure. An awareness of genre will also affect your decisions about the design of your document. In fact, the characteristic design of a particular type of document—for example, the use of columns, headings, and photographs in a magazine article—can help you distinguish one genre from another. Learning about genre and design will help you confidently anticipate your readers' expectations about the document you are producing.

Be Aware of New Technological Opportunities and Challenges

The technological landscape that shapes the work of research writers has undergone more change in the past twenty-five years than at any other time in recorded history. Not even the innovations in printing technologies that brought about the Gutenberg Bible, despite their undeniably important contributions to the growth of literacy, had such immediate and far-reaching effects on reading, writing, and learning. The emergence of the World Wide Web, the development of blogs and Wikis, the shift toward digital music and video, the growth in wireless access, and the changes to libraries brought about by online library catalogs, databases, digital books, and online journals have significantly changed how research writers locate, manage, and work with sources.

For the foreseeable future, we can expect even more changes in how we access and work with information. Five years ago, who would have thought that a telephone could help us browse the Web and take notes on sources? Yet the latest smart phones not only connect us to the Web, they allow us to listen to music at the same time—and take photos, schedule appointments, and record voice memos. What will the next year bring? And how will it affect our work as writers?

Information Literacy
You can increase your ability to write with confidence by paying attention to the choices you make as you search for and use information. Throughout this book, you'll find Information Literacy callouts that indicate an important opportunity or challenge associated with information and information technology. The advice you find will help you improve your ability to work with technology, and as a result will help you become a better writer.

Prepare to Manage Your Time

Time management should be a high priority as you begin your research writing project. If you don't schedule your time well, for example, you might spend far too much time collecting information and far too little working with it.

As you begin thinking about your research writing project, consider creating a project timeline. A timeline can help you identify important milestones in your project and determine when you need to meet them.

My Research Project

CREATE A PROJECT TIMELINE

In your research log, start a project timeline like the one shown here. The steps in your process might be slightly different, but most research writing projects follow this general process. As you create your timeline, keep in mind any specific requirements of your assignment, such as handing in a first draft, revised drafts, and so on.

PROJECT TIMELINE		
ACTIVITY	**START DATE**	**COMPLETION DATE**
Select your topic		
Explore your topic		
Narrow your topic		
Develop your research question		
Read and evaluate information		
Take notes		
Plan your search for information		
Collect information		
Organize your information		
Develop your thesis statement		
Identify supporting points, reasoning, and evidence		
Organize your document		
Write the first draft of your document		
Review and revise your first draft		
Write and revise additional drafts		
Edit your draft		
Design your document		
Finalize in-text and end-of-text citations		
Publish and submit your document		

You can download or print this activity at **bedfordresearcher.com**. Click on Activities > Create a Project Timeline.

FEATURED WRITERS

Discussions throughout this book are illustrated by six featured writers — real students who crafted a variety of research projects, including traditional essays, Web sites, and feature articles. You can learn from these real-life examples as you plan and conduct your own research, and draft and revise your own document.

Alexis Alvarez • Writing about the Impact of Competitive Sports on Adolescent Girls
Alexis wrote a research essay about the effects competitive sports can have on adolescent girls. She explored the general topic of competitive sports and women before narrowing her topic to the use of steroids by female teenaged athletes. You can read her essay on p. 333.

Patrick Crossland • Writing an Informative Research Paper about College Admissions Standards
Patrick wrote a research essay about college admissions standards. Throughout the semester, Patrick worked in a group with four classmates. Although each student wrote his or her own essay, the students shared ideas and sources. You can read his essay on p. 363.

Kevin Fahey • Writing an Analytic Research Essay about Ernest Hemingway's Characterization of Nick Adams
Kevin wrote a research essay about Ernest Hemingway's description and development of Nick Adams, the character Hemingway scholars agree most closely resembles Hemingway himself.

Pete Jacquez • Writing about the Benefits of Wind Power
Pete created a Web site about the benefits of wind-generated electrical power. His site provides both information about wind power and an argument in favor of increasing reliance on wind power.

Elizabeth Leontiev • Writing about the Impact of the U.S. War on Drugs on Coca Farmers in South America
Elizabeth wrote an argumentative research essay for her composition course. She explored the general topic of the war on drugs and then joined a conversation about the effects of U.S. efforts to eradicate coca farming in South America. You can read her research essay on p. 317.

Chris Norris • Writing a Multimodal Essay about Metal Music
Chris wrote a multimodal essay — an essay created in PowerPoint that used text, images, audio, and video to convey his argument — about the resurgence in popularity of metal music. Chris conducted research into the history of metal music, interviewed a local metal band, and created a complex and engaging essay that has to be seen (and heard) to be fully appreciated.

You can follow the featured writers' research writing process by visiting the *Bedford Researcher* Web site at **bedfordresearcher.com** and clicking on Featured Writers. Here you'll find interviews in which the writers discuss their work, and you can read their assignments, the notes they took as they worked on their projects, and drafts of their documents.

1b

How can I choose an appropriate topic?

In the most general sense, your topic is what you will research and write about—it is the foundation on which your research writing project is built. An appropriate topic, however, is much more than a simple subject heading in an almanac or encyclopedia. It is a subject of debate, discussion, and discovery.

Thinking of your topic as a topic of conversation is critical to your success as a research writer. Research writing goes beyond merely locating and reporting information. Instead, it is an ongoing process of inquiry in which you must consider your purposes, your readers, and the conventions associated with the type of document you plan to write.

Although locating a topic is as easy as visiting your library, reading the newspaper, or browsing the Web, choosing a topic that is well suited to your research writing project requires additional work. It involves reflecting on your assignment, your interests, and your readers.

To choose a suitable topic, analyze your assignment, generate ideas about appropriate topics, and consider the level of interest you and your readers might have in each topic.

Step 1: Analyze Your Assignment

Research writers in academic and professional settings usually work in response to an assignment. You might be given general guidelines, such as "choose a topic in your major"; you might be asked to choose a topic within a general subject area, such as race relations; or you might be given complete freedom in your choice of topic.

Be aware, however, that no matter how much freedom you have, your assignment will provide important clues about what your instructor and your other readers will expect. To analyze your assignment, ask yourself the following questions about your research writing situation.

? WHAT'S MY PURPOSE?

Every writer has a purpose, or reason, for writing. In fact, most writers have multiple purposes. If you are writing a research project for a class, your purposes might include completing the assignment as required, learning something new, improving your writing skills, convincing others to adopt your point of view about an issue, and getting a good grade. If you are an employee working on a project status report, your purposes might include conveying key information to your superiors, performing well enough to earn a promotion, and gaining valuable experience in project management. Whatever your purposes for conducting a research project, your topic should help you accomplish them.

"What's My Purpose?" boxes like this one, located throughout this book, will help you consider and reconsider your purpose throughout your research writing process.

Who Are My Readers and Why Would They Read My Document?   Your assignment might identify your readers, or audience, for you. If you are writing a research project for a class, one of your most important readers will be your instructor. You are also likely to have additional readers, such as your classmates, people who have a professional or personal interest in your topic, or, if your project will be published in print or online, the readers of a particular newspaper, magazine, or Web site. If you are writing in a business or professional setting, your readers might include supervisors, customers, or other people associated with the organization. In some cases, you might be asked to define your own audience. As you consider possible topics, ask yourself which subjects these readers would be most interested in learning about. Featured writer Kevin Fahey, for example, would probably not have written about the literature of Ernest Hemingway if his target audience had been the readers of a magazine such as *PC World* or *Street Rod*.

Regardless of who your readers are, remember that they aren't empty vessels waiting to be filled with information. They will have their own purposes for reading your document. If the topic you select doesn't fit those purposes, they're likely to stop reading.

What Will Influence Me and What Will Influence My Readers?   Research writers aren't mindless robots who churn through sources and create documents without emotion or conviction—or at least they shouldn't be. Your topic should interest you. An appropriate topic will keep you motivated as you carry out the work needed to complete your research project successfully. Your project should also be your own, even if it's been assigned to you. One of the most important things you can do as a research writer is to make a personal connection with the topic. To make that connection, look for topics that can help you pursue your personal, professional, and academic interests.

Readers are influenced by their interest in a particular topic, their knowledge of the topic, and their values and beliefs. If your readers have no interest in your topic, know little about it, or are offended by it, you aren't likely to meet with much success.

What Type of Document Am I Writing?   Assignments often specify the type of document—or *genre*—you will be writing. You might be asked to write essays, reports, or Web sites. You might be asked to write articles, opinion columns, letters to the editor, multimedia presentations, brochures, or flyers. The genre of your document will have an impact on the kinds of topics you choose. For example, consider the differences among the topics addressed in articles in news magazines such as *TIME* and *Newsweek*, the topics addressed in scholarly journals in biology, and the topics addressed on Web sites published by the U.S. Department of Education. Genre will also affect your decisions about the design of your document. To better understand the relationships among genre, design, and topic, review the research essay written by featured writer Alexis Alvarez, the Web site developed by featured writer Pete Jacquez, and the multimodal

TUTORIAL

How do I analyze the audience for a research writing assignment?

Learn about your readers by looking for clues about their needs, interests, and expectations.

COCC150: College Composition Portfolio 3: Engaging in a Public Issue
Due Date: May 2nd at the beginning of class

1 Analyze the assignment's purpose for clues about your audience.

2 Look for terms such as *reader* and *audience*. Then examine the text near those terms for clues about your readers' expectations.

3 Identify clues about the assignment's genre; look for terms such as *essay, report, argument, article*, or *Web site*.

In this essay, you will write a public response — an article or essay directed to a specific publication — for readers who are interested in the issue you analyzed in your last portfolio. To accomplish this goal, you will: (1) assess the writing situation surrounding the issue; (2) collect information from a variety of sources, including written texts, personal experience, and, if appropriate, field research; (3) evaluate your sources to choose those that best support your argument; and (4) make a sufficiently narrow argumentative claim and support that claim with sound reasoning and evidence.

You should address your article or essay to readers of a publication that has published work about your issue. You will need to analyze the publication, its readers (specifically, their needs, interests, experiences, assumptions, and values), and the writing situation that has shaped discourse about this issue. In general, your audience is likely to expect you to thoroughly explain the points you are making and to support your argument using appropriate forms of evidence. In addition, it is likely that your audience will expect you to use a reasonable tone, to respect your readers and sources, and to avoid slang. Your readers are also likely to expect you to acknowledge and cite your sources in a manner consistent with other sources published by your target publication.

Review another example and work on analyzing your own research writing assignment at **bedfordresearcher.com**. Click on Interactive Exercises.

essay written by featured writer Chris Norris. As you reflect on potential topics for your research writing project, keep in mind the type of document specified in your assignment.

What Role Will I Adopt Toward My Readers?   A role is a way of relating to your readers. The roles you take on will reflect your purpose, your understanding of your readers, and the type of document you plan to write. If you hope to convince or persuade your readers, for example, you would take on the role of an advocate. Advocates are likely to write documents such as argumentative essays, blogs, opinion columns, editorials, funding proposals, and sales plans. If you hope to help your readers understand the significance of a particular work of art or to understand the workings of a complex organization such as the stock market, you would take on the role of interpreter. As you consider which topics might interest you, think about how you plan to relate to your readers. Some topics will be more appropriate for an assignment that asks you to interpret an object, event, or process to your readers, while others will be more appropriate for assignments that ask you to inform or persuade or solve problems. You can read more about roles on p. 36.

What Will Affect My Ability to Work on This Project?   The requirements of your assignment, the limitations you will face as you work, and the opportunities you can capitalize upon will affect your ability to work on your research project.

Requirements and Limitations   If you are writing your research project for a class, examine the requirements of your assignment:

- the type of document — or *genre*
- the required length or page count
- the project due date
- the number and type of sources you can use (electronic, print, and field)
- any suggested or required resources, such as a library catalog or database
- specific requirements about the organization and structure of your document (a title page, introduction, body, conclusion, works cited list, and so on)
- expected documentation format (such as MLA, APA, *Chicago*, or CSE)
- any intermediate reports or activities due before you turn in the final project document (such as thesis statements, notes, outlines, and rough drafts)

You might also face limitations, such as lack of access to information or lack of time to work.

Determining your requirements and limitations will help you weigh the potential drawbacks of a topic. You might find that you need to narrow the scope of your topic significantly given your time and page limit.

Opportunities   Sometimes writers get so wrapped up in the requirements and limitations of the assignment that they overlook their opportunities. As you think about your topic, ask yourself whether you can take advantage of opportunities such as

- access to a specialized or particularly good library
- personal experience with and knowledge about a topic
- access to people who are experts on a topic

For example, Alexis Alvarez thought about her personal experiences and those of her friends before deciding to focus on the impact of competitive sports programs on adolescent girls.

Step 2: Generate Ideas about Appropriate Topics

By now you might have some ideas of topics that interest you and that fit your research writing situation. Your next step is to think more carefully about potential topics by using prewriting activities such as brainstorming, freewriting, looping, and clustering. You can use these activities to generate possible topics and narrow your focus from broad, general topics to those that would be more appropriate for a research project.

Brainstorming   Brainstorming involves listing ideas as they occur to you. This list should not consist of complete sentences—in fact, brainstorming lists are meant to record the many ideas that come into your head as you think of them. Brainstorming is most successful when you avoid censoring yourself. Although you'll end up using only a few of the ideas you generate during brainstorming, don't worry until later about weeding out the useful ideas from the less promising ones.

Brainstorming sessions are usually conducted in response to a specific question. Featured writer Patrick Crossland generated the following list in response to the question, "What interests me personally about this project?"

how people decide they like colleges

who goes to which colleges? Breakdown by academic ability, income, social class, race?

how colleges select students

what colleges look for in students

secret standards used by colleges?

Freewriting   When freewriting, you write full sentences quickly, without stopping and—most important—without editing what you write. You might want to start with one of the ideas you generated in your brainstorming activity, or you can begin your freewriting session with a phrase such as "I am interested in my topic because. . . ." After brainstorming about the general topic of college admissions, Patrick Crossland focused his freewriting on his readers' purposes and interest. The following is an excerpt from Patrick's freewriting:

> *People love stats. My readers may want to know about the statistics of who's getting into what colleges and why. My readers may want to use my info as a source for their own writing or thinking about the subject—they may want to contest/agree with my stand and viewpoints about how students are admitted to college—may even think they know how schools go about the process, like using SAT scores and activities and sometimes race.*

Patrick did not edit his work or worry about spelling, grammar, or style.

Some writers set a timer and freewrite for five, ten, or fifteen minutes; others set a goal of a certain number of pages and keep writing until they have met that goal. (Hint: If you find it difficult to write without editing, try blindwriting—freewriting on a computer with the monitor turned off.)

Looping   Looping is an alternative form of freewriting. During a looping session, you write for a set amount of time (say five minutes) and then read what you've written. As you read, identify one key idea in what you've written and then write for five minutes with the new key idea as your starting point. Patrick Crossland, for example, wrote in response to a sentence he had generated during freewriting, "My readers may want to know about the statistics of who's getting into what colleges and why."

> *My readers will be both my professor, who has already gone through college, and my fellow students, who may be looking to transfer to other colleges or apply to graduate schools someday—what aspect of college admissions will all of these readers be interested in?*

Clustering   Clustering involves presenting your ideas about a potential topic in graphical form. Clustering can help you gain a different perspective on a topic by helping you map out the relationships among your ideas. It can also help you generate new ideas. Patrick Crossland used clustering to map out his ideas and further narrow his topic (see Figure 1.2).

When you have completed your brainstorming, freewriting, looping, and clustering activities, review what you've written. You'll most likely find that these prewriting techniques have generated a useful list of ideas for a topic.

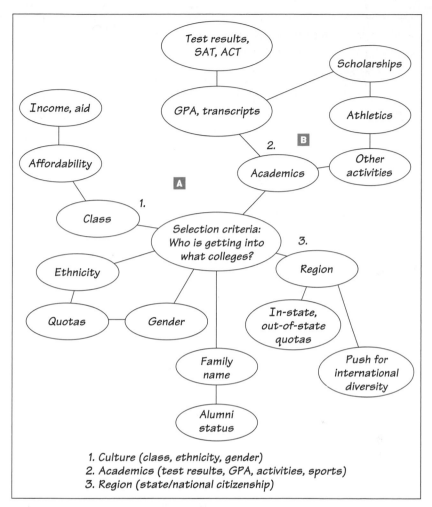

FIGURE 1.2 A Cluster of Ideas Created by Patrick Crossland

A Patrick listed a central idea and three key areas to explore.

B Key areas are also linked to related ideas.

My Research Project

GENERATE IDEAS ABOUT A TOPIC

In your research log, use brainstorming, freewriting, looping, and clustering to generate ideas for a topic.

Brainstorm responses to the following questions.

• What do I want to accomplish with this project?

• What interests me personally about this project?

- What interests me academically about this project?
- Who are my readers?
- What topics do my readers need to read about?
- What topics would my readers like to read about?

Freewrite in response to one of the following prompts, replacing the X's with the ideas for topics that you generated during your brainstorming session. Before you begin, set a goal of a certain number of minutes or a set amount of pages you will write.

- Writing about X will help me accomplish the following purposes:
- I am personally interested in X because . . .
- I am academically interested in X because . . .
- My readers need or would like to know about X because . . .

Select a response from your freewriting activity and carry out the following **looping** exercise.

1. Paste the response at the top of your word processing file or write it at the top of a page in your notebook. Then freewrite for five minutes about the response.

2. Identify the best idea in this freewriting.

3. Freewrite for five more minutes about the idea you've identified.

4. Repeat the process until you've refined your idea into a potential topic.

Generate additional ideas about your potential topic by using a **clustering** exercise.

1. In the middle of a sheet of paper, or in the center of an electronic document (word processing file or graphics file), write your potential topic.

2. Identify ideas that are related to your central topic and list them near it. Think about the importance and relevance of each related idea, and draw lines and circles to show the relationships among your ideas.

3. Write additional ideas related to the ideas in Step 2. In turn, draw lines and circles to show their relationships to the other ideas in your cluster.

4. Repeat the process until you've created a cluster of ideas that represents your current understanding of the topic you are considering.

You can download or print this activity at **bedfordresearcher.com**. Click on Activities > Generate Ideas about a Topic.

[**FRAMING MY ARGUMENT**]

Step 3: Consider Your Writing Situation

After you've spent time thinking and prewriting about potential topics for your research project, you should select the strongest candidate.

As you make your choice, think carefully again about the level of interest both you and your readers might have in the topic. Some topics, such as college admissions standards, which is addressed by Patrick Crossland, will appeal to a large number of people, including high school students applying to colleges, college students who might not have been accepted by their top choices, and the parents of these students. Other topics, such as the work of Ernest Hemingway, which was addressed by Kevin Fahey, will appeal to a smaller group of readers—in this case, literary scholars or devoted fans of Hemingway's short stories. The key is to identify which topics—regardless of whether they will attract many readers or only a handful of researchers—are compatible with your writing situation.

In addition, remember that your topic is subject to change. It's a starting point, not a final destination. As you explore your topic, you'll begin to narrow it to a specific issue—a point of disagreement, uncertainty, concern, or curiosity—that is being discussed by a community of readers and writers.

A search for *college admissions*, for example, produces nearly 50 times as many results as a search for *Hemingway* and *"Nick Adams"*. Both topics, however, resulted in successful research projects.

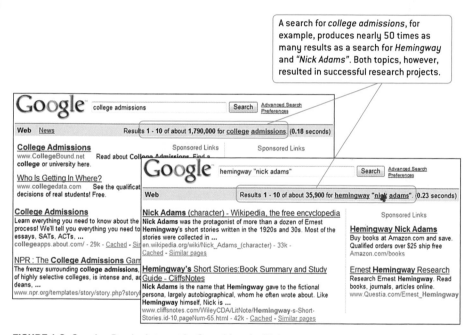

FIGURE 1.3 Gauging Reader Interest by Searching the Web

> **QUICK REFERENCE**

Getting Started

☑ Gain confidence about research writing by becoming acquainted with the research writing process. (p. 3)

☑ Create a research log to manage information and ideas as you work. (p. 5)

☑ Develop a project timeline to help manage your time. (p. 7)

☑ Analyze your assignment by reflecting on your research writing situation—purposes, influences, type of document (genre), requirements, limitations, and opportunities. (p. 9)

☑ Generate ideas about appropriate topics by brainstorming, freewriting, looping, and clustering. (p. 13)

☑ Choose the most promising and appropriate topic. (p. 16)

Part I
Joining the Conversation

1 Getting Started

 2 Exploring and Narrowing Your Topic

3 Developing Your Research Question
   and Proposal

2

Exploring and Narrowing Your Topic

> **Key Questions**
>
> **2a. How can I explore my topic? 19**
>   Create a plan to explore your topic
>   Discuss your topic with others
>   Conduct preliminary observations
>   Find and review sources
>
> **2b. How can I narrow my topic? 30**
>   Identify conversations about issues in your sources
>   Assess your interest in the issues
>   Choose an issue

Exploring involves gaining a general understanding of the issues—points of disagreement, uncertainty, concern, or curiosity—within a topic. Narrowing your focus to a single issue lays the groundwork for developing the research question that will frame your thinking about that issue and guides your efforts to gain a comprehensive understanding of it.

2a

How can I explore my topic?

Beginning to explore your topic is similar to attending a public meeting on a controversial issue. Imagine yourself at a meeting about a proposed development in your neighborhood. You're uncertain about whether to support or oppose its construction, but it seems as though all the others at the meeting have made up their minds. After an hour of people shouting back and forth, the moderator suggests a break to allow tempers to cool.

During the break, you wander from one group of people to another. Everyone is talking about the same topic, but the conversations are radically different.

Joining the Conversation

In one group, four people who bitterly oppose the development are talking about how to stop it. In another group, a developer is explaining the steps that will be taken to minimize the project's impact on the neighborhood. Yet another group is discussing alternative uses of the building site. As you walk around the room, you listen for information to help you decide which conversation you want to join. Eventually, you join the group discussing alternatives to development because this issue interests you most.

This process is similar to the strategies you'll use to explore and narrow your topic. At this early stage in your research project, you are listening in on conversations about specific issues in order to choose one that most intrigues you.

To explore your topic, create a plan, discuss your topic with others, conduct preliminary observations, and find and review sources.

Step 1: Create a Plan to Explore Your Topic

Before you start exploring your topic, create an informal research plan.

? WHAT'S MY PURPOSE?

Review your purpose in your research log. As you develop your research plan, remember that it should reflect your purpose for working on the project and provide directions for locating, collecting, and managing information.

The most common elements of a research plan include:

- a list of people with whom you can discuss your topic, including people who know a great deal about or have been involved with the topic, and people, such as librarians, who can help you locate information about your topic
- a list of questions to ask people who can help you explore your topic
- a list of settings you might observe to learn more about your topic
- a list of resources to search and browse, such as library catalogs, databases, Web search sites, and Web directories
- a system for keeping track of the information you collect

After you create your plan, use it to guide your work and to remind yourself of steps you might overlook. A note such as "talk to Professor Chapman about recent clinical studies" can come in handy if you've become so busy searching the Web or your library's catalog that you forget about your other plans for exploring your topic. After you've drafted your plan, share it with your instructor, your supervisor, or a librarian, who might suggest additional resources, shortcuts, and alternative strategies. Take notes on the feedback you receive and, if necessary, revise your plan.

My Research Project

CREATE A PLAN TO EXPLORE YOUR TOPIC

In your research log, answer the following questions.

- Who can help me learn more about my topic?
- What questions should I ask people on my list?
- What settings can I observe to learn more about my topic?
- What resources can I search or browse to learn more about my topic?
- How can I keep track of information I collect as I explore my topic?

Using your responses, write your plan as a series of steps and ask your instructor, your supervisor, or a librarian to review it.

You can download or print this activity at **bedfordresearcher.com**. Click on Activities > Create a plan to explore your topic.

Joining the Conversation

Step 2: Discuss Your Topic with Others

Talking about your topic with people who know about it or have been affected by it can provide you with insights that are not available through other sources. An instructor, a supervisor, or a librarian can also help you identify additional resources.

Featured writer Alexis Alvarez explored her topic—women and competitive sports—in part by talking with family members and friends who had competed in organized sports. These discussions helped Alexis better see the many different issues she could pursue within her topic.

You can also explore a topic by conducting formal interviews (see p. 151) or by writing letters and email messages (see p. 160). If you are uncertain about how to find people you can interview about your topic, you might start by visiting a Web discussion forum or newsgroup devoted to discussion of serious issues. (For an example, visit the Google Groups newsgroup, World_Politics, at groups.google.com/group/World_Politics/topic.)

> Learn more about newsgroups, electronic mailing lists, and Web discussion forums at bedfordresearcher.com. Click on Guides > How to Search the Web > Discussion Group Searches.

Step 3: Conduct Preliminary Observations

Observation is a powerful tool, especially when you are just getting started on a research project. Like discussing your topic with others, observing can provide you with valuable information that isn't available from other sources.

Featured writer Chris Norris used observation to help explore his topic, the growing interest among young adults in metal music. Chris observed shows featuring local metal bands, which provided him with a different perspective than he could have gained through other information-gathering techniques.

Step 4: Find and Review Sources

After you've talked with others about your topic and observed relevant settings, take advantage of the work other writers have done on the topic by finding and reviewing sources.

Search Your Library's Online Catalog. Online library catalogs allow you to search for sources by keyword, title, and author. Before you begin your search, generate a list of words and phrases associated with your topic. If you already know the names of authors or the titles of books or periodicals related to your topic, search for them. At this point, however, you'll usually conduct a keyword search on your topic.

Featured writer Patrick Crossland wrote a research essay about college admissions standards. He began exploring his topic by conducting a keyword search in his library's online catalog on the broad topic of college admissions (see Figure 2.1). For more about searching online library catalogs, see p. 109.

Browse Your Library's Shelves. Once you've located a relevant book or periodical through your library's online catalog, you can usually find other sources about your topic on the same or nearby shelves (see Figure 2.2). Scan the titles of those works to locate additional sources you might not have found in your online catalog search.

As you browse your library, be aware of differences in the types of sources you find. Depending on your topic, some types of sources will be more appropriate than others. For example, if you are interested in a topic such as featured writer Pete Jacquez's (wind-generated electrical power), and want to learn about the latest developments in wind turbine design, you might focus on trade and

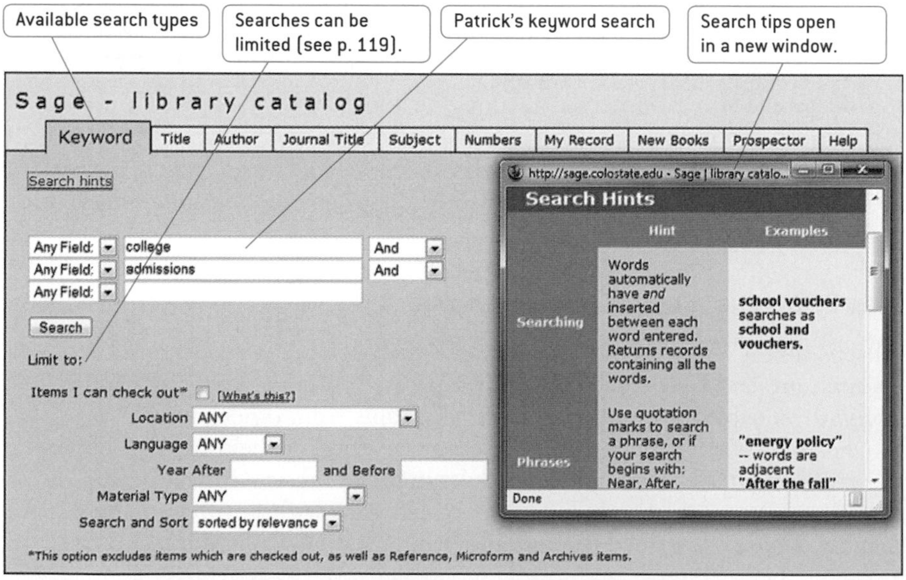

FIGURE 2.1 Patrick Crossland's Initial Search in His Library's Online Catalog

FIGURE 2.2 Browsing the Shelves in a Library

A If you located the book *Bolivia & Coca* . . .

B . . . browse the shelves to find related works such as *The Coca Boom and Rural Social Change in Bolivia*.

professional journals, newspapers, and magazines. If you are interested in a topic such as Ernest Hemingway, as Kevin Fahey was, you would focus on books and articles in scholarly journals. Note the following characteristics of sources you might find as you browse the shelves at your library.

- **Books** undergo a lengthy editorial process before they are published, and librarians evaluate them before adding them to the library collection.

- **Articles in scholarly journals** also undergo a lengthy editorial process before they are published. Most are reviewed—evaluated for accuracy, completeness, and methodological soundness—by experts in the field before they are accepted for publication. You can usually recognize a scholarly journal by its listing of an editorial board, the use of works cited lists and in-text citation in articles found in the journal, and the presence of the words *peer reviewed, blind reviewed,* or *refereed*.

- **Articles in trade and other professional journals** do not always go through a strict review process. You can find out whether articles are reviewed by looking at the submission policies printed in the journal.

- **Articles in magazines and newspapers** are usually reviewed only by the editors of the publication. Editorials typically represent an editor's or editorial board's opinion on an issue and are not subject to review. Similarly, opinion columns and letters to the editor seldom go through a review process.

- **Theses and dissertations** are final projects for students in graduate programs. Theses and dissertations vary in quality and reliability, although they have been reviewed and approved by committees of professors.

- **Microfilm and microfiche** are methods of storing documents such as older issues of newspapers and magazines or government documents and reports.
- **Other sources** include maps, videotapes, audiotapes, and multimedia items such as CD-ROMs and DVDs.

When you locate a source that seems particularly useful, read its works cited list, footnotes, endnotes, or in-text citations for related sources and then find and evaluate them.

Browse Newsstands and Bookstores.   If your topic is a current one, browse at a newsstand for specialty newspapers and magazines to which your library doesn't subscribe. If your topic has a broad, popular appeal, you might look at the books in a large bookstore or on a bookseller's Web site.

Search Available Databases.   Databases organize information as records (or entries) on a particular topic. Most databases provide publication information about articles in journals, magazines, and newspapers. You can search databases in much the same way that you can search an online library catalog (see Figure 2.3). If you have difficulty locating databases or aren't sure which databases are appropriate for your topic, ask a reference librarian for assistance. To learn more about searching databases, see p. 113.

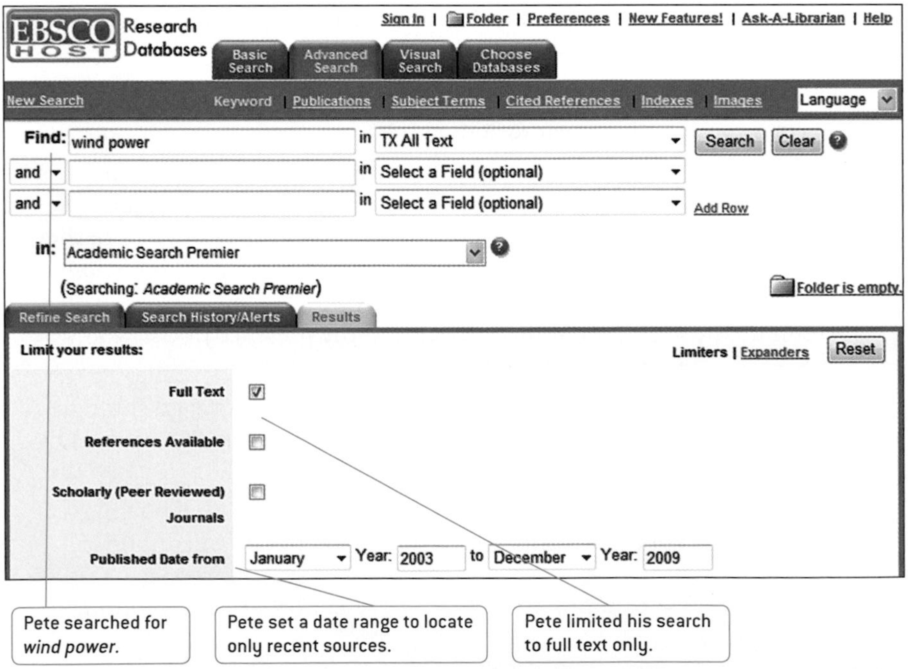

FIGURE 2.3 Pete Jacquez's Initial Search in the Academic Search Premier Database

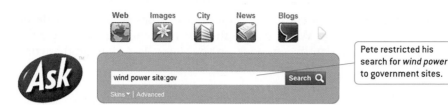

FIGURE 2.4 Pete Jacquez's Initial Search on Ask.com

Search the Web and Consult Web Directories. Web searches allow you to locate quickly a great deal of information about your topic — although not all of it will be as reliable as the sources you locate through a library catalog or database. To start searching the Web, visit one of the leading search sites (see Figure 2.4), such as Ask (ask.com), Google (google.com), Live Search (live.com), or Yahoo! (yahoo.com).

You can also use Web directories, which employ editors — real people — to organize links to Web sites in categories and subcategories (see p. 124 to learn more about Web directories). Leading Web directories include Open Directory (dmoz.org) and Google Directory (directory.google.com). When Pete Jacquez visited Open Directory, he found information on his topic by clicking on the general category Science and then by clicking in succession on the subcategories Energy and Wind Power (see Figure 2.5).

Browse Electronic Mailing Lists, Newsgroups, Web Discussion Forums, Blogs, and Wikis. Electronic mailing lists, newsgroups, Web discussion forums, blogs, and Wikis can be excellent sources of information, but they can also contain some outrageous misinformation. Because most of these resources are unmoderated — that is, anything sent to them is published — you'll find

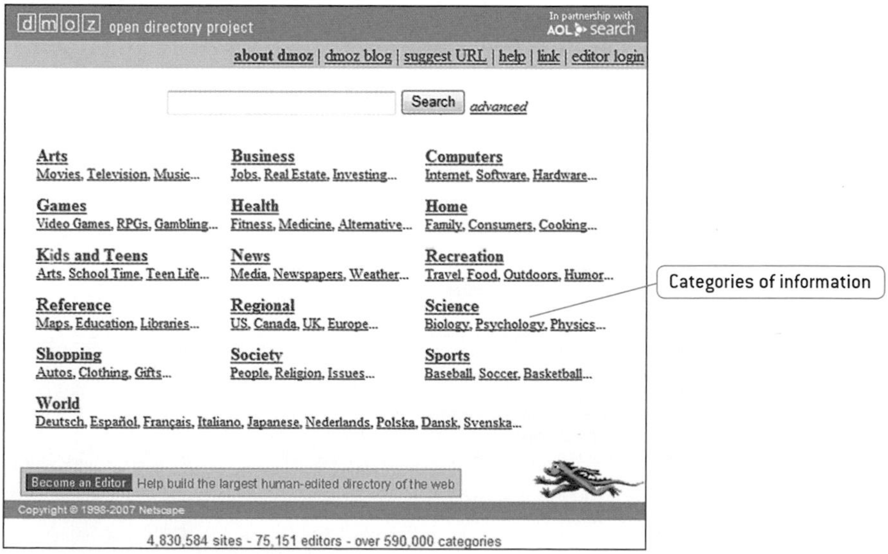

FIGURE 2.5 Searching the Open Directory

everything from expert opinions to the musings of folks who know little or nothing about your topic. When read with a bit of skepticism, however, the messages can help you identify issues within your topic. For more on these on-line resources, see Chapter 9.

Record Your Search Results.   As you explore your topic, record your searches: Identify the library catalogs, databases, and Web sites you search; list the words and phrases you use in your searches; and note the quality and quantity of results produced by each search. This information will be useful if, later on, you want to conduct these searches again or conduct the same searches on different search sites or databases.

> @ Learn more about locating information on the Web at **bedfordresearcher.com**. Click on Guides > How to Search the Web.

Skim Your Sources.   Skimming—reading just enough to get a general idea of what a document is about—enables you to gather information quickly from the sources you've located as you've explored your topic. You can skim books, articles, Web pages, newsgroups, chat transcripts, interview notes, observation

---

Information Literacy

Once you visit a site, you can begin to browse the Web. Browsing the Web is similar to browsing the shelves in the library. That is, once you've located a Web site that is relevant to your research question, you can usually follow links from that site to related sites. For instance, one of the Web sites Pete Jacquez visited as a result of his initial search on ask.com (see Figure 2.4) was the National Renewable Energy Laboratory's National Wind Technology Center Web site, which contains a list of Web sites related to wind power (see Figure 2.6). For more on Web searches, see Chapter 9.

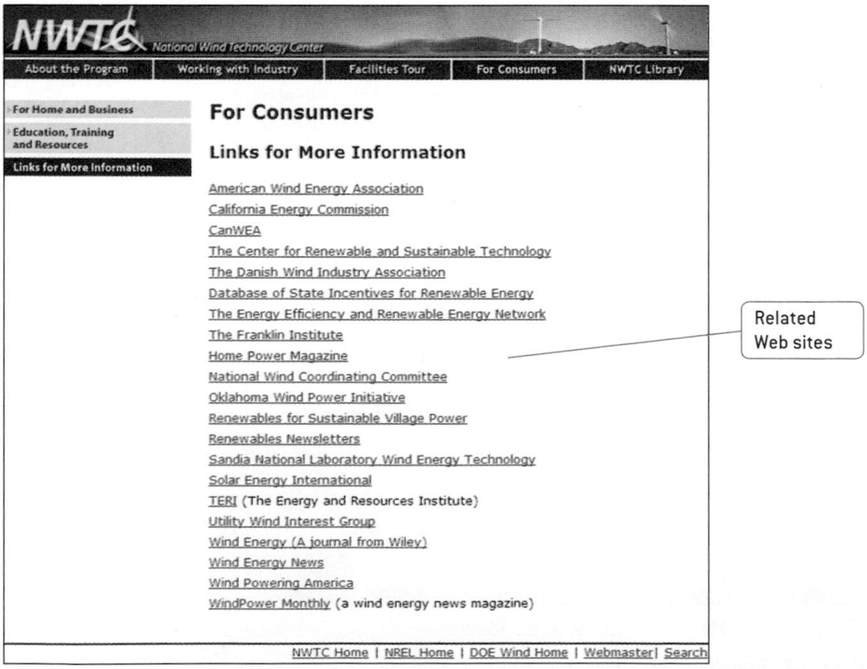

FIGURE 2.6 A Site Listed in Pete Jacquez's Initial Search Results

Check the title for cues about content.

Skim opening paragraphs for the purpose and scope of the document.

ENERGY'S WIND OF CHANGE

▶ Birger T. Madsen

Wind energy is rapidly developing as an environmentally sound and cost-effective option for power generation. Here, one of its champions describes an industry with wind in its sales

The prime motors of expansion are increasing environmental awareness and political commitments to reduce greenhouse gas emissions made under the Kyoto Protocol of 1997. Wind is free and supplies of it are inexhaustible, and when it produces energy it doesn't release heat or greenhouse gases.

There is enough wind to provide twice the expected global electricity demand for 2020

A 'doped' market

Read the first and last sentences of paragraphs to find key information.

Skim captions of photos and figures, which often highlight important information, ideas, and arguments.

Check headings and subheadings to learn about content and organization.

FIGURE 2.7 Skimming a Print Document

notes, or anything else in written form. Figures 2.7 and 2.8 illustrate strategies for skimming brief print documents and Web pages. Key strategies include identifying the type of document—or genre—you are skimming; scanning titles, headings and subheadings, and figure captions; reading the first and last sentences of paragraphs; scanning menus and other navigation aids; and looking for information about authors and publishers. If you are reading a longer document, such as a book or report, consider these additional strategies:

@ Learn more at bedfordresearcher.com. Click on Guides > How to Search the Web > Discussion Group Searches.

- **Check the table of contents,** if one is provided. This provides a useful overview of the document's content and organization.

- **Check the index,** if one is provided, to learn more about the content of the document.

- **Check the glossary,** if one is provided. The terms that are defined can provide clues about the focus of the document.

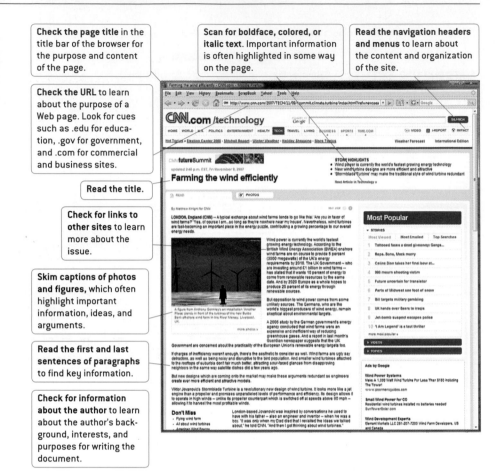

Check the page title in the title bar of the browser for the purpose and content of the page.

Scan for boldface, colored, or italic text. Important information is often highlighted in some way on the page.

Read the navigation headers and menus to learn about the content and organization of the site.

Check the URL to learn about the purpose of a Web page. Look for cues such as .edu for education, .gov for government, and .com for commercial and business sites.

Read the title.

Check for links to other sites to learn more about the issue.

Skim captions of photos and figures, which often highlight important information, ideas, and arguments.

Read the first and last sentences of paragraphs to find key information.

Check for information about the author to learn about the author's background, interests, and purposes for writing the document.

FIGURE 2.8 Skimming a Web Page

- **Check the works cited list,** if one is provided, to learn about the types of evidence used in the document.
- **Check for pull quotes** (quotations or brief passages pulled out of the text and set in larger type elsewhere on the page), which often call attention to important information, ideas, and arguments in a document.
- **Check for information about the author** to learn about the writer's background, interests, and purposes for writing the document.

Mark, Annotate, and Take Brief Notes on Your Sources.   As you skim your sources, do the following:

- Mark them by highlighting or underlining important passages so that you'll be able to locate key passages easily later in your research writing process (see Figure 2.9).

FIGURE 2.9
Pete Jacquez's Annotations and Highlighting on a Printout of a Page from an Online Magazine

- Annotate them by briefly recording in the margins your initial reactions to a source.
- Take brief notes in your research log. For example, you might note similarities or differences among your sources, such as different proposals for solving a problem or different interpretations of an issue. These notes allow you to start to pull together the information, ideas, and arguments that several of your sources touch on.

My Research Project

EXPLORE YOUR TOPIC

As you work through the strategies discussed in this chapter, use the following activity to keep track of your topic exploration in your research log.

1. What is my topic?

2. Have I discussed my topic with others? If so, what have I learned? If not, who are likely candidates for interviews — such as librarians, instructors, and people involved with or affected by my topic — and what questions should I ask them?

3. Are there any preliminary observations I should conduct? Have I done so? If so, what have I learned?

4. Have I found and reviewed sources? Have I searched the library catalog and browsed the shelves? Have I searched databases and the Web? Have I skimmed, marked, annotated, and taken brief notes on the sources I've found? If so, what have I learned about my topic?

You can download or print this activity at **bedfordresearcher.com**. Click on Activities > Explore Your Topic.

2b

How can I narrow my topic?

Once you've explored your topic, your most important goal is to narrow it to a specific issue. Issues are points of disagreement, uncertainty, concern, or curiosity that are being discussed by communities of readers and writers.

As he explored the general topic of metal music, Chris Norris read sources, listened to music, talked with his professor about his topic, and kept a running list of ideas and information that interested him. Chris started to make connections among the wide range of information, ideas, and arguments he encountered, and he was ultimately able to focus on the single issue that interested him most: the rebirth in the popularity of metal music.

Moving from your topic to a single issue about that topic involves identifying conversations about issues in your sources, assessing your interest in the issues, and asking whether writing about this issue will allow you to achieve your purposes as a writer.

Step 1: Identify Conversations about Issues in Your Sources

Identifying conversations about issues in your topic is the first step in determining which issue is most appropriate for your research project. As you work through this process, look for patterns in the information, ideas, and arguments you encounter.

Find Central Concepts Repeated in Your Sources.   When several sources refer to the same idea, you can assume that this information is central to the topic. For instance, as Alexis Alvarez looked at articles and Web sites about the impact of competitive athletics on adolescent girls, she found repeated references to self-esteem, confidence, and performance-enhancing drugs. Noticing this repetition enabled Alexis to identify some of the important conversations about her topic.

Find Broad Themes Discussed in Your Sources.   Sources that discuss the same general theme are most likely involved in the same conversation. Among the sources that featured writer Elizabeth Leontiev explored, she found that some focused on the history of the U.S. war on drugs, some focused on its cost, others focused on its effectiveness, and still others focused on the impact of the war on drugs both in Central and South America. By noting these broad themes, Elizabeth was able to identify some of the key conversations taking place about her topic.

Find Disagreements among Your Sources.   Some sources will explicitly indicate that they disagree with arguments, ideas, or information in other sources. For example, Pete Jacquez found that some sources reported on the cost effectiveness of wind-generated electrical power, while others argued that electricity generated from burning gas, coal, or oil is more cost-effective. Looking for such explicit statements of disagreement helped Pete identify a group of sources that were engaged in conversation with one another.

TUTORIAL

How can I identify conversations in my sources?

You can identify conversations taking place in your sources by looking for patterns. Creating a four-column table like the one below can help you sort things out. In this example, Elizabeth Leontiev notes that three of her sources talk about the effectiveness of the U.S. war on drugs. She used this conversation as the basis for her research on the impact of U.S. drug policy on South American coca farmers.

1 Record the source. Here, the writer uses the authors' last names.

2 Record concepts that are repeated in your sources.

3 Record other broad themes that you've noticed in your sources.

4 Note points on which the sources disagree.

5 Note the sources that these sources are citing. (You might use them later.)

Source	Gordon	Forero	Logan
Repeated Concepts	"zero cocaine, not zero coca"	"zero cocaine, not zero coca"	
Broad Themes	Overall effectiveness of U.S. war on drugs	Overall effectiveness of U.S. war on drugs	U.S. interference in affairs of other countries
Disagreements	U.S. policy of coca extermination — argues it has failed	U.S. policy of coca extermination — focuses on political issues	U.S. policy of coca extermination — argues policy is likely to change
Key Voices	Forero, Chipana, Morales	Morales	Morales, Reinicke

Review another example and work on identifying conversations in your sources at **bedfordresearcher.com**. Click on Interactive Exercises.

Find Recurring Voices in Your Sources.   As you read sources, you might find that some authors write frequently about your topic or that some authors are referred to frequently by other writers. These authors might have significant experience or expertise related to the topic, or they might represent particular perspectives on the topic. Stay alert for these recurring voices.

Step 2: Assess Your Interest in the Issues

After you have identified issues that are being discussed in your sources, you are ready to assess the importance and relevance of those issues. Determine your personal interest in each issue by asking what interests you most about each one. By identifying personal connections between your sources and your own interests, you are more likely to focus on an issue that will sustain your interest throughout the course of your research project.

[**FRAMING MY ARGUMENT**]

Step 3: Choose an Issue

After you've assessed the issues you've found during your exploration of your topic, select the strongest candidate and the one that interests you most. Think, too, about the level of interest your readers might have in the issue and whether writing about this issue will allow you to achieve your purposes as a writer.

Evaluate each issue by asking yourself the following questions:

- **Will selecting this issue help me achieve my purposes as a writer?** Review your purpose and examine how each of the issues you have identified will help you best accomplish it.

- **Will my readers want or need to read about this issue?** Ask yourself which issue your readers would be most interested in or would most need to know about.

- **Is this issue appropriate for the type of document I plan to write?** Some issues that are well suited for editorials and opinion columns in your school newspaper, for example, might not be suitable for an academic or professional paper.

- **Is this issue compatible with my requirements and limitations?** Determine whether you can address an issue reasonably, given your assignment due date.

- **What opportunities do I have if I choose this issue?** Identify any special resources that might be available to you, such as access to a special collection in a library, experts on an issue, or individuals who have been affected by it.

To assess the importance and relevance of issues discussed in his sources, Pete Jacquez brainstormed one of the issues that interested him most, strategies for increasing U.S. use of wind-generated electrical power. He listed five aspects of his writing situation and generated ideas about each one (see Figure 2.10).

Table 2.1 shows the topics explored by the featured writers and the issues they addressed.

Purpose:

Seems to fit. I want to figure out how we can use wind power, so focusing on strategies would help us increase use. It would be good to look at how new laws (fed? State?) might encourage development of wind farms. Look at tax breaks, new technologies, research and development funding.

Readers:

Lots of folks are worried about global warming, so even if they think "environmentalist" is a bad word, they probably won't see wind power as some ridiculous scheme. And it's getting almost as cheap as coal, and with gas prices getting so high maybe we'll be moving to electric cars, so maybe they'll see the value of having more, eco-friendly power sources (well, aside from the birds).

Type of Document:

People can find a Web site a lot easier than an essay, and if they read what I write, that's a good thing. I shouldn't have too much trouble putting up a small site. I can probably just use Word to make the pages.

Requirements/Limitations:

I might need to focus this more. Maybe look only at Colorado.

Opportunities:

CSU is the first school to give students an option of paying for wind power, and there are some profs here who were involved in that. I could interview one of them.

FIGURE 2.10 Pete Jacquez's Brainstorming about Issues

TABLE 2.1 THE PROGRESSION FROM TOPIC TO CONVERSATION		
FEATURED WRITER	**TOPIC**	**ISSUE**
Alexis Alvarez	Women and competitive sports	Steroid use among adolescent girls involved in competitive sports
Patrick Crossland	College admissions	Impact of college admissions standards on the makeup of U.S. colleges and universities
Kevin Fahey	Ernest Hemingway	Varying interpretations of Hemingway's characterization of Nick Adams
Pete Jacquez	Wind-generated electrical power	Best strategies for increasing U.S. use of wind-generated electrical power
Elizabeth Leontiev	The war on drugs	Impact of U.S. war on drugs on South American coca farmers
Chris Norris	Contemporary music	Resurgence in popularity of metal music

My Research Project

NARROW YOUR TOPIC TO AN ISSUE

In your research log, complete the following activity to narrow your topic to a single issue.

1. What are the three most important issues I have identified so far?

2. Of these issues, which one will best help me sustain my interest in this project?

3. Which one will best help me achieve my purposes as a writer?

4. Which one will best address my readers' needs, interests, values, and beliefs?

5. Which one best fits the requirements of my assignment?

6. Which one is most appropriate for the type of document I plan to write?

7. Which one has the fewest limitations?

8. Which one allows me to best take advantage of opportunities?

9. Based on these answers, the issue I want to choose is:

You can download or print this activity at **bedfordresearcher.com**. Click on Activities > Narrow Your Topic to an Issue.

> **QUICK REFERENCE**

Exploring and Narrowing Your Topic

☑ Get organized by creating a plan to explore your topic. (p. 20)

☑ Discuss your topic with people who know about or have been affected by it. (p. 21)

☑ Conduct preliminary observations. (p. 21)

☑ Find and review written sources by searching your library catalog, browsing its shelves, searching databases, searching the Web, and skimming your sources. (p. 22)

☑ Identify issues related to your topic. (p. 30)

☑ Evaluate the issues in light of your research writing situation. (p. 32)

☑ Select an issue. (p. 32)

Part I
Joining the Conversation

1	Getting Started
2	Exploring and Narrowing Your Topic
3	Developing Your Research Question and Proposal

3

Developing Your Research Question and Proposal

> **Key Questions**
>

Your research question directs your efforts to develop a research proposal, create a search plan, and collect information. It also provides the foundation for your thesis statement—a statement designed to help your readers understand your view of the issue—which you'll develop and refine as you work with sources and draft your document.

3a

How can I develop my research question?

A research question is a brief question that directs your efforts to collect, critically read, evaluate, and take notes on your sources. An effective research question focuses on a specific issue, reflects your writing situation, and is narrow enough to allow you to collect information in time to meet your deadlines. Most research questions begin with the word *what, why, when, where, who,* or *how.* Some research questions use the word *would* or *could* to ask whether something is possible. Still others use the word *should* to analyze the appropriateness of a particular action, policy, procedure, or decision. Since your research question may change as you learn more about your issue, it's best to think of it as a flexible guide. By revising your research question to reflect your growing understanding of the issue you've decided to address, you will build a solid foundation for the thesis statement you'll create when you begin planning and drafting your document (see p. 177).

Developing your research question involves considering your roles; generating ideas about potential research questions; assessing each question in light of your interests, roles, and research writing situation; and choosing and refining the question.

Step 1: Consider Your Roles

A role is a way of relating to your readers. The roles you take on will reflect your purpose, your understanding of your readers, and the type of document—or genre—that you plan to write.

? WHAT'S MY PURPOSE?

To help them achieve their purpose, research writers typically adopt one or more of the following roles.

- *Advocates* present evidence in favor of their side of an argument and, in many cases, offer evidence that undermines opposing views. If you plan to write an argument, you'll most likely adopt the role of advocate.

- *Reporters* often present themselves as experts and present detailed but neutral information on a topic. Their writing is authoritative and suggests that they are knowledgeable. A reporter might also write a document that provides an overview of competing ideas about a topic, such as a guide to the positions of candidates for public office.

- *Observers* focus on learning about and exploring the implications of an individual, event, object, idea, or issue. Writers who adopt this role typically reflect on their topic, and often write documents that trace their thinking about it. Observers often refer to their observation process in their documents, and typically focus on their personal reactions to and understanding of their topic.

- *Interpreters* analyze and explain the significance of ideas or events. In some ways an interpreter acts like a reporter or an observer. However, while reporters tend to present the information they've found in their sources as factual, and observers tend to focus on personal reactions to a topic, interpreters are more likely to consider the accuracy and meaning of the sources they cite.

- *Evaluators* focus primarily on considering how well something meets a given set of criteria. Their writing is usually balanced, and they usually offer evidence and reasoning to support their evaluation.

- *Problem solvers* focus on one or more of the following activities: identifying and defining a problem, discussing the impact of the problem, and offering one or more solutions to the problem. Writers who address problems typically present the problem in a straightforward, apparently objective manner, although they sometimes use emotionally charged language to shape their readers' interpretation of the problem. They offer evidence and reasoning to support their analysis of a problem.

- *Inquirers* present new information about a topic. For instance, a scientist might conduct a study that tests the effects of a new diet; the report that emerged from the study would present the results. If you plan to conduct your own laboratory or field studies, you will most likely take on the role of inquirer.

↓

- *Entertainers* attempt to amuse or divert their readers. Although entertainment is not a primary goal in academic or professional writing, it is often an important part of articles written for magazines, newspapers, and Web sites. Research writers often write informative articles in an entertaining way in an attempt to keep their readers interested.

Note that these roles are not mutually exclusive. For example, featured writer Pete Jacquez's initial purpose was to inform his readers about the potential benefits of wind power. Eventually he decided that he also wanted to advocate its use, suggesting strategies for increasing our reliance on wind power.

My Research Project

SELECT ROLES CONSISTENT WITH YOUR PURPOSE

The following activity can help you rank the relative importance of the potential roles you might adopt as you work on your project.

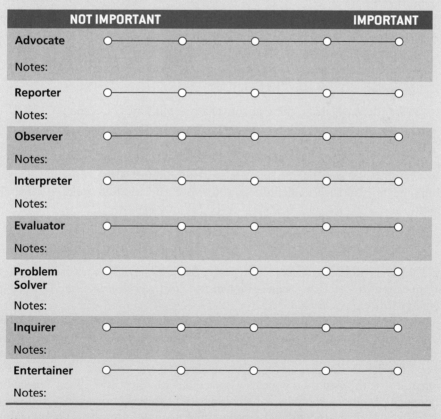

NOT IMPORTANT				IMPORTANT
Advocate	O———O———O———O———O			
Notes:				
Reporter	O———O———O———O———O			
Notes:				
Observer	O———O———O———O———O			
Notes:				
Interpreter	O———O———O———O———O			
Notes:				
Evaluator	O———O———O———O———O			
Notes:				
Problem Solver	O———O———O———O———O			
Notes:				
Inquirer	O———O———O———O———O			
Notes:				
Entertainer	O———O———O———O———O			
Notes:				

You can download or print this activity at **bedfordresearcher.com**.
Click on <u>Activities</u> > <u>Select Roles Consistent with Your Purpose</u>.

Step 2: Generate Potential Research Questions

Your next step is to generate a list of questions about the issue you've decided to address. Questions can focus on the following:

- **Information.** What is known — and not known — about an issue?
- **History.** What has occurred in the past that is relevant to an issue?
- **Assumptions.** What conclusions — merited or not — have writers and readers already made about an issue?
- **Goals.** What do the writers and readers involved in conversation about this issue want to see happen (or not happen)?
- **Outcomes.** What has happened so far? What is likely to happen?
- **Policies.** What are the best procedures for carrying out actions? For making decisions?

Questions can lead you to engage in the following kinds of thinking processes:

- **Definition.** Describing specific aspects of an issue.
- **Evaluation.** Asking about strengths and weaknesses or appropriateness.
- **Comparison/Contrast.** Asking about distinctions between aspects of an issue.
- **Cause/Effect Analysis.** Asking what leads to a specific result.
- **Problem/Solution Analysis or Advocacy.** Defining problems, considering outcomes of a problem, assessing potential solutions, and/or offering solutions.
- **Sequential Analysis.** Asking about step-by-step series of events.
- **Inquiry.** Seeking new information; conducting original research.
- **Reporting.** Conveying what is known about an event, idea, or phenomenon.

By combining a specific focus, such as assumptions, with a specific type of thinking process, such as definition, you can create carefully tailored research questions.

> What assumptions have shaped debate about this issue?
> What assumptions have worked against a resolution of this issue?

In Table 3.1, different focuses and types of thinking processes are used to generate questions about Pete Jacquez's issue, *best strategies for increasing U.S. use of wind-generated electrical power.*

As you begin generating potential research questions, ask yourself whether you are interested in focusing on such concerns as the current state of knowledge about your issue, its history, the assumptions informing the conversation about the issue, the goals of writers involved in the conversation, the likely outcomes of the issue, or policies associated with the issue. Then reflect on the range of options you have for thinking about these concerns. Are you interested, for example, in defining or evaluating? Are you interested in conducting such analyses as comparing alternatives, looking for cause/effect relationships, defining or solving problems, or tracing a sequence of events? Are you interested in conducting your own study? Are you interested in reporting what others have done or are doing?

Specific question words might also help you get started. If you are interested in conducting an analysis, for example, you might use the words *what, why, when, where, who,* and *how.* If you are interested in exploring goals and outcomes, you might use the words *would* or *could.* If the conversation focuses on determining an appropriate course of action, generate questions using the word *should.* Consider the differences between these questions:

- **What** are the benefits of wind power?
- **Would** it be feasible to require electrical companies to generate 20 percent of their power through wind turbines?
- **Should** the federal government pursue legislation to support wind power?

Each question would lead to differences in how to search for sources of information, which sources to use in a project document, what role to adopt as a writer, and how to organize and draft the document.

Step 3: Select and Refine Your Research Question

Review your potential research questions and select a question that interests you, is consistent with the roles you have adopted, and is appropriate for your research writing situation. Then refine your question by referring to shared assumptions and existing conditions, narrowing its scope, and conducting preliminary searches.

[**FRAMING MY ARGUMENT**]

Refer to Shared Assumptions and Existing Conditions   You can refine your research question by using qualifying words and phrases to narrow its scope, by calling attention to assumptions that have been made by the community of writers and readers who are addressing your issue, or by referring to existing conditions relevant to your issue. Note the difference between these three versions of featured writer Alexis Alvarez's research question:

Original Question

What should be done about steroid use by adolescent girls involved in competitive sports?

Alternative 1

Even though we know that widespread drug testing of all athletes, younger and older, is impossible, what should be done about steroid use by adolescent girls involved in competitive sports?

(continued on p. 42)

TABLE 3.1 GENERATING RESEARCH QUESTIONS

	DEFINITION	EVALUATION	COMPARISON/ CONTRAST	CAUSE/ EFFECT	PROBLEM/ SOLUTION	SEQUENCE	INQUIRY	REPORTING
Information	Where are the best locations for generating wind power?	How effective are current strategies for increasing use of wind power?	What are the similarities and differences among strategies to increase use of wind power?	What will lead to increased use of wind power?	What are the primary obstacles to increasing use of wind power?	What process is likely to be most effective at increasing use of wind power?	How could we increase U.S. use of wind power?	What strategies are now being tried to increase use of wind power?
History	Which strategies have been used to increase use of wind power?	Which strategies have been most effective at increasing use of wind power?	When will the costs of wind-generated electrical power rival that of power generated by natural gas, coal, and oil?	What has led to efforts to increase use of wind power?	How have obstacles to increased use of wind power been overcome?	What process has been followed to successfully implement wind power in other countries?	What can we learn from the past to increase use of wind power?	How are people using lessons from the past to increase current use of wind power?
Assumptions	Which values drive efforts to increase use of wind power?	Which assumptions have proven most damaging in efforts to increase use of wind power?	Which assumptions are driving efforts to increase use of wind power?	What faulty assumptions have led to failures in the wind power industry?	What can be done to rescue efforts to increase reliance on wind power?	What has led to current assumptions about wind power?	How can we change assumptions about use of wind power?	What are the focuses of the debate about use of wind power?

	DEFINITION	EVALUATION	COMPARISON/CONTRAST	CAUSE/EFFECT	PROBLEM/SOLUTION	SEQUENCE	INQUIRY	REPORTING
Goals	What are the goals of wind power advocates?	Which goals are most likely to be realized by advocates of wind power?	What are the differences among the goals pursued by different groups of wind power advocates?	What is likely to occur if current goals of wind power advocates are realized?	What are the primary obstacles to wind power and how can they be overcome?	How have the goals pursued by wind power advocates developed over time?	Would advocates of wind power respond positively to a shift in short-term goals?	How is the goal of greater use of wind power being pursued by its advocates?
Outcomes	What is likely to result from efforts to increase use of wind power?	What are the best outcomes that can be expected from efforts to increase use of wind power?	Compared to the use of coal-based power plants, what are the advantages of outcomes from efforts to increase use of wind power?	Could advertising campaigns increase the likelihood of widespread adoption of wind power?	What undesirable consequences are likely to result from efforts to increase use of wind power?	When will wind power be an economically viable alternative to power from coal?	Why are legislators hesitant about supporting increased use of wind power?	Who are the most likely users of wind power?
Policies	What policies should the government implement to support wind power?	What are the advantages of pursuing a policy of increased use of wind power?	How do policy initiatives led by wind-power advocates differ from those of the coal industry?	What are the likely results of government support for wind power?	To what extent can a policy of greater reliance on wind power reduce reliance on petroleum imports?	How will the energy industry respond to passage of a national energy policy favoring wind power?	How do consumers respond to "extra-cost" wind power initiatives?	Would it be feasible to require electrical companies to generate 20% of their power through wind turbines?

Alternative 2

Given the lack of knowledge among athletes and their parents about the health consequences of steroid use, what should be done about steroid use by adolescent girls involved in competitive sports?

As you refine your research question, you might use conditional words and phrases such as the following:

Mix . . .	and Match
Although	we know that . . .
Because	it is uncertain . . .
Even though	it is clear that . . .
Given that	studies indicate . . .
In light of	recent events . . .
Now that	it has been shown . . .
Since	the lack of . . .
While	we cannot . . .

Narrow the Scope of Your Research Question   Early research questions typically suffer from lack of focus. You can narrow the scope of your question by looking for vague words and phrases and replacing them with more specific words or phrases. The process of moving from a broad research question to one that might be addressed effectively in a research essay might produce the following sequence.

Original Research Question

What is behind the increased popularity in women's sports?

Refined

What has led to the increased popularity of women's sports in colleges and universities?

Further Refined

How has Title IX increased opportunities for women athletes in American colleges and universities?

In this example, the writer has narrowed the scope of the research question in two ways. First, the writer has shifted its focus from women's sports in general to women's sports in American colleges and universities. Second, the writer has moved from a general focus on increased popularity of women's sports to a more specific focus on opportunities brought about by Title IX, federal legislation that mandated equal opportunities for women athletes.

Information Literacy
Conduct Preliminary Searches. One of the best ways to test your research question is to conduct some preliminary searches in an online library catalog or database or on the Web. If you locate a vast amount of information in your searches, you might need to revise your question so that it focuses on a more manageable aspect of the issue. In contrast, if you find almost nothing in your search, you might need to expand the scope of your research question.

TUTORIAL

How do I refine my research question?

The first draft of your research question might be too broad, which can make it difficult for you to focus your research efforts. Refine your initial research question so that you can collect information efficiently.

In this example, Pete Jacquez refines his research question about the use of wind-generated electrical power. He used his research question as he collected and worked with sources, and later, he developed his thesis statement to answer his question.

Preliminary Research Question:
How can we increase our reliance on alternative energy?

1 Refer to shared assumptions and existing conditions by using phrases such as *although it is clear that ...*, *because we cannot ...*, and *given that studies have shown....*

In light of consumer demand for low-cost electricity, how can we increase our reliance on alternative energy?

2 Identify vague words and phrases, such as *alternative* and *reliance on*, and replace them with more specific words.

In light of consumer demand for low-cost electricity, what steps can U.S. citizens take to encourage local, state, and federal governments to support increased use of wind-generated electrical energy?

3 Using these specific terms, conduct preliminary searches in your library catalog, databases, and on the Web. If you get too many results, narrow your focus even further. (Here, Pete narrows his target audience from *U.S. citizens* to *Colorado citizens* and focuses on passing a statewide referendum.)

In light of consumer demand for low-cost electricity, what steps can Colorado citizens take to pass a statewide referendum requiring increased use of reliance on wind-generated electrical energy?

Review another example and work on narrowing your own research question at **bedfordresearcher.com**. Click on Interactive Exercises.

Joining the Conversation

TABLE 3.2 THE FEATURED WRITERS' RESEARCH QUESTIONS

FEATURED WRITER	TOPIC	ISSUE	RESEARCH QUESTION
Alexis Alvarez	Women and competitive sports	Steroid use among adolescent girls involved in competitive sports	What should be done about steroid use by adolescent girls involved in competitive sports?
Patrick Crossland	College admissions	Impact of college admissions standards on the makeup of U.S. colleges and universities	What cultural, academic, and regional factors affect college admissions decisions?
Kevin Fahey	Ernest Hemingway	Varying interpretations of Hemingway's characterization of Nick Adams	How is Nick Adams characterized by Ernest Hemingway?
Pete Jacquez	Wind-generated electrical power	Best strategies for increasing U.S. use of wind-generated electrical power	What strategies, if any, should Coloradoans use to encourage local, state, and federal governments to increase U.S. use of wind-generated electrical power?
Elizabeth Leontiev	The war on drugs	Impact of U.S. war on drugs on South American coca farmers	How can we reduce the economic impact of the war on drugs on South American coca farmers?
Chris Norris	Contemporary music	Resurgence in popularity of metal music	What accounts for the resurgence in popularity of metal music?

3b

What is a research proposal and how can I create one?

A research proposal—sometimes called a prospectus—is a formal presentation of your plan for your research writing project. A proposal helps you pull together the planning you've done on your project and identify areas where you need additional planning.

Unlike a research plan (see p. 20), which is designed primarily to help *you* decide how to collect information, a research proposal is addressed to someone else, usually an instructor, supervisor, or funding agency. A research proposal typically includes the following parts.

- **A title page** serves as a cover for your research proposal. It should include the working title of your research writing project, your name and contact information, and the date.

- **An introduction** should identify the issue you've decided to address; state your research question and, if you have created one, your preliminary thesis statement; describe your purpose; and identify your readers and describe their needs, interests, values, and beliefs.

- **A review of literature** provides a brief overview of the key information, ideas, and arguments in the sources you've collected so far. You should identify useful sources found during your exploration of your topic and explain why you've found them useful.

- **A plan to collect information** offers a brief description of the types of resources you'll use to locate information relevant to your issue and outlines the steps you'll take to collect it. You should indicate whether you'll consult reference librarians; whether you'll use library catalogs, databases, and Web sites; and whether you'll conduct field research.

- **A project timeline** will give your reader an indication of the range of days, weeks, or months over which you will be completing your research and writing your document.

- **A working bibliography** lists the sources you've collected so far. Sometimes you will be asked to create an annotated working bibliography, which contains a brief description of each source. Your working bibliography should conform to the documentation system (MLA, APA, *Chicago*, CSE) specified by your instructor, supervisor, or funding agency. For more information on bibliographies, see p. 169.

Optional elements include the following:

- **An abstract or executive summary** provides a brief summary—usually fifty to two hundred words—of your project. You should identify the issue you've decided to address and your research question. You should also indicate what type of document—such as a research essay, informative Web site, or magazine article—you'll write.

- **An overview of key challenges** encourages you to think about potential problems you will need to address as you work on your project. This section of your research proposal might discuss such difficulties as locating or collecting specific types of sources. It also provides an opportunity for your instructor, supervisor, or potential funder to respond by suggesting strategies for meeting specific challenges.

- **A funding request and rationale** provides a budget that identifies costs for key project activities, such as conducting your search, reviewing the sources you collect, writing and designing the document, and publishing the document.

A formal research proposal allows you to consolidate the work you've done so far and get feedback on your plans to carry out your project.

My Research Project

CREATE A RESEARCH PROPOSAL

Use the following activity to create a formal research proposal.

1. Provide the working title for your project.

2. Describe your issue.

3. Describe your purpose for working on this project.

4. Describe your readers' needs, interests, values, and beliefs.

5. State your research question.

6. Briefly review key findings about your issue from the sources you found as you explored your topic.

7. Indicate how you'll locate additional information, ideas, and arguments about your issue.

8. Include your project timeline.

9. Include your working bibliography.

10. Discuss the key challenges you face (optional).

11. Identify specific funding requests (optional).

You can download or print this activity at **bedfordresearcher.com**. Click on Activities > Create a Research Proposal.

> QUICK REFERENCE

Developing Your Research Question and Proposal

☑ Define your role as a research writer. (p. 36)

☑ Generate potential research questions. (p. 38)

☑ Select and refine your research question. (p. 39)

☑ If necessary, develop a research proposal. (p. 44)

The Bedford Researcher

I	Joining the Conversation
II	**Working with Sources**
III	Collecting Information
IV	Writing Your Document
V	Documenting Sources

PART II

Working with Sources

As you collect information, you'll read critically, evaluate sources, take notes, and guard against unintentional plagiarism. The next four chapters lead you through the process of engaging with the information, ideas, and arguments you will encounter as you work on your research writing project.

Part II
Working with Sources

> **4**   **Reading Critically**
> 5   Evaluating Sources
> 6   Taking Notes
> 7   Avoiding Plagiarism

4

Reading Critically

> **Key Questions**

Critical readers read actively and with an attitude. Reading actively means working with a text as you read: skimming, reading for meaning, and rereading passages that leave you with questions. It means underlining and highlighting text, noting your reactions in the margins, and responding to information, ideas, and arguments. Reading with an attitude means never taking what you read at face value. It means asking questions, looking for implications, making inferences, and making connections to other sources.

How does reading critically differ from evaluating?

At first glance, reading critically might seem to be the same as evaluating, which is discussed in detail in the next chapter. Although the two processes are related, they're not identical. Critically reading a source—questioning what it says and thinking about what it means—focuses your attention on making sense of the source. In contrast, evaluation focuses your attention on determining how reliably a source presents its information and how well it meets your needs as a research writer.

4b

How can I use my research question to read critically?

Your research question focuses your attention on your issue, provides the foundation for your search plan, and directs you to specific sources as you collect information. Your research question also provides the basis for creating a preliminary thesis statement, which you will use to guide your critical reading.

A preliminary thesis statement is an answer to your research question. At this point in your research writing process, your answer to your research question is preliminary because it is neither as formal nor as complete as the thesis statement you'll use when you draft your document. However, a preliminary thesis statement is an important first step toward developing your thesis statement—your statement of your main point. Figure 4.1 shows the progression from research question to preliminary thesis statement to thesis statement in the context of the research writing process.

As an early response to your research question, your preliminary thesis statement can help you decide whether you agree or disagree with an author—and,

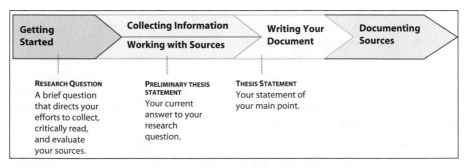

FIGURE 4.1 Moving from a Research Question to a Preliminary Thesis Statement to a Thesis Statement

thus, whether you want to align yourself with his or her position on the issue. It will also help you judge whether the evidence provided in a source might be of use to you as you develop your argument—either to support your own argument or to illustrate an alternative approach to the issue.

Use your preliminary thesis statement to test your ideas against the information, ideas, and arguments you encounter in your reading. As your ideas change, revise your preliminary thesis statement.

Develop a Preliminary Thesis Statement

To draft your preliminary thesis statement, brainstorm or freewrite in response to your research question. After reviewing your response, settle on a preliminary thesis statement and use it to guide your critical reading.

Featured Writer Alexis Alvarez's Research Question:

What should be done about steroid use by adolescent girls involved in competitive sports?

Responses:

The typical response to steroid use in sports, such as the Olympics or professional football, seems to be some sort of punishment—losing a medal or being banned from competition for a period of time. But will this work with kids—especially kids who don't seem to have the same level of maturity as older athletes? And what about parents who encourage kids—and most likely provide the funds—to use steroids to get ahead (parents with college scholarship dollars in their eyes, no doubt)? So . . . maybe punishment isn't the answer—or at least it's only part of the answer. It seems from my reading so far that most kids don't understand the negative consequences of using steroids. They only see the potential benefits (making a team, performing at a higher level, getting famous, getting a scholarship, etc.). And parents might not understand those consequences as well. And then some coaches might even get into the act, "helping" kids compete at a higher level, and getting the wins they "need." If kids don't understand the consequences, then education might be useful. And most kids don't like to cheat, so maybe part of the answer is putting more of an emphasis on fair play. And you need to get parents and coaches into some sort of solution too.

Preliminary thesis statement:

Steroid use by adolescent girls involved in competitive sports might be addressed by educating athletes, parents, and coaches about health consequences and emphasizing fair play.

This statement is too vague to use as a thesis statement, but it would serve as an effective guide for critically reading sources. For example, if you read a source that argues for a solution to the problem of steroid use by young athletes, you could ask whether that solution makes sense in light of what you had read in other sources or whether it is based on a different set of assumptions.

Table 4.1 presents the movement from research question to preliminary thesis statement in the featured writers' projects. Note how the preliminary thesis statement attempts to answer the research question and thus lets readers know what the writer thinks an answer to the research question might be. The development of their preliminary thesis statements marked a significant step for the featured writers in their progress toward writing their final documents. By offering a preliminary answer to their research questions, they began to take ownership of their work: They shifted their focus from learning about the conversations they had decided to join to beginning to develop their contribution to the conversation.

> @ Read more about the Featured Writers at **bedfordresearcher.com**.

TABLE 4.1 THE FEATURED WRITERS' PRELIMINARY THESIS STATEMENTS

FEATURED WRITER	RESEARCH QUESTION	PRELIMINARY THESIS STATEMENT
Alexis Alvarez	What should be done about steroid use by adolescent girls involved in competitive sports?	Steroid use by adolescent girls involved in competitive sports should be addressed by educating athletes, parents, and coaches about health consequences and emphasizing fair play.
Patrick Crossland	What cultural, academic, and regional factors affect college admissions decisions?	Factors affecting college admissions decisions include race, gender, and intellectual ability.
Kevin Fahey	How is Nick Adams characterized by Ernest Hemingway?	Nick Adams is a flawed character with whom readers can identify.
Pete Jacquez	What strategies, if any, should Coloradoans use to encourage local, state, and federal governments to increase U.S. use of wind-generated electrical power?	Coloradoans should encourage local, state, and federal governments to increase reliance on wind-generated electrical power through a mix of tax incentives and reduced regulation.
Elizabeth Leontiev	How can we reduce the economic impact of the war on drugs on South American coca farmers?	The U.S. and South American governments should adopt the "zero cocaine, not zero coca" policy.
Chris Norris	What accounts for the resurgence in popularity of metal music?	Metal music has a political message, musical diversity, and a strong fan base.

My Research Project

DRAFT A PRELIMINARY THESIS STATEMENT

In your research log, complete the following activity to draft your preliminary thesis statement.

1. Write your current research question.

2. Brainstorm or freewrite in response to your research question.

3. Select the response that best reflects your current understanding of the conversation you have decided to join. If appropriate, combine responses into one preliminary thesis statement.

4. Write your preliminary thesis statement.

You can print or download this activity at **bedfordresearcher.com**. Click on Activities > Develop and Refine Your Thesis Statement.

4c

How can I read with an attitude?

Reading critically means reading with an attitude. Your attitude will change during your research writing process. As you begin to read your sources critically, your attitude might be one of curiosity. You'll note new information and mark key passages that provide you with insights into the conversation you're joining. You will adopt a more questioning attitude as you try to determine whether sources fit in your project or are reliable. Later, after you begin to draw conclusions about the conversation, you might take on a more skeptical attitude, becoming more aggressive in challenging arguments made in sources than you were at first.

Regardless of where you are in your research writing process, you should always adopt a critical attitude. Accept nothing at face value; ask questions about your topic; look for similarities and differences in the sources you read; examine the implications of what you read for your research project; be on the alert for unusual information; and note relevant sources and information. Most important, be open to ideas and arguments, even if you don't agree with them. Give them a chance to affect how you think about the conversation you've decided to join.

Approach a Source with Your Writing Situation in Mind

One way to get into the habit of reading critically is to approach a source with your writing situation in mind. To do so, think about your research question and preliminary thesis statement; your purpose; your readers' needs, interests, values, and beliefs; the type of document you've decided to write; the design of your document and the context in which it will be read; your requirements and limitations; and your opportunities.

Your Research Question and Preliminary Thesis Statement   As you critically read your sources, answer the following questions:

- Are the information, ideas, and arguments in this source relevant to my research question and preliminary thesis statement?
- Does this source present information, ideas, and arguments that make me reconsider my research question or preliminary thesis statement?
- Does this source provide any new arguments, ideas, or information?
- Does this source offer a new perspective on the conversation?

? WHAT'S MY PURPOSE?

Return to your research log and review your purpose. Keeping your purpose in mind as you read will make it easier to recognize useful information when you come across it. As you read, ask yourself the following questions:

- Will the information in this source help me accomplish my purpose? Can I use the information in this source as support for points I want to make? Can I use it to illustrate ideas that differ from mine?
- Is the information in this source more useful for my purpose than what I've found in other sources?
- Does the source provide a good model of a convincing argument or an effective presentation of information? Can I learn anything from the presentation of the points and evidence in this source?

Your Readers' Needs, Interests, Values, and Beliefs   Consider your readers' needs, interests, values, and beliefs by asking the following questions as you read:

- Would my readers want to know about the information, ideas, and arguments found in this source?
- Would my readers find the source's information convincing or compelling?
- Would my readers benefit from a review of the argument and evidence presented in this source?
- What are my readers likely to think about the argument and evidence presented in this source? How will they respond to them?

The Type of Document You Will Write   Consider the conventions associated with the type of document, or genre, you've decided to write. Ask yourself:

- What type of evidence is usually provided in this type of document?
- Will I be expected to provide charts, graphics, photographs, or other types of illustrations? If so, can I learn anything from how illustrations are used in the source?

- How are documents of this type typically organized? Can I find examples of effective organizational strategies in the sources I read?

The Design of Your Document and the Context in Which It Will Be Read Research documents are presented in a variety of formats — for example, as printed texts, Web pages, or multimedia presentations. They're also read in a wide range of settings: in an office by someone sitting at a desk; on a bus or train by someone commuting to or from work; on a computer with a large, high-resolution monitor or a cramped screen. As you read your sources, be alert to what you can learn about organizing and formatting your document effectively. Answer the following questions about your document and the context in which it will be read:

- Does this source provide a useful model for designing my document?
- Does this source help me understand how I might address the context in which my document will be read?

Your Requirements and Limitations As you read, keep your requirements and limitations in mind:

- If I find useful information in a source, will I be able to follow up on it with additional research? Will I have enough time to follow up on that information?
- How much information can I include in my document? Will my readers be looking for a general overview or a detailed report?

Your Opportunities Instead of limiting your options, take advantage of them. As you read, ask yourself whether a source presents any possibilities or opportunities you have not discovered yet.

4d

What strategies can I use to read actively?

Once you have drafted your preliminary thesis statement and thought about your writing situation, you are ready to start reading actively. Reading actively means interacting with sources and considering them in light of the conversation you've decided to join. When you read actively, you might do one or more of the following:

- identify key information, ideas, and arguments
- write questions in the margins
- jot down reactions to information, ideas, and arguments
- note how you might use information, ideas, and arguments in your project document

- link one part of the source to another visually
- identify important passages for later rereading

As you read sources, use two active-reading strategies: marking a source and annotating a source.

Mark Sources

Marking a source to identify key information, ideas, and arguments is a simple yet powerful active-reading strategy. Common marking techniques include

- using a highlighter, a pen, or a pencil to identify key passages in a print source
- attaching notes or flags to printed pages
- highlighting passages in electronic texts with your word processor

Annotate Sources

You can further engage with your sources by writing brief annotations, or notes, in the margins of print sources and by using commenting tools for electronic sources. Many research writers use annotations in combination with marking (see Figure 4.2). If you have highlighted a passage (marking) with which you disagree, for instance, you can write a brief note about why you disagree with the passage (annotating). You might make note of another source you've read that could support your argument, or you might write a reminder about the need to look for information that will help you argue against the passage.

> @ Learn more about electronically highlighting text at bedfordresearcher.com. Click on Guides > How to Use Your Word Processor.

4e

What should I pay attention to as I read?

Different projects will require you to pay attention to different things as you read. In general, however, you should pay attention to the following:

- the type of source — or genre — you are reading
- whether the source is a primary or secondary source
- the author's main point and other key points
- reasons and evidence offered to support points
- new information (information you haven't read before)
- ideas and information that you find difficult to understand
- ideas and information that are similar to or different from those you have found in other sources

Getting to the ivy league: How family composition affects college choice

go to Web site

Author: Lillard, Dean; Gerner, Jennifer **Source:** Journal of Higher Education 706–730 70, no. 6 (Nov/Dec 1999): p. 706–730 **ISSN:** 0022-1546 **Number:** 46386576 **Copyright:** Copyright Ohio State University Press Nov/Dec 1999

Introduction

A primary tenet of American society revolves around access to positions of influence and equality of opportunity. Educational attainment provides the central vehicle through which upward mobility can occur. Consequently, educational researchers have long been concerned about the extent to which higher education has been accessible to all students regardless of socioeconomic and racial characteristics. This study examines patterns of attendance at four-year and selective four-year colleges across students from single- and two-parent families. In particular, we examine whether these students differ in their choice of colleges to which they apply, are admitted, and which they attend.

A student's home life has an impact on college apps.

The college-aged population is increasingly characterized by the experience of family disruption. Rising rates of divorce and illegitimate births imply that an increasing number of children either directly experience the breakup of their parents' marriage or never live in traditional two-parent families. Among those children born in 1950, 28% of whites and 60% of blacks had at some time lived with only one (or no) parent by age 17. Of children born twenty years later, 41% of whites and 75% of blacks can expect to live with fewer than two parents by age 17. These figures imply that, in contrast to earlier cohorts, the experience of living in a single-parent home is increasingly common among children growing up in the late 1970s and 1980s.

Children from dysfunctional families less likely to apply

Two reasons why access to college varies with family makeup

As family disruption becomes more prevalent, questions of equity and access arise if children from disrupted families are less likely to apply to and attend four-year colleges and selective four-year colleges. Differences in access might arise from two possible sources. First, disrupted and intact families may differ in the resources they can bring to bear to prepare their children for college. Second, the impact of these resources on college choices of children from disrupted and intact families may differ. Our results suggest that although both influences are present, differences in the levels of resources account for the largest proportion of the difference in the college choices between children from disrupted and intact families.

Review of the Literature

In a general review of the college choice literature, Hossler, Braxton, and Coopersmith (1989) identify several important correlates of college choice. These include family socioeconomic status, student academic ability and achievement, parental levels of education, parental encouragement and support, student educational aspirations about career plans, and quality of the high school. Although many of these factors vary with family composition, little attention is paid in this literature to the role family composition plays in college choices.

FIGURE 4.2 A Source Highlighted and Annotated by Featured Writer Patrick Crossland

Noting these aspects of a source during your active reading will help you better understand the source, its role in the conversation you've decided to join, and how you might use it in your document.

TUTORIAL

How can I read actively?

Marking and annotating allow you to identify key ideas, information, and arguments, record your reactions to a source, question the source, connect the source to other sources, and note how you might use arguments, ideas, and information.

In this example, featured writer Chris Norris marks and annotates an article from msnbc.com about current trends in contemporary music. Later, he would use passages from the article to support his argument about the resurgence of metal music.

1 Identify key information, ideas, and arguments.

2 Write questions in the margins.

3 Record your reactions to information, ideas, and arguments in the margins.

4 Note how you might use information, ideas, and arguments in your project document.

5 Link parts of the text visually.

6 Identify important passages for later rereading.

Heavy metal becoming increasingly political
As genre nears 30, social commentary weaves its way among power chords

What other bands address animal rights?

Cattle Decapitation — from left, Josh Elmore, Travis Ryan and Troy Oftedal — perform metallic odes to animal rights.
Jeff Chiu / AP

AP Associated Press
updated 12:59 p.m. MT, Thurs., Aug. 10, 2006

SAN FRANCISCO - Heavy metal singer Chris Barnes didn't know what people would think of "Amerika the Brutal," an anti-war song he wrote after his cousin deployed to Iraq in 2003.

He heard a number of complaints — but also received supportive e-mails from American troops in the war zone.

"It kind of sent a shiver up my spine because those are the guys I didn't want to offend by sounding anti-war," said Barnes, vocalist for the death metal band Six Feet Under.

The messages even reach overseas.

Lamb of God's albums criticize American foreign policy. Cattle Decapitation are ardent vegetarians who use explicit album covers and songs like "Veal and the Cult of Torture" to condemn the meat industry. Serj Tankian of System of a Down is co-founder of a nonprofit organization that works on social issues.

Political engagement

More than three decades after Black Sabbath conjured images of the dark arts, heavy metal is growing up. The genre is increasingly incorporating social and political messages into its dense power chords.

Cattle Decapitation vocalist Travis Ryan said his San Diego band's mix of charging guitars and an animal rights message is drawing a diverse crowd that includes activists as well as traditional metal fans.

"We've always had a lot of crazy crossover going on," he said before a recent show. "It's a pretty diverse crowd we have. I've never known what to make of it."

Twenty artists recently displayed art inspired by the band's last album "Humanure," in an online exhibit. Proceeds from sales of the art will be donated to animal rights causes.

Metal bands are also branching out into literature and mythology. Mastodon, which is headlining a summer tour with metal stalwart Slayer, patterned the concept album "Leviathan" around the story of Moby Dick. Death metal band Nile bases its songs and image around Egyptian mythology and iconography.

Use for section on diversity of metal music

"Metal is expanding and evolving and becoming more diverse," said Canadian anthropologist and filmmaker Sam Dunn, who directed "Metal: A Headbanger's Journey," released on DVD this summer. "It's at a much more vibrant state than it was even five or 10 years ago."

Dunn is working on a sequel to the film with the working title "Global Metal" which will trace the popularity of metal overseas, especially in developing countries like Brazil, Columbia and Indonesia.

CONTINUED: "A tool for social and political commentary"

Most popular
Most viewed | Top rated | Most e-mailed

Black-hole pioneer John Wheeler dies at 96
Incontinence drugs linked to memory problems
Neighbor saves three after plane hits house
Sheriff's office pays tow bill for good Samaritan
Surviving son denied health benefits post-Iraq
Most viewed on msnbc.com

Review another example and read one of your sources actively by viewing this tutorial at **bedfordresearcher.com**. Click on <u>Interactive Exercises</u>.

Identify the Type of Source You Are Reading

One of the most important things to pay attention to as you read is the type of source — or genre — you are reading. If a source is an opinion column rather than an objective summary of an argument, for example, you'll be less likely to be taken in by a questionable use of logic or analysis. If you are reading an annual corporate report for stockholders in a company, you'll recognize that the primary concern of the writers is to present the company in as positive a light as possible. If an article comes from a peer-reviewed scholarly journal, you'll be sure that it's been judged by experts in the field as well founded and worthy of publishing.

Recognizing the type of source you are reading will help you create a context for understanding and questioning the information, ideas, and arguments presented in the source.

Identify Primary and Secondary Sources

Primary sources are either original works or evidence provided directly by an observer of an event. Primary sources include

- poems, short stories, novels, essays, paintings, musical scores and recordings, sculpture, and other works of art or literature
- diaries, journals, memoirs, and autobiographies
- interviews, speeches, government and business records, letters, and memos
- reports, drawings, photographs, films, or video and audio recordings of an event
- physical artifacts associated with an event, such as a weapon used in a crime or a piece of pottery found in an archaeological dig

Secondary sources comment on or interpret an event, often using primary sources as evidence (see Table 4.2).

As a research writer, you should attempt to obtain as many primary sources as possible so that you can come to your own conclusions about your issue. Remember that your goal is to develop your own ideas about an issue, so that

TABLE 4.2 EXAMPLES OF PRIMARY AND SECONDARY SOURCES	
PRIMARY SOURCES	**SECONDARY SOURCES**
A short story by Ernest Hemingway	An article that presents an analysis of the short story
A transcript of the statement made by President George W. Bush on September 11, 2001	A recording of an interview in which a historian discusses the significance of the statement
A report of a laboratory study concerning the benefits of strength training for women with osteoporosis	A Web site that presents a review of recent research about prevention and treatment of osteoporosis

Working with Sources

you can create an original, well-supported contribution to the conversation you've decided to join. If you rely entirely or mostly on secondary sources, you'll be viewing the issue through the eyes of other researchers. Be sure to ask yourself, when you read a secondary source, what factors might have affected the author's argument, presentation, or analysis.

‖ Working with Sources

Identify Main Points

Most sources, whether they are informative or argumentative, make a main point that you should pay attention to as you read critically:

- An editorial in a local newspaper urges voters to approve financing of a new school.
- An article reports a new advance in automobile emissions testing.
- A Web page provides information about the benefits of a new technique for treating a sports injury.

Identify Supporting Points

Once you've identified a main point, look for key points that support it. If an author is arguing, for instance, that English should be the only language used for official government business in the United States, that author might support his or her argument with the following additional points:

- Use of multiple languages erodes patriotism.
- Use of multiple languages keeps people apart—if they can't talk to each other they won't learn to respect each other.
- Use of multiple languages in government business costs taxpayers money because so many alternative forms need to be printed.

Identify Reasons and Evidence

A point is only as good as the reasons and evidence that are offered to support it. Reasons and evidence can take many forms, including the following:

- **Appeals to authority.** Appeals to authority ask a reader to accept a point because someone in a position of authority supports it. The evidence used to support this kind of appeal typically takes the form of quotations, paraphrases, or summaries of the ideas of experts on an issue. As you read a source, ask yourself which authorities the writer has identified and how the writer has used information from those authorities to support a point. Ask whether the authority is an appropriate choice, and whether information from the authority is presented fairly and effectively.
- **Appeals to emotion.** Writers frequently use emotional appeals to frame an argument. A writer might introduce an article with a brief description of

a situation that affects one or more people, for example, in the hope that readers will be more sympathetic to the argument that follows. As you read sources, be aware of the uses to which emotional appeals can be put and consider whether you might accept the writer's argument if the emotional appeal were not made.

- **Appeals to principles, values, and beliefs.** Writers frequently rely on the assumption that their readers share with them particular principles, values, and beliefs. Religious and ethical arguments are often based on this kind of appeal, such as the belief that you should treat others as you would have them treat you, to believe that men and women should be treated equally, or to believe that every vote should count. When you encounter an appeal to principles, values, or beliefs, ask yourself what you can learn about the writer's principles, values, and beliefs, and then decide whether you share them.

- **Appeals to character.** Appeals to character might be referred to as the "trust me" strategy. This kind of appeal asks the reader to consider the writer's character as a reason to accept an argument. It can also ask the reader to consider their own character—to trust, as it were, in themselves.

- **Appeals to logic.** When writers make logical appeals, they present a set of propositions in the hope that you will accept them and agree with their conclusion. Appeals to logic often occur in the form of if/then reasoning, as in, "If this is true, then we can expect such and such to happen." As you read a source, identify the assumptions that lie behind a writer's logical appeals about an issue. You might find that, despite a well-reasoned argument, you can't accept the argument because you don't share the writer's assumptions.

- **Reasoning based on empirical evidence.** Many of us think of empirical evidence as information presented in numerical form. We think of it as "data." In fact, empirical evidence is any sort of information obtained through observation. A first-hand account of an event should be thought of as empirical evidence. So should results from surveys. So should measurements from an experiment. So should observation notes and transcripts of interviews. In many cases writers will present general conclusions based on empirical evidence rather than present a detailed discussion of the evidence. For example, a writer is much more likely to point out that more than half of the respondents to a survey agreed with a particular solution to a problem, rather than explain that 11 percent strongly disagreed, 22 percent disagreed, 7 percent had no opinion, 42 percent agreed, and 18 percent strongly agreed. When you encounter empirical evidence in a source, consider where the evidence comes from and how it is being used. If the information appears to be presented fairly, ask whether you might be able to use it to support your own argument, and attempt to verify its accuracy by consulting additional sources.

Identify New Information

As you read, mark and annotate passages that contain information that is new to you. Keep track of new information in your research log in the form of a list or as a series of brief descriptions of what you've learned and where you learned it.

Identify Hard-to-Understand Information

As you read, you might be tempted to ignore information that's hard to understand. If you skip over this information, you might miss something that is critical to the success of your research project. When you encounter information that's difficult to understand, mark it and make a brief annotation reminding yourself to check it out later.

Sometimes you'll learn enough from your reading of other sources that the passage won't seem as difficult when you come back to it later. And sometimes you'll still be faced with a passage that's impossible to figure out on your own. In this case, turn to someone else for advice.

- Search a database, library catalog, or the Web using words you didn't understand in the source.
- Ask your instructor or a librarian for help.
- Ask a question about the passage on a newsgroup or electronic mailing list.
- Interview an expert in the area.

Identify Similarities and Differences

You can learn a lot by looking for similarities and differences among the sources you read. For example, you might identify a group of authors who share a position on an issue, such as favoring increased government support for wind energy. You could then contrast this group with other groups of authors, such as those who believe that market forces should be the primary factor encouraging wind power and those who believe we should focus on other forms of energy. Similarly, you can make note of information in one source that agrees or disagrees with information in another. These notes can help you build your own argument or identify information that will allow you (and potentially your readers) to better understand the issue.

My Research Project

NOTE CONNECTIONS AMONG SOURCES

In your research log, identify connections among your sources. Ask whether information in one source agrees or disagrees with information in another. How might you handle these connections in your research project?

You can print or download this activity at **bedfordresearcher.com**. Click on Activities > Note Connections among Sources.

4f

How many times should I read a source?

As you work through your sources, you'll find that many are less relevant to your research project than you'd hoped when you collected them. When you come across one of these sources, move on to the next source. Other sources are worth reading more carefully. When a source offers what seems like good arguments, ideas, or information, use a three-pass approach:

1. Skim the source to get a general idea of its organization and content.
2. Read actively, marking and annotating relevant passages in the text.
3. Reread passages that are either particularly promising or difficult to understand.

First Pass: Skim for Organization and Content

Before investing too much time in a source, skim it. Skimming—reading just enough to get a general idea of what a source is about—can tell you a great deal in a minimal amount of time.

Skimming is an important first step in reading a source critically. Skimming helps you understand how a source is organized, which can help you more quickly assess its usefulness and relevance. If the source uses a familiar organizational pattern, you'll find it easier to locate key information.

You can also learn a great deal about the content of a source through skimming.

Skimming is most effective when you approach your sources with your writing situation and specific questions in mind. Before you skim a source, write a list of questions about the source in your research log. As you skim, add questions to your list. When you're finished, write answers to your questions. Your questions might include the following:

- What is the main point of this source?
- What additional points are offered to support the main point?
- What evidence is offered to support the points?
- Who is it written for?
- Why was it written?

CHECKLIST FOR SKIMMING SOURCES

☑ Identify the type of document — for example, book, magazine article, opinion column, scholarly journal article, personal Web site, blog entry.

☑ Check the title.

☑ Look at the table of contents, if one is provided.

Working with Sources

CHECKLIST FOR SKIMMING SOURCES (continued)

☑ Read the abstract, if one is provided, or the introduction.

☑ Check major headings and subheadings.

☑ Read the titles or captions of any figures and tables.

☑ Look for pull quotes (quotations or brief passages pulled out into the margins or set somewhere on the page in larger type).

☑ Scan the first sentences and last sentences of paragraphs for key information.

☑ Check the works cited list, if one is provided.

My Research Project

USE QUESTIONS TO GUIDE CRITICAL READING

Before you read a source, generate a list of questions about it. As you read, keep those questions in mind and ask additional questions. After you've read the source, use this activity to keep track of the answers to your questions. In your research log, create a table like the one shown here. For each source, write the name of the source and questions you would like to answer as you read the source. After you read the source, write your responses to your questions in the appropriate column.

SOURCE	
Question 1:	Response:
Question 2:	Response:
Question 3:	Response:
Question 4:	Response:

You can print or download this activity at **bedfordresearcher.com**. Click on Activities > Use Questions to Guide Critical Reading.

Second Pass: Read Actively

After you've skimmed the source and identified promising sections, read those sections actively—highlighting or underlining key passages, making notes in the margin, or recording observations in your research log. You should read either the entire source or at least enough to know that you don't need to read any more.

Third Pass: Reread Important Passages

If you decide that a source is valuable—or if you still have questions about the source—reread passages that you've identified as important. Again, read actively, continuing to note your reactions and ideas as you read. Rereading key passages in this way can help you gain a better understanding of the source, which can make a tremendous difference as you begin writing. Rereading passages—indeed, even an entire source—can also be useful as you plan, draft, and revise your document. As you refine your argument, return to your sources to determine whether you are presenting information, ideas, and arguments from them fairly and accurately and whether you might find additional material to support your argument.

[FRAMING MY ARGUMENT]

Mark and Annotate Sources with Your Argument in Mind   As you read critically, remember that you'll need to advance and support an argument in your project document. You'll need to understand what others have written so that you can fairly represent the issue to your readers, differentiate your argument from those made by other writers, and identify evidence to support your argument. As you read, mark key passages by highlighting or underlining, and make annotations to remind yourself of the importance or potential uses of the information, ideas, and arguments in the passage (see Figure 4.3). Keep your writing situation in mind as you make your annotations. Consider your purpose and role as a writer, and think about your readers' needs, interests, values, and beliefs. Use your annotations to call attention to how you might use the information in each marked or highlighted passage to accomplish your goals as a writer.

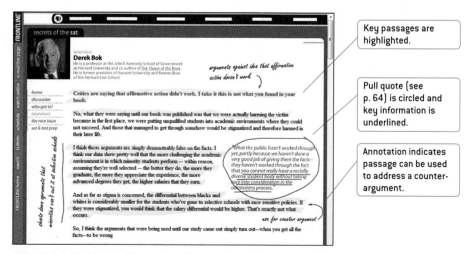

FIGURE 4.3 Marking and Annotating Sources with Your Argument in Mind

> **QUICK REFERENCE**

Reading Critically

☑ Draft a preliminary thesis statement. (p. 51)

☑ Read with an attitude, keeping in mind the following: your research question and preliminary thesis statement; your purpose; your readers' needs, interests, values, and beliefs; the type of document you will write and the context in which it will be read; your requirements and limitations; and your opportunities. (p. 53)

☑ Mark and annotate your sources. (p. 56)

☑ Identify primary and secondary sources, main and supporting points, evidence, new and hard-to-understand information, and similarities and differences among sources. (p. 56)

☑ Read the source multiple times, first skimming, then reading actively, then rereading important passages. (p. 63)

Part II
Working with Sources

4	Reading Critically
5	**Evaluating Sources**
6	Taking Notes
7	Avoiding Plagiarism

5

Evaluating Sources

> **Key Questions**
>
> **5a.** **What factors should I use to evaluate a source?** 67
> Evaluate relevance
> Evaluate evidence
> Evaluate the author
> Evaluate the publisher
> Evaluate timeliness
> Evaluate comprehensiveness
> Evaluate genre
>
> **5b.** **Should I evaluate all types of sources in the same way?** 73
> Evaluate the relevance and credibility of electronic sources
> Evaluate the relevance and accuracy of field sources

At the beginning of a research project, you'll most likely make quick judgments about your sources. Skimming an article, book, or Web site might be enough to tell you that spending more time with the source would be wasted effort. As you encounter a new source, determine how well it meets your needs as a research writer and how reliably it presents information, ideas, and arguments.

5a

What factors should I use to evaluate a source?

Evaluating a source means examining its relevance, evidence, author, publisher, timeliness, comprehensiveness, and genre.

Evaluate Relevance

Relevance is the extent to which a source provides information you can use in your research writing project. The most important questions you should ask to determine the relevance of a source are about your purpose and audience.

? WHAT'S MY PURPOSE?

Determine if the information in a source will help you accomplish your purpose. In the course of your research, you might find a number of information-filled sources. If the information is not relevant, however, it won't help you fulfill your purpose. For example, an analysis of the new user interface in the latest iPod might contain accurate and up-to-date information, but if you're writing about the monopolistic practices of leading digital music publishers, this source probably won't be of much use to you.

Determine if the Information in a Source Will Help You Address Your Readers' Needs, Interests, Values, and Beliefs   The information in a source should be useful to your readers. You might be tempted to include a beautifully worded quotation, but if your readers won't see how it contributes to your document, don't use it. Your readers will expect information that meets their needs. If they want to read about downloading music online, for instance, pass up sources that focus only on traditional music publishers.

Evaluate Evidence

Evidence is information offered to support a point (see p. 60). Evidence can include appeals to authority, emotion, principles, values, beliefs, character, and logic. It can also include measurements and observations, typically referred to as empirical evidence. An argument in favor of charging local sales tax on Web-based purchases might use statistics—a form of empirical evidence. It could calculate the revenue a town of fifty thousand might lose if five percent of its citizens made fifteen online purchases in a given year. As a research writer, you can evaluate not only the kind of information offered to support points made in a source but also the quality, amount, and appropriateness of that evidence. Ask the following questions about each source:

- **Is enough evidence offered?** A lack of evidence might indicate fundamental flaws in the author's argument.

- **Is the right kind of evidence offered?** More evidence isn't always better evidence. As you evaluate a source, ask yourself whether the evidence is appropriate for the points being made. Ask as well whether more than one type of evidence is being used. Many sources rely far too heavily on a single type, such as personal experience or anecdotal evidence.

- **Is the evidence used ethically?** If statistics are offered as evidence, ask yourself whether they are interpreted fairly or presented clearly. If a quotation is used to support a point, try to determine whether it is used appropriately.

- **Is the evidence convincing?** There are several signs that an argument isn't convincing. Among the most important are the absence of reasonable alternative interpretations of the evidence, questionable or inappropriate use of evidence, and evidence that seems to contradict points made elsewhere in the source. In addition, ask yourself whether the author mentions and attempts to refute opposing viewpoints or evidence. If the author hasn't done so, his or her argument might not be strong.

- **Is the source of the evidence provided?** Knowing the origins of evidence used in a source can make a significant difference in your evaluation of it. For example, if a source quotes a political poll but doesn't indicate which organization conducted the poll, you won't be able to determine the reliability of that evidence.

Evaluate the Author

In addition to relevance and evidence, you can evaluate a source based on who wrote it. Take for example two editorials published in your local newspaper that make similar arguments and offer similar evidence. One is written by a 14-year-old middle school student, the other by a U.S. senator. You would certainly favor an editorial written by the senator if the subject was U.S. foreign policy. If the subject was student perceptions about drug abuse prevention in schools, however, you might value the middle schooler's opinion more highly.

The importance of authorship as an evaluation criterion varies from source to source. In some cases, including many Web sites, you won't even know who the author is. In other cases, such as signed opinion columns in a newspaper or magazine, your evaluation could be affected by knowing that the author is politically conservative, liberal, or moderate. Similarly, you might find it useful to know that a message published on a Web discussion forum was written by someone who is recognized as an expert in the field.

Ask the following questions about the author of a source:

- **Is the author knowledgeable about the topic?** It can be difficult to judge an author because expertise can be gained in many ways. An author might be an acknowledged expert in a field; he or she might be a reporter who has written extensively about a topic; or he or she might be recounting firsthand experiences. Then again, an author might have little or no experience with a topic beyond a desire to say something about it. How can you tell the difference? Look for a description of the author in the source. If none is provided, the source might give a URL for the author's home page, and you can check out his or her credentials there. Or perhaps you can locate information about the author on the Web or in a biographical reference such as *Who's Who*.

- **What is the author's affiliation?** Knowing the institution, agency, or organization that employs the author or the political party or organizations to which the author belongs can help you evaluate the assumptions that inform a source.

- **How do the author's biases affect the information, ideas, and arguments in the source?** We all have a bias—a set of interests that shapes our perceptions of a topic. As you evaluate a source, consider the extent to which the author's biases affect the presentation of information, ideas, and arguments in the source. To uncover an author's biases, try to learn more about his or her affiliations. You might infer a bias, for instance, if you learn that an author writes frequently about gun control regulations and works for the National Firearms Association.

Evaluate the Publisher

A publisher is a person or group that prints or produces the documents written by authors. Publishers provide access to print or electronic sources, including books, newspapers, journals, Web sites, sound and video files, and databases. Some documents — such as messages posted to newsgroups or sources obtained through field research — have no publisher.

You can make informed judgments about publishers in much the same way that you can evaluate authors. Ask the following questions about the publisher of a source:

- **How can I locate information about the publisher?** If a publisher is listed in a print document, search for information about the publisher on the Web. You can often tell whether a publisher is reputable by looking at the types of material it publishes. If you are viewing a document on the Web, search for a link to the site's home page.

- **How do the publisher's biases affect the information, ideas, and arguments in the source?** Like authors, publishers have biases. Unlike authors, they often advertise them. Many publishers have a mission statement on their Web sites, while others present information on their Web pages that can help you figure out their bias. You might already know a fair amount about the biases of a publisher, particularly if the publisher is a major newspaper or magazine, such as the *New York Times* (regarded as liberal) or the *Wall Street Journal* (regarded as conservative). If the publisher is a scholarly or professional journal, you can often gain an understanding of its biases by looking over the contents of several issues or by reading a few of its articles.

Evaluate Timeliness

The importance of timeliness — when a source was published — varies according to your writing situation. If your research project would benefit from sources that have recently been published, then evaluate recent sources more favorably than dated ones. If you're writing an article on the use of superconducting materials in new mass transportation projects, you probably won't want to spend a lot of time with articles published in 1968. On the other hand, if you're writing about the 1968 presidential contest between Hubert Humphrey and Richard Nixon, sources published during that time period will take on greater importance.

Print sources usually list a publication date, but it can be more difficult to tell when Web sources were created. When in doubt, back up undated information found on the Web with a dated source.

Evaluate Comprehensiveness

Comprehensiveness is the extent to which a source provides a complete and balanced view of a topic. Like timeliness, the importance of comprehensiveness varies according to the demands of your writing situation. If you are working on a narrowly focused project, such as the role played by shifts in Pacific Ocean currents on snowfall patterns in Colorado in the winter of 2008, you might not find this evaluation criterion as useful as the others. However, comprehensiveness can be a guide if you need to provide a complete and balanced treatment of a general topic, such as the potential effects of global climate change on agricultural production in North America, or if you are still learning as much as you can about your topic.

Evaluate Genre

Identifying the genre—or document type—of the source you are evaluating can help you understand a great deal about its intended readers, the kind of appeals and evidence it is likely to use, and the kind of argument it is likely to make. Genres, such as an environmental impact statement, a newspaper editorial, or a magazine article, emerge from general kinds of writing situations. For example, an article in a professional journal will adopt conventions—ways of addressing readers, using sources, and presenting an argument—that reflect the needs and purposes of individuals who work in that area. An article appearing in the journal will almost certainly rely on published sources or information from a scientific study, for instance, and it will carefully document its sources so that its readers can locate related sources easily. In contrast, a blog entry is more likely to rely on personal observation and reflection. A blog entry would also be more likely to employ a more sensational approach to presenting an argument than a journal article, which usually makes claims cautiously and only with a great deal of hedging (as in, "it would appear that . . ." and "based on the evidence, it seems likely that . . .").

By understanding the conventions of a particular genre, you can determine whether a source is a good representative of that kind of document, and you can understand whether the information, ideas, and arguments found in it might be of use to you as you work on your writing project.

CHECKLIST FOR EVALUATING SOURCES

✔ **Determine whether the source is relevant.** Will the source help you accomplish your purpose and address your readers' needs, interests, values, and beliefs?

✔ **Determine whether the source provides evidence and uses it appropriately.** Is enough evidence of the right kind offered? Is evidence used fairly, is it convincing, and is its source provided?

↓

CHECKLIST FOR EVALUATING SOURCES (continued)

✓ **Learn about the author of the source.** Ask whether the author is knowledge-able. Try to determine the author's affiliation and consider how the author's biases affect the information, ideas, and arguments in the source.

✓ **Learn about the publisher of the source.** Try to locate information about the publisher, and reflect on how the publisher's biases affect the information, ideas, and arguments in the source.

✓ **Think about the timeliness of the source** and its impact on and relevance to your project.

✓ **Consider the comprehensiveness of the source** and its impact on and rel-evance to your project.

✓ **Consider the genre of the source** and its impact on the kind of information included in the source, the manner in which information is used by the author, and the likely audience for which the source was written.

[FRAMING MY ARGUMENT]

Consider Genre in Your Decisions about Sources for Your Writing Project
As you consider which sources are best suited for your writing project, keep in mind the importance of referring to sources that your readers will recognize as relevant, reliable, and author-itative. An important part of your purpose as a writer is to influence your readers, and the types of sources you use to support your argu-ment will have an impact on them. Featured writer Pete Jacquez, for example, might have drawn support-ing evidence for his argu-ment about wind-generated electrical power from a wide range of blogs, personal Web sites, discussion forums, and magazine articles. Instead, he chose to rely primarily on government reports, such as the National Renewable

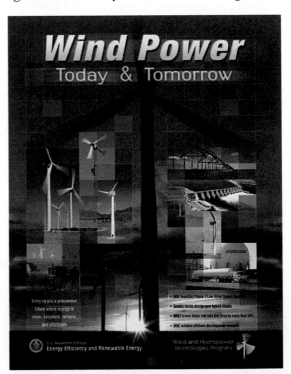

FIGURE 5.1 Pete Jacquez Relied Heavily on Government Reports

Energy Laboratory's *Wind Power: Today and Tomorrow*, because he knew government reports are generally recognized as credible, reliable, and authoritative (see Figure 5.1).

By choosing sources that your readers will recognize as appropriate and reasonable, you can increase the chances that your project will be successful. Understanding the types of documents that are typically used in the genre you've selected for your project document can help you make an effective argument.

5b

Should I evaluate all types of sources in the same way?

You can apply the general evaluative criteria discussed in the previous section to most types of sources. However, two sets of sources — electronic and field sources — can pose challenges during evaluation. The following discussion highlights additional factors to keep in mind as you evaluate electronic and field sources.

Evaluate the Relevance and Credibility of Electronic Sources

Because anyone can create a Web site, start a blog, contribute to a Wiki, or post a message to a newsgroup, email list, or Web discussion forum, approach these sources with more caution than you would reserve for print sources such as books and journal articles, which are typically published only after a lengthy editorial review process.

Web Sites and Blogs To assess the relevance and credibility of a Web site or a blog, examine its domain (.edu, .com, and so on) and look for information about the site (often available through an About This Site or Site Information page). The following tutorial provides information about evaluating Web sites.

TUTORIAL

How do I evaluate a Web site?

Because Web sites can be published without having gone through a rigorous review process, you'll want to evaluate them carefully. Evaluate a Web site by learning about its author, publisher, purpose, publication date, use of evidence, relevance, timeliness, and credibility. This example shows how you can evaluate a Web page that featured writer Alexis Alvarez found as she explored her topic: steroid use by adolescent girls involved in competitive sports.

1 Check its domain (.edu, .gov, .com, and so on) to learn about its purpose and publisher:

.biz, .com, .coop	business	**.mil**	military
.edu	higher education	**.gov**	government
.org	nonprofit organization	**.pro**	professional
.net	network organization	**.name**	personal

2 Check the title bar, page header, and page titles to learn about the site's purpose, publisher (p. 70), and relevance (p. 67).

3 Search for information — on the site or through a separate Web search — about the author (p. 69) or publisher (p. 70), if identified.

4 Check timeliness (p. 70) by looking for a publication or a "last modified" date.

5 Read the body text and review illustrations to evaluate relevance (p. 67), evidence (p. 68), and comprehensiveness (p. 71).

6 Check page footers for information about the publisher and author. Look for *About this Site* or *Contact* links.

Review another example and evaluate your Web sources at **bedfordresearcher.com**. Click on Interactive Exercises.

Newsgroups, Email Lists, Discussion Forums To assess the relevance and credibility of a message on a newsgroup, email list, or Web discussion forum, check for a "signature" at the end of the message and try to locate a Frequently Asked Questions (FAQ) list. A signature can provide information about the sender, such as a professional title, and the URL for a personal home page where you can learn more about the author. An FAQ can tell you about the purpose of a newsgroup, email list, or discussion forum; whether messages are moderated (reviewed prior to posting); and whether membership is open to all or restricted to a particular group.

> @ Learn more at bedfordresearcher.com. Click on Guides > Searching Newsgroups, Email Lists, and Discussion Forums.

Wikis Wikis are Web sites that can be added to or edited by visitors to the site. Wikis such as Wikipedia (en.wikipedia.org) have grown in importance on the Web, and many Wikipedia pages are highly ranked by Web search sites such as Ask, Yahoo!, and Google. Unfortunately, it can be difficult to evaluate the credibility of Wiki pages because their creators and editors are often difficult to identify and because changes to Wiki pages can occur quickly. Susan Kruglinski, in an article in *Discover magazine* (discovermagazine.com/2006/jul/evolutionmap/), reports that the Wikipedia entry for evolution was changed more than 2,000 times by 68 editors over a five year period. Her discussion of those changes calls attention to the difficulty of treating Wiki pages as authoritative and stable.

Evaluate the Relevance and Accuracy of Field Sources

With some adjustment, most of the criteria discussed in this chapter can be applied to field sources such as interviews, correspondence, observations, and surveys. Relevance and the accuracy of the information you collect deserve additional attention. Ask the following questions as you evaluate information collected through field research.

- Are the questions you asked in an interview, a survey, or correspondence still relevant to your research project?

- Is the information you collected in an observation still relevant? Are your observation notes as complete as you had hoped they would be?

- Are the individuals you interviewed or corresponded with as qualified and knowledgeable as you expected?

- Were questions in interviews, surveys, and correspondence answered fully and honestly?

- Did survey respondents have adequate time to complete the survey? Did they appear to believe their privacy would be respected?

> **Information Literacy**
> In most cases, it is best to use Wikis when you are beginning to learn about an issue, and to avoid citing them as the "last word" on a topic. In fact, those last words might change before you submit your final draft.

Working with Sources

My Research Project

USE EVALUATION TO TRIM A WORKING BIBLIOGRAPHY

Use the bibliography tools at **bedfordresearcher.com** to evaluate sources on the criteria defined in this chapter, enter publication information, create annotations, save text from electronic sources, and generate a bibliography.

You can use your evaluations to determine which sources should be added to or removed from your working bibliography. If you decide that a source is no longer relevant to your project, however, don't throw it away. There's always a chance that you'll decide you need it later. Instead of deleting it, put it in a category named "irrelevant," or move it into a new bibliography named "other sources" or "unused sources."

> ### QUICK REFERENCE

Evaluating Your Sources

☑ Evaluate the relevance, evidence, author, publisher, timeliness, comprehensiveness, and genre of your sources. (p. 67)

☑ Evaluate Web sources for relevance and credibility. (p. 73)

☑ Evaluate field research for relevance and accuracy. (p. 75)

Part II
Working with Sources

4	Reading Critically
5	Evaluating Sources
6	Taking Notes
7	Avoiding Plagiarism

6

Taking Notes

 Key Questions

Taking notes allows you to focus more closely on what your sources tell you about your topic and how each source can help you answer your research question. By studying a source and noting the key points it makes, you'll gain a clearer understanding of the source. Careful note taking also helps you avoid plagiarism and lays the foundation for drafting your document. For these reasons, note taking is one of the most important research writing skills.

6a

How can I record my notes?

Some research writers take notes by hand, on note cards, on photocopies of sources, in a notebook, on loose sheets of paper, on the transcript of an interview, or on correspondence. Other researchers choose to take notes electronically, in a word processing program, in a database program, in a bibliographic citation program such as EndNote or Reference Manager, in email messages, or in a blog.

Your notes will be most useful if you take them systematically and consistently. For example, instead of taking some notes on Post-It Notes, some on note cards, and the rest in a word processing file, take all of your notes in one form. A consistent

> **Information Literacy**
> Still other researchers have turned to Web-based tools, such as Google Notebook (see p. 162), which allow you to create notes, save Web-based materials (including images) for later viewing, and organize notes with folders and labels. Using these kinds of tools, you can save "clips" (all or part of a page) for later viewing, annotate your clips, and create notes to manage your project.

note-taking system will make it easier to find information later and will reduce the time and effort you'll need when you organize your ideas and draft your document. It will also reduce the chances that you'll plagiarize unintentionally (see p. 88).

What methods can I use to take notes and avoid plagiarism?

Notes—in the form of direct quotations, paraphrases, and summaries—provide you with a record of your reactions to your sources. Notes can also include comparisons among sources and your thoughts about how to use them later in your document.

> **? WHAT'S MY PURPOSE?**
>
> Review your purpose in your research log. As you take notes, remember that they should reflect your purpose for working on a project and provide direction for quoting, paraphrasing, and summarizing information. Keeping your purpose as writer in mind should help you avoid wasting time taking notes that won't be useful to you later.

Quote Directly

A direct quotation is an exact copy of words found in a source. When you quote directly in your notes, you should enclose the passage in quotation marks, identify the source, and list the number of the page (or paragraph, if you are using a digital source that does not indicate page numbers) where the quotation can be found. Proofread what you have written to make sure it matches the original source exactly—including wording, punctuation, and spelling.

You should take direct-quotation notes when

- a passage in a source features an idea that you want to argue for or against
- a passage in a source provides a clear and concise statement that would enhance your project document
- you want to use an authority's or expert's exact words
- you want to use the exact words of someone who has firsthand experience with the issue you are researching

Be sure to place quotation marks around a quoted passage when you take a note. If you don't use quotation marks, you might later think the passage is a paraphrase or summary and unintentionally plagiarize it when you draft your document. To learn more about avoiding plagiarism, see Chapter 7 (p. 87) and Chapter 15 (p. 222).

Modifying a Direct Quotation Using an Ellipsis   When only part of a passage relates to your project, you might want to quote only that part in your notes. To indicate that you have changed a quotation by deleting words, use three spaced periods, called an ellipsis (. . .). If you don't use an ellipsis, your readers will assume that a quotation you are presenting is identical to the text found in the source.

Original Passage

> Anderson is convinced that this is the right way to do it because he's seen all of the ways that aren't. A girls' basketball coach for more than two decades, he'd already experienced firsthand all that modern youth sports had to offer. It wasn't pretty: Screaming, red-faced parents who shuffle their children from program to program because Junior or Jane doesn't get enough court time. Elite squads that serve as showcases for a few super-star players trying to attract the attention of a Division 1 program. Eight-year-old prima donnas factory-installed with a sense of entitlement simply because they know their way around a ball and a pair of high-tops.
>
> Source: Eric Dexheimer, "Nothing to Lose," retrieved from http://www.westword.com/issues/2004-05-13/news/sports_print.html, paragraph 15.

Quotation Modified Correctly Using an Ellipsis

> *"Anderson is convinced that this is the right way to do it because he's seen all of the ways that aren't. A girls' basketball coach for more than two decades, he'd already experienced firsthand all that modern youth sports had to offer. . . . Screaming, red-faced parents who shuffle their children from program to program because Junior or Jane doesn't get enough court time. Elite squads that serve as showcases for a few superstar players. . . . Eight-year-old prima donnas . . . with a sense of entitlement simply because they know their way around a ball and a pair of high-tops"* (paragraph 15).

Four periods indicate the deletion of a full sentence or more. Three periods indicate material deleted from a sentence.

Modifying a Direct Quotation Using Brackets   Sometimes you'll need to modify a quotation so that it will be easier for your readers to understand it. For example, a passage you want to quote might refer to an individual mentioned in a previous paragraph as "he" or "she." Because your readers will not be able to see that paragraph, you'll want to add the person's name. To modify a direct quotation by changing or adding words, use brackets: [ ]. If you don't use brackets when you change or add words, readers will assume the quotation you are presenting is identical to the text found in the source.

Quotation Modified Correctly Using Brackets

> *"At many magazines, editors have a hand in fashioning them [the advertisements]"* (paragraph 37).

The words added in brackets clarify "them," which refers to a noun in an earlier sentence.

Remember that using brackets and ellipses does not entitle you to change the meaning of a quotation. Check your notes against the original passages to be sure you aren't misrepresenting the source by changing, adding, or deleting words.

Modifying Quotations Using "Sic"   If a passage you are quoting contains a misspelled word or an incorrect fact, use the word "sic" in brackets to indicate that the error occurred in the original passage. If you don't use "sic," your readers will think that the mistake is yours.

> **Quotation Modified Correctly Using "Sic"**
>
> *"Bill Clinten's [sic] last year in office was beset with nearly as many problems as any of his first seven years" (Richards 22).*

Avoiding Unintentional Plagiarism When Quoting from Sources   Unintentional plagiarism occurs when a writer inadvertently fails to acknowledge the source of information, ideas, and arguments in a document (see p. 88). If a writer quotes a passage in a note but neglects to include quotation marks, the quotation might be used in the final document without acknowledgement. The solution to this problem is simple: Take careful notes by using the following checklist. Be aware, however, that mistakes can happen, particularly if you are taking notes in a hurry. As you draft your document, remember to look for notes that differ from your usual style of writing. More often than not, if a note doesn't sound like your own writing, it isn't.

CHECKLIST FOR QUOTING

To quote accurately when taking notes, follow these guidelines:

✔ Identify the author, title, and the page or paragraph where the passage can be found.

✔ Avoid unintentional plagiarism by using quotation marks.

✔ Use ellipses, brackets, and "sic" as necessary.

✔ Check your note against the original passage to be sure you aren't introducing errors or misrepresenting the source.

Paraphrase

If you restate a passage from a source in your own words, you are paraphrasing the source. Typically, a paraphrase is roughly as long as the original passage. You can use paraphrases to illustrate or support points you make in your document or to refer to ideas with which you disagree. Even though you are using your own words when you paraphrase, you must still cite the source because the paraphrase presents ideas and information that are not your own.

One of the most common problems with using source material is paraphrasing too closely—that is, making such minor changes to the words of a source that your paraphrase remains nearly identical to the original passage. To avoid plagiarizing unintentionally by paraphrasing too closely, focus on understanding the key ideas in the passage and then restate them in your own words.

The following examples of paraphrasing are drawn from featured writer Patrick Crossland's research writing project.

Original Passage

"High school grades and test scores are not the only factors considered by colleges and universities in the admissions process. Other factors that influence college admissions decisions include high school rank, being an athlete, alumni connection, extracurricular activities, special talents, and other personal characteristics of applicants."

Source: William H. Gray III, "In the Best Interest of America, Affirmative Action Is a Must," p. 144.

Appropriate Paraphrase

William H. Gray III notes that, in addition to high school grades and standardized test scores, most colleges and universities make admissions decisions based on an applicant's participation in sports, involvement in extracurricular activities, personal qualities, talents, relations to alumni, and class rank (144).

Preserves the meaning of the original passage without replicating sentence structure and wording

Inappropriate Paraphrase

William H. Gray III notes that high school grades and test scores are not the only issues weighed by colleges and universities during college admissions decisions. Other factors that influence those decisions are high school rank, participating in athletics, connections to alumni, out-of-school activities, unique talents, and other personal qualities of applicants (144).

Does not differ sufficiently from original; uses the same sentence structure and changes only some key words

Inappropriate Paraphrase

William H. Gray III notes that participation in sports and involvement in extracurricular activities are among the most important factors affecting college admissions decisions (144).

Distorts the meaning of the original passage

Avoiding Unintentional Plagiarism When Paraphrasing Sources Begin a paraphrase with "In other words." This strategy reminds you that it's important to do more than simply rephrase the passage. You might also want to set the original source aside while you paraphrase so that you won't be tempted to copy sentences directly from it. After you've completed your paraphrase, check it for accuracy.

Working with Sources

TUTORIAL

How do I paraphrase a source?

Paraphrasing a source involves restating the ideas and information in a passage in your own words. Use different words and sentence structure to help ensure that your paraphrase isn't too close to the original passage. In this example, Alexis Alvarez identifies a relevant passage in one of her sources and creates a note that paraphrases the passage.

1 Select the passage you want to paraphrase.

Original Passage: Why do athletes risk chronic debilitating diseases and death by taking steroids? Because these drugs work. In very short order, they pack on pounds of muscle and increase strength dramatically. Weight training while using steroids maximizes your gains.

Source: Kendrick, C. (n.d.). *Seduced by steroids.* Retrieved from http://www.familyeducation.com/drugs-and-alcohol/sports/36182.html.

2 Identify relevant information and ideas in the passage.

Why do athletes risk chronic debilitating diseases and death by taking steroids? Because these drugs work. In very short order, they pack on pounds of muscle and increase strength dramatically. Weight training while using steroids maximizes your gains.

3 Draft a paraphrase that identifies the source and includes the information.

Kendrick (n.d.) asks why athletes use steroids, which can lead to serious illness and death. He responds to his own question by noting that steroids increase muscle mass and strength and are particularly effective when used with weight training.

4 Revise the paraphrase so that it uses wording and sentence structure that differs from the original passage.

Kendrick (n.d.) notes that, despite longterm and potentially lethal health risks, athletes use steroids because, in combination with weight training, they can dramatically increase strength and muscle mass.

Review another example and work on creating your own paraphrases at **bedfordresearcher.com**. Click on Interactive Exercises.

CHECKLIST FOR PARAPHRASING

To paraphrase, follow these guidelines:

✔ Be sure that you understand the passage by reading it and the surrounding text carefully.

✔ Restate the passage in your own words. Make sure that you do more than simply change a few key words.

✔ Avoid unintentional plagiarism by comparing the original passage with your paraphrase. Make sure that you've conveyed the meaning of the passage but that the wording and sentence structure differ from those in the original passage.

✔ Note the author, title, and the page or paragraph where the passage can be found.

Summarize

A summary is a concise statement of information in a source. Research writers often summarize an entire source, but they can also summarize lengthy passages. You can write summaries to capture the overall argument and information in a source, and to record a writer's argument so that you can later refute it. Keep in mind that summaries must include a citation of the source.

Here is an original passage from a source one might consult while researching television addiction. A note containing a summary of the passage, which appeared in *Scientific American*, follows the original.

Original Passage

> What is more surprising is that the sense of relaxation ends when the set is turned off, but the feelings of passivity and lowered alertness continue. Survey participants commonly reflect that television has somehow absorbed or sucked out their energy, leaving them depleted. They say they have more difficulty concentrating after viewing than before. In contrast, they rarely indicate such difficulty after reading. After playing sports or engaging in hobbies, people report improvements in mood. After watching TV, people's moods are about the same or worse than before.
>
> Source: Robert Kubey and Mihaly Csikszentmihalyi, "Television Addiction," p. 76

Appropriate Summary

> *Kubey and Csikszentmihalyi, "Television Addiction," p. 76*
>
> *Although watching television may relax a viewer, studies have shown it does little to improve a viewer's alertness, energy level, or mood. (summary)*

Problems can arise when a writer fails to summarize ideas and instead either creates a close paraphrase or writes a patchwork paraphrase that is little more than a series of passages copied from the source. The following examples of paraphrasing are drawn from Patrick Crossland's research writing project.

Original Passages from the Source's Introduction

A primary tenet of American society revolves around access to positions of influence and equality of opportunity. Educational attainment provides the central vehicle through which upward mobility can occur. . . . This study examines patterns of attendance at four-year and selective four-year colleges across students from single- and two-parent families. In particular, we examine whether these students differ in their choice of colleges to which they apply, are admitted, and which they attend. . . . Differences in access might arise from two possible sources. First, disrupted and intact families may differ in the resources they can bring to bear to prepare their children for college. Second, the impact of these resources on college choices of children from disrupted and intact families may differ. Our results suggest that although both influences are present, differences in the levels of resources account for the largest proportion of the difference in the college choices between children from disrupted and intact families.

Source: Dean Lillard and Jennifer Gerner, "Getting to the Ivy League: How Family Composition Affects College Choice," p. 709.

Inappropriate Summary

Lillard and Gerner, "Getting to the Ivy League," p. 709

Lillard and Gerner argue that *higher education provides the primary means through which upward mobility occurs* in the United States. They *studied patterns of attendance at four-year and selective four-year colleges across college applicants from single- and two-parent families,* focusing in particular on differences in *decisions about which college to apply to, admissions decision, and colleges attended.* They found that *differences in the financial and educational resources accounted for the primary difference in college choices between children from single- and two-parent families.* (summary)

The highlighted passages are paraphrased too closely.

Appropriate Summary

Lillard and Gerner, "Getting to the Ivy League," p. 709

In the article "Getting to the Ivy League: How Family Composition Affects College Choice," Dean Lillard and Jennifer Gerner stress that a student's ability to obtain loans, his or her likelihood of getting financial aid, and family support all affect college admissions choices. Students who grow up in poor families or weak school districts are at a disadvantage compared to students from affluent families and schools, and may not be given the resources they need to help them with the college application process. (summary)

The summary gives a broad overview of the article's argument and avoids close paraphrases of key points.

Avoiding Unintentional Plagiarism When Summarizing a Source Remind yourself to summarize, rather than mirror the language and sentence structure of the source, by beginning your summary with "The author argues that" or "The author found that." You might want to set the original source aside while you write your summary so that you won't be tempted to copy sentences directly from it. After you've completed your summary, check it for accuracy.

CHECKLIST FOR SUMMARIZING

To summarize, follow these guidelines:

✔ Be sure that you understand the source by reading it carefully.

✔ Summarize main and supporting points in your own words. Make sure that you do more than string together a series of close paraphrases of key passages.

✔ Check for unintentional plagiarism by comparing the original source with your summary.

✔ Note the author, title, and, if you are summarizing only part of a source, the page or paragraphs where the information can be found.

Compare Sources

Your notes can indicate connections among your sources by identifying relationships among ideas, information, and arguments. Paying attention to your sources as a group—not just to individual sources—helps you gain a more complete understanding of your issue. It also can be useful when you begin planning and organizing your document. Featured writer Chris Norris reviewed his notes and identified connections he saw between what he'd observed at shows and what he'd learned from his interviews with the musicians in Last Word, a local metal band. In his observation notes, Chris added a comparison note: "This ties in with Adler's interview."

Start Planning Your Document

Planning notes are directions to yourself about how you might use a source in your project document, how you might organize the document, or ideas you should remember later. Chris Norris wrote planning notes—such as, "How will this tie in? Use on opening screen?"—as he prepared to write his multimodal essay.

[FRAMING MY ARGUMENT]

Look for Disagreements among Your Sources Although your argument will develop more fully as you plan and draft your essay, you probably have some idea by now of the overall point you'd like to make in your document. As you take notes, pay attention to how the authors of each source might respond to your point and to the points made in the other sources you collect. Once you've finished taking notes, review them to identify patterns in the authors' responses. Look in particular for disagreements among the authors. As you learn more about the central points of disagreement in a conversation, you'll begin to understand how writers align themselves with an issue. As a result, you'll be prepared to decide which sources might provide support for your argument and which sources will serve best to illustrate alternative approaches to the issue (see Figure 6.1).

Patrick Crossland reminds himself how he might use a source to support his argument.

Derek Bok, PBS Online, Frontline Interview

http://www.pbs.org/wgbh/pages/frontline/shows/sats/interviews/bok.html

In the interview, Bok states, "I think our data show pretty well that the more challenging the academic environment is in which minority students perform — within reason, assuming they're well selected — the better they do, the more they graduate, the more they appreciate the experience, the more advanced degrees they get, the higher salaries that they earn.

Line up this argument against Krauthammer's claim that admission decisions should be race blind.

"And as far as stigma is concerned, the differential between blacks and whites is considerably smaller for the students who've gone to selective schools with race sensitive policies. If they were stigmatized, you would think that the salary differential would be higher. That's exactly not what occurs.

"So, I think the arguments that were being used until our study came out simply turn out — when you get all the facts — to be wrong." (paragraphs 3-5)

FIGURE 6.1 An Annotation about a Disagreement among Sources

My Research Project

TAKE NOTES

Take notes and save them in your research log. Be careful to avoid plagiarizing your sources as you quote, paraphrase, and summarize them.

> **QUICK REFERENCE**

Taking Notes

☑ Decide how you will record your notes; then take notes systematically and consistently. (p. 77)

☑ Take notes that quote sources directly. (p. 78)

☑ Take notes that paraphrase passages in sources. (p. 80)

☑ Take notes that summarize sources. (p. 83)

☑ Write notes that compare the information, ideas, and arguments in sources. (p. 85)

☑ Write notes that help you plan your document. (p. 85)

Part II
Working with Sources
4   Reading Critically
5   Evaluating Sources
6   Taking Notes
> 7 Avoiding Plagiarism

7

Avoiding Plagiarism

 **Key Questions**

Few writers intentionally try to pass off the work of others as their own. However, deadlines and other pressures can lead writers to take notes poorly and cite sources improperly. In addition, easy access to documents through the Web and full-text databases has made it tempting to copy and paste work from other writers without acknowledging its source.

Failing to cite your sources can lead to serious problems. Your readers will not be able to determine which ideas and information in your text are your own or which are drawn from your sources. If they suspect you are failing to acknowledge your sources, they are likely to doubt your credibility and suspect your competence, and they might even stop reading your document. More seriously, submitting academic work that does not include proper identification of sources might result in failure in a course or some other disciplinary action.

7a

What is plagiarism?

Plagiarism is a form of intellectual dishonesty. It involves either unintentionally using someone else's work without properly acknowledging where the ideas or information came from (the most common form of plagiarism) or intentionally passing off someone else's work as your own (the most serious form of plagiarism).

Plagiarism is based on the notion of "copyright," or ownership of a document or idea. Like a patent, which protects an invention, a copyright protects an author's investment of time and energy in the creation of a document. Essentially, it assures authors that, when they create a document, someone else won't be able to steal ideas from it and profit from that theft without penalty.

Unintentional Plagiarism

In most cases, plagiarism is unintentional, and most cases of unintentional plagiarism result from taking poor notes or failing to use notes properly. You are plagiarizing if you

- quote a passage in a note but neglect to include quotation marks and then later insert the quotation into your document without remembering that it is a direct quotation.
- include a paraphrase that differs so slightly from the original passage that it might as well be a direct quotation.
- don't clearly distinguish between your ideas and ideas that come from your sources.
- neglect to list the source of a paraphrase, quotation, or summary in your text or in your works cited list.

Although unintentional plagiarism is, by definition, something that the writer hasn't planned to do, it is nonetheless a serious issue and, when detected, is likely to have consequences. Some instructors might require that an assignment be rewritten; others might impose a penalty, such as a lowered grade or failure on the assignment.

Intentional Plagiarism

Intentional plagiarism, although less common than unintentional plagiarism, can lead to academic penalties ranging from a reduced grade on an assignment to failure of a course to expulsion. Intentional plagiarism includes

- engaging in "patchwork writing," which involves piecing together passages from two or more sources without acknowledging the source and without properly quoting or paraphrasing.

TUTORIAL

How can I avoid unintentional plagiarism?

Unintentional plagiarism is the use of another writer's work without properly acknowledging the source of the ideas or information. Unintentional plagiarism is often the result of rushed work on a project. It can sometimes result from inadequate research writing skills or honest mistakes. In this example, featured writer Patrick Crossland checks his rough draft for unintentional plagiarism.

To avoid unintentional plagiarism, follow these steps:

1 Check for a works cited or reference list.

2 Identify each quotation, paraphrase, and summary.

3 Check for appropriate attributions.

4 Check for appropriate in-text citation.

5 Ensure that each source is included in your works cited or reference list.

6 Check for changes in writing style. If you find changes, check your notes to identify the source of the passage and ensure that you haven't neglected to include quotation marks or paraphrased too closely.

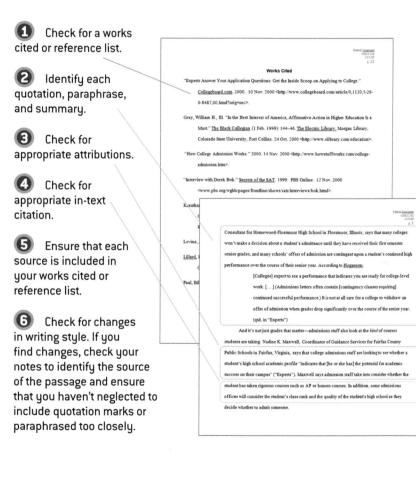

Review another example and assess your own draft for unintentional plagiarism at **bedfordresearcher.com**. Click on Interactive Exercises.

- creating fake citations to mislead a reader about the sources of information used in a document.

> For additional help, consult the St. Martin's Tutorial on Avoiding Plagiarism at bedfordstmartins.com/plagiarismtutorial.

- copying or closely paraphrasing extended passages from another document and passing them off as the writer's original work.

- copying an entire document and passing it off as the writer's original work.

- purchasing a document and passing it off as the writer's original work.

7b

What are research ethics?

Research ethics are based on the notion that writing — and in particular research writing — is an honest exchange of information, ideas, and arguments among writers and readers who share an interest in an issue. As a research writer, you'll want to behave honestly and ethically. In general, you should

- acknowledge the sources of the information, ideas, and arguments used in your document. By doing so, you show respect for the work that others have done before you.

- accurately and fairly represent the information, ideas, and arguments — to ensure that you do not misrepresent that work to your readers.

- provide citation information for your sources. These citations help your readers understand how you have drawn your conclusions and where they can locate those sources should they want to consult them.

These three rules are the essence of research ethics. If your readers suspect that you have acted unethically, they will question the accuracy and credibility of the information, ideas, and arguments in your document. Ultimately, failing to act ethically — even when the failure is unintentional — can reflect poorly on you and your document.

[FRAMING MY ARGUMENT]

Safeguard the Effectiveness of Your Argument Through Ethical Research Practices   Few readers will give you credit for being a good researcher. If they notice that you've cut a few corners, however, they'll start to question your credibility. If they suspect you've sacrificed research ethics altogether, they'll probably stop reading your document. By attending to research ethics — by acknowledging your sources, representing them fairly, and citing them accurately — you can safeguard the trust of your readers and increase the chances that they'll pay attention to your argument. Figure 7.1 shows how featured writer Kevin Fahey attended to research ethics in his essay about Ernest Hemingway's characterization of Nick Adams.

Hannum points out, the theme of submergence as a defense mechanism recurs throughout

the Nick Adams stories: "Even on the threshold of adult life, [Nick] has not yet learned

that submergence merely shelves problems, without solving them for him (47)." The

repetition of this theme throughout the story suggests that Nick dislikes swimming on the

surface because it requires more discipline and endurance than swimming underwater.

Underwater, Nick might also feel that he can temporarily "escape society's rules about

sexual behavior" (Comley 70), which would require him to face his fear of commitment.

Nick is "forever seeking a pristine boyhood paradise free from the responsibility of adult,

heterosexual relationships" (Strychacz 67).

   Not only does Nick lack the code hero's self-awareness and courage, but he also

> An attribution is used to identify the source of a paraphrase and a subsequent quotation.

> Quotation marks and parenthetical source citation indicate partial quotation.

Jain, S. P. *Hemingway: A Study of his Short Stories.* New Delhi: Arnold-Heinemann,

   1985. Print.

Schafer, Nancy Imelda. "Ernest Hemingway." *Empirezine.com*. N.P., 2001. Web.

   3 Oct. 2001.

Strychacz, Thomas. "In Our Time, Out of Season." *The Cambridge Companion to*

   Hemingway. Ed. Scott Donaldson. Cambridge: Cambridge UP, 1996. 55–86. Print.

Wilt, Judith. Personal interview. 16 Oct. 2001.

Young, Philip. *Ernest Hemingway: A Reconsideration*. University Park: The

> Complete source information is included in the works cited list.

> Sources are cited in MLA style.

FIGURE 7.1 Attending to Research Ethics

Working with Sources

7c

What is common knowledge?

Although crediting other authors for their work is important, you almost certainly won't need to document every fact and idea used in your document, because some of the information you'll use falls under the category of common knowledge. Common knowledge is information that is widely known, such as the fact that the Declaration of Independence was signed in 1776. Or it might be the kind of knowledge that people working in a particular field, such as petroleum engineering, use on a regular basis.

  If you're relatively new to your topic, it can be difficult to determine whether information in a source is common knowledge. As you explore your topic, however, you will begin to identify what is generally known. For instance, if three or more sources use the same information without citing its source, you can assume that the information is common knowledge. If those sources use the information and cite the source, however, make sure you cite it as well.

7d

What is fair use and when should I ask permission to use a source?

The concept of fair use deals with how much of a source you can borrow or quote. According to Section 107 of the Copyright Act of 1976—the fair use provision, available at copyright.gov/title17/—writers can use copyrighted

---

Dear Ms. Jackson:

I am a student and am completing a research project for my writing class, English Composition 200, at Colorado State University. The research project will be used only for educational purposes and will be distributed only to my **A** instructor and members of my class for a period of three weeks during April and May of this year.

B I would like to include in my project the following image, which is displayed on your site at www.westernliving.org/images/2302a.jpg, and would greatly appreciate your permission to do so:

C If you are able to grant me the requested permission, please respond to this email message. My deadline for completing my project is April 22nd. I appreciate your quick response.

If you are not the copyright holder or do not have authority to grant this request, I would appreciate any information you can provide concerning the current copyright holder.

Thank you for considering this request.

Sincerely,

Glenn Choi   **D**

GlennChoi@students.colostate.edu

(970) 555–1515

FIGURE 7.2 Sample Permission Request

A Or " . . . on the Web at www.myschool.edu."

B Insert or describe passage or image. For example: "paragraphs 3 through 5 of the article," a thumbnail of the image, the URL of a document or image on the Web.

C Or " . . . sign the enclosed copy of this letter and return it to me."

D Provide contact information, such as name, address, email address, phone number, fax number.

materials for purposes of "criticism, comment, news reporting, teaching (including multiple copies for classroom use), scholarship, or research." In other words, writers generally don't need to seek permission to make brief quotations from a source or to summarize or paraphrase a source.

Writers who plan to publish their work should seek permission to use material from a source if they want to quote a lengthy passage or, in the case of shorter works such as poems and song lyrics, if they want to quote a significant percentage of the source. If you are working on an assignment for a course — and do not plan to publish the assignment on the Web or in print — you are generally allowed to use material from another source without seeking permission to do so. Remember, however, that in all cases you must still cite the source of the material you use.

If you seek permission to use a source, explain why and how you want to use it. Many authors and publishers allow academic use of their work but frown on commercial uses. When you contact an author or publisher, send a permission agreement that includes your name and contact information, the source you wish to use, the purpose for which you will use the source, and the time during which it will be used (see Figure 7.2).

If you contact an author or publisher by mail, include a self-addressed, stamped envelope. It will save the author or publisher the cost of responding by mail, indicates that you are serious, and, perhaps most important, shows good manners.

■■ Working with Sources

7e

Why do writers plagiarize?

The causes of intentional plagiarism range from running out of time to seeing little value in a course. The most common reasons offered to explain intentional plagiarism — and steps you can take to avoid falling victim to its temptation — are listed below.

The Top Seven Reasons Students Plagiarize — and Why They Don't Pay Off

"It's easy to plagiarize."   Some people believe it takes less work to cheat than to create an original document. That's probably true — but only in the short term. If you are pursuing a college degree, the odds are high that your profession will require writing ability or an understanding of how to work with information. When you're assigned a report or a proposal down the road, you might regret not taking the time to hone your writing and research skills.

Information Literacy
Writers who wish to use multimedia sources, such as images, audio, or video, should consider either seeking permission to use the source or linking directly to it. Be cautious about linking directly to multimedia sources, however, since some Web sites specifically ask that you not link to content on their site (typically because doing so increases the demand on Web servers).

"I ran out of time."   If you're among the select group of people who carefully budget their time and complete their assignments early, congratulations. You probably won't be tempted to plagiarize because you've run out of time to work on an assignment. If you're like the rest of us, however, you'll occasionally find yourself wondering where all the time has gone and how you can possibly complete the assignment. If you find yourself in this situation, contact your instructor about a revised deadline for the assignment. You might find that you'll face a penalty for turning in work late, but that penalty will almost certainly be less severe than a penalty for intentional plagiarism.

"I couldn't care less about this assignment."   It's not unusual to put off assignments that don't interest you. Rather than simply putting off the assignment, review the discussion of "taking ownership of an assignment" (see p. 4) to determine whether you can focus the assignment in a way that interests you. If that fails, contact your instructor to see if you can customize the assignment so that it better aligns with your interests.

"I'm no good at writing."   A surprisingly large number of people have doubts about their ability to write well enough to earn a good grade in a writing course. With time, effort, and support, however, most of them do well in their courses. Occasionally, however, people convince themselves that plagiarizing is a reasonable alternative to writing their own document. If you lack confidence in your writing skills, seek assistance from your instructor, a campus writing center, a tutoring center, one of the many online writing centers on the Web (such as the Writing@CSU Web site at writing.colostate.edu), or a friend or family member. You're likely to find that, even with only modest support, you'll be able to accomplish your goals as a writer.

"I didn't think I'd get caught."   Some writing students believe—and might even have experiences to support their belief—that they won't get caught. If instructors do not regularly see student writing, that might be the case. Most writing courses, however, allow instructors to become familiar with their students' writing styles. If instructors notice a sudden change in style, or encounter varying styles in the same document, they might become suspicious about the originality of the document. In addition, a growing number of colleges and universities are starting to rely on plagiarism detection software, which increases the likelihood that plagiarism can be detected. Indeed, even "original, unplagiarized essays" available for a reasonable price on the Web can turn out to be less original than advertised.

"Everybody plagiarizes."   Some people plagiarize intentionally because they believe everyone else (or at least a substantial number of their classmates) is doing so. In fact, however, the number of students who plagiarize in writing courses is quite low. Despite reports that as many as 87 percent of college students have admitted to cheating at least once in high school, the number of students who cheat in college is significantly lower than that, and cheating is far more likely to occur on tests and in homework assignments in math and science courses than in writing courses. In addition, the students most likely to cheat are those who earn lower grades in the courses. Don't be persuaded by dramatic statistics that plagiarism is the norm in writing classes. The reality is that few students plagiarize intentionally, and those who do still tend to earn lower grades than most students in the course.

"This course is a waste of my time."   If you view a course as little more than a box that needs to be checked, rather than an opportunity to learn something of value, you might attempt to check that box with as little effort as possible. If you find yourself questioning the value of a course that requires writing assignments, you might be tempted to turn in work that isn't your own. Doing so, however, can backfire in significant ways. If you are caught plagiarizing, you'll most likely receive a reduced grade for the assignment or the course, and it's possible you'll fail the course and need to retake it. Instead of plagiarizing, talk with the instructor about your concerns about the relevance of the course, or discuss the situation with an academic advisor. You might find, as a result of those discussions, that the course actually has some relevance to your interests and career plans.

7f

How can I avoid plagiarism?

In most cases, writers who plagiarize do so unintentionally. You can avoid unintentional plagiarism by learning how to

- take notes accurately (see Chapter 6)
- integrate quotations, paraphrases, and summaries into a document (see Chapter 15)
- cite sources in the text and in a works cited or reference list (see Chapters 19–23)

Gaining control over these three sets of research writing skills can reduce the risk of plagiarizing unintentionally. Taking notes accurately will reduce the chance that, during drafting, you'll think a direct quotation from a source is a paraphrase or summary written in your own words. Learning how to integrate information from your sources will help you ensure that the information and ideas from a source don't mistakenly read as if they are your own work. And citing sources in your text and in a list at the end of your document will let your readers know that you want to give credit to the sources from which you've drawn information, ideas, and arguments.

You can also avoid unintentional plagiarism by ensuring that you have a clear understanding of your issue. When you are just beginning to learn about an issue, you might find it difficult not only to express your own ideas clearly and effectively, but also to restate or reframe the information, ideas, and arguments

Working with Sources

you've encountered in your sources. The result might be a document composed of passages that have been copied without attribution or paraphrased too closely. To address difficulties understanding an issue, conduct a knowledge inventory to gain insights into what you do and don't understand about the issue. Conducting a knowledge inventory involves answering three questions.

1. What do you already know about the issue?
2. What don't you know?
3. What do you want to know?

Your knowledge inventory can serve as a starting point for brainstorming, collecting and working with sources, and planning. It can also serve as a guide for discussing the issue with others.

My Research Project

CONDUCT A KNOWLEDGE INVENTORY

In your research log, answer the following questions about the issue you've decided to address in your project document.

1. What do I already know about the issue?

2. What don't I know?

3. What do I want to know?

Review your answers, then identify the concepts that, if you understood them more fully, would allow you to work on your assignment more effectively. Learn about those concepts by discussing them with an instructor, librarian, or someone who knows about or has been affected by the issue.

You can print or download this activity at **bedfordresearcher.com**. Click on Activities > Conduct a Knowledge Inventory.

Avoid Plagiarism During Group Work   Peer review and other collaborative activities raise important questions about plagiarism.

-   If another writer suggests changes to your document and you subsequently incorporate them into your document, are you plagiarizing?
-   What if those suggestions significantly change your document?
-   If you work with a group of writers on a project, do you need to identify the parts that each of you wrote?
-   Is it ethical to list yourself as a coauthor if another writer does most of the work on a collaborative writing project?

Information Literacy

Once you've completed your knowledge inventory, meet with your instructor, consult a librarian, or talk with people who are knowledgeable about the issue. Use the results of your knowledge inventory to frame your discussion. It might, for example, help you identify key concepts that, once understood, will help you write about your issue more effectively. Ideally, your discussions will help you determine the most productive way to learn more about your issue.

The answers to these questions will vary from situation to situation. In general, it's appropriate to use comments from reviewers in your document without citing them. If a reviewer's comments are particularly helpful, acknowledge his or her contributions in your document; writers often thank reviewers in a footnote or endnote or in an acknowledgments section. It is usually appropriate to list coauthors on a collaboratively written document without individually identifying the text that was written by each coauthor, although some instructors ask that individual contributions be noted in the document or on a cover page. If you are uncertain about what is appropriate, ask your instructor.

7g

What should I do if I'm accused of plagiarism?

If your instructor expresses concerns about the originality of your work or the manner in which you've documented your use of information, ideas, and arguments from sources, ask for a meeting to discuss the situation. To prepare for the meeting

- review your document to identify passages that might have raised suspicions.
- collect the materials you've used in your writing project, such as copies of your sources, responses to surveys, interview transcripts, and so on.
- collect materials you've written during the project, such as the results of brainstorming and freewriting sessions; organizational materials you've created, such as clusters, maps, and outlines; and rough and final drafts of your document.
- reflect on your research writing process.

During the meeting, listen to the concerns of your instructor before responding. It will be natural to feel defensive about the situation, but you'll probably be more comfortable if you take notes and try to understand why your instructor has concerns about your document. Once your instructor is finished expressing his or her concerns, think carefully about what has been said and respond as clearly as possible. You'll probably find that your instructor will have follow-up questions, most likely about the sources you've used, your research writing process, and the document you've written.

If you find that you have engaged in unintentional plagiarism, ask your instructor for guidance about how to avoid it in the future and ask what sort of penalty you will face for doing so. Ask, as well, what consequences you might face should it be determined that you have plagiarized intentionally.

If you and your instructor are unable to resolve the situation, you might face a disciplinary process. To prepare for that process, learn as much as you can about the academic integrity policies at your institution.

> **QUICK REFERENCE**

Avoiding Plagiarism

☑ Understand the definition of plagiarism and the concept of copyright. (p. 87)

☑ Understand the meaning of research ethics. (p. 90)

☑ Understand the concept of common knowledge. (p. 91)

☑ Understand the concept of fair use and, if necessary, seek permission to use sources. (p. 92)

☑ Understand why you might be tempted to plagiarize intentionally and reflect on strategies for avoiding temptation. (p. 93)

☑ Understand how to reduce the chance that you'll plagiarize unintentionally. (p. 95)

☑ Understand what to do if you are accused of plagiarism. (p. 97)

Working with Sources

The Bedford Researcher

I	Joining the Conversation
II	Working with Sources
III	**Collecting Information**
IV	Writing Your Document
V	Documenting Sources

PART III

Collecting Information

 8   Planning Your Search for Information   101

 9   Searching for Information with Electronic Resources   108

 10   Searching for Information with Print Resources   140

 11   Searching for Information with Field Research Methods   150

 12   Managing Information   162

Learning how to collect information provides the foundation for a successful research project. As you begin to answer your research question, you'll want to know more about how and where to look for useful sources of information. In this section you'll learn how to develop a plan to guide your search for information; how to search for information using electronic resources, print resources, and field research methods; and how to keep track of the information you collect.

8

Planning Your Search for Information

Key Questions

8a. How can I identify relevant sources?   102

8b. How can I identify and use the best search tools and research methods?   104

8c. How can I get ready to carry out my plan?   106

Getting ready to search for information involves making decisions about

- the types of sources you want to collect (such as books, articles, and opinion columns)

- the types of search tools (such as library catalogs, databases, and Web search sites) and research methods (such as browsing library shelves, consulting librarians, and conducting surveys) you will use to collect information

- the types of searches you will carry out (such as keyword and phrase searches)

- the schedule you will follow as you conduct your research

To make these decisions, reflect on the plan you created in Chapter 2 to explore your topic. The goal of that plan was to gain a broad understanding of the conversations taking place about issues in your topic. Now you are ready to develop a research plan—a brief, informal plan that records your ideas about how to locate and collect information on a specific conversation about your issue. Unlike a research proposal (see p. 44), which is addressed to an instructor, supervisor, or potential funding agency, a research plan is written for *you*.

? WHAT'S MY PURPOSE?

Your research question focuses your attention on a specific aspect of the issue you've decided to address. Your decisions about how to search for information should reflect that focus.

Consider Elizabeth Leontiev's research question and the different plans she might have used to locate and collect information. Elizabeth's research question asks how we can reduce the economic impact of the war on drugs on South American coca farmers. Her research plan led her to collect information through interviews with faculty at her university, searches of U.S. and South American government Web sites, searches of news Web sites, database searches of articles and editorials in newspapers and magazines, and database searches for articles in scholarly journals. If she had developed a different research question, Elizabeth would have developed a different research plan. For instance, if she had focused on the effectiveness of U.S. policy at reducing the importation of cocaine, she would have decided to search U.S. government Web sites and her keyword and phrase searches (see p. 132) would have concentrated on cocaine smuggling as opposed to the plight of South American farmers.

As you decide how to collect and manage information, keep your research question in mind. Doing so will help you determine the types of sources, resources, and search strategies you'll need to investigate the issue you've decided to address.

8a

How can I identify relevant sources?

Research writers use information found in a variety of sources—electronic, print, and field—to support the points they make in their documents. To identify relevant sources, consider the scope and timeliness of your

> @ Read more about Elizabeth Leontiev at bedfordresearcher.com. Click on Featured Writers.

issue, the nature of the conversation you are joining, and the type of evidence you'll need to learn about and frame your argument.

- **Consider the scope and timeliness of your issue.** Issues that are of interest to a large number of readers and writers, such as funding for higher education or reducing alcohol consumption by college students, tend to be discussed over an extended period of time in a wide range of sources. Binge drinking by college students, for example, has been addressed for decades by writers of scholarly books and scholarly journal articles, and the issue has been the subject of countless newspaper and magazine articles, Web sites, and blogs. If your issue involves a recent or highly localized incident, however, such as the death of a local college student from alcohol poisoning, you're less likely to find the incident discussed in books or scholarly journals, since months or even years can pass between the time an article is written and the time it is published. It is typically more effective, in the case of issues that involve recent events or "breaking news," to turn to magazine and newspaper articles, the Web, blogs, observation, surveys, or interviews.

- **Consider the nature of the conversation you plan to join.** Ask yourself whether you are joining a conversation taking place among the general public, a group of enthusiasts or concerned citizens, or a group of scholars within a particular discipline. If, for example, you are joining a conversation about a highly specialized issue within a scholarly discipline, such as a discussion of gene splicing in biochemistry, you're likely to find that the best sources will be scholarly books and scholarly journal articles. In contrast, if the conversation focuses on an issue that has broad appeal, such as how best to address transportation problems in your state or region, you'll be able to draw on a much wider range of sources, including newspaper and magazine articles, editorials and opinion columns, blogs, and Web sites.

- **Consider what you'll need to learn about an issue.** If the issue you will write about is unfamiliar to you, look for sources that offer general overviews or discuss important aspects of the issue. The introductory chapters of scholarly books, for example, often provide general overviews of an issue, even when the majority of the book might focus on only a narrow aspect of the issue. You can also look for overviews of an issue in magazine articles, in professional journal articles, and on the Web.

Collecting Information

[FRAMING MY ARGUMENT]

Consider the Type of Evidence You'll Need to Frame an Argument. As you consider how you'll construct your argument, think about the kind of evidence other writers have used to address the issue. If you've found that most writers have referred to information, ideas, and arguments found in scholarly journal articles, for example, be sure to search for those kinds of articles (see Figure 8.1).

Family Composition and College Choice 715

biological parents (52% compared to 62%), and many fewer ever attended a four-year college (37% compared to 51%). Although it is well documented that children from disrupted families acquire less education, it is remarkable that the association shows up at every decision point for postsecondary education.

> Sources are cited in parentheses, following APA style.

The differences we observe between disrupted and nondisrupted families are consistent with the evidence from the education literature which finds that children from low-income families are less likely to attend selective schools (Kingston & Lewis, 1989; Hearn, 1989). If disrupted families have lower incomes than nondisrupted families, we would expect to see lower probabilities of attendance at more selective schools for children from disrupted families.

The association between family disruption and college choice is also reflected in the quality of the colleges to which students apply, are admitted, and attend. Figure 2 shows that, conditional on having applied to

---

FIGURE 8.1 Scholarly Journal Article Found by Patrick Crossland as He Explored His Topic

a college, a student was 33% less likely to apply to a selective college if he or she did not live with both biological parents while in high school (3.9% versus 2.6%). Those experiencing family disruption were less likely to be admitted to a selective school given they applied, and given that they attended any four-year school, they were 20% less likely to attend a selective school immediately after high school and 22% less likely to ever attend a selective school.

> Numerical data is used throughout the article.

The differences shown in Figures 1 and 2 can be decomposed into differences in impact and differences in levels of resources discussed earlier. The equation we use to decompose observed differences is given by:

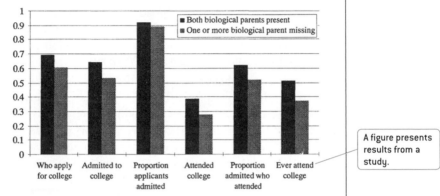

> A figure presents results from a study.

FIGURE 8.1 *continued*

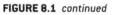

8b

How can I identify and use the best search tools and research methods?

Once you've identified the types of sources that seem most relevant, determine which search tools and research methods you might use to locate those sources. In general, you can use three sets of resources to locate information:

- **Electronic search tools,** such as online library catalogs, databases, and Web search sites, allow you to search and browse for sources using a computer. Electronic search tools provide access to publication information about—and in some cases to the complete text of—print and digital sources.

- **Print resources,** such as bibliographies, indexes, encyclopedias, dictionaries, handbooks, almanacs, and atlases, can be found in library reference and periodicals rooms. Unlike electronic search tools, which typically cover recent publications, many print resources provide information about publications over several decades—and in some cases over more than a century.

- **Field research methods** allow you to collect information firsthand. These methods include conducting observations, interviews, and surveys; corresponding with experts; attending public events and performances; and viewing or listening to television and radio programs.

TUTORIAL

How can I identify relevant types of sources?

Locate the types of resources you might use to locate information by considering the scope and timeliness of your issue, the nature of the conversation you are join-ing, and the type of evidence you'll need to learn about and frame your argument.

In this example, Chris Norris began the process of deciding what kinds of sources to search for by brainstorming. He used the results of his brainstorming to create his search plan.

1 Consider the scope and timeliness of your issue.

Scope and Timeliness: The scope is pretty narrow, I think. I'm focusing on a particular type of contemporary music, rather than everything that's new. But timeliness is interesting, because it's both current and historic. There's a sense of revival, with plenty of play off of old ideas. Metal's been around for a while, so I'll need to look at older sources.

2 Consider the nature of the conversation you are joining.

Nature of the Conversation: The conversation is mostly among fans and a few music critics, usually on the Web and mostly through blogs. There are a few sites, but the real action is taking place in blogs. There are also some magazines, but they're not as widely read as the blogs.

3 Consider the type of sources needed to learn about an issue.

Learning about the Issues: I'll need to figure out who's who, get a sense of the key critics and the leading artists (besides my faves).

4 Consider the type of evidence needed to frame your argument.

Framing the Issue: Sources I've read so far seem to be mostly personal opinion and analysis of new music. People quote some of the more popular artists and the more respected bloggers/critics.

Review another example and work on creating your search plan at **bedfordresearcher.com**. Click on Interactive Exercises.

Collecting Information

Your research plan should identify the strategies you will use for each type of search tool and research method. Research strategies include keyword searches, interview questions, and observation forms. If your topic lends itself to Web searches, for instance, your research plan should define the keyword searches you will use. If you need to interview people, your research plan should identify the questions you want to ask each person.

Because Chris Norris wanted to understand why musicians and fans had developed a renewed interest in metal music, he needed to develop interview questions; create a means of collecting information during his observations; and compile a list of potential search terms for databases, Web search sites, and directories. In contrast, because Kevin Fahey was searching primarily for books and journal articles, he based his research plan almost exclusively on searches in library catalogs and databases.

My Research Project Activity

CREATE A RESEARCH PLAN

In your research log, create a research plan using the following questions.

1. What types of sources are most relevant to my issue?

2. What types of search tools and research methods should I use to locate information?

3. What research strategies should I use with each tool and method?

You can download or print this activity at **bedfordresearcher.com**. Click on Activities > Create a Research Plan.

8c

How can I get ready to carry out my plan?

After developing your research plan, schedule time to search for and collect information. Next to each activity—such as searching databases, searching the Web, searching a library catalog, and conducting an interview—identify start dates and projected completion dates. Creating a schedule will help you budget and manage your time.

Share your research plan with your instructor, your supervisor, or a librarian. Each might suggest additional search tools, research methods, shortcuts, and alternative research strategies for your project. Take notes on the feedback you receive and, if necessary, revise your plan.

Collecting Information

Planning Your Search for Information

☑ Prepare to collect information by reflecting on your purpose. (p. 102)

☑ Create a research plan. (p. 106)

☑ Create a schedule for carrying out your research plan. (p. 106)

☑ Ask your instructor, your supervisor, or a librarian to review your plan. (p. 106)

Collecting Information

Part III
Collecting Information

8 Planning Your Search for
   Information

9 Searching for Information with
   Electronic Resources

10 Searching for Information with
   Print Resources

11 Searching for Information with
   Field Research Methods

12 Managing Information

9

Searching for Information with Electronic Resources

> **Key Questions**
>
> **9a. How can I search for sources with online library catalogs?   109**
> Search by author
> Search by title
> Search by keyword
> Search by subject
> Search by publication date
> Search by call number
> Search by a combination of terms
>
> **9b. How can I search for sources with databases?   113**
> Identify relevant databases
> Search within database fields
> Search with wildcards
> Conduct Boolean searches
> Set search limits
>
> **9c. How can I search for sources with Web search sites?   123**
> Identify relevant Web search sites
> Search with keywords and phrases
> Conduct advanced Web searches
> Use special symbols and operators
>
> **9d. How can I search for sources with media search sites?   136**
> Use image search sites and directories
> Use audio search sites
> Use video search sites

Since the computer became a research tool, the primary challenge associated with collecting information has changed. Research writers no longer worry about locating *enough* sources; instead, they worry about finding the *right* sources. This chapter addresses the important differences among online library catalogs, databases, Web search sites, and media search sites that you can use to locate information, and explains how to use these resources to locate the best sources for your research writing project.

How can I search for sources with online library catalogs?

Library catalogs provide information about the materials in a library's collection. Most libraries provide access to their catalogs through the Web, although some smaller libraries rely on traditional print catalogs. At a minimum, an online catalog will provide information about the author(s), title, publication date, subject, and call number for each source in the library's collection. Often it will also indicate the location of the source in the library and whether the source is available for checkout.

Online library catalogs give information on the print publications in a library collection. They can also provide information about publications in other media. Online catalogs typically help you locate

> **@** Find other sites that list online library catalogs at bedfordresearcher.com. Click on Links > Resources for Conducting Electronic Searches.

- books
- journals owned by the library (although not individual articles)
- newspapers and magazines owned by the library (although not individual articles)
- documents stored on microfilm or microfiche
- videotapes, audiotapes, CDs, DVDs, and other multimedia items owned by the library
- maps
- theses and dissertations completed by college or university graduate students

Note that library catalogs are not well suited for locating journal, magazine, or newspaper articles or online sources such as Web pages.

Most online library catalogs at colleges and universities allow you to search for sources by author(s), title, keyword, subject, publication date, and call number.

> **Information Literacy**
> Although you can limit your search to the online library catalog at your college or university, you can benefit from searching other catalogs available on the Web. The Library of Congress online catalog, for example, presents a comprehensive list of publications on a particular subject or by a particular author (visit catalog.loc.gov). Some sites, such as the Karlsruhe Virtual Catalog (www.ubka.uni-karlsruhe .de/hylib/en/kvk.html), allow you to locate or search multiple online library catalogs. If your library doesn't have a listed publication in its collection, you can request it through interlibrary loan.

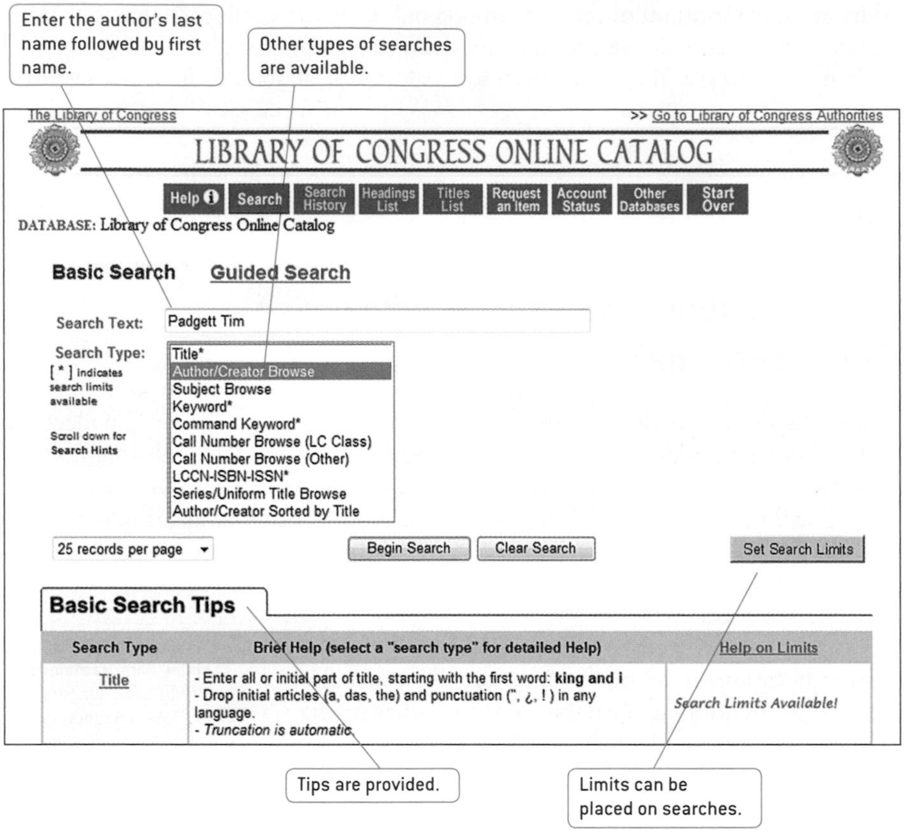

FIGURE 9.1 Searching by Author at the Library of Congress Online Catalog (catalog.loc.gov)

Search by Author

Searching by author means looking for sources written by a specific author or authors. Most library catalogs assume that you will enter the last name of the author first, followed by a first name or initial. Some library catalogs and databases allow you to browse sources by entering all or part of the last name or by using wildcard symbols (symbols such as * or ? that stand in for one or more letters in a word; see p. 117). Figure 9.1 shows a search Elizabeth Leontiev conducted for sources written by Tim Padgett, one of the writers she'd learned about as she explored her topic.

Search by Title

If you know the exact title of a source, such as *Hemingway: A Study of His Short Stories,* you can enter the entire title. If you know only part of the title, such as *Hemingway* or *His Short Stories,* you might have to sift through a list of books whose titles contain the phrase or word you enter.

> **Information Literacy**
> Most online library catalogs do not include articles — *a, an, the,* and so on — at the beginning of titles. They typically move them to the end, as in *Twentieth Century: A Century of Chaos, The.* If you search for sources using a title, be sure to omit initial articles.

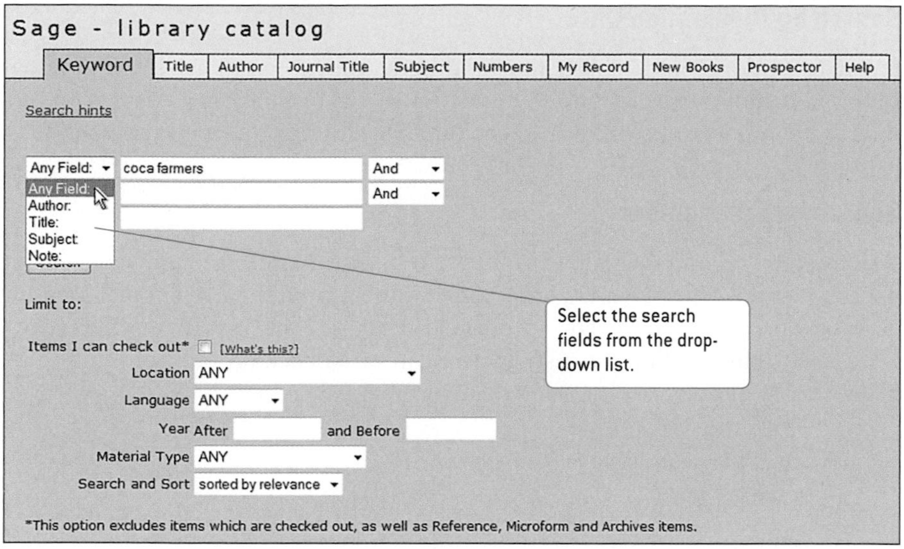

FIGURE 9.2 Searching by Keyword in an Online Library Catalog

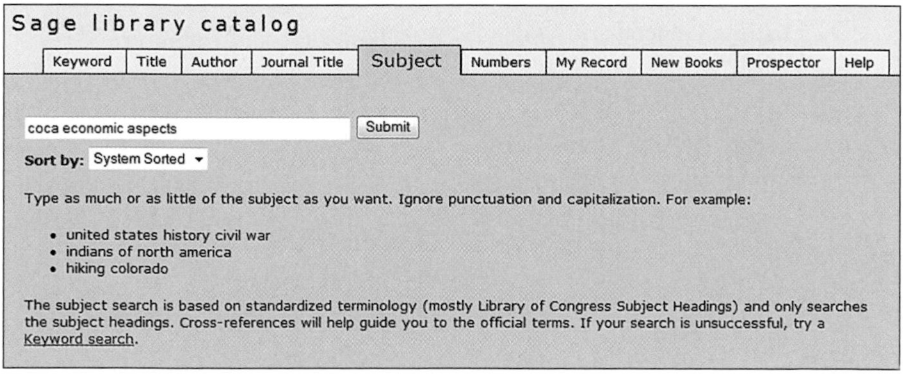

FIGURE 9.3 Searching by Library of Congress Subject Heading

Search by Keyword

Searching by keyword allows you to search for a specific word or phrase. In many online library catalogs, you can decide whether to search in all or only some parts (or fields) of a catalog record, such as title or subject (see Figure 9.2).

Search by Subject

When you search by subject, you look for sources cataloged under specific subject headings (see Figure 9.3). Many college and university libraries use the Library of Congress classification system to organize their collections, while others use the Dewey decimal classification system.

Information Literacy
Because subject searches use the subject headings of the Library of Congress or Dewey decimal classification systems, your subject search must be exactly tailored to the classification system used. If not, your search will be unsuccessful. If you do not know the relevant subject headings for your issue, keyword searches are likely to be more effective.

Search by Publication Date

If you're working on a subject that is time-sensitive—such as recent developments in health care legislation—limit your search by publication date. You can reduce the number of sources to those published during a certain time period.

Search by Call Number

Searching by call number allows you to take a virtual stroll through your library. To conduct this type of search, enter a call number from the Library of Congress classification system or the Dewey decimal system. If you are viewing the record for a book that you find interesting, you can often click on the call number to browse a list of sources with nearby call numbers.

Library of Congress Classification System

A	General Works	K	Law
B	Philosophy, Psychology, Religion	L	Education
		M	Music and Books on Music
C	Auxiliary Sciences of History	N	Fine Arts
D	History: General and Old World	P	Language and Literature
		Q	Science
E	History: United States	R	Medicine
F	History: United States Local and America	S	Agriculture
		T	Technology
G	Geography, Anthropology, Recreation	U	Military Science
		V	Naval Science
H	Social Sciences	Z	Library Science and Information Resources
J	Political Science		

Dewey Decimal Classification System

000	Computers, Internet, and Systems	500	Science
		600	Technology
100	Philosophy	700	Arts
200	Religion	800	Literature, Rhetoric, and Criticism
300	Social Sciences, Sociology, and Anthropology	900	History
400	Language		

Search by a Combination of Terms

Online library catalogs can help you locate sources quickly, especially when you conduct simple searches, such as an author search by last name. If the last name is a common one such as Smith, Garcia, or Chen, however, your search might produce far more results than you would like. In this case, it might help to search for more than one type of information—such as author and keyword—at the same time. The Library of Congress online catalog, for example, allows you to conduct this type of search through its Guided Search page.

My Research Project

PREPARE TO SEARCH ONLINE LIBRARY CATALOGS

As you get ready to search online library catalogs, return to your research plan and make a list of names, keywords, and phrases. Examine your working bibliography to identify the authors, titles, and subjects of your best sources. Then answer the following questions.

1. What are the names of authors I can use to search by author?

2. What are the titles of works that have been referred to me or that I have found in works cited pages that I can use to search by title?

3. What words and phrases can I use to search by keyword?

4. What words and phrases can I use to search by subject?

5. Does it make sense to search by date? If so, what are the dates I should search within?

6. Would call numbers in the Library of Congress or Dewey decimal classification systems be useful for me to browse? If so, what are these call numbers?

You can download or print this activity at **bedfordresearcher.com**. Click on Activities > Prepare to Search Online Library Catalogs.

9b

How can I search for sources with databases?

Databases operate much like online library catalogs, although they focus on a different collection of sources. Whereas an online catalog allows you to search for publications owned by the library, a database allows you to search for sources that have been published on a particular topic or in a particular discipline regardless of whether the library owns the sources. Although some databases can be accessed publicly through the Web, such as ERIC (eric.ed.gov), most are available only through subscription services on library computers or a library Web site.

Databases vary in the topics they cover and the information they provide. The major types of databases include

- **News and Information Databases,** which focus on recently published articles in newspapers, such as the *New York Times*, and popular magazines, such as *TIME* and *Newsweek*. Some databases of this type, such as LexisNexis

Academic, also allow you to search articles distributed by news services, such as the Associated Press, and transcripts of radio and television programs.

- **Subject databases,** which provide information and abstracts (brief summaries) on sources about a broad subject area, such as education, business, or government. Academic Search Premier, for example, identifies sources published in a wide range of academic and professional journals.

- **Bibliographies,** which provide publication information about publications in a specific discipline or profession, such as literary studies, computational linguistics, or the social sciences. The MLA Bibliography, for example, provides information about sources published in the field of English literature.

- **Citation indexes,** which provide publication information and abstracts on sources that have referenced a specific publication. A list of these citations can lead you to other relevant sources on your issue, and they can expand your understanding of the conversation you are joining. If you have already located sources on your issue, you can search a citation database, such as the Web of Science, for articles that cite your sources.

Most databases supply only publication information and brief descriptions of the information in a source; they do not reproduce the full text of the source. Using the citation information provided by the database, you can check your library's online catalog for the title of the publication in which it appears. If your library does not own the publication, you can request it through interlibrary loan (see p. 141).

Identify Relevant Databases

To identify databases that might be relevant to the issue you are addressing in your research writing project, review your library's list of databases or consult a reference librarian. Ask yourself the following questions:

Am I Focusing on an Issue That Is Likely to Have Been Addressed in Recent News Coverage?   If so, consider searching databases that focus on newspapers and weekly magazines, such as:

- LexisNexis Academic
- ProQuest Newspapers
- Alternative Press Index
- Newspaper Source

Information Literacy
A growing number of databases — often called "full–text" databases — allow you to view the complete text of a source. In some full-text databases, sources are provided in the form of a fully formatted PDF file (a type of file that can be viewed in Adobe's Acrobat Reader). These files provide exact copies of the source as it appeared when it was originally published. In other cases, the text of the source is provided, but the document is formatted in a way that differs from its original publication format, usually either in HTML format or as plain text.

Am I Focusing on an Issue That Is Related to a Broad Area of Interest, Such as Business, Education, or Government? If so, consider searching databases that focus on more general issues, such as:

- Academic Search Premier
- Article First
- Catalog of U.S. Government Publications
- WorldCat

Am I Focusing on an Issue That Is Related to a Particular Profession or Academic Discipline? If so, consult bibliographies that focus on that area. Many libraries provide advice about databases that are relevant to a particular profession or discipline. For example, if you are interested in an issue related to sociology, you might consult the following databases:

- Family and Society Studies Worldwide
- Social Science Abstracts
- Sociological Abstracts

Have I Already Identified Sources About My Issue? If you have already located promising sources, you can search citation indexes to identify sources that refer to your sources. Depending on your area, you might search the following databases:

- Science Citation Index
- Social Sciences Citation Index
- Arts & Humanities Citation Index

Is the Full Text of the Source Available? Full-text databases offer the complete source for viewing or download. They cut out the middle step of needing to search for the specific periodical that published the article. If you are not sure that your library will own the sources provided by a database, or if you'd simply like to locate them more quickly, consider using full-text databases. Databases that offer some or all of their sources in full text include:

- Academic Search Premier
- ERIC
- IEEE Xplore
- LexisNexis Academic
- ScienceDirect

Information Literacy
Access to most databases is purchased by a library in a manner similar to subscribing to a journal or magazine. Large research libraries often subscribe to hundreds of databases, while smaller libraries might subscribe to only a handful. Because libraries must purchase subscriptions to databases, they typically restrict access to the databases to library patrons, such as students, staff, and faculty. The general public cannot access these databases unless they connect to them through computers that are in the library or in a campus office or computer lab. If your library does not subscribe to databases that meet your needs, consider using Deep Web search sites such as Academic Info (academicinfo.net) and Complete Planet (aip.completeplanet.com), which offer access to Web-based databases and specialized directories (see p. 124).

Collecting Information

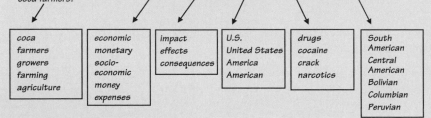

My Research Project

USE YOUR RESEARCH QUESTION TO GENERATE SEARCH TERMS

To generate keywords for your searches, write your research question on a piece of paper or in a word processor and then underline or boldface the most important words and phrases in the sentence. Brainstorm a list of related words and phrases.

Example: How can we reduce the economic impact of the U.S. war on drugs on South American coca farmers?

| coca farmers growers farming agriculture | economic monetary socio-economic money expenses | impact effects consequences | U.S. United States America American | drugs cocaine crack narcotics | South American Central American Bolivian Columbian Peruvian |

You can print or download this activity at **bedfordresearcher.com**. Click on Activities > Use Your Research Question to Generate Search Terms.

Search within Database Fields

To search for sources, research writers type words and phrases in the search fields of a database. If you are conducting a basic search, your search will appear to be similar to a search of a Web search site (see p. 123). Figure 9.4 shows a keyword search conducted by Patrick Crossland on the basic search page of Academic Search Premier. Figure 9.5 shows the results returned by the search.

As with online library catalogs, you can also focus your search on specific fields, such as title or author. Common database fields that can be searched include:

- author
- title
- abstract
- publication in which an article appears

Keywords are entered in the Find box.

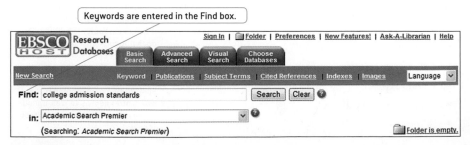

FIGURE 9.4 A Basic Search Using Keywords

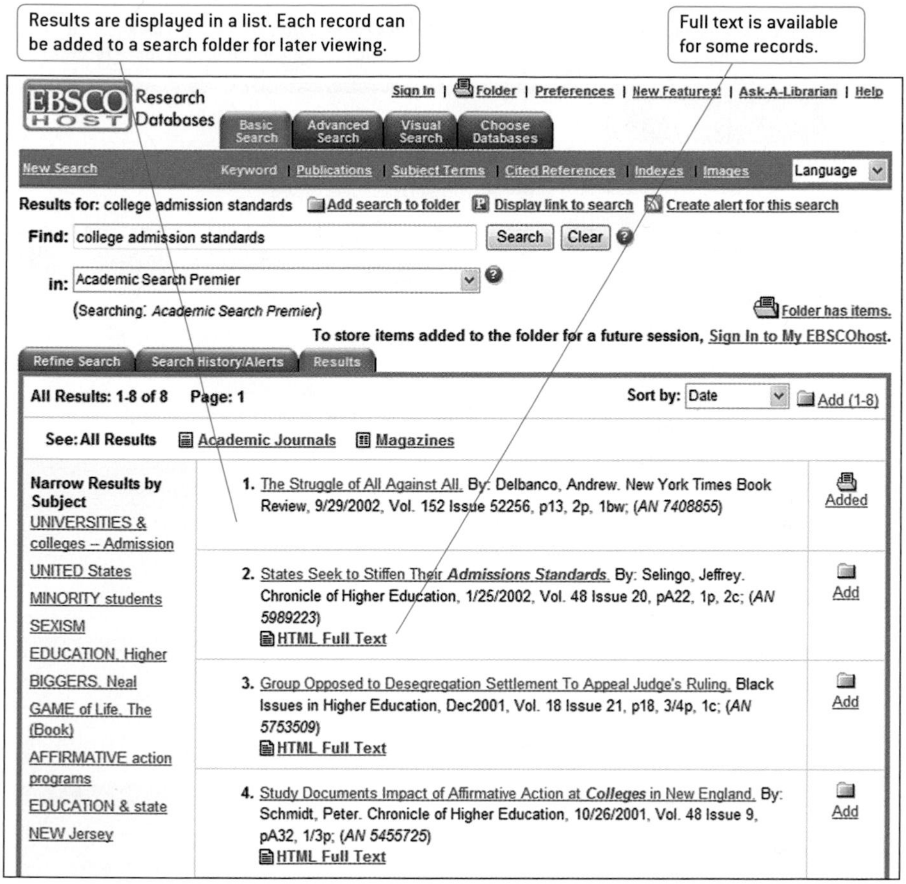

> Results are displayed in a list. Each record can be added to a search folder for later viewing.

> Full text is available for some records.

FIGURE 9.5 Search Results

Most databases also allow you to search all fields of a database record, much as you would search the Web (see p. 123). EBSCO databases, for example, allow you to search "all text," while OCLC databases use the term "keyword" to refer to searches of all fields.

Alexis Alvarez had found a useful article by Costello about steroid use among younger competitive athletes. She combined a search for articles written by authors named Costello with keyword searches for *soccer* and *steroids* (see Figure 9.6).

Search with Wildcards

Sometimes you're not sure what form of a word is most likely to occur. Rather than conducting several searches for *compete, competes, competitive, competitiveness, competition,* and *competitions,* for example, you can combine your search into a single wildcard search. Wildcards are symbols that take the place of letters or strings of letters. By standing in for multiple letters, they allow you to expand the scope of your search.

> The Author field is selected for the first entry in the search.

> *Soccer* and *steroids* are used for keyword searches of all text in the database records.

OCLC FirstSearch   **Colorado State University Libraries**

ArticleFirst Advanced Search

• Enter search terms in one or more boxes and click on **Search**. (Or **Browse Journals and Magazines**)

| Home | Databases | Searching | | Staff View | My Account | Options | Comments | Exit | Hide tips |

| Basic Search | Advanced Search | Expert Search | Previous Searches | Go to page |

Browse Titles   News   Help   Current database: **ArticleFirst**

| Search | Clear |

Search in database: ArticleFirst ▾ ⓘ (Updated: 2007-12-01)
OCLC index of articles from the contents pages of journals

Search for: costello — Author ▾
and ▾ soccer — Keyword ▾
and ▾ steroids — Keyword ▾

Limit to: Year _____ (format: YYYY-YYYY)

Limit availability to: ☐ 🔖 Subscriptions held by my library (COF, COLORADO STATE UNIV) ❷
match any of the following Library Code _____ Find codes ...

Rank by: No ranking ▾ ❷

| Search | Clear |

| English | Español | Français | عربي | 日本語 | 한국어 | 中文（繁體）| 中文（简体）| Options | Comments | Exit |

FIGURE 9.6 Searching within Fields in a Database

The two most commonly used wildcard symbols are as follows:

* usually takes the place of one or more characters, such as *compet**

? usually takes the place of a single character, such as *wom?n*

Other wildcard symbols include !, +, #, and $. Consult the help section in a database to learn whether wildcard symbols are supported.

Conduct Boolean Searches

Boolean searches let you focus your search by specifying whether keywords or phrases *can* appear in the results of a search, *must* appear in the results, or *must not* appear in the results. Some forms of Boolean search also allow you to search for keywords or phrases that appear next to, before or after, or within a certain distance from one another within a document. Table 9.1 lists commonly used Boolean operators and their functions.

Many databases, online catalogs, and Web search sites include the use of Boolean search terms—typically AND, OR, and NOT or plus (+) and minus (–) signs—in their advanced search forms (see Figure 9.8) or in expert search forms (see Figure 9.9).

Set Search Limits

Most databases allow you to set search limits, such as the type of document or the period of time during which a document was published (see Figure 9.10). Depending on the database, you might be able to set the following types of limits in a search:

- language
- publication date
- document type (genre)
- whether the document is peer reviewed
- whether references are included in the document
- whether the document is available in full text

Information Literacy

In addition to linking to online versions of articles, a number of subscription services allow you to save your searches and search results for later viewing. EBSCOhost, for example, allows you to create an account on its "My EBSCOhost" site. Once you've created an account, you can save your work in a folder that you can access as you use the database (see Figure 9.7).

Results saved from searches are displayed.

Searches can be saved.

EBSCO HOST Research Databases	Sign In | Folder | Preferences | New Features! | Ask-A-Librarian | Help
Basic Search | Advanced Search | Visual Search | Choose Databases	
New Search	Keyword | Publications | Subject Terms | Cited References | Indexes | Images Language ▼

Folder Contents

◀ Back

To store these items in the folder for a future session, Sign In.

Folder List

▶ Articles (5)

Images (0)

Videos (0)

Persistent Links to Searches (2)

Saved Searches (0)

Search Alerts (0)

Journal Alerts (0)

Web Pages (0)

Articles

1-5 of 5   Page: 1

Select: All \| None   Delete: All \| Selected   🖨 Print ✉ E-mail 💾 Save 📤 Export

Sort by: Name ▼

☐ 1. Diversity by Any Other Name: Are There Viable Alternatives to Affirmative Action in Higher Education? By: Long, Bridget Terry. Western Journal of Black Studies, Spring2003, Vol. 27 Issue 1, p30-34, 5p; *(AN 10693271)*
Cited References (11)
📄 PDF Full Text *(900K)*

☐ 2. Getting into college taxes kids, parents By: Mary Beth Marklein. USA Today, 10/09/2006; *(AN J0E338780112906)*
📄 HTML Full Text

☐ 3. Is It Grade Inflation, or Are Students Just Smarter? By: Arenson, Karen W.. New York Times, 4/18/2004, Vol. 153 Issue 52823, Week in Review p2-2, 1/3p; *(AN 12990642)*

☐ 4. Kentucky Moves Toward College Test for All. By: Hoff, David J.. Education Week, 3/22/2006, Vol. 25 Issue 28, p28-30, 2p; *(AN 20789529)*
📄 HTML Full Text

☐ 5. Make College Admissions Colorblind. By: Chavez, Linda. Human Events, 12/9/2002, Vol. 58 Issue 45, p1, 2p, 1c; *(AN 8642591)*
📄 HTML Full Text 📄 PDF Full Text *(848K)*

FIGURE 9.7 The EBSCOhost Folder

Collecting Information

TABLE 9.1 COMMONLY USED BOOLEAN OPERATORS

BOOLEAN OPERATOR	FUNCTION	EXAMPLE
AND/+ (plus)	Finds sources that include both terms	adolescent AND girls
OR	Finds sources that include either term	sports OR athletics
NOT/– (minus)	Finds sources that include one term but not the other	girls NOT boys
ADJ (adjacent)	Finds sources in which the keywords appear next to each other	competitive ADJ athletics
NEAR	Finds sources in which the keywords appear within a certain number of words of each other (usually twenty-five; depending on the database, you may be able to change the default setting)	adolescent NEAR athlete
BEFORE	Finds sources in which keywords appear in a particular order	competitive BEFORE athletics
Parentheses ( )	Although not strictly a Boolean search term, parentheses are used to group keywords and Boolean operators	competitive AND (athletics OR sports) AND (girls NOT boys)

AND indicates that the phrase *adolescent girls* must be in the record.

Search in database: ArticleFirst (Updated: 2007-12-01)
OCLC index of articles from the contents pages of journals

Search for: competitive sports Keyword

NOT excludes records that include the word *boys*.

and — adolescent girls Keyword

not — boys Keyword

FIGURE 9.8 Boolean Search in an Advanced Search Form

AND requires both phrases to be present.

Search in database: ArticleFirst (Updated: 2007-12-01)
OCLC index of articles from the contents pages of journals

Search for: ("competitive sports" AND "adolescent girls") NOT boys

NOT excludes records that include the word *boys*.

Parentheses group two phrases.

Indexed in: Keyword (kw:)

FIGURE 9.9 Boolean Search in an Expert Search Form

TUTORIAL

How do I conduct a Boolean search in a database?

Use the advanced search in a database to conduct a Boolean search. In this example, Pete Jacquez conducted a Boolean search with limits on the Academic Search Premier database.

1. Use Boolean operators to specify which terms **must** be in the source (AND), **can** be in the source (OR), or **must not** be in the source (NOT).

2. Enter your keywords and phrases. This search looks for articles about wind power and legislation in Colorado that do not involve discussions of lobbying.

3. Choose the database fields that should be searched. Here, the author field is chosen to exclude authors named Owens, since he already has that source.

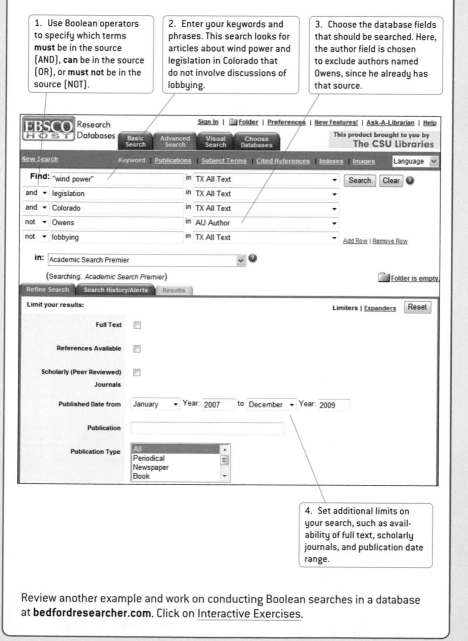

4. Set additional limits on your search, such as availability of full text, scholarly journals, and publication date range.

Review another example and work on conducting Boolean searches in a database at **bedfordresearcher.com**. Click on Interactive Exercises.

Collecting Information

Now Selected: ❓ PAIS International

> The search is limited to sources published in 2007 or 2008.

Change: Technology ▼ or Specific Databases

Date Range: 2007 ▼ to 2008 ▼

> The search is limited to journal articles in English.

Limited to: ☐ Latest Update   ☑ Journal Articles Only   ☑ English Only

FIGURE 9.10 Setting Search Limits in a Database

[**FRAMING MY ARGUMENT**]

Craft Searches That Reflect Your Writing Situation. As you develop your searches, keep your writing situation in mind. The keywords and phrases you use in your searches should help you accomplish your purposes and address the needs, interests, values, and beliefs of your readers, while the type of resources you search—library catalogs, databases, and particular types of Web search sites and directories—should reflect the type of document you plan to write. Some databases, such as LexisNexis Academic, will direct you to sources in newspapers and magazines, while others, such as ArticleFirst and Web of Science, will direct you to articles in scholarly journals.

Kevin Fahey had learned, by exploring his topic and talking with his instructor, that he should search for scholarly books and articles from scholarly journals that addressed his issue, Hemingway's characterization of Nick Adams. He began his search with the Modern Language Association's Directory of Periodicals (see Figure 9.11).

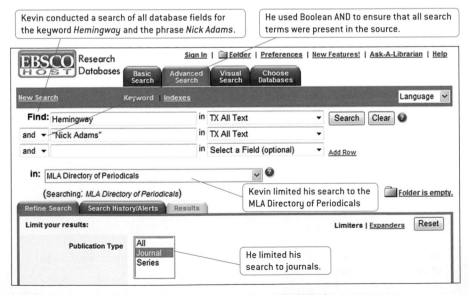

> Kevin conducted a search of all database fields for the keyword *Hemingway* and the phrase *Nick Adams*.

> He used Boolean AND to ensure that all search terms were present in the source.

FIGURE 9.11 Kevin Fahey's Search of the MLA Directory of Periodicals

9c

How can I search for sources with Web search sites?

The Web has become the largest and most accessible "library" in the world. In addition to content developed for online use, the Web is home to a great deal of material that was once available only in print. For example, many magazines and journals are placing their back issues on the Web, and others are moving completely to online publication. In addition, groups such as Project Gutenberg (gutenberg .org) are providing access to literature published long before the information age.

Unfortunately, the Web is also the most disorganized library in the world, since it's being built by millions of people without a common plan or much communication among them. Thus, to locate sources, researchers have turned to Web search sites. Like online library catalogs and databases, Web search sites help you to locate information quickly and easily. However, while library catalogs and databases provide results that have been carefully selected by librarians and database editors, the Web pages produced by Web search sites can be uneven in quality, ranging from refereed articles in scholarly journals to home pages written by fifth graders. As you prepare to search the Web, consider the types of Web search sites that are available and the types of searches you'll conduct on them.

Identify Relevant Web Search Sites

A surprisingly large number of Web search sites can help you locate sources about the written conversation you've decided to join. Established search sites, such as Google, Ask, and Yahoo!, constantly compete with new sites, each hoping that you'll turn to them when you wish to conduct a search. To determine which search sites might be best suited to the needs of your research writing situation, learn about the types of Web search sites that are available.

Web Search Engines   When you use a Web search engine, you obtain information about Web pages and other forms of information on the Internet, including PDF files, PowerPoint files, Word files, blogs, and newsgroups (see p. 128). Web search engines keep track of these sources by locating documents on Web sites and entering them in a searchable database. Leading Web search engines include

AlltheWeb:	alltheweb.com
AltaVista:	altavista.com
Ask:	ask.com
Excite:	excite.com
Gigablast:	gigablast.com
Google:	google.com
Live Search:	live.com

> @ Find a list of additional Web search engines at bedfordresearcher.com. Click on Links > Resources for Conducting Electronic Searches.

Information Literacy
Keep two cautions in mind as you use Web search engines. First, because most search engines index only a portion of the Web — sometimes as much as 50 percent and sometimes as little as 5 percent — you should use more than one search engine to search the Web. If you don't find what you're looking for on one, it doesn't mean you won't find it on another. Second, because Web pages can be moved, deleted, or revised, you might find that a search engine's results are inaccurate. Some search sites, such as Google, provide access to cached versions of older Web pages.

Collecting Information

FIGURE 9.12 Google is the leading Web search engine.

Mojeek:	mojeek.com
MozDex:	mozdex.com
Yahoo! Search:	search.yahoo.com

Web Directories   Unlike Web search sites, Web directories employ human editors to organize information about Web pages into categories and subcategories. Directories allow you to browse lists of Web sites by clicking on general topics, such as Health or Education, and then successively narrow your search by clicking on subtopics. Many directories also permit you to conduct keyword searches within specific categories (see Figure 9.13). This enables you to search

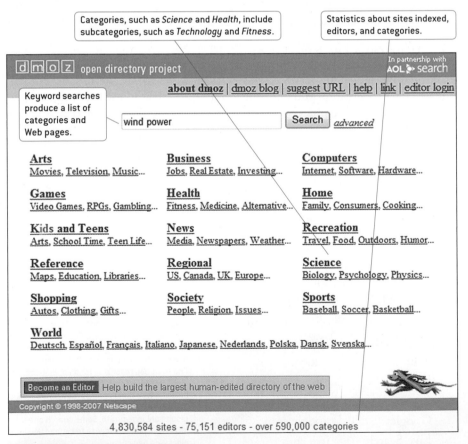

FIGURE 9.13a Searching a Web Directory

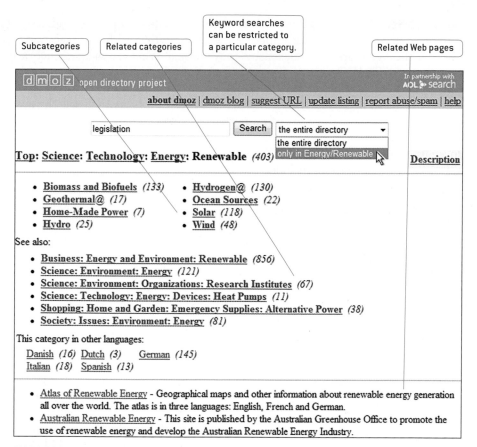

FIGURE 9.13b Searching a Web Directory

within a collection of Web sites that have already been judged by real people to be relevant to your topic. Leading Web directories include

About.com:	about.com
Best of the Web:	botw.org
Google Directory:	google.com/dirhp
Hoppa:	hoppa.com
InfoMine:	infomine.ucr.edu
Internet Public Library:	ipl.org
JoeAnt:	joeant.com
Librarians' Index to the Internet:	lii.org
Open Directory Project:	dmoz.org
Web World:	webworldindex.com
WWW Virtual Library:	vlib.org
Yahoo! Directory:	dir.yahoo.com

Collecting Information

Deep Web Search Sites and Directories   Many specialized topics are addressed through databases or database-supported Web sites that, although accessible through the Web, are not indexed by conventional Web search sites such as Google or AllTheWeb. These sites are referred to collectively as the Deep Web or the Invisible Web because they are not easily found by the search technologies used by leading search sites. To search the Deep Web, try such search sites as Complete Planet, a directory of more than seventy thousand searchable databases and specialty search engines, and Turbo10, a meta search site focusing on specialized sites, directories, and Web-accessible databases. Leading Deep Web search sites and directories include

Academic Info:	academicinfo.net
Complete Planet:	aip.completeplanet.com
Direct Search:	freepint.com/gary/direct.htm
Turbo10.com:	turbo10.com

Meta Search Sites   On a meta search site you can conduct a search on several Web search engines or Web directories at the same time. These sites typically search the major search engines and directories and then present a limited number of results on a single page.

Use a meta search site early in your search for information on the Web. You might use a meta search site to do a side-by-side comparison of various search sites and directories. When Pete Jacquez searched for the phrase *wind power* on search.com, for example, he found that the search sites Google and Yahoo! produced more useful sets of results than the Alexa and Mojeek search sites. On many meta search sites, you can choose to search the entire Web or limit your results to those Web pages that have images, audio, or video files. Clusty groups results into clusters by topic or by type of Web site (.gov, .com, .org, etc.), while Kartoo presents results as a visual map, rather than a list of records. Surfwax provides abstracts of the results, so you don't have to navigate directly to each particular page. Leading meta search sites include

> @ Find a list of additional meta search sites at bedfordresearcher.com. Click on Links > Resources for Conducting Electronic Searches.

Clusty:	clusty.com
Dogpile:	dogpile.com
ixquick:	ixquick.com
Kartoo:	kartoo.com
Mamma:	mamma.com
Metacrawler:	metacrawler.com
Search.com:	search.com
SRCHR:	srchr.com
SurfWax:	surfwax.com
Zuula:	zuula.com

> **Information Literacy**
> Some estimates indicate that the amount of information available through the Deep Web exceeds that on the publicly searchable World Wide Web by a factor of 10. You can access this information by using Deep Web search sites and the databases to which your library subscribes (see p. 113).

News Search Sites   You can search for news on most major Web search sites and directories, such as Google, Ask, and Yahoo!. In addition, specialized news search sites allow you to conduct focused searches for current and archived news reports. Leading news search sites include

AlltheWeb News:	alltheweb.com/?cat=news
AltaVista News:	altavista.com/news/
Ask News:	news.ask.com
Google News:	news.google.com
Live Search:	live.com/?&scope=news
RocketInfo.com:	rocketnews.com
World News:	wn.com
Yahoo! News:	news.yahoo.com

Reference Search Sites   On a reference search site you can search for information that has been collected in encyclopedias, almanacs, atlases, dictionaries, and other reference resources. Some reference sites, such as MSN Encarta and Encyclopedia Britannica Online, offer limited access to information from their encyclopedias for no charge and complete access for a fee. Other sites, such as Information Please and Bartleby.com allow unrestricted access to recently published reference works, including the *Columbia Encyclopedia, The Encyclopedia of World History,* and *The World Factbook.* One widely used reference site is Wikipedia (en.wikipedia.org), a site that is collaboratively written by its readers. Because of its comprehensiveness, Wikipedia can serve as a useful starting point for research on a topic. However, because any reader can make changes to the site, it's best to double-check the information you find there. For more information about the drawbacks of relying on Wikis as authoritative sources of information, see p. 75. Leading reference search sites include

Bartleby.com Reference:	bartleby.com/reference
Encyclopedia.com:	encyclopedia.com
Encyclopedia Britannica Online:	britannica.com
Information Please:	infoplease.com
MSN Encarta:	encarta.msn.com
Wikipedia:	en.wikipedia.org

Government Documents Search Sites and Directories   Many government agencies and institutions have turned to the Web as their primary means of distributing their publications. FirstGov, sponsored by the U.S. government, allows you to search the federal government's network of online resources. Government Printing Office Access provides publication information about print documents and links to those publications when they are available online. Sites such as

FedStats and FedWorld give access to a wide range of government-related materials. In addition to these specialized government Web sites, you can locate government publications through many Web directories, such as Yahoo!. Leading government documents sites include

About.com's U.S. Government Information Directory:	usgovinfo.about.com
Canadian Government Search Engines:	canada.gc.ca/search/srcind_e.html
FedStats:	fedstats.gov
FedWorld:	fedworld.gov
Google U.S. Government Search:	google.com/ig/usgov
Government Printing Office Access:	gpoaccess.gov
GovSpot.com:	govspot.com
SearchGov.com:	searchgov.com
State and Local Government Directory:	statelocalgov.net
USA.gov:	usa.gov

Blog Search Sites   Blogs—short for Weblogs—consist of chronologically ordered entries on a Web site and most closely resemble entries in a diary or journal. Blog entries usually include a title and a text message, and can also incorporate images, audio, video, and other types of media. Many entries provide links to other pages on the Web. The purposes of blogs vary.

- Some blogs report on events and issues (see Figure 9.14). The bloggers who provided daily—sometimes hourly—reports on the 2008 political conventions offered valuable, firsthand insights into aspects of the conventions that were not addressed through the mainstream media. The bloggers who reported on the Iraq war, similarly, offered a perspective on events in Iraq and elsewhere that would not have been available otherwise.

- Some blogs alert readers to information elsewhere on the Web. These blogs cite recently published news reports and articles, newly revealed developments in a particular discipline, and new contributions to an ongoing debate—and provide commentary on that information. Blogs created to serve this purpose often publish news and commentary from other Web sites and blogs.

- Some blogs serve as public relations spaces for institutions and organizations, such as corporations, government agencies, and colleges. Blogs that serve this purpose typically focus on services or activities associated with the institution or organization.

⫴ Collecting Information

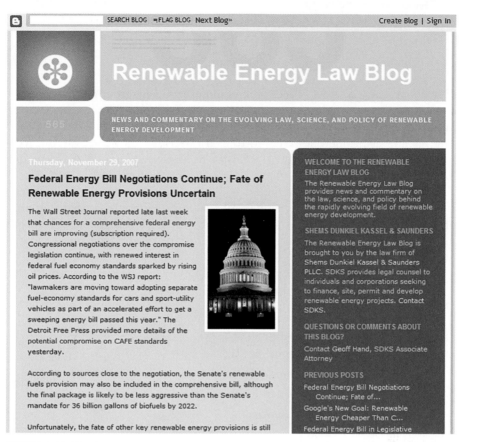

FIGURE 9.14 Blog Entry on Renewable Energy Law

- Some blogs serve largely as a space for personal reflection and expression. A blogger might share his or her thoughts about each day, current events, or other issues with friends and family.

Research writers can use blogs as sources of information and commentary on an issue and as sources of firsthand accounts by individuals involved in or affected by an issue. If you find blogs by experts in the field, you can begin a dialogue with people involved in or knowledgeable about your topic. To locate blogs that are relevant to your research question, use the following blog search sites and directories.

Ask.com Blogs:	ask.com/?tool=bls
BlogCatalog:	blogcatalog.com
Blogdigger:	blogdigger.com
BlogLines:	bloglines.com
Globe of Blogs:	globeofblogs.com
Google Blogsearch:	blogsearch.google.com

IceRocket:	icerocket.com
Noocle:	blog.noocle.com
Technorati:	technorati.com

Discussion Search Sites   Electronic mailing lists, newsgroups, and Web discussion forums support conversations among individuals who share an interest in an issue or belong to a particular community. You can read a message sent to a mailing list, sometimes referred to as a listserv, in the same way that you read other email messages. Messages posted to newsgroups and Web discussion forums can be read using most Web browsers.

In addition to reading messages, you can post your own. Although there is no guarantee that you'll receive helpful responses, experts in a particular area often read and contribute to these forums. If you are fortunate enough to get into a discussion with one or more knowledgeable people, you might obtain useful information.

Mailing lists, newsgroups, and discussion forums can be located through the following search engines and directories.

Catalist:	lsoft.com/lists/listref.html
CyberFiber:	cyberfiber.com
Forum Zilla:	forumzilla.com
Google Groups:	groups.google.com
Newzbot:	newzbot.com
Tile.net:	tile.net/lists

> @ Find a list of additional search sites for newsgroups and mailing lists at **bedfordresearcher.com**. Click on Links > Resources for Conducting Electronic Searches.

Social Network Search   Sites such as MySpace, Facebook, Hi5, and Bebo provide opportunities to identify people who share your interest in an issue. By searching these sites, you can identify individuals who might be knowledgeable about an issue or have been affected by it. You can search social networks using the following sites:

Bebo Search:	bebo.com/Search.jsp
Facebook Search:	facebook.com/srch.php
Hi5 Search:	hi5.com/friend/displaySearch.do
IceRocket:	icerocket.com/index?tab=myspace&q=
MySpace Search:	search.myspace.com
Noocle:	social.noocle.com
ProfileLinker:	profilelinker.com
Wink:	wink.com

Alternative Search   The Web is anything but static — it changes all the time. It shouldn't come as a surprise that search tools will change as well. The following sites approach searching the Web in new and promising ways.

Collecting Information

Grokker (grokker.com) presents search results in the form of an outline or map of related sites (see Figure 9.15).

Lexxe (lexxe.com) uses natural language processing to create clusters of results.

LyGO Visual Search (lygo.com) clusters search results and provides an image and summary of each Web page returned by the search (see Figure 9.16).

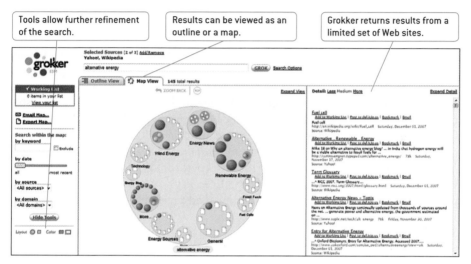

FIGURE 9.15 Grokker: www.grokker.com

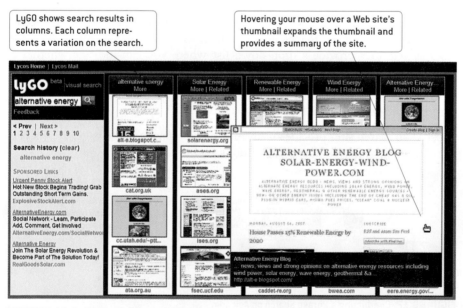

FIGURE 9.16 LyGO Visual Search: lygo.com

Rollyo (rollyo.com) allows you to build custom search lists, which contain only the sites you want to search. You can also search sites created by Rollyo staff and users.

Snap (snap.com) shows visual previews of the Web pages returned by the search.

WebBrain (webbrain.com) creates a visual map based on your search and lists sites relevant to the part of the map you are exploring.

Search with Keywords and Phrases

Like database searches, most Web searches are conducted with keywords and phrases.

Keyword Searches   In most Web search sites, adding keywords will reduce the number of results returned by your search. For example, adding *wind* to a search for the keywords *alternative* and *energy* on Google will reduce the number of results by roughly 97 percent. Adding *legislation* to a search for *alternative*, *energy*, and *wind* will reduce it by a further two percent. You can find out how the Web search site you are using treats multiple keywords by consulting its help page — or by conducting some test searches and reviewing your results.

Searches for Exact Phrases   Sometimes the best way to locate information is to search for an exact phrase (see Figure 9.17). If you're interested in the economic impact of a damaging hurricane, such as Hurricane Katrina, for instance, you might search for sources containing the exact phrase *Hurricane Katrina*. This would eliminate sources in which the words *Hurricane* and *Katrina* both appear, but are separated by other words. Many Web search sites permit you to specify phrases using quotation marks, and a number of the advanced search pages for Web search sites provide a drop-down list where you can indicate whether a string of words consists of separate keywords or is a phrase.

Conduct Advanced Web Searches

Most Web search sites provide an advanced search page. These pages allows you to refine your search by specifying options such as

FIGURE 9.17 Conducting a Phrase Search on Ask.com

- whether all, some, or none of the words in the search box should appear on a page or in a document
- whether words should be treated as a phrase
- where the words should be found (for example, in the title, the page content, or the URL)
- when the page or document was first found by the search site
- when the page or document was last modified
- the language in which a page or document is published
- the format (html, PDF, PowerPoint, Word, and so on) in which the page or document is published
- the domain containing the page or document
- whether results should be screened for sexual content

Advanced search pages for Web search sites offer tools that are similar to those provided by the advanced search forms in most databases (see Figure 9.18). They support Boolean searches (see p. 118) as well as the ability to limit searches (see p. 119).

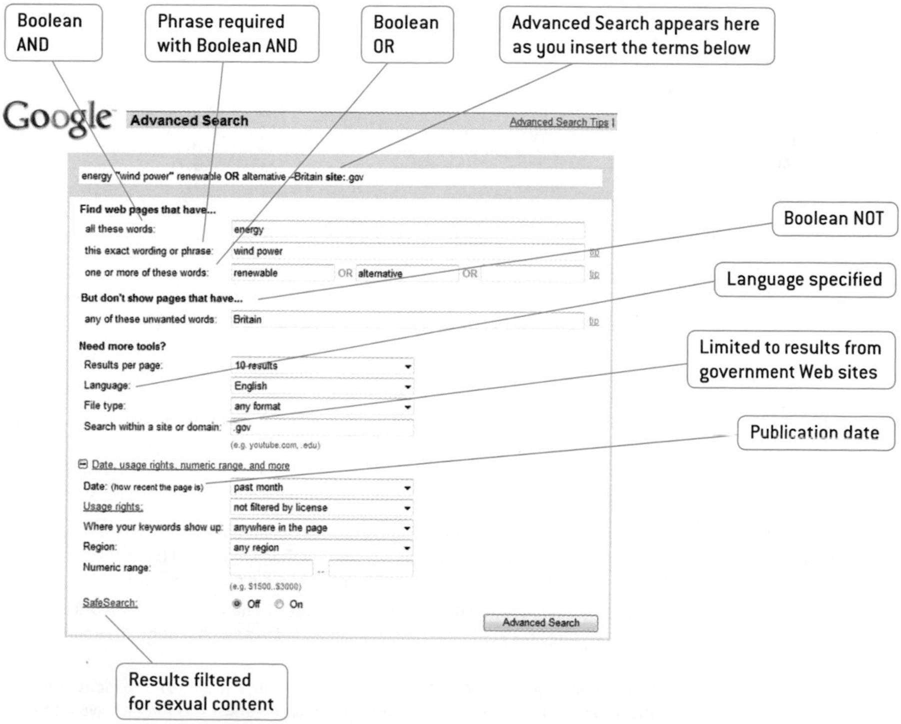

FIGURE 9.18 Google's Advanced Search Page

FIGURE 9.19 Searching with Special Symbols

Use Special Symbols and Operators

A number of leading Web sites, such as Google, Yahoo!, Ask, and Live.com offer special symbols and operators that allow you to fine-tune a Web search (see Figure 9.19). These special symbols and operators can be used in combination with keyword, phrase, wildcard, and Boolean searches. Table 9.2 lists special symbols and Boolean commands. Table 9.3 illustrates the use of several special operators in Web searches.

TABLE 9.2 SPECIAL SYMBOLS				
FUNCTION	ASK	GOOGLE	LIVE	YAHOO!
Boolean AND	+	+	AND or & or +	AND or +
Boolean OR	OR		OR or |	OR
Boolean NOT	–	–	NOT or –	NOT or –
Boolean Group			( )	( )
Phrase	"phrase"	"phrase"	"phrase"	"phrase"
Words Near Each Other		steroids * kids		

Information Literacy

Many advanced search pages allow you to search for pages or documents that have been modified within a specific period of time. Others allow you to identify pages or documents that were found by the search site during a specific period of time. These options differ in important ways and are subject to critical limitations.

- Modification date is not the same as publication date. Adding an image or changing a single word on a page constitutes a modification. A page created in 1997 will be included in search results if a spelling error was corrected last week.

- The "found on date" is not the same as publication date. It takes a while for a search site to locate new pages — sometimes as little as an hour after the page is released and sometimes as long as two weeks. In addition, some pages and documents might have been created several years ago but have been found only recently because they have just been made public on a Web site.

Collecting Information

TABLE 9.3 SPECIAL OPERATORS

Words in body text

Google	intext:steroid
Live	Inbody:steroid

Words in title of page

Ask	Intitle:steroid allintitle:steroid or drugs
Google	intitle:steroid
Live	Title:steroid
Yahoo!	intitle:steroid

Words in URL

Ask	Inurl:steroids
Google	inurl:writing
Live	Inurl:writing
Yahoo!	inurl:writing

Search a single domain

Ask	site:www.theantidrug.com
Google	site:www.theantidrug.com
Live	site:www.theantidrug.com
Yahoo!	site:www.theantidrug.com

Locate pages linking to a page

Ask	Inlink:www.theantidrug.com
Google	link:http://www.theantidrug.com
Live	link:http://www.theantidrug.com
Yahoo!	link:http://www.theantidrug.com

Find documents in a specific format

Google	filetype:pdf
Live	filetype:pdf
Yahoo!	originurlextension:pdf

Find synonyms

Google	~writing
Yahoo!	synonym writing

Find a definition

Google	define:steroid
Yahoo!	define steroid

Collecting Information

My Research Project

RECORD SEARCHES

One of the most important research strategies you can use as you collect information is keeping track of your searches. Note not only the keywords or phrases and the search strategies you used with them (wildcards, Boolean search, author search, and so on) but also how many sources the search turned up and whether those sources were relevant to your research project.

In your research log, record the following information for each source you search.

1. Resource that was searched

2. Search terms used (keywords, phrases, publication information)

3. Search strategies used (simple search, wildcard search, exact phrase search, Boolean search)

4. Date search was conducted

5. Number of results produced by the search

6. Relevance of the results

7. Notes about the search

You can download or print this activity at **bedfordresearcher.com**. Click <u>Activities</u> > <u>Record Searches</u>.

9d

How can I search for sources with media search sites?

The Web is home not only to textual information, such as articles and books, but also to a growing collection of other types of media, such as photographs, podcasts, and streaming video. Image search sites have been available on the Web for a number of years. More recently, search sites have turned their attention to audio and video as well. You can locate useful information about your conversation by searching for recordings of radio broadcasts, television shows, documentaries, podcasts, and other media.

You can search for media using established search sites, such as Ask, Google, and Yahoo!, as well as with a growing number of newer media search sites.

Use Image Search Sites and Directories

Image searches have long been among the search tools available to research writers. Using Google's image search (images.google.com), for example, you can search for images using keywords and phrases, and you can conduct advanced searches by specifying the size and kind of image you desire. The following search sites and directories allow you to locate images.

AltaVista Image Search:	altavista.com/image/
Ask Image Search:	ask.com/?tool=img
Ditto:	ditto.com
Fagan Finder Image Search Engines:	faganfinder.com/img/
Google Image Search:	images.google.com
Live Image Search:	live.com/?scope=images
Picsearch:	picsearch.com
Wikimedia Commons – Images:	commons.wikimedia.org/wiki/ Category:Images
Yahoo! Image Search:	images.search.yahoo.com
Yotophoto:	yotophoto.com

Use Audio Search Sites

Thinking of the Web as the first place to visit for new music has become second nature for many of us. But the audio content available through the Web includes more than music alone. Radio broadcasts, recordings of speeches, recordings of natural phenomena, and other forms of sound, are also available on the Web. Sites such as Seeqpod (seeqpod.com) allow you to search for sounds and listen to them before downloading. Leading audio search sites include:

AlltheWeb Audio:	alltheweb.com/?cat=mp3
AltaVista Audio Search:	altavista.com/audio/
Digital Audio Search:	digitalaudiosearch.com
FindSounds:	findsounds.com
Seeqpod:	seeqpod.com
Wikimedia Commons – Sound:	commons.wikimedia.org/wiki/ Category:Sounds
Yahoo! Audio Search:	audio.search.yahoo.com

Use Video Search Sites

Through sites such as YouTube (youtube.com) and Yahoo! Video (video.yahoo .com) Web-based video has become one of the fastest-growing parts of the Web. You can view everything from news reports on CNN.com to a video about the effects of a recent hurricane to documentaries about the Iraq war. And, of course, you can view a lot of material that will most likely be of little use in a research project. With careful selection and evaluation, however, you might find

Collecting Information

materials that will help you better understand and contribute to the discussion of your issue. Leading video search sites include

AlltheWeb Video:	alltheweb.com/?cat=vid
AOL Video:	video.aol.com
Ask Video Search:	ask.com/?tool=vid
Blinkx:	blinkx.com
ClipBlast:	clipblast.com
Google Video:	video.google.com
Live Video Search:	live.com/?&scope=video
Wikimedia Commons – Video:	commons.wikimedia.org/wiki/ Category:Video
Yahoo! Video Search:	video.search.yahoo.com
YouTube:	youtube.com

Collecting Information

? WHAT'S MY PURPOSE?

As you decide which of the electronic resources discussed in this chapter you will use, keep in mind the differences among them. Understanding the different types of materials these resources offer will help you judge how much time to spend using them. If you are addressing an issue that is currently being debated in the popular press, news search sites might offer a good starting point. If you have chosen a historical topic, consider starting with your library's online catalog. If you are researching a topic that is addressed in scholarly articles, turn to databases. Your purpose as a writer will affect your decisions about which resources to use and how to use them.

My Research Project

DISCUSS YOUR RESEARCH PROJECT WITH OTHERS

Return to your research log and review your research plan. As you collect information about your issue, reconsider how your plan capitalizes on available electronic resources. If you are uncertain about how you might use these resources, discuss your project with a reference librarian or your instructor. Given the wide range of electronic resources available, a few minutes of discussion could save you a great deal of time searching for useful sources.

> **QUICK REFERENCE**

Searching for Information with Electronic Resources

☑ Search your library's online catalog. (p. 109)

☑ Identify and search relevant databases. (p. 114)

☑ Identify and use appropriate Web search sites. (p. 123)

☑ Identify and use appropriate media search sites. (p. 136)

Collecting Information

10

Searching for Information with Print Resources

> **Key Questions**

Contrary to recent claims, there is life (and information) beyond the World Wide Web. Print resources can help you locate a wealth of information relevant to your research project.

? WHAT'S MY PURPOSE?

To make the most effective use of the print resources available in a library, ask how the information they can point you toward will help you achieve your purpose as a writer. If you are working on a research project that has a historical component, as was the case with Elizabeth Leontiev and Kevin Fahey, you'll find that print bibliographies and indexes can point you toward sources that cannot be located

↓

> **WHAT'S MY PURPOSE?** (continued)
>
> using a database. Moreover, because libraries organize their collections by subject, you can use the sources you locate through print resources as starting points for browsing the library stacks. By relying on the careful selections librarians make when adding to a library collection, you will be able to find useful, credible sources that reflect your purpose and address your issue.

10a

How can I use the library stacks to locate sources?

The library stacks—or shelves—house the library's collection of bound publications. You can locate publications by browsing the stacks and checking works cited pages for related publications. Once you've decided a source is relevant to your issue, you can check it out or request it through interlibrary loan.

Browse the Stacks

One of the advantages of the classification systems used by most libraries—typically either the Library of Congress or Dewey decimal classification systems—is that they are subject based. As a result, you can browse the stacks to look for sources on a topic because books on similar subjects are shelved together. For example, if your research takes you to the stacks for books about alcohol abuse, you're likely to find books about drug abuse, treatment programs, and codependency nearby.

When you find a publication that seems useful, check the works cited page for related works. The combination of browsing the stacks for sources and checking the works cited pages of those sources can lead you to publications relevant to your issue.

Check Out Books and Periodicals

In some cases, you'll discover that a publication you want is not available because it has been checked out, reserved for a course, or placed in off-site storage. If a publication is checked out, you may be able to recall it—that is, ask that it be returned to the library and held for you. If it has been placed on reserve, you may be able to photocopy or take notes on it. If it has been placed in off-site storage, you can usually request it at the circulation desk.

Use Interlibrary Loan

If you can't obtain the book or periodical you need from your library, use interlibrary loan to borrow materials from another library. Most libraries allow you to request materials in person or on the Web. Some libraries let you check the status of your interlibrary loan request or renew interlibrary loan materials through the Web. You can learn how to use interlibrary loan at your library by consulting its Web site or a librarian.

10b

How can I use a library periodicals room to locate sources?

Periodicals include newspapers, magazines, and scholarly and professional journals. A periodicals room—or journals room—contains recent issues for library visitors to browse. Many libraries also have a separate room for newspapers published in the last few weeks or months.

To ensure everyone's access to recently published issues, most libraries don't allow you to check out periodicals published within the last year, and they usually don't allow newspapers to be checked out at all. Older periodicals are sometimes placed in bound volumes in the stacks. Few libraries, however, keep back issues of newspapers in paper form. Instead, you can often find back issues of leading newspapers in full-text databases or in microforms. Microform is a generic name for both microfilm, a strip of film containing greatly reduced images of printed pages, and microfiche, film roughly the shape and size of an index card containing the same kinds of miniaturized images. You view these images using a microform reader, a projection unit that looks something like a large computer monitor. Many microform readers allow you to print full-size copies of the pages.

Information Literacy
To help you locate articles in periodicals, most periodicals rooms provide access to electronic databases, which are more likely than print indexes and bibliographies to contain listings of recent publications. Once you've identified articles you want to review, you'll need to find the periodicals containing those articles. Most online library catalogs allow you to conduct a title search for a periodical, in the same way you conduct a title search for a book. The online catalog will tell you the call number of the periodical, and most online catalogs will give information about its location in the library. In addition, some libraries provide a printed list that identifies where periodicals are located. If you have difficulty finding a periodical or judging which publications are likely to contain articles relevant to your research project, ask a librarian for assistance.

@ Learn more about using databases to locate sources at **bedfordresearcher .com**. Click on Guides > How to Search a Database.

[FRAMING MY ARGUMENT]

Use Works Cited Lists to Identify Key Voices in a Conversation. Many of the articles you'll find in your library's periodicals room will contain works cited or reference lists. When you find an article that is relevant to your argument, check the list of sources for related articles. As you find new sources, check for authors whose work is cited frequently (see Figure 10.1). This will help identify key voices in the conversation, writers whose work is either controversial, groundbreaking, fundamental, or in some other way central to the conversation.

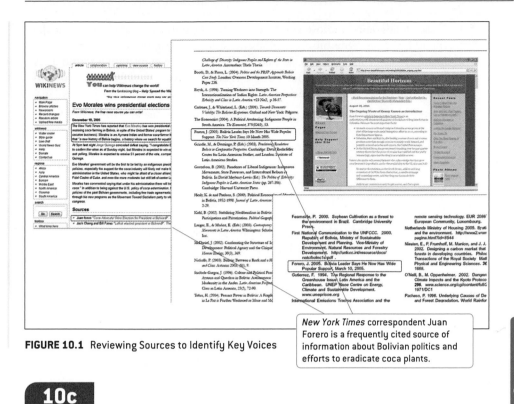

FIGURE 10.1 Reviewing Sources to Identify Key Voices

New York Times correspondent Juan Forero is a frequently cited source of information about Bolivian politics and efforts to eradicate coca plants.

10c

How can I use a library reference room to locate sources?

Reference rooms contain print resources on a range of topics, from government to finance to philosophy to science. Some of the most important print resources you can consult in a reference room include bibliographies, indexes, biographies, general and specialized encyclopedias, handbooks, almanacs, and atlases.

Consult Bibliographies

Bibliographies list books, articles, and other publications that have been judged relevant to a topic. Some bibliographies provide only citations, while others include abstracts—brief descriptions—of listed sources. Complete bibliographies attempt to list all of the sources published about a topic, while selective bibliographies attempt to list only the best sources published about a topic. Some bibliographies limit their inclusion of sources by time period, often focusing on sources published during a given year.

Types of Bibliographies You're likely to find several types of bibliographies in your library's reference room or stacks, including trade bibliographies, general bibliographies, and specialized bibliographies.

Collecting Information

- **Trade Bibliographies** allow you to locate books published about a particular topic. Leading trade bibliographies include *The Subject Guide to Books in Print*, *Books in Print*, and *Cumulative Book Index*. Kevin Fahey found a large number of books about Ernest Hemingway in the *Annual Bibliography of English Language and Literature* (see Figure 10.2).

- **General Bibliographies** cover a wide range of topics, usually in selective lists. For sources on humanities topics, consult *The Humanities: A Selective Guide to Information Sources*. For sources on social science topics, see *Social Science Reference Sources: A Practical Guide*. For sources on science topics, go to bibliographies such as *Information Sources in Science and Technology*, *Guide to Information Sources in the Botanical Sciences*, and *Guide to Information Sources in the Physical Sciences*.

- **Specialized Bibliographies** typically provide lists of sources—often annotated—about a topic. For example, *Art Books: A Basic Bibliography of Monographs on Artists*, edited by Wolfgang M. Freitag, focuses on sources about important artists.

Locating Bibliographies   Although most general and trade bibliographies can be found in your library reference room, specialized bibliographies are likely to be located in your library's stacks. To locate bibliographies, follow these steps.

1. *Consult a cumulative bibliography.* Cumulative bibliographies provide an index of published bibliographies. *The Bibliographic Index: A Cumulative Bibliography of Bibliographies*, for instance, identifies bibliographies on a wide range of topics and is updated annually.

2. *Consult your library's online catalog.* When you search your library's online catalog, use keywords related to your issue plus the keyword *bibliography*. Kevin Fahey searched his college's online catalog using the keywords *Hemingway* and *bibliography*.

3. *If necessary, seek advice from a reference librarian.* Reference librarians will help you find bibliographies that are relevant to your issue.

Consult Indexes

Indexes provide citation information for sources found in a particular set of publications. Many indexes also include abstracts—brief descriptions—that can help you determine whether a source is worth locating and reviewing. The following types of indexes can be found in libraries.

Information Literacy

Although many of the reference books in library reference rooms serve the same purposes as the electronic databases discussed in Chapter 9, others offer information not available in databases. Using reference books to locate print resources has several benefits.

- **Most databases have short memories.** Databases seldom index sources published before 1970, and typically index sources only as far back as the mid-1980s. Depending on the conversation you've decided to join, a database might not allow you to locate important sources.

- **Most databases focus on short works.** In contrast, many of the print resources in library reference rooms will refer you to books and longer publications as well as to articles in periodicals.

- **Many library reference resources are unavailable in electronic form.** For instance, the *Encyclopedia of Creativity*, which offers more than two hundred articles, is available only in print form.

- **Entries in print indexes are easier to browse.** Despite efforts to aid browsing, databases support searching far better than they do browsing.

Collecting Information

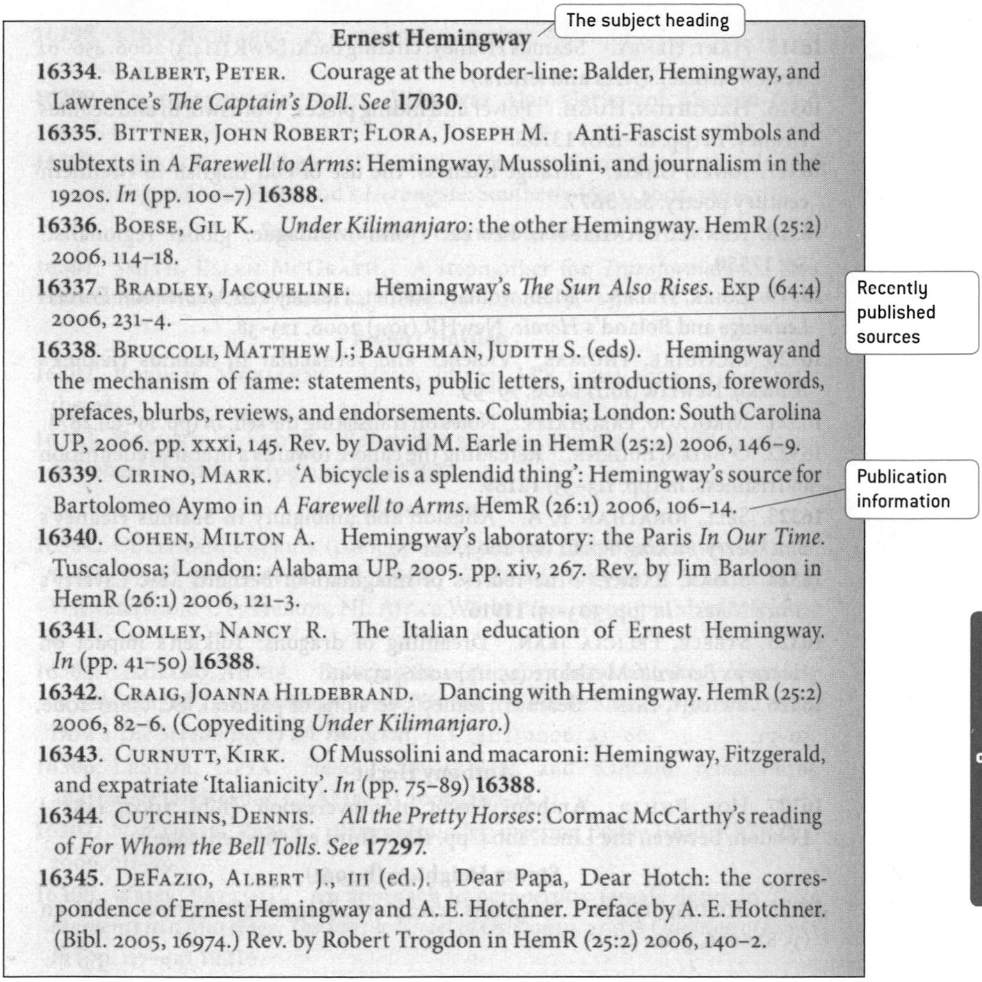

Ernest Hemingway — The subject heading

16334. BALBERT, PETER.   Courage at the border-line: Balder, Hemingway, and Lawrence's *The Captain's Doll*. See **17030**.

16335. BITTNER, JOHN ROBERT; FLORA, JOSEPH M.   Anti-Fascist symbols and subtexts in *A Farewell to Arms*: Hemingway, Mussolini, and journalism in the 1920s. *In* (pp. 100–7) **16388**.

16336. BOESE, GIL K.   *Under Kilimanjaro*: the other Hemingway. HemR (25:2) 2006, 114–18.

16337. BRADLEY, JACQUELINE.   Hemingway's *The Sun Also Rises*. Exp (64:4) 2006, 231–4. — Recently published sources

16338. BRUCCOLI, MATTHEW J.; BAUGHMAN, JUDITH S. (eds).   Hemingway and the mechanism of fame: statements, public letters, introductions, forewords, prefaces, blurbs, reviews, and endorsements. Columbia; London: South Carolina UP, 2006. pp. xxxi, 145. Rev. by David M. Earle in HemR (25:2) 2006, 146–9.

16339. CIRINO, MARK.   'A bicycle is a splendid thing': Hemingway's source for Bartolomeo Aymo in *A Farewell to Arms*. HemR (26:1) 2006, 106–14. — Publication information

16340. COHEN, MILTON A.   Hemingway's laboratory: the Paris *In Our Time*. Tuscaloosa; London: Alabama UP, 2005. pp. xiv, 267. Rev. by Jim Barloon in HemR (26:1) 2006, 121–3.

16341. COMLEY, NANCY R.   The Italian education of Ernest Hemingway. *In* (pp. 41–50) **16388**.

16342. CRAIG, JOANNA HILDEBRAND.   Dancing with Hemingway. HemR (25:2) 2006, 82–6. (Copyediting *Under Kilimanjaro*.)

16343. CURNUTT, KIRK.   Of Mussolini and macaroni: Hemingway, Fitzgerald, and expatriate 'Italianicity'. *In* (pp. 75–89) **16388**.

16344. CUTCHINS, DENNIS.   *All the Pretty Horses*: Cormac McCarthy's reading of *For Whom the Bell Tolls*. See **17297**.

16345. DEFAZIO, ALBERT J., III (ed.).   Dear Papa, Dear Hotch: the correspondence of Ernest Hemingway and A. E. Hotchner. Preface by A. E. Hotchner. (Bibl. 2005, 16974.) Rev. by Robert Trogdon in HemR (25:2) 2006, 140–2.

FIGURE 10.2 An Entry from the *Annual Bibliography of English Language and Literature* on Ernest Hemingway

Periodical Indexes   Periodical indexes list sources published in magazines, trade journals, scholarly journals, and newspapers. Some periodical indexes cover a wide range of periodicals, others focus on periodicals that address a single subject, and still others focus on a small set or even an individual periodical.

- *The Readers' Guide to Periodical Literature* indexes roughly two hundred general-interest magazines. Updated monthly, the *Readers' Guide* organizes entries by author and subject.

- *Art Index* provides information about sources published only in art magazines and journals. Updated quarterly, *Art Index* organizes entries by author and subject.

- The *New York Times Index* lists articles published only in that newspaper. Updated twice a month, the *Index* organizes entries by subject, geography, organization, and references to individuals.

Collecting Information

TUTORIAL

How do I use a bibliography?

Use a bibliography to locate important publications about a subject. In this example, Kevin Fahey used *The Humanities: A Selective Guide to Information Sources* to locate information about Ernest Hemingway.

1 Locate your subject through the index or page headings, as you would in a phone book.

2 If it is provided, read background information about the subject.

3 Review the bibliography to identify sources that are judged by the author of the subject entry or the editors of the bibliography to be relevant to the subject.

4 Entries in specialized bibliographies are often written by leading scholars. If the author of an entry is identified, search for publications by that author.

Subject heading

Background information

Bibliography

Review another example and work on using bibliographies at **bedfordresearcher .com.** Click on Interactive Exercises.

Patrick Crossland used *The Readers' Guide to Periodical Literature* to locate sources about college admissions (see Figure 10.3).

Significant differences can exist between the print and electronic database versions of periodical indexes. For example, while the printed *Readers' Guide to Periodical Literature* covers publications since 1900, the *Readers' Guide* database only contains information on articles published since 1983.

> @ Find an annotated list of periodical indexes at **bedfordresearcher.com**. Click on Links > Resources for Specific Disciplines.

Indexes of Materials in Books   To locate articles in edited books, turn to resources such as the *Essay and General Literature Index*, which indexes nearly five thousand book-length collections of articles and essays in the arts, humanities, and social sciences. You might also find subject-specific indexes of materials in books. *The Cumulative Bibliography of Asian Studies*, for example, covers articles in edited books.

Pamphlet Indexes   Libraries frequently collect pamphlets of various kinds. To help patrons find these materials, many libraries create a pamphlet index. Ask a reference librarian whether your library has a pamphlet index and where it is. You can also consult the *Vertical File Index*. Updated monthly, this index lists roughly three thousand brief sources on ten to fifteen newsworthy topics each month.

Government Documents Indexes   Government documents indexes list documents published by federal, state, and local governments.

- To find documents published by the federal government, consult the *Monthly Catalog of United States Government Publications*.

- To locate documents published by the U.S. Congress, look in the *CIS Index to Publications of the United States Congress*.

- To obtain information about the daily proceedings of the House of Representatives and the Senate, consult the *Congressional Record*.

- For documents published by the Supreme Court, consult *United States Reports*, the cumulative index of the *Official Reports of the Supreme Court*.

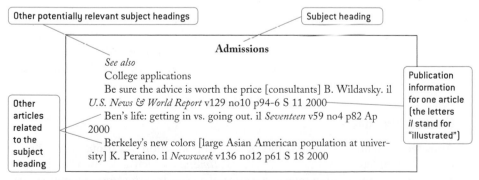

FIGURE 10.3 A Listing in *The Readers' Guide to Periodical Literature*

- To locate government documents containing statistical information, including census reports, look in the *Statistical Abstract of the United States.*

Many larger college and university libraries serve as depositories of government documents. As a result, indexes to government documents might be found in either the reference room or a separate government documents collection in your library. Ask a reference librarian for help.

Citation Indexes   Citation indexes allow you to determine which publications make reference to other publications, a useful strategy for finding sources that are engaged in the same conversation. To learn which sources refer to an article published in a scientific journal, for example, you could consult the *Science Citation Index.*

Consult Biographies

Biographies cover key figures in a field, time period, or geographic region. *Who's Who in America,* for instance, provides brief biographies of important figures in the United States during a given year, while *Great Lives from History* takes a broader view, offering biographies of key figures in world history.

Consult General and Specialized Encyclopedias

General encyclopedias attempt to provide a little knowledge about a lot of things. The idea behind a general encyclopedia, such as the *New Encyclopaedia Britannica,* is to present enough information about a topic to get you started on a more detailed search.

Specialized encyclopedias such as *The MIT Encyclopedia of the Cognitive Sciences,* for example, take a narrower focus than general encyclopedias, usually of a field of study or a narrow historical period. In addition, articles in specialized encyclopedias are typically longer than articles in general encyclopedias and offer more detailed coverage of topics.

Consult Handbooks

Like encyclopedias, handbooks provide useful background information about a topic in a compact form. Unlike encyclopedias, most handbooks, such as *The Engineering Handbook* and the *International Handbook of Psychology,* cover a narrow topic area. Entries in handbooks are also much shorter than the articles found in encyclopedias.

Consult Almanacs

Almanacs contain lists, charts, and tables of information of various types. You're probably familiar with *The Old Farmer's Almanac,* which is known for its accuracy in predicting weather over the course of a year. Information in almanacs can range from the average rainfall in Australia to the batting averages of the 1927 Yankees to the average income of Germans and Poles prior to World War II.

Consult Atlases

Atlases provide maps and related information about a region or country. Some atlases take a historical perspective, while others take a topical perspective.

My Research Project

DISCUSS YOUR RESEARCH PROJECT WITH OTHERS

Return to your research log and review your research plan. As you collect information about your issue, reconsider how your plan capitalizes on the print resources available in your library reference room. If you are uncertain about how you might use these resources, discuss your project with a reference librarian. Given the wide range of specialized print resources that are available, a few minutes of discussion with a knowledgeable librarian could save you a great deal of time.

> **QUICK REFERENCE**

Searching for Information with Print Resources

☑ Use the library stacks to locate sources. (p. 141)

☑ Use the periodicals room to locate sources. (p. 142)

☑ Use the reference room to locate sources. (p. 143)

Collecting Information

11

Searching for Information with Field Research Methods

 Key Questions

Published documents aren't the only source of information for a research project. Nor are they always the best. Publications—such as books, articles, Web sites, or television reports—offer someone else's interpretation of an event or an issue. By relying on another person's interpretation, you're looking through that person's eyes rather than through your own.

Experienced research writers know that you don't have to use published reports to find out how an event or issue has affected people—you can ask the people yourself. You don't have to view television or radio coverage of an event—you can go to the event yourself. And you don't have to rely on someone else's survey of public opinion—you can conduct your own.

III Collecting Information

> ### ❓ WHAT'S MY PURPOSE?
>
> Your preparations for using field research methods will be most effective if you clearly understand your purpose for carrying out your research project and your purpose for using field research. Before committing yourself to designing and administering a survey, for example, ask yourself what kind of results you can expect to gain and what role those results will play in your project. Ask as well whether a certain field research method is the best technique for gaining that information, or whether you might gain it more effectively and efficiently in another way.

11a

How can I use interviews to collect information?

Interviews — in which one person seeks information from another — can provide firsthand accounts of an event, authoritative interpretations of events and issues, and reactions to an event or issue from the people who have been affected by it. Most interviews follow a question-and-answer format, but some more closely resemble a free-flowing discussion. You can conduct interviews face to face, over the telephone, via email, and even through an instant messaging program.

Decide Whether to Conduct an Interview

Thinking carefully about the role an interview might play in your research project can help you decide whether and how to conduct it. Sometimes the decision to interview is a natural extension of the kind of work you're doing. For example, although Alexis Alvarez was able to find plenty of information from other sources about the pressures that would lead adolescent female athletes to use performance-enhancing drugs, she decided to interview friends and family members who had played competitive sports because she knew that firsthand reports would strengthen her argument. Sometimes interviews are conducted because an issue is so current that little authoritative information is available to a writer. Conducting an interview can provide needed information about the issue.

Sometimes the decision to conduct an interview isn't so much the result of careful planning as it is the recognition of an available opportunity. Pete Jacquez, who created a Web site about wind-generated electrical power, learned that one of his friends had recently signed up for a wind power program offered by his university. His interviews produced a personal perspective about wind power that he wouldn't have been able to find through print or electronic sources.

@ Read more about Alexis Alvarez and Pete Jacquez at bedfordresearcher.com. Click on Featured Writers.

Plan Your Interview

The most important things to consider as you plan your interview are whom to interview and what to ask.

Deciding Whom to Interview   Your decisions about whom to interview should be based on the kind of information you want for your research project.

- If you're trying to better understand a specific aspect of a conversation, interview an expert in the field.
- If you want to learn what people in general think about an issue, interview a number of people who are affected by the issue.
- If you're hoping to collect quotations from people who are authorities on a subject, interview someone who will be recognized as an authority.

Once you've decided what sorts of people you want to interview, you'll need to identify and contact interview candidates. If you're working on a research project for a class, ask your instructor and classmates for suggestions. Then ask whether they can introduce you to the people they suggest. Before you call to set up an interview, make some preparations.

1. Write a script to help you remember what to say.
2. Prepare a list of dates and times that work for you.
3. Estimate how much time you'll need to complete the interview.
4. Be ready to suggest a location for the interview.
5. Leave your phone number or email address so that your interview candidate can get in touch with you if a conflict arises.

> @ Find a list of Web sites about conducting interviews at bedfordresearcher.com. Click on Links > Resources for Conducting Field Research.

[**FRAMING MY ARGUMENT**]

Deciding What You Should Ask   Your interview questions should focus on the issue you want to address in your project. As you prepare your questions, keep the following principles in mind.

1. *Consider your research question, the role you are adopting, and the kind of information you want to collect.* Are you seeking background information, or do you want someone's opinion? An answer to the question, "How did this situation come about?" will be quite different from an answer to the question, "What do you think about this situation?"
2. *Ask questions that require more than a yes or no answer.* You'll learn much more from an answer to a question such as, "What factors will affect your vote on referendum X?" than from an answer to, "Will you vote for referendum X?"
3. *Prepare a limited number of main questions and many follow-up questions.* Good interviews seldom involve more than eight to ten main questions, but experienced interviewers know that each question can lead to several follow-up questions.
4. *Be flexible.* Be prepared to tailor your follow-up questions to the interviewee's responses.

Conduct Your Interview

Consult the following checklist before you conduct your interview.

CHECKLIST FOR CONDUCTING INTERVIEWS

☑ **Arrive early and review your questions.** If you are conducting your interview over the phone, set time aside before the call to review your questions and then call the person you are interviewing at the agreed-upon time.

☑ **Introduce yourself and ask for permission to record the interview.** Explain why you are conducting the interview. Ask for permission to record and use quotes from the interview.

☑ **Set up and test your recording equipment.** Ideally, use an audio or video recorder to make a complete record of your interview. At a later time, you can review what was said and carefully transcribe exact quotations from the tape.

☑ **Ask your questions clearly and be ready to respond with follow-up questions.** Allow the person you are interviewing a chance to answer your questions fully. Don't insist on strictly following your list of interview questions; if discussion naturally flows in another, useful direction, be prepared to shift your line of questioning.

☑ **Take notes, even if you are using a video or audio recorder.** A set of handwritten notes will serve as a backup if there are technical glitches and will help you remember ideas you had during the interview. You should write down key points made during the interview as well as any important ideas that come to mind.

☑ **Be alert for related sources mentioned in the interview.** If specific sources that might be relevant to your research writing project are mentioned during the interview, ask for copies of those sources, or for the exact titles and where you might find them.

☑ **Leave your contact information when the interview is over.** Provide a way for the person you interviewed to reach you to change or add anything to his or her comments.

☑ **Send a thank-you note.** Let the person you interviewed know how much you appreciated the opportunity to learn from him or her.

III Collecting Information

11b

How can I use observation to collect information?

Like interviewing, observing a setting can provide you with valuable information you would not be able to find in other sources. Although some observations can involve a significant amount of time and effort, an observation need not be complicated to be useful.

Decide Whether to Conduct an Observation

The most important decision you'll make regarding an observation is whether to conduct it in the first place. Some topics are more suited for observation than others. For example, before writing his multimodal essay on the resurgence of metal music, Chris Norris observed musicians and fans at two concerts. Observing gave Chris insights that he couldn't have gained simply by reading about metal music or interviewing musicians and fans.

Plan Your Observation

As you plan your observation, determine the following:

What You Should Observe and How Often You Should Observe It   If, for example, you've decided to observe children in a day-care center, you'll quickly learn that there are not only many day-care providers in your community but also several different kinds of providers. Clearly, observing a large day-care center won't tell you much about what happens in a small center operated out of a home. In addition, there's no guarantee that what you'll see in one day-care center on any given day will be typical. Should you conduct multiple observations? Should you observe multiple types of day-care providers?

The answers to these questions will depend largely on what role the information you collect during your observations will play in your research writing project. If you want to learn more about the topic but don't plan to use anything you observe as a source of evidence in your project, then you might want to conduct a fairly limited observation. If you decide to use evidence from your observations throughout your project, then you will need to conduct multiple observations, possibly in more than one setting.

What to Look For   The biggest limitation of observation is that you can see only one thing at a time. Experienced observers focus their observations on activities that are most relevant to their research projects. As a result, their observations are somewhat selective. Spreading yourself too thin will result in fairly "thin" results. Then again, narrowing in too quickly can mean that you miss important aspects of the setting. Your reasons for conducting an observation and what you hope to gain from it are probably your best guide to what to focus on.

Whether You Need Permission to Observe   Seeking permission to observe someone can be complicated. People have expectations about privacy, but people can (and often do) change their behavior when they know they are being observed. As you consider whether to ask for permission, imagine yourself in the position of someone who is being observed. If you are still uncertain, ask your instructor for advice.

> **@** Find a list of Web sites about conducting observations at bedfordresearcher.com. Click on Links > Resources for Conducting Field Research.

Conduct Your Observation

You'll find a number of similarities between collecting information in an interview and collecting information during an observation. The checklist that follows will help you conduct your observation.

CHECKLIST FOR CONDUCTING OBSERVATIONS

✔ **Arrive early.** Give yourself time to get prepared.

✔ **Review your planning notes.** Remind yourself what you're looking for and how you will record your observations.

✔ **Introduce yourself.** If you have asked for permission to observe a setting (such as a class or a day-care center), introduce yourself before you begin your observation. Use your introduction as an opportunity to obtain signatures or consent forms if you need them.

✔ **Set up your recording equipment.** You'll certainly want to make sure you've got a notepad and pens or pencils. You might also have an audio or video recorder, a laptop computer, or a handheld, such as a Palm or Pocket PC. Test whatever you've brought with you to make sure it's working properly.

✔ **Take notes.** As with interviews, take notes during your observation even if you're using an audio or video recorder. Noting your impressions and ideas while conducting an observation can help you keep track of critical events. In addition, if your recorder doesn't work as expected, a set of notes can mean the difference between salvaging something from the observation and having to do it all over again. If you find yourself in a situation where you can't take notes — such as at a swimming lesson, when you're taking part in the lesson — try to write down your thoughts about what you've observed immediately after the session.

✔ **Leave contact information and send thank-you notes.** If you have asked someone for permission to observe the setting, give the person a way to contact you, and send a thank-you note after you have completed the observation.

11c

How can I use surveys to collect information?

Surveys allow you to collect information about beliefs, attitudes, and behaviors from a group of people. Typically, surveys help you answer *what* or *who* questions—such as "Who will you vote for in the next election?" Surveys are less useful in obtaining the answers to *why* questions. In an interview, for instance, you can ask, "Why did you vote the way you did in the last election?"

and expect to get a reasonably well-thought-out answer. In a survey, however, people often neglect to write lengthy, careful responses. If you conduct a survey, remember to include a copy of your survey questions in an appendix to your project document.

Decide Whether to Conduct a Survey

Your decision about whether to conduct a survey should be based on the role it will play in your research project, the amount of work required to do a good job, and the kind of information you are seeking. In many cases, you'll find that other field research methods are more appropriate than surveys. Surveys are useful if you want to collect information about the attitudes and behaviors of a large group of people (more than five or ten). If you simply want opinions from a handful of people, you can gain that information more efficiently by interviewing or corresponding with them.

Plan Your Survey

As you plan your survey, determine the following:

Whom to Survey   You must decide whom and how many people to survey. For instance, if you're interested in what students in a specific class think about an issue, survey all of them. Even if the class is fairly large (say, one hundred students), you probably won't have too much trouble tabulating the results of a brief survey. Keep in mind, however, that most surveys aren't given to everyone in a group. National polls, for instance, seldom survey more than one thousand people, yet they are used to assess the opinions of everyone in the country. So how will you select your representative sample? One way is to choose people from the group at random. You could open your school's telephone book and then pick, say, every twentieth name. Another option is to stratify your sample. For example, you could randomly select a specific number of first-year, second-year, third-year, and fourth-year students—and you could make sure that the number of men and women in each group is proportional to their enrollment at the school.

Find a list of Web sites about conducting surveys at bedfordresearcher.com. Click on Links > Resources for Conducting Field Research.

What to Ask and How to Ask It   Designing effective surveys can be challenging. Understanding the strengths and weaknesses of the kinds of questions that are frequently asked on surveys is a good way to get started. Figure 11.1 illustrates the main types of questions found on surveys.

Whether You Are Asking Your Questions Clearly   Test your survey items before administering your survey by asking your classmates or family members to read your questions. A question that seems perfectly clear to you might cause confusion to someone else. Try to rewrite the questions that confuse your "testers" and

Election Survey

Thank you for completing this survey.

A 1. Did you vote in the last presidential election? ☐ yes ☐ no

2. I vote:

In every election	In most elections	In about half of the elections	Rarely	Never
☐	☐	☐	☐	☐

B 3. I have voted in the following types of elections (check all that apply):
   ☐ Regular local elections
   ☐ Special local elections
   ☐ Regular statewide elections
   ☐ National elections

C 4. Voting is a civic duty: ☐ true ☐ false

D 5. All eligible voters should participate in local, state, and national elections:

Strongly Agree	Agree	Not Sure	Disagree	Strongly Disagree
☐	☐	☐	☐	☐

6. Please rate the following reasons for voting on a 1-to-5 scale, in which 5 indicates very important and 1 indicates not at all important:

	1	2	3	4	5
To be a good citizen	☐	☐	☐	☐	☐
To have a say in how government affects my life	☐	☐	☐	☐	☐
To support a particular cause	☐	☐	☐	☐	☐
To vote against particular candidates	☐	☐	☐	☐	☐

E 7. Please rank the following types of elections from most important (4) to least important (1):
   _____ Presidential elections
   _____ Statewide elections
   _____ Locale (city and county) elections
   _____ Student government elections

F 8. Please tell us what influenced your decision to vote or not vote in the last election.

FIGURE 11.1 Sample Survey

A Yes/no items divide respondents into two groups.

B Multiple-choice items indicate whether a respondent knows something or engages in specific behaviors. Because they seldom include every possible answer, be careful when including them.

C True/false items more often deal with attitudes or beliefs than with behaviors or events.

D Likert scales measure respondents' level of agreement with a statement, their assessment of something's importance, or how frequently they engage in a behavior.

E Ranking forces respondents to place items along a continuum.

F Short-answer items allow greater freedom of response, but can be difficult to tabulate.

Collecting Information

TUTORIAL

How do I write a good survey question?

Developing a good survey question is challenging. The process is similar to writing an essay. The first drafts of survey questions serve to express your thoughts. Subsequent revisions help clarify questions for survey respondents. Keep your purpose in mind to be sure your question will elicit the information you need.

In this example, Chris Norris devised a survey question to find out how fellow students view heavy metal music.

1 Write a first draft of the question:

Do you listen to heavy metal music and why or why not?

2 Simplify the question:

Why do you listen — or not listen — to heavy metal music?

3 Consider alternative ways of asking a question — including whether it should be a question:

What are your reasons for listening — or not listening — to music by heavy metal bands like Slayer and Pantera?

4 Identify and then clarify key words and phrases:

List five words to describe music by heavy metal bands like Slayer and Pantera.

5 Ask for feedback from potential respondents. Review and clarify key words and phrases. Consider potential reactions to phrasing:

Please describe your reaction when you hear a song by heavy metal bands like Slayer or Pantera.

Review another example and work on refining survey questions at **bedfordresearcher.com**. Click on Interactive Exercises.

then test them again. Doing so will help you improve the clarity of your survey. Consider the evolution of the following question.

Original Question:

What can be done about voter turnout among younger voters?

> Does "about voter turnout" mean increasing voter turnout, decreasing voter turnout, or encouraging younger voters to be better informed about candidates? Does the phrase "younger voters" mean 18-year-olds or 30-year-olds?

Revised Question:

In your opinion, what can be done to increase turnout among 18- to 24-year-old voters?

Conduct Your Survey

The sheer number of surveys people are asked to complete these days has reduced the public's willingness to respond to them. In fact, a "good" response rate for a survey is 60 percent, and many professional pollsters find lower response rates acceptable. The checklist that follows can help you achieve a reasonable response rate.

CHECKLIST FOR CONDUCTING SURVEYS

☑ **Keep it short.** Surveys are most effective when they are brief. Don't exceed one page.

☑ **Format and distribute your survey appropriately.** If your survey is on paper, make sure the text is readable, there is plenty of room to write, and the page isn't crowded with questions. If you are distributing your survey through email, you can either insert the survey questions into the body of your email message or attach the survey as a word processing file. If you are distributing your survey on the Web, you can

- code your survey so that survey responses are added to a database (if you can create Web pages of this kind or know someone who can).

- ask respondents to copy the text on the page and paste it into an email message that they then send to you.

- link a word processing file containing your survey to a Web page and ask respondents to fill it out and return it to you as an email attachment.

- ask respondents to print the survey and fax or mail it back to you.

☑ **Explain the purpose of your survey.** Explaining who you are and how you will use the results of the survey in your research writing project can help increase a respondent's willingness to complete and return your survey.

☑ **Treat survey respondents with respect.** People respond more favorably when they think you are treating them as individuals rather than simply as part of a mailing list. When possible, use first-class stamps on surveys sent through the

↓

> **CHECKLIST FOR CONDUCTING SURVEYS** (continued)
>
> mail and, when appropriate, address potential respondents by name in cover letters or email messages.
>
> ☑ **Make it easy to return the survey.** If you are conducting a survey through the mail, be sure to include a stamped, self-addressed envelope. If you are conducting your survey on the Web or via email, be sure to provide directions for returning completed surveys.

Analyze Your Results

Once you've collected your surveys, you must tabulate your responses. It's usually best to tabulate survey responses using a spreadsheet program, which provides flexibility when you want to analyze your results. You can also organize the results in a table in a word processing program. Once you've tabulated the responses, spend time analyzing the results. You should look for trends in your data. For example, ask whether groups respond differently on particular questions, or whether age or experience seems to predict responses. Look as well for surprising results, such as unexpectedly high levels of agreement or disagreement with Likert-scale items or striking differences in the responses to short-answer questions.

11d

How can I use correspondence to collect information?

Correspondence includes any textual communication, such as letters, faxes, and email. Correspondence can also take place through real-time communication using chat or instant messaging. If you use chat or instant messaging, be sure to save a record—or transcript—of the exchange.

Although many research writers benefit from corresponding with experts, correspondence need not be sent only to experts. If you are writing an article about the effects of recent flooding in the Midwest, you could correspond with relatives, friends, or even strangers to ask them about their experiences with the floods. You can use their responses to illustrate the impact of the flood on average folks. You can also correspond with staff at government agencies, corporations, and organizations. Many of these institutions hire public relations personnel to respond to inquiries from the public.

Courtesy is essential when corresponding. Introduce yourself and explain the goals of your research project. Make sure that you are clear and ask specific questions. Thank your reader and indicate that you look forward to hearing from him or her. If you decide to send a letter via regular mail, include a self-addressed, stamped envelope to increase your chances of getting a response.

Printing   Printing articles or Web pages allows you to highlight key passages, write comments in the margins, and circle text and graphics on a page. When you print a Web page, make sure the URL and date are included on the printout and are readable. If they're not included or if they're incomplete (which can happen when URLs are very long), write them down on the first page of the printout.

Copying and Pasting   You can use the COPY and PASTE commands in your browser and word processor to save electronic documents and graphics. Note that you also need to copy and paste the URL and record the date on which you accessed the page so that you can return to it if necessary and cite it appropriately.

> Learn more about copying and pasting at **bedfordresearcher.com**. Click on Guides > How to Use Your Word Processor.

Saving   Toward the end of your research writing project, particularly when you are drafting your document, you might find yourself wishing that you'd saved all of your electronic sources on a hard drive, a USB flash drive, or a writable CD or DVD. Saving sources allows you to open them in a Web browser or word processor at a later time.

How you save your sources will vary according to the type of electronic source you're viewing. Web pages can be saved using the FILE > SAVE AS . . . or FILE > SAVE PAGE AS . . . menu command in your browser. Images and other media materials from the Web can be saved by right-clicking (in Windows) or control-clicking (on the Macintosh) on the item you want to save and selecting SAVE IMAGE AS . . . or SAVE PICTURE AS . . . or some variation of that command from the pop-up menu. Depending on the database, you might be able to mark a record returned by your search. Saving a source does not automatically record the URL or the date on which you viewed the source for the first time. Be sure to record that information.

As you save information, keep it organized. The simplest organizational strategy is to save your work in a single folder (see Figure 12.1). As you save

FIGURE 12.1 A Project Workspace Using a Single Folder

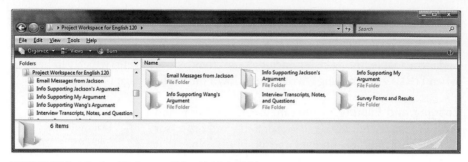

FIGURE 12.2 A Project Workspace Using Multiple Folders

your work, use descriptive file names. Rather than naming a file "Notes 1," for instance, name it "Interview Notes from John Garcia, April 22." Keep in mind that the single-folder approach might not work well for larger projects. At some point, the sheer number of files in the folder makes it difficult to find a single file easily. Rather than scrolling through several screens of files, you might find it more efficient to create multiple folders to hold related files (see Figure 12.2).

Using Email   You can email yourself messages containing electronic documents you've found in your research. Some databases, such as those from EBSCO and OCLC/FirstSearch, allow you to email the text of selected records directly from the database (see Figure 12.3).

Saving Bookmarks and Favorites in Your Browser   You can use a Bookmarks or Favorites list in your Web browser to keep track of your sources (see Figure 12.4).

Be aware that Bookmarks and Favorites lists can become disorganized. To avoid this problem, put related items into folders, and give the items on your list descriptive names.

Using Personal Bookmarking Sites   Personal bookmarking sites allow you to save your bookmarks to a Web site at no charge and view them from any computer with a connection to the Web. Some of these sites, such as Google Bookmarks, allow you to access your bookmarks through a toolbar. The Google toolbar (toolbar.google.com) not only provides access to your bookmarks, but also to tools for organizing them, such as tags, a notebook, and the ability to save clippings from Web pages (see Figure 12.5).

Information Literacy

There are drawbacks to relying on a Bookmarks or Favorites list as a place to "store" your sources. First, pages on the Web can and do change. If you suspect that the page you want to mark might change before you complete your research project, save it to disk or print it so that you won't lose its content. Second, some Web pages are generated by database programs. In such cases, you might not be able to return to the page using a Bookmarks or Favorites list. A URL like the following usually indicates that a Web page is generated by a database program:

> http://firstsearch.oclc.org/FUNC/
> QUERY:%7Fnext=NEXTCMD%7F%
> 22/FUNC/SRCH_RESULTS%22%
> 7FentityListType=0

The majority of the characters in such URLs are used by the database program to determine which records to display on a page. In many cases, the URL works only while you are conducting your search. If you add such a URL to your Bookmarks or Favorites list, there's a good chance it won't work later.

EBSCO Research Databases

Sign In | Folder | Preferences | New Features! | Ask-A-Librarian | Help

Basic Search | Advanced Search | Visual Search | Choose Databases

New Search   Keyword | Publications | Subject Terms | Cited References | Indexes | Images   Language ▾

Results for: sports *AND* steroids *AND* adolescents   Add search to folder Display link to search
                                                            Create alert for this search

Find: sports   in Select a Field (optional) ▾   Search   Clear ❓
and ▾ steroids   in Select a Field (optional) ▾
and ▾ adolescents   in Select a Field (optional) ▾   Add Row   Folder has items.

Refine Search | Search History/Alerts | Results

All Results: 1-4 of 4   Page: 1   Sort by: Date ▾   Add (1-4)

See: All Results   Academic Journals   ┌──────────────────────────────┐
                                                          │ Add records you want to email │
sports and steroids and a... > TEENAGERS   │ to the results folder.   │
                                                          └──────────────────────────────┘

Narrow Results by Subject

ANABOLIC steroids

DRUG abuse

NORWAY

STRAIN theory (Chemistry)

SMOKING

Risk factors

ANDR

SMOK

1. Adolescent Anabolic Steroid Use, Gender, Physical Activity, and Other Problem Behaviors*. By: Miller, Kathleen E.; Hoffman, Joseph H.; Barnes, Grace M.; Sabo, Don; Melnick, Merrill J.; Farrell, Michael P.. Substance Use & Misuse, 2005, Vol. 40 Issue 11, p1637-1657, 21p, 6bw; DOI: 10.1080/10826080500222727; (AN 18686012)
   PDF Full Text (1.9MB)   Add

2. Use of Anabolic-Androgenic *Steroids* in Adolescence: Winning, Looking Good or Being Bad? By: Wichstrom, Lars; Pedersen, Willy. Journal of Studies on Alcohol, Jan2001, Vol. 62 Issue 1, p5, 9p, 2 charts; (AN 4100746)   Add

┌──────────────────────────────┐
│ Click on the email icon.   │
└──────────────────────────────┘

Folder List

▶ **Articles** (3)   **Articles**

  Images (0)   1-3 of 3 Page: 1

  Videos (0)   Select: All | None   Delete: All | Selected   Print E-mail Save Export

┌────────────────────────────────┐   Sort by: Name ▾
│ Provide the email address,   │
│ subject, and notes, and set   │ ☑ 1. For the Record. Sports Illustrated, 5/7/2007, Vol. 106 Issue 19, p26-28, 2p; (AN
│ other options.   │   24987485)
└────────────────────────────────┘   HTML Full Text

  Search Alerts (0)   ☑ 2. Girls and steroids. Teacher Magazine, Feb98, Vol. 9 Issue 5, p11, 1/9p; (AN 184821)
                                 HTML Full Text
  Journal Alerts (0)

Articles

Number of items to be e-mailed: 3   **Include when sending:**
E-mail Address: alexis.alvarez@colostate.edu   ☑ HTML Full Text (when available)

Separate each e-mail address with a semicolon.

Subject: Search Results   ○ Standard Field Format
Comments: Three useful articles.   Detailed Citation and Abstract ▾

                                                ● Citation Format
                                                  APA (American Psychological Assoc.) ▾

                                                ○ Customized Field Format

Format: ● Rich Text   ○ Plain Text
                                                ┌──────────────────────────────────┐
        ☑ Remove these items from folder after e-mailing   │ Some databases allow you to   │
                                                │ choose a citation format for   │
        Send   │ your record, but check it to be   │
                                                │ sure it follows the documen-   │
For information on e-mailing Linked Full Text, see online help. *For*   │ tation style correctly.   │
information on using Citation Formats, see online citation help   └──────────────────────────────────┘

FIGURE 12.3 Sending Database Records via *Electronic Mail*

Collecting Information

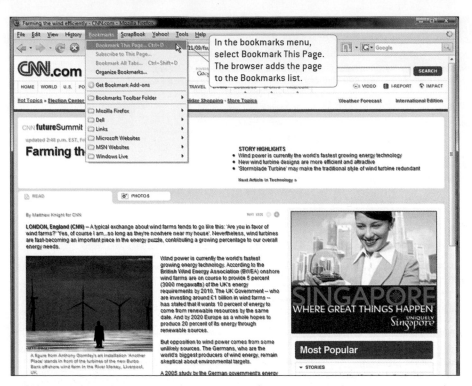

FIGURE 12.4 Adding an Item to Your Bookmarks List (Firefox, Mozilla, and Netscape Navigator)

If you use multiple computers, you can benefit from the following sites.

Ask.com's MyStuff:	mystuff.ask.com
Google Bookmarks:	google.com/bookmarks/
Yahoo! Bookmarks:	bookmarks.yahoo.com

Using Social Bookmarking Sites   Social bookmarking sites allow you to create lists of bookmarks at no charge that other Web users can view. Most of these sites also allow you to create private bookmarks. The advantages of these sites for research writers include (1) the ability to save bookmarks and then view them at any time from any computer connected to the Web and (2) the ability to browse bookmarks collections created by other users who share your interest in an issue. Leading social bookmarking Web sites include:

BlinkList:	blinklist.com
ClipMarks:	clipmarks.com
Del.icio.us:	del.icio.us
Webaroo:	webaroo.com

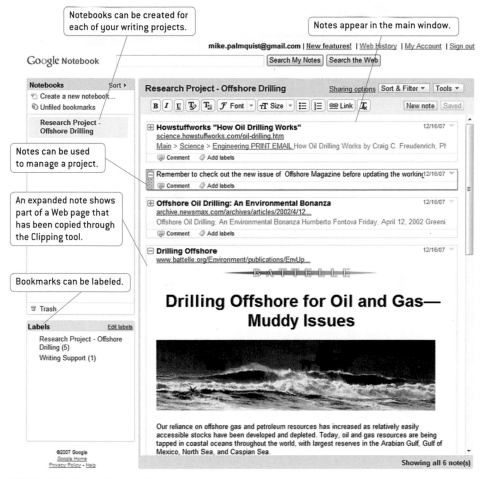

FIGURE 12.5 Google Notebook

Using Web Capture Tools A wide range of programs have been created to help writers keep track of the information they find online. Some of these programs work with your browser as toolbars or "add-ons" (a term used for programs that work within the Firefox browser). Most leading social bookmarking sites, for example, have created free tools that can be added to Internet Explorer and Firefox (See Figure 12.6). By clicking on the ClipMark button, for instance, you can add a Web page—or portions of a page—to your collection of materials on ClipMarks. Some add-ons in Firefox offer powerful sets of tools for managing information. Zotero and ScrapBook both allow you to save entire pages or parts of pages to your local computer, while Zotero also provides support for citing sources.

Information Literacy
Whatever strategies you use to save and organize electronic sources, be sure to back up your work. Replacing lost information takes time and effort. Avoid the risk of lost information by taking the time to make copies of your electronic files, saved Web pages, email messages, and Bookmarks or Favorites list.

FIGURE 12.6 Scrapbook Firefox Add-on

Leading no-fee Web capture tools include

BlinkList Button:	blinklist.com
ClipMarks Toolbar:	clipmarks.com/install/
Del.icio.us Tools:	del.icio.us/help/
ScrapBook Firefox Add-on:	amb.vis.ne.jp/mozilla/scrapbook/
Zotero Firefox Add-on:	zotero.org

Using bedfordresearcher.com   Use the bibliography tools at bedfordresearcher
.com to save bibliographic information about each of your sources, write a brief
note or annotation about each source, evaluate each source, and save text from
electronic sources. You can also create a bibliography formatted in MLA, APA,
Chicago, or CSE style. Read more about bibliographies later in this chapter on
p. 169.

Decide How to Save and Organize Print Sources

During your research project, you'll accumulate a great deal of print information,
such as:

* your written notes (in a notebook, on loose pieces of paper, on Post-It
  Notes, and so on)

- printouts from Web pages and databases
- articles sent through a library's fax-on-demand service
- printed word processing documents, such as various drafts of your research question
- books, magazines, newspapers, brochures, pamphlets, and government documents
- photocopies of articles, book chapters, and other documents
- letters, printed email messages, survey results, and so on

Rather than letting all this information build up in messy piles on your desk or stuffing it into folders in your backpack, create a filing system to keep track of your print documents. Filing systems can range from well-organized piles of paper labeled with Post-it Notes to three-ring binders to file cabinets filled with neatly labeled files and folders.

Regardless of the approach you take, keep the following principles in mind.

- **Create an organizational scheme that allows you to locate your print materials.** Decide whether you want to group material by topic, by date, by pro versus con, by type of material (Web pages, photocopies, original documents, field sources, and so on), or by author.
- **Stick with your organizational scheme.** You'll find it difficult to locate materials if you use different approaches at different points in your research project.
- **Make sure printed documents provide complete publication information.** If a source doesn't contain publication information, write it on the document yourself.
- **Date your notes.** Indicating dates when you recorded information can help you reconstruct what you might have been doing while you took the notes. Dates are also essential for documenting Web sources and other sources obtained online.
- **Write a brief note on each of your print materials.** Indicate how it might contribute to your project.

Collecting Information

12b

How can I create a bibliography?

A bibliography is a list of sources with complete publication information, usually formatted according to the rules of a documentation system such as those created by the Modern Language Association (see Chapter 20), the American Psychological Association (see Chapter 21), or the Council of Science Editors (see Chapter 23), or found in books such as the *Chicago Manual of Style* (see Chapter 22). As you prepare to collect information, consider creating a working bibliography or an annotated bibliography.

Create a Working Bibliography

A working bibliography is a running list of the sources you collect as you work on your research project—with publication information for each source. The organization of your working bibliography can vary according to your needs and preferences. You can organize your sources in any of the following ways.

- in the order in which you collected your sources
- in categories
- by author
- by publication title
- according to an outline of your project document

The entries in a working bibliography should include as much publication information about a source as you can gather (see Table 12.1).

TABLE 12.1 INFORMATION YOU SHOULD LIST IN A WORKING BIBLIOGRAPHY	
TYPE OF SOURCE	**INFORMATION YOU SHOULD LIST**
All Sources	Author(s) Title Publication year Medium consulted
Book	Editor(s) of book (if applicable) Publication city Publisher Series and series editor (if applicable) Translator (if applicable) Volume (if applicable) Edition (if applicable)
Chapter in an Edited Book	Publication city Publisher Editor(s) of book Book title Page numbers
Journal, Magazine, and Newspaper Article	Journal title Volume number or date Issue number or date Page numbers
Web Page, Newsgroup Post, Email Message, Blog Entry, and Wiki Page	URL Access date (the date you read the source) Sponsoring organization (if listed)
Field Research	Title (usually a description of the source, such as "Personal Interview with Jessica Lynn Richards" or "Observation of June Allison's Class at Tavelli Elementary School") Date (usually the date on which the field research was conducted)

Your working bibliography will change significantly as you work on your research writing project. As you explore and narrow your topic, collect sources, and work with sources, you will add potentially useful sources and delete sources that are no longer relevant. Eventually, your working bibliography will become one of the following:

- a *works cited* or *reference list*—a formal list of the sources you have referred to in a document.

- a *bibliography* or *works consulted list*—a formal list of the sources that contributed to your thinking about an issue, even if those sources were not referred to explicitly in the text of the document.

Keeping your working bibliography up-to-date is a critical part of your research writing process. Your working bibliography helps you keep track of your sources and increases the likelihood that you will cite all the sources you use in your document—an important contribution to your efforts to avoid plagiarism.

The first five sources from featured writer Elizabeth Leontiev's working bibliography are found in Figure 12.7.

Entries follow MLA style (see p. 294).

Borwick, Phoebe, and Amy Donohue. "Drugs: Nobody's Winning the War." *Just Focus*. Global Education Centre, 10 Oct. 2006. Web. 5 June 2007.

Forero, Juan. "Coca Advocate Wins Election for President in Bolivia." *New York Times*. New York Times, 19 Dec. 2005. Web. 3 June 2007.

Gordon, Gretchen. "The United States, Bolivia, and the Political Economy of Coca." *Multinational Monitor* 27.1 (2006): 15-20. *Expanded Academic ASAP*. Web. 15 May 2007.

Harman, Danna. "In Bolivia, a Setback for US Anti-Coca Drive." *Christian Science Monitor*. Christian Science Monitor, 22 Dec. 2005. Web. 12 May 2007.

United States. Office of National Drug Control Policy. "Drug Facts: Cocaine." *Office of National Drug Control Policy*. Executive Office of the President of the United States, n.d. Web. 8 June 2007.

When authors are not listed, the sponsoring organization is listed as the author.

FIGURE 12.7 Part of Elizabeth Leontiev's Working Bibliography

My Research Project

CREATE A WORKING BIBLIOGRAPHY

You can create your working bibliography in print form (such as, in a notebook) or in electronic form (for example, in a word processing file). You can also use the bibliography tools at **bedfordresearcher.com**, which allow you to

- create entries for new sources
- annotate sources
- evaluate sources
- copy and save some or all of the text from a source
- display your working bibliography in MLA, APA, *Chicago*, or CSE style
- print your working bibliography, save it as a file, or send it via email

Create an Annotated Bibliography

You may be asked to create an *annotated bibliography*, a formal document that provides a brief note about each of the sources you've listed, in addition to its complete citation information. These notes, or annotations, are typically brief—usually no more than two or three sentences. The content, focus, and length of your annotations will reflect your purposes for creating an annotated bibliography.

- In some research writing projects, you will submit an annotated bibliography to an instructor for review and comment. In this situation, your instructor will most likely expect a clear description of the content of each source and some indication of how you might use the source.

- In other research writing projects, the annotated bibliography might serve simply as a planning tool—a more detailed version of a working bibliography. As a result, your annotations might call your attention to key passages or information in a source, suggest where you might use information or ideas from the source in your project document, or emphasize relationships between this source and others you've collected.

- In still other research writing projects, the annotated bibliography might be the end product of your research efforts. In this case, you will write your annotations for your readers, keeping their needs, interests, values, and beliefs in mind.

Alexis Alvarez created an annotated bibliography that she used to record her ideas about how to use her sources and that her instructor used to assess her progress on her research writing project (see Figure 12.8).

In contrast, featured writer Pete Jacquez created an annotated bibliography that he included on his Web site about wind-generated electrical power. Because his bibliography was intended for readers who were interested in learning more about wind power, his annotations focused primarily on describing the information, ideas, and arguments in each source. The first four entries in his annotated bibliography are found in Figure 12.9.

Entries follow APA style (see p. 332).

Costello, B. (2004, July 4). Too late? Survey suggests millions of kids could be juicing. *New York Post.* **Retrieved from http://www.nypost.com**

This article discusses steroid and other performance-enhancing drugs used by eighth- through twelfth-grade boys and girls and provides a number of relevant statistics. I'll use this source to support statements about steroid use among young female athletes.

Annotations provide brief summaries of the purpose and content of the sources.

Davies, D., & Armstrong, M. (1989). *Psychological factors in competitive sport.* **New York, NY: Falmer Press.**

This book addresses various psychological factors in sports including learning, motivation, anxiety, stress, and performance. I'll use it to support my discussion of why sports can have negative effects on girls.

DeNoon, D. (2004, August 4). *Steroid use: Hitting closer to home.* **Retrieved from http://webmd.com/fitness-exercise/features/ steroid-use-hitting-closer-to-home**

Annotations are intended for Alexis and her teacher. They indicate how and where she will use them in her document.

This Web page provides information about increasing steroid use in America as well as the latest statistical figures regarding this use. I'll use it for statistical evidence and to drive home the point that this problem needs to be addressed.

Dexheimer, E. (2004, May 13). Nothing to lose: The Colorado Impact teaches girls about life — then hoops. *Denver Westword.* **Retrieved from http://www.westword.com**

Article about a different way of coaching club basketball focusing mainly on the Colorado Impact club and their policies on practice and community service. I'll use it to provide the basketball coach's viewpoint of club basketball and the effects of it on parents, athletes, etc.

FIGURE 12.8 Part of Alexis Alvarez's Annotated Bibliography

[FRAMING MY ARGUMENT]

Refine Your Argument by Turning Your Working Bibliography Into an Annotated Bibliography. Your working bibliography is simply a list of sources. If you've forgotten what the source is about, you'll need to consult your notes or review the source before you can think about how to use it in your project document. By turning your working bibliography into an annotated bibliography, however, you can remind yourself of the role each source might play in your argument. Create annotations that (1) remind you of the information, ideas, and arguments in the source and (2) record your ideas about how the source might be used to frame your argument. The following tutorial can help you turn your working bibliography into an annotated bibliography.

III Collecting Information

Entries follow APA style (see p. 333).

Bisbee, D. W. (2004). NEPA review of offshore wind farms. *Boston College Environmental Affairs Law Review 31*(2), 349–385.

This review focuses on offshore wind farms and their efficiency at producing electricity. The article notes that offshore wind farms can sometimes be inconsistent in their output of electrical power due to variable winds. The article speculates about the extent to which this inefficiency resulting from inconsistent winds reduces the viability of offshore wind farms as an alternative to fossil fuel plants.

Annotations provide brief summaries of the purpose and content of the sources.

Bohlander, B. (2004, April 26). *Colorado State first university in the United States to offer choice of wind power to campus residents.* Retrieved from http://www.newsinfo.colostate.edu/index.asp?page=news_item_display&news_item_id=627126272

This news release announces that Colorado State University is the first university to offer students the option of purchasing wind-generated electrical power for their use in dormitories and other campus housing. The news release discusses the future of wind power and provides information about the specific costs for students who choose to utilize wind power while living on campus.

Brown, L. R. (2003). Wind power is set to become world's leading energy source. *Humanist 63*(5), 5.

This article addresses advancements in wind power technology and how further advancements will help in the push for wind-generated electricity. This article supports the idea that wind power can and should be utilized as an alternative to fossil fuels.

Annotations are intended for visitors to Pete's Web site, rather than for his instructor or himself.

Chasteen, S. (2004). Who owns wind? *Science and Spirit 15*(1), 12–15.

This article focuses on the economic aspect of implementing wind power. The author identifies the issue of economic motives behind wind power, which has become more relevant as large firms look to move into the wind power market.

FIGURE 12.9 Part of Pete Jacquez's Annotated Bibliography

How do I create an annotated bibliography?

Descriptive annotations are usually three-to-five-sentence summaries of the source. For graded annotated bibliographies, ask your instructor about what is expected. In this example, part of the annotated bibliography created by Pete Jacquez is used to illustrate the type of information that can be included in an annotated bibliography.

1 Provide a complete source citation, following the guidelines of your documentation system (such as MLA, APA, *Chicago*, or CSE). This example uses APA style.

2 Format each citation so that it stands out from its annotation. Bold or a contrasting color are often used.

3 In the annotation, identify the information and ideas that are most relevant to your project, such as significant arguments and findings.

4 If relevant, include information about the background and qualifications of the author or key authorities mentioned in the source.

5 Indicate how you might use the source in your research project.

Hill, A., & West, A. (2004). Wind farms: The debate. *Ecologist 34*(2), 24–28.

This article uses a debate format to address questions about the environmental and economic costs and benefits of wind farms. The answers to the questions come from two knowledgeable sources. Hill is head of communications for the British Wind Energy Association and West is vice-chairperson of Country Guardian, a conservative organization opposed to commercial wind farms. I will use this in the wind power economics section of my Web site.

Stone, B. (2004, September 20). The master of wind. *Newsweek 144*(12), E34.

This article profiles Jim Dehlson, who owns Clipper Windpower. Dehlson explains that the implementation of wind power has been difficult, with the main obstacle being cost. Dehlson believes that wind power will not fully succeed without a proactive approach from the government. The article presents a cost analysis comparing relative costs of electricity generated from fossil fuels with that generated by wind. I will probably use this article to illustrate the economic and environmental trade-offs of wind power.

Collecting Information

Review another example and work on your annotated bibliography at **bedfordresearcher.com**. Click on Interactive Exercises.

QUICK REFERENCE

Managing Information

☑ Decide how you will save and organize electronic sources. (p. 162)

☑ Decide how you will save and organize print sources. (p. 168)

☑ Create a working bibliography (p. 170) or annotated bibliography (p. 172).

||| Collecting Information

The Bedford Researcher

I	Joining the Conversation
II	Working with Sources
III	Collecting Information
IV	**Writing Your Document**
V	Documenting Sources

PART IV

Writing Your Document

After you have collected information, you'll have a better understanding of the scope of your issue. In the chapters that follow, you'll learn how to use your new knowledge to create a well-written, well-designed document.

13

Developing, Supporting, and Organizing Your Ideas

> **Key Questions**
>
> **13a. How can I develop my thesis statement?** 180
>
> Review your research question and preliminary thesis statement
> Reflect on your readers
> Consider the type of document you will write
> Identify important words in your research question and preliminary
>   thesis statement
> Focus your thesis statement
>
> **13b. How can I support my thesis statement?** 185
>
> Choose supporting points
> Develop reasons for your points
> Select and organize evidence
> Arrange your argument
> Assess the integrity of your argument
>
> **13c. How should I organize my document?** 196
>
> Choose an appropriate organizational pattern
> Create an outline

As you shift your attention away from collecting and working with sources and toward crafting your own contribution to the conversation about your issue, you'll begin the process of planning your argument. That process includes developing and supporting your thesis statement, deciding how to organize your document, and creating an outline.

13a

How can I develop my thesis statement?

Up to this point, your research question and preliminary thesis statement have helped focus your efforts to learn about an issue. Now it's time to develop a thesis statement that answers your research question in a definitive manner. If you've asked, for example, about the causes of a problem, then your thesis statement should identify those causes. If you've asked what the best solution to a problem might be, your thesis statement should identify that solution.

Sample Research Question:

What should be done to address the growing number of antibiotic-resistant infections?

Sample Thesis Statement:

State and federal governments should increase funding for research into the development of new antibiotics.

In addition to answering your research question, your thesis statement can invite your readers to learn something new, suggest that they change their attitudes or beliefs, or argue that they should take action of some kind.

Sample Research Question:

What should be done to address the growing number of antibiotic-resistant infections?

Sample Thesis Statement: Asking Readers to Learn Something New:

We should understand how antibiotic-resistant infections occur and how we can avoid them.

Sample Thesis Statement: Asking Readers to Change Their Attitudes or Beliefs:

The challenges posed by the growing number of antibiotic-resistant infections can be met only through a thoughtful and thorough examination of our public-health funding priorities.

Sample Thesis Statement: Asking Readers to Take Action:

Each of us should ask our state and federal representatives to increase funding for research into the development of new antibiotics.

Table 13.1 presents the featured writers' movements from research question to preliminary thesis statement to thesis statement. Note how each thesis statement answers its research question and either directs readers' attention to one aspect of the conversation, encourages them to change their attitudes or beliefs,

TABLE 13.1 THE FEATURED WRITERS' MOVEMENT FROM RESEARCH QUESTION TO THESIS STATEMENT

FEATURED WRITER	RESEARCH QUESTION	PRELIMINARY THESIS STATEMENT	THESIS STATEMENT
Alexis Alvarez	What are the effects of competitive soccer on adolescent girls?	Steroid use by adolescent girls involved in competitive sports should be addressed by educating athletes, parents, and coaches about health consequences and emphasizing fair play.	Although competitive sports can provide young female athletes with many benefits, they can also have negative effects, the worst of which is increasing drug use.
Patrick Crossland	What cultural, academic, and regional factors affect college admissions decisions?	Factors affecting college admissions decisions include race, gender, and intellectual ability.	Getting into college is like entering a contest in which each applicant is pitted against thousands of others.
Kevin Fahey	How is Nick Adams characterized by Ernest Hemingway?	Nick Adams is a flawed character with whom readers can identify.	By portraying Nick Adams as befuddled, intimidated, and even self-serving, Hemingway gives us a hero with whom most readers can identify.
Pete Jacquez	What strategies, if any, should Coloradoans use to encourage local, state, and federal governments to increase U.S. use of wind-generated electrical power?	Coloradoans should encourage local, state, and federal governments to increase reliance on wind-generated electrical power through a mix of tax incentives and reduced regulation.	Coloradoans should lead a national movement toward increased use of wind power.
Elizabeth Leontiev	How can we reduce the economic impact of the war on drugs on South American coca farmers?	The U.S. and South American governments should adopt the "zero cocaine, not zero coca" policy.	The "zero cocaine, not zero coca" policy will boost the Bolivian economy, allow native Andeans to maintain their cultural practices, and reduce cocaine trafficking into the United States.
Chris Norris	What accounts for the resurgence in popularity of metal music?	Metal music has a political message, musical diversity, and a strong fan base.	With its political consciousness, diversity of musical subgenres, and thriving fan community, metal music today is undergoing a rebirth.

or urges them to take action of some kind. Developing an effective thesis statement involves five steps:

1. Reviewing your research question and preliminary thesis statement.

2. Reflecting on your readers.

3. Considering the type of document—or genre— you plan to write.

> @ Read about the student writers discussed in this chapter at bedfordresearcher .com. Click on Featured Writers.

4. Identifying important words in your research question and your preliminary thesis statement.

5. Focusing your thesis statement.

Step 1: Review Your Research Question and Preliminary Thesis Statement

Begin your review by reading quickly through your notes to gain an overall sense of the information, ideas, and arguments in your sources. You'll probably come to realize that you've gained a more complete understanding of your issue—an understanding that might affect your purpose and role as a writer and, by extension, your understanding of your writing situation. The review might also affect the main point you want to make in your document. Use the following questions to determine whether you should refine your research question and preliminary thesis statement.

- How have the sources you've consulted changed your thinking about the issue?

- Have your purposes—the reasons you are working on this project— changed since you started your project? If so, how do you view your purposes now?

- Are you adequately addressing your readers' purposes, needs, interests, values, and beliefs?

- Can you address this idea given the requirements and limitations of your writing project?

IV Writing Your Document

? WHAT'S MY PURPOSE?

Make sure your preliminary thesis statement still fits the purpose of your research writing project and the role (or roles) you've adopted as a research writer. Kevin Fahey, for example, wanted to analyze Ernest Hemingway's characterization of Nick Adams. His preliminary thesis statement, "Nick Adams is a flawed character with whom readers can identify," answered the research question, "How is Nick Adams characterized by Ernest Hemingway?" Nick decided that his preliminary thesis statement was consistent with his purpose (to conduct a literary analysis) and his role (interpreter).

Step 2: Reflect on Your Readers

A thesis statement should invite your readers to learn something new, to change their attitudes or beliefs about a topic, or to take action of some kind. Patrick Crossland could assume that his readers—classmates in his composition class—had experienced the college admissions process. He knew, however, that they might not understand fully the factors that affect admissions decisions. Most important, if any of his classmates were thinking of transferring to another school, they might need to be aware of those factors.

Step 3: Consider the Type of Document You Will Write

An effective thesis statement will reflect the type—or genre—of document you plan to write. Depending on the genre, your readers will have different expectations about how you present your thesis statement. Readers of an academic essay are likely to expect a calm, clearly written statement of what you want them to learn, believe, or do. Readers of an informative newspaper article will expect you to identify, in a balanced and seemingly unbiased manner, what you want them to learn. Readers of an opinion column will expect you to be more assertive, and perhaps even more entertaining, about your main point. Consider how the following thesis statements, all addressing problems with the recruitment of athletes at a college or university, reflect the type of document the writer plans to draft:

Argumentative Academic Essay:

The University should ensure that its recruiting practices are fully in compliance with NCAA regulations.

Informative Newspaper Article:

The University is taking steps to bring its recruiting practices in line with NCAA regulations.

Opinion Column:

The University's coaches need to get their act together before the NCAA slaps them with sanctions.

Step 4: Identify Important Words in Your Research Question and Preliminary Thesis Statement

Identify the key words and phrases you have relied on so far and use them to craft your thesis statement. Consider the following example, which indicates how words and phrases from a research question and preliminary thesis statement are used in a thesis statement:

Research Question:

What is the cause of recent declines in the state's brown trout population?

> Calls attention to a problem and introduces three key phrases.

Preliminary Thesis Statement:

Disease linked to hatchery-raised rainbow trout seems to be causing the decline in the state's brown trout population.

> Identifies the cause of the problem — "disease" carried by "hatchery-raised rainbow trout."

Thesis Statement:

The Department of Natural Resources should determine whether the recent decline of brown trout populations in state streams is caused by disease spread by rainbow trout released from state fish hatcheries.

> Suggests a course of action to solve the problem.

Step 5: Focus Your Thesis Statement

[FRAMING MY ARGUMENT]

A broad thesis statement does not encourage your readers to learn anything new, to change their attitudes or beliefs, or to take action. The following thesis statement is too broad:

Broad Thesis Statement:

We should ensure that every American receives adequate health care coverage.

There's no conversation to be had about this topic because few people would argue with such a statement. A more focused thesis statement would define what should be done and who should do it. To focus your thesis statement, ask what your readers would want to know about the issue, what attitudes should be changed, or what action should be taken. Consider their likely responses to your thesis statement and attempt to head off potential counter-arguments or questions.

Focused Thesis Statement:

The U.S. Congress should allow all Americans to enroll in the health care plan offered to federal employees.

My Research Project

DEVELOP AND REFINE YOUR THESIS STATEMENT

In your research log, complete the following activity to draft your thesis statement.

1. My research question is:

2. My preliminary thesis statement is:

3. My purpose for writing is:

4. My role is:

5. I want my thesis statement to reflect the following needs, interests, values, and beliefs of my readers:

↓

6. I want my readers to do one or more of the following:
- learn about . . .
- change their attitudes or beliefs about . . .
- take the following action:

7. I plan to write the following type of document:

8. The most important words and phrases in my research question are:

9. The most important words and phrases in my preliminary thesis statement are:

10. Building on my research question and preliminary thesis statement, my thesis statement is:

11. My readers are likely to respond to this thesis statement by asking the following questions or raising the following objections:

12. I can focus my thesis statement by rephrasing it:

You can print or download this activity at **bedfordresearcher.com.** Click on Activities > Develop and Refine Your Thesis Statement.

13b

How can I support my thesis statement?

Presenting your thesis statement effectively involves far more than knowing what you want others to understand or believe or how you want them to act. It requires the development of a strategy to accomplish your goal. That strategy should reflect not only your purposes as a writer, but also your readers' needs, interests, values, beliefs, and knowledge of an issue. It should also take into account the conventions typically used in the type of document you plan to write. Deciding how to support your thesis statement involves the following:

- Choosing supporting points
- Developing reasons for your points
- Selecting and organizing evidence
- Arranging your argument
- Assessing the integrity of your argument

Step 1: Choose Supporting Points

In longer documents, such as essays, reports, and Web sites, writers usually present several points to support their thesis statement. The kinds of supporting points writers choose will vary according to the type of document they are writing. In informative documents, writers are likely to focus on the three or four most important aspects of the issue they want readers to understand. In analytical documents, writers are likely to choose points that help readers understand the results of the analysis. In argumentative documents, writers usually offer a series of claims that will lead readers to accept the argument advanced in the thesis statement.

To choose the points you'll make to support your thesis statement, consider brainstorming, freewriting, looping, or clustering. As you generate ideas, reflect on your purpose, your role as a writer, the type of document you intend to write, and your readers.

- If you are writing to inform, ask what you want to convey to your readers and what they are most likely to want to know about the issue.

- If you are writing to evaluate, reflect on how best to present your criteria and the results of your evaluation.

- If you are writing to analyze, consider how you'll present the results of your analysis and the questions your readers might have about each part of your analysis.

- If you are writing to solve a problem, decide how to define the problem and how to present your solution. Try to predict the questions your readers will have about your problem definition, your proposed solution, and alternative solutions.

- If you are writing to convince or persuade, ask how you can convince your readers to accept your thesis statement, how they are likely to respond to your argument, and what sort of counter-arguments they might propose.

Step 2: Develop Reasons for Your Points

For thousands of years, writers have appealed to readers to accept their ideas as reasonable and valid. Much of the work of ancient Greek and Roman thinkers, such as Aristotle and Cicero, for example, revolved around strategies for presenting an argument to an audience. Their work continues to serve as a foundation for how we think about conveying information, ideas, and argument to readers. In particular, the concept of an *appeal* to an audience plays a central role in thinking about how to develop an argument. Essentially, when you ask someone to accept your argument, you are appealing to them—you are asking them to consider what you have to say and, if they accept it as appropriate and valid, to believe or act in a certain way.

You can persuade your readers to accept your points by appealing to authority, emotion, principles, values, beliefs, character, and logic.

Appeals to Authority   When you make an appeal to authority, you ask a reader to accept a point because someone in a position of authority supports it. The evidence used to support this kind of appeal typically takes the form of quotations, paraphrases, or summaries of the ideas of experts on an issue, of political leaders, or of people who have been affected by an issue. As you consider potential reasons for accepting a point, reflect on the notes you've taken on your sources. Ask whether you've identified experts, leaders, or people who have been affected by an issue, and then ask whether you can use them to convince your readers that your point has merit.

Appeals to Emotion   Appeals to emotion attempt to elicit an emotional response to an issue. The famous "win one for the Gipper" speech delivered by Pat O'Brien, who was playing the part of Notre Dame coach Knute Rockne in the 1940 film *Knute Rockne: All American*, is an example of an appeal to emotion. At halftime during a game with Army, with Notre Dame trailing, he said:

> Well, boys . . . I haven't a thing to say. Played a great game . . . all of you. Great game. I guess we just can't expect to win 'em all.
> I'm going to tell you something I've kept to myself for years. None of you ever knew George Gipp. It was long before your time. But you know what a tradition he is at Notre Dame . . . And the last thing he said to me — "Rock," he said, "sometime, when the team is up against it — and the breaks are beating the boys — tell them to go out there with all they got and win just one for the Gipper . . . I don't know where I'll be then, Rock", he said, "but I'll know about it — and I'll be happy."

Using emotional appeals to frame an argument — that is, to help readers view an issue in a particular way — is a tried and true strategy. But use it carefully, if you use it all. In some types of documents, such as scholarly articles and essays, emotional appeals are used infrequently, and readers of such documents are likely to ask why you would play on their emotions instead of making a logical appeal or appeals to authority.

Appeals to Principles, Values, and Beliefs   Appeals to principles, values, and beliefs rely on the assumption that your readers value a given set of principles. Religious and ethical arguments are often based on appeals to principles, such as the need to respect God, to love one another, to trust in the innate goodness of individuals, to believe that all of us are created equal, or to believe that security should never be purchased at the price of individual liberty. If you consider making an appeal to principles, values, or beliefs, be sure your readers are likely to share the particular principle, value, or belief you will use.

Appeals to Character   Writers frequently use appeals to character. When politicians refer to their military experience, for example, they are saying, "Look at me. I'm a patriotic person who has served our country." When a celebrity endorses a product, he or she is saying, "You know and like me, so please believe me when I say that this product is worth purchasing." Appeals to character can also reflect a person's professional accomplishment. When a scientist or philosopher presents an argument, for example, they sometimes refer to their background and experience, or perhaps to their previous publications. In doing so, they are implicitly telling their readers that they have proven to be accurate and truthful in the past, and that readers can continue to trust them. Essentially, you can think of appeals to character as the "trust me" strategy. As you consider this kind of appeal, reflect on your character, accomplishments, and experiences, and ask how they might persuade your readers to trust you.

IV

Writing Your Document

Appeals to Logic   When someone talks about a logical appeal, they mean reasoning through a set of propositions to reach a considered conclusion. For example, you might argue that a suspect is guilty of murder because police found her fingerprints on a murder weapon, her DNA in blood under the murder victim's fingernails, scratches on the suspect's face, and video of the murder from a surveillance camera. Your argument would rely on the logical presentation of evidence to convince a jury that the suspect was the murderer and to persuade them to return a verdict of guilty. As you develop reasons to support your points, consider using logical appeals such as if/then reasoning, cause/effect reasoning, and problem/solution reasoning.

You can use different types of appeals to support your points. Emotional appeals can be mixed with appeals to character. A coach's address to a team before an important athletic competition often relies not only on appeals to emotion but also on appeals to character, calling attention to their need to trust what the coach has to say and to trust in themselves and their own abilities. Similarly, appeals to principle can be combined with appeals to emotion and logic.

My Research Project

DEVELOP REASONS FOR YOUR POINTS

To develop an argumentative strategy, reflect on your purpose, your readers, and your overall claim. In your research log, record your responses to the following:

1. List each of your points.

2. Ask what sorts of appeals are best suited to each point.

3. Sketch out promising appeals. Ask, for example, how you would appeal to authority, or how you would appeal to logic.

4. Ask how your readers are likely to respond to a given appeal.

5. Ask whether the kind of document you are writing lends itself to the use of particular appeals.

You can download or print this activity at **bedfordresearcher.com**. Click on Activities > Develop Reasons for Your Points.

Step 3: Select and Organize Evidence

Consider using the following types of evidence to support your points:

- textual, in the form of quotations, paraphrases, and summaries
- numerical and statistical information
- images—including photographs, drawings, animations, and video—and sound
- tables, charts, and graphs
- information from personal interviews and observations
- personal experience

You can use evidence to

- introduce or contrast ideas and arguments
- provide examples and illustrations
- define ideas and concepts
- illustrate processes
- associate particular ideas and concepts with authorities, such as political leaders, subject-matter experts, or people who have been affected by an issue
- call attention to similarities and differences

As you select supporting evidence, consider the type of document—or genre—you plan to write. The type of evidence used in various genres can differ in important ways. Articles in magazines, newspapers, and Web sites, for example, are more likely to rely on interviews, observation, and illustrations as primary sources of evidence than are academic essays, whose writers tend to draw information from published sources found in a library or database. Multimodal essays, in contrast, are likely to use not only textual information and images, but also audio, video, and animation.

My Research Project

SELECT EVIDENCE TO SUPPORT YOUR THESIS STATEMENT

Use the following prompts to help identify evidence to support your thesis statement:

1. List the points you are using to support your thesis statement.

2. Identify relevant evidence, and then list the evidence below each point. You might need to review your sources to locate additional evidence, or even obtain additional sources.

3. Determine whether you are relying too heavily on information from a single source.

4. Determine whether you are relying too heavily on one type of evidence.

5. Determine whether you've chosen evidence that is consistent with the type of document you plan to write.

You can download or print this activity at **bedfordresearcher.com**. Click on Activities > Select Evidence to Support Your Thesis Statement.

Once you have chosen your evidence, strategies such as labeling, grouping, clustering, and mapping can help you determine how to present that evidence to support your points. These strategies will also help you later as you develop an outline of your document.

Labeling Evidence Labeling can help you understand at a glance how and where you will use your evidence. For example, you might label notes or sources containing the evidence you want to use in your introduction with "Introduction," those that you plan to use to define a concept with the name of that concept, and so on. If you have taken electronic notes or saved electronic sources, as Pete Jacquez did, you have a number of options (see Figure 13.1). Once you've labeled your notes and sources, you can organize them into groups or order them according to the outline you will create.

@ Read about the student writers discussed in this chapter at **bedfordresearcher.com**. Click on Featured Writers.

Grouping Evidence Grouping involves categorizing the evidence you've selected to support your points. Paper-based notes and copies of sources can be placed in related piles or file folders; sources and notes in word processing files or a personal digital assistant can be saved in larger files or placed in electronic folders; items in Bookmarks or Favorites lists can be sorted by category (see Figure 13.2).

Economic Issues — Label at the top of a note in a word processing file

Chasteen, Stephanie. (2004). Who Owns Wind? *Science and Spirit 15*(1), 12-15.

Focuses on the economic aspects, particularly motivations and market potential, of implementing wind power.

Key quotes:

"Technological advancements and federal tax credits have made wind energy potentially profitable, landing it on the radar screen of private developers and utilities" (p. 12).

"On a dollar-for-dollar basis, wind is cost-competitive with the soaring prices of natural gas. It's still more expensive than nuclear and coal power, but studies suggest that when all costs (such as health care for coal miners stricken by black lung disease or federal subsidies of nuclear power) are taken into account, wind energy is actually cheaper" (p. 13).

FIGURE 13.1 Labeling Electronic Notes and Sources

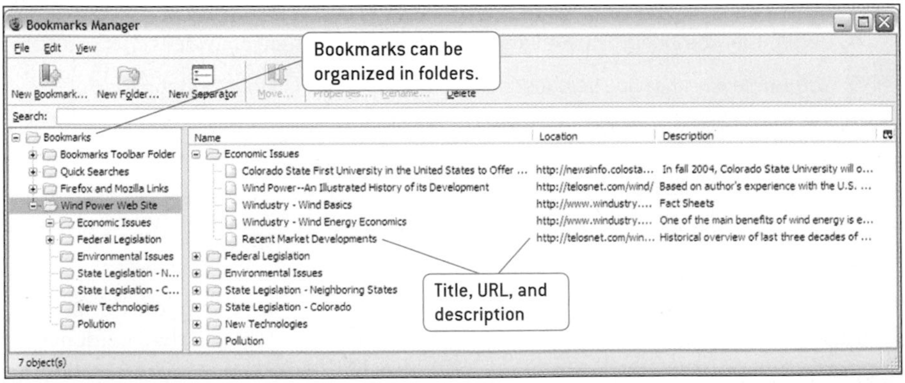

FIGURE 13.2 Grouping Electronic Notes and Sources

Step 4: Arrange Your Argument

Clustering and mapping allow you to develop a visual arrangement of the supporting points, reasons, and evidence you'll use to support your thesis statement.

Clustering   You can use clustering to explore the relationships among your thesis statement, supporting points, reasons, and evidence. Clustering involves arranging these elements of your argument visually on a sheet of paper or on a computer screen. By putting your thesis statement at the center of the cluster and your supporting points around it, you can explore how reasons and evidence relate to a supporting point, and how the supporting points relate to each other and to the thesis statement.

   Clustering can be used at several points in a research writing projects: as you begin to explore your topic, as you brainstorm to come up with ideas, as you explore relationships among the material you've collected, and now as you begin to arrange your argument.

My Research Project

ARRANGE AN ARGUMENT BY CLUSTERING

Clustering can help you explore the relationships among your thesis statement, supporting points, reasons, and evidence. To create a cluster:

1. In the middle of a sheet of paper, or in the center of an electronic document (word processing file or graphics file), list your thesis statement.

2. Place your supporting points around your thesis statement.

3. Place your reasons for accepting your supporting points next to each point.

4. List the evidence you'll present to support your reasons next to each reason.

5. Think about the relationships among your supporting points, reasons, and evidence, and draw lines and circles to show those relationships.

6. Annotate your cluster to indicate the nature of the relationships you've identified.

You can print or download this activity at **bedfordresearcher.com**. Click on Activities > Arrange an Argument by Clustering.

Mapping   You can use mapping to explore sequences of supporting points, reasons, and evidence. For example, you might use mapping to create a timeline or to show how an argument builds on one supporting point after another. This use of mapping is particularly effective as you begin to think about organizing your project document, and it often relies on the organizing patterns discussed on p. 255, such as chronology, cause/effect, comparison/contrast, cost/benefit, and problem/solution.

   The following tutorial shows a map that Alexis Alvarez created to organize her thoughts about the supporting points, reasons, and evidence in her research essay about steroid use among adolescent girls.

TUTORIAL

How can I map my argument?

You can map your argument by arranging your supporting points, reasons, and evidence to bolster your thesis statement. In this example, Alexis Alvarez maps the key points, reasons, and supporting evidence in her argumentative essay about steroid use among adolescent girls. Later, she will use this map as she develops her outline.

1 List your thesis statement.

2 Review your notes to identify supporting points that help advance your thesis statement.

3 Choose an organizational pattern (see p. 196) based on your reasoning. Here, the writer uses a problem/solution pattern to arrange her argument.

4 Following your organizational pattern, list the issues you want to discuss. Here, the writer focuses on the positive effects of sports and the negative consequences of using performance-enhancing drugs.

5 Identify the evidence for each issue. Here, the writer includes references to sources in parentheses.

Review another example and work on

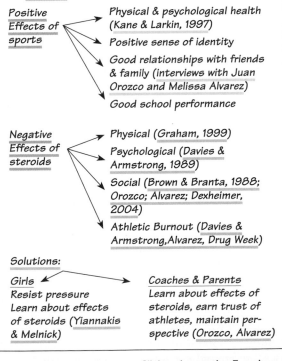

Thesis Statement: Although competitive sports can provide young female athletes with many benefits, they can also have negative effects, the worst of which is increasing drug use.

Problem: Girls in sports are using steroids to improve their athletic performance. In many cases, coaches and parents are involved.

___ *Use CDC report (2004) and Mundell (2004) for stats about usage and to show that girls in sports are as likely as boys to use steroids*

___ *Use "Girls and Steroids" (1998) and Manning (2002) to show growth in steroid use among girl athletes*

Positive Effects of sports →
- *Physical & psychological health (Kane & Larkin, 1997)*
- *Positive sense of identity*
- *Good relationships with friends & family (interviews with Juan Orozco and Melissa Alvarez)*
- *Good school performance*

Negative Effects of steroids →
- *Physical (Graham, 1999)*
- *Psychological (Davies & Armstrong, 1989)*
- *Social (Brown & Branta, 1988; Orozco; Alvarez; Dexheimer, 2004)*
- *Athletic Burnout (Davies & Armstrong, Alvarez, Drug Week)*

Solutions:

Girls ←
Resist pressure
Learn about effects of steroids (Yiannakis & Melnick)

Coaches & Parents
Learn about effects of steroids, earn trust of athletes, maintain perspective (Orozco, Alvarez)

mapping your own argument at **bedfordresearcher.com**. Click on Interactive Exercises.

IV Writing Your Document

Step 5: Assess the Integrity of Your Argument

If you're familiar with the "Buy this car, get a date with this girl (or guy)" school of advertising, you're aware of arguments that lack integrity. These kinds of arguments show a lack of respect toward readers. They also have a high likelihood of backfiring (the longstanding success of automobile ads filled with attractive young men and women notwithstanding), and readers who recognize errors in logic or the use of inappropriate emotional appeals are likely to reject an argument out of hand.

To ensure the integrity of your argument, acquaint yourself with common logical fallacies. Then check that your argument does not fall victim to them. Some of the most common logical fallacies are described below.

Fallacies Based on Distraction

A red herring refers to the practice of introducing an irrelevant and distracting issue into a discussion in an attempt to win an argument. The term originated with the practice of sweeping a red herring (a particularly fragrant type of fish) across the trail being followed by a pack of hunting dogs. The smell, as you might imagine, distracted the dogs from the real object of their hunt. A question such as, "Why worry about the rising cost of tuition when the government is tapping our cell phones?", is an example of a red herring. In this case, government surveillance has nothing to do with increases in college tuition.

Ad hominem attacks are based on the idea of guilt by association. They are also a type of red herring. Suggesting that we should all question the merits of shiatsu massage because Saddam Hussein received a massage on a daily basis is an example of an ad hominem attack. The goal of an ad hominem attack is to distract the reader from the real issue by associating an idea with someone the writer believes should not be trusted. These kinds of attacks are used on a regular basis. When you hear someone say that you shouldn't trust alternative energy because Ted Kennedy endorses it, or that school vouchers are bad because George Bush supports them, you're listening to an ad hominem attack.

Irrelevant history is another form of a red herring fallacy. Arguing that a proposal is bad because someone came up with the idea while he was using cocaine, for example, suggests that the state of mind of the person who originates an idea has something to do with its merits. It might well be the case that the idea is flawed, but your assessment should be based on an analysis of its strengths and weaknesses. Otherwise, you might as well say that an idea is undoubtedly sound because someone thought of it while they were sober.

Fallacies Based on Questionable Assumptions

Sweeping generalizations, sometimes known as hasty generalizations, ignore the fact that there are exceptions to the rules. Arguing that the rich are conservative and always vote for Republicans, for example, is based on an assumption

IV Writing Your Document

that anyone who is rich is just like everyone else who is rich. These kinds of arguments don't account for variation within a group, nor do they account for unusual situations that would mean the generalization doesn't apply.

Straw-man attacks are based on a description of an opponent that is designed to be easy to discredit. An attack on a "straw man's" position is similar to a boxer taking on a scarecrow. Scarecrows don't fight back. Straw-man attacks include characterizing an opposing position as more extreme than it actually is, or using evidence that is far easier to refute than evidence that would be offered by a real opponent.

Citing inappropriate authorities can take several forms. You might provide evidence, in the form of a quotation or paraphrase, from an individual who is not actually an expert on a subject. You might provide evidence from an authority who has a strong bias on an issue. You might provide evidence from an authority as if he or she is representative of the overall consensus of authorities on the subject, when in fact the individual is far from the mainstream.

Celebrity endorsements are sometimes treated as though they are statements from authorities on an issue. Celebrities are not typically experts on a subject, however, and in many cases they are paid for their endorsement.

Jumping on a bandwagon is based on the idea that, if everyone seems to believe something, it must be true. Also known as argument from consensus, it is an example of substituting careful analysis for group thinking. The idea of jumping on a bandwagon refers to the practice, in early American politics, of parading a candidate through town on a bandwagon. To show support for the candidate, people would climb aboard the wagon.

Fallacies Based on Misrepresentation

Stacking the deck, which has its origins in the shady behavior of card sharks, refers to the practice of presenting evidence for only one side of an argument. Most readers will wonder whether you've done this deliberately and, if so, what you are trying to hide.

Base-rate fallacies are commonly used to make arguments based on statistics. If you read that drinking coffee will triple your risk of developing a particular form of cancer, you might be alarmed. If you read that drinking coffee raises your risk from one in a billion to three in a billion, however, you might rest easier.

Questionable analogies, also known as false analogies, involve inappropriate comparisons. They are based on the assumption that, if two things are similar in one way, they must be similar in others. For example, you might argue that global warming is like a fever, and then argue that just as a fever usually runs its course and the patient recovers, so too will global warming run its course and the climate will recover.

Fallacies Based on Careless Reasoning

Post hoc fallacies offer a false causal model. Formally known as *post hoc, ergo propter hoc* fallacies ("after this, so because of this"), they argue that, because something happened first, it caused something else. In fact, there might be no causal relationship. Most people would recognize the following type of post hoc argument as fallacious: "People who own large, expensive homes often drive large, expensive cars. To obtain a large, expensive car, buy a large, expensive house."

Slippery slope arguments are based on the idea that a single step toward a bad situation will inevitably lead to that situation. These kinds of arguments usually urge us to "hold the line" against taking that step. One of the most common slippery slope arguments against the use of marijuana, for example, is that it leads to the use of stronger narcotics. It might be that some users of heroin or cocaine would never have used the drug if they hadn't first tried marijuana, but there is no evidence that all users of marijuana inevitably try harder drugs.

Either/or arguments typically present two choices, one of which is usually characterized as extremely undesirable. In fact, there might be a third choice, or a fourth, or a fifth.

Non sequiturs are statements that do not follow logically from what has just been presented. Arguing, for example, that any politician who is wealthy is corrupt assumes that the only way a politician can become wealthy is to take money from lobbyists or special interest groups or to accept bribes.

Circular reasoning, also known as begging the question, relies on restating a point that has just been made. Arguing that a decline in voter turnout is a result of fewer people voting is an example of circular reasoning.

Appeals to ignorance are based on the idea that you should believe something because there's no evidence not to believe it. You might argue, for example, that we should believe in Santa Claus because there's no definitive evidence that he does not exist.

Appeals to consequences are based on the idea that, if there are benefits to behaving as though a proposition is true, we should accept that proposition. For example, believing that a new cancer treatment will be effective is likely to help cancer patients feel better about their chances of surviving the disease, but that belief has nothing to do with whether the treatment is actually effective.

13c

How should I organize my document?

As you've read about your issue, you've encountered new information, ideas, and arguments. Your thesis statement reflects your overall response to those ideas. It might urge your readers to learn something new, to change their beliefs about your issue, or to take action. Choose an appropriate organizing pattern by reflecting on your writing situation, thesis statement, supporting points, reasons, and evidence. Then start organizing your document by creating a formal or informal outline.

Step 1: Choose an Appropriate Organizational Pattern

Common organizational patterns include the following:

Chronology   The document's organization reflects the sequence in which events occur over time. For example, you might focus attention on a sequence of events in a recent election.

Description   The document provides a point-by-point description of the characteristics of an issue. For example, you might focus on the typical architectural features of a suburb.

Cause/Effect   The document is organized according to factors that lead to (cause) an outcome (effect). For example, you might identify the reasons behind a recent strike by grocery store employees.

Pro/Con   The document presents ideas and information to favor one side of an argument. You might argue, for example, in favor of legislation calling for increased reliance on wind power.

Multiple Perspectives   The document arranges information, ideas, and arguments according to a range of perspectives about an issue. Documents using this organizational pattern frequently provide an analysis supporting one perspective. For example, a document addressing the use of alternative energy might argue in favor of one form of power, such as tidal or solar power.

Comparison/Contrast   The document identifies similarities and differences among the information, ideas, and arguments relevant to an issue. For example, a document offering an analysis of a specific policy initiative, such as raising the voting age, might attempt to pull together the arguments made by several sources arguing against change.

Strengths/Weaknesses   The document contrasts the strengths and weaknesses of one or more arguments about an issue, such as increasing federal funding for higher education by instituting a national lottery. Documents using this organizing principle typically make the claim that one argument is superior to the others.

Costs/Benefits   The document presents costs and benefits associated with an issue. For example, an analytical essay might discuss the costs and benefits of implementing a particular educational initiative.

Problem/Solution   The document defines a problem and discusses the appropriateness of one or more solutions to the problem. If multiple solutions are proposed, the document usually endorses one particular solution.

 WHAT'S MY PURPOSE?

Your choice of organizing pattern will reflect your purpose and the role or roles you adopt as a writer.

- If you're adopting the role of *observer,* you might select chronology, description, comparison/contrast, or cause/effect to reflect on an individual, event, object, idea, or issue.

- If you're adopting the role of *reporter,* you might select chronology, cause/effect, or comparison/contrast.

- If you're adopting the role of *interpreter,* you might choose cause/effect to ask, "What causes something to happen?"

- If you're adopting the role of *evaluator,* you're likely to choose from patterns such as strengths/weaknesses, pro/con, comparison/contrast, or multiple perspectives.

- If you're adopting the role of *problem solver,* you're likely to use a problem/ solution pattern to address your issue. If you're focusing on the causes or status of a problem, however, you might also use chronology, cause/effect, or multiple perspectives.

- If you're adopting the role of *advocate,* you might opt for an organizing principle that is well suited to argumentation, such as pro/con or strengths/weaknesses.

Your choice of organizational pattern should also reflect the points you are making in your document and the reasons and evidence you use to support those points.

Step 2: Create an Outline

An outline represents the sequence in which your supporting points, reasons, and evidence will appear in your document. As you develop an outline, you'll make decisions about the order in which you will present your supporting points and the evidence you'll use to back them up. Later, as you draft, your outline can serve as a plan for creating your document.

1. *Introduction – what is coca? where is it grown?*

2. *Cultural and economic importance of coca crop*

3. *Evo Morales's plan: "zero cocaine, not zero coca"*
   - Benefits of the Morales plan

4. *Brief history of other plans and their failures*
   - U.S. "war on drugs"
   - aerial fumigation / coca eradication
   - alternative cropping

5. *Conclusion supporting the Morales plan*

FIGURE 13.3 Elizabeth Leontiev's Informal Outline

Create an Informal Outline

Informal outlines can take many forms: a brief list of words, a series of short phrases, or even a series of sentences. You can use informal outlines to remind yourself of key points to address in your document or of notes you should refer to when you begin drafting. Elizabeth Leontiev, who wrote a research essay about the impact of the U.S. war on drugs on South American coca farmers, created the following informal outline. In her outline, each item represents a section she planned to include in her essay (see Figure 13.3).

Patrick Crossland wrote the following "thumbnail outline," a type of informal outline, as he worked on his research essay about college admissions decisions. Patrick identified the major sections he would include in his research essay and noted which sources he would use to provide background information and to support his argument (see Figure 13.4).

Create a Formal Outline

A formal outline provides a complete and accurate list of the points you want to address in your document. Formal outlines use Arabic numerals, letters, and Roman numerals to indicate the hierarchy of information. An alternative approach, common in business and the sciences, uses numbering with decimal points:

I.
   A.
      1.
      2.
   B.
      1.
      2.
II.

1.
   1.1
      1.1.1
      1.1.2
   1.2
      1.2.1
      1.2.2
2.

Intro

Present problem; offer an introductory look at the question of who's getting into college and what the factors are that affect this. Introduce the various admittance issues to be examined.

Section 1

Examine the notion of competition through the "Caleb" analogy. Look at the college application process through the perspective of a game (therefore beating the competitors). Present the tier system and analogy by Miller.

Section 2

Look at the issue of race, the history of the problem, and the introduction of equal opportunity policies. Present the Krauthammer view of who it hurts or helps (is it fair in that sense?).

Section 3

Discuss family situations and their relation to the ability to succeed in higher education. Use Lillard and Gerner source covering the issues of family makeup.

Section 4

Examine the role that gender plays in getting accepted and succeeding in college. Look at issues of equality of the sexes.

Section 5

Look at mental/physical capabilities and their relation to college success. Discuss a change in curricula to suit people of all different mental capabilities.

Conclusion

FIGURE 13.4 Patrick Crossland's Thumbnail Outline

IV Writing Your Document

Writers use formal outlines to identify the hierarchy of information, ideas, and arguments. You can create a formal outline to identify

- your thesis statement
- your supporting points
- the sequence in which those points should be presented
- evidence for your points
- the notes and sources you should refer to as you work on your document

The most common types of formal outlines are topical outlines and sentence outlines.

Topical Outlines   Topical outlines present the topics and subtopics you plan to include in your research document as a series of words and phrases. Items at the same level of importance should be phrased in parallel grammatical form.

Thesis statement: Although competitive sports can provide young female athletes with many benefits, they can also have negative effects, the worst of which is increasing drug use.

I. **Female Participation in Competitive Athletics**
    A. Short history and current trends
    B. Understanding the female athlete
II. **Positive Impact of Competitive Athletics**
    A. Physiological (Kane & Larkin)
        1. Reduced risk of obesity and heart disease
        2. Increased immune functioning and prevention of certain cancers
        3. Improved flexibility, strength, and aerobic power
    B. Psychological (Kane & Larkin)
        1. Improved self-esteem
        2. Enhanced mental health
        3. Effective in reducing symptoms of stress, anxiety, and depression
    C. Sociological
        1. Expansion of social boundaries
        2. Teaches responsibility, discipline, and determination
        3. Educational asset
III. **Negative Impact of Competitive Athletics**
    A. Physiological (Graham)
        1. Overtraining
        2. Eating disorders
        3. Exercise-induced amenorrhea and osteoporosis
    B. Psychological (Davies & Armstrong)
        1. Unrealistic personal expectations
        2. Loss of self-confidence and emotional trauma
        3. Increased stress and anxiety
    C. Sociological (Orozco; Dexheimer)
        1. Pressure to win at any cost
        2. Pressure to attain an unrealistic body
IV. **Repercussions of Negative Impact**
    A. Burnout (Davies & Armstrong; *Drug Week*)
        1. Causes
        2. Consequences
    B. Drug use (CDC report; Manning)
        1. Causes
        2. Consequences
V. **Avoiding the Pitfalls in Competitive Athletics**
    A. Parents
        1. Supporting your athlete in every situation
        2. Awareness
        3. Communication
    B. Coaches (Orozco)
        1. Looking beyond triumph and defeat
        2. Knowing your players
    C. Athletes (Yiannakis & Melnick)
        1. Believing in yourself
        2. Balancing life and competitive athletics

FIGURE 13.5 Alexis Alvarez's Topical Outline

In her topical outline for her research essay on steroid use among adolescent girls, Alexis Alvarez includes her thesis statement, suggests the key points she wants to make in her document, maps out the support for her points, and uses a conventional system of numbers and letters (see Figure 13.5).

Sentence Outlines Sentence outlines use complete sentences to identify the points you want to cover (see Figure 13.6). Sentence outlines typically serve two purposes:

1. They begin the process of converting an outline into a draft of your document.

2. They help you assess the structure of a document that you have already written.

> Learn how to use bullets, numbering, and indentation to create outlines at bedfordresearcher.com. Click on Guides > How to Use Your Word Processor.

When you've created your outline, ask whether it can serve as a blueprint for the first draft of your document. Taking the time to create an effective outline now will reduce the time needed to write your first draft later.

Thesis statement: Although competitive sports can provide young female athletes with many benefits, they can also have negative effects, the worst of which is increasing drug use.

    I.   Society has been concerned with the use of performance-enhancing drugs among younger male athletes, but many don't know that these drugs are also used by younger female athletes.

        A.   Women began participating in sports in the mid-19th century, although participation was not encouraged until recently. Millions of girls are involved in a wide range of physical activities and are participating in school-sponsored sports.

        B.   In response to pressures of competitive sports, girls' steroid use has increased and younger and younger girls are taking steroids.

    II. Sports can benefit a girl's growth and development physiologically as well as psychologically and sociologically.

        A.   Participation in sports has a wide range of positive physiological effects on adolescent girls.

            1.   Studies have shown that participation in sports can reduce the risk of obesity and heart disease.

            2.   Studies have shown that participation in sports appear to increase immune functioning and prevent certain cancers.

            3.   Participation in sports has also been linked to improved flexibility, strength, and aerobic power.

FIGURE 13.6 Part of Alexis Alvarez's Sentence Outline

IV Writing Your Document

My Research Project

CREATE AND REVIEW YOUR OUTLINE

In your word processing program or in your research log, create an outline.

- If your word processing program has an outlining tool, use it to create a formal outline. In Microsoft Word, use the VIEW > OUTLINE menu command to view your document in outline mode. Use the PROMOTE and DEMOTE buttons on the outlining toolbar to set the levels for entries in your outline. Use the COLLAPSE and EXPAND buttons to hide and show parts of your outline.

Review your outline by asking yourself the following questions.

1. Does my outline provide an effective organization for my document?

2. Have I covered all of my key points?

3. Have I addressed my key points in sufficient detail?

4. Do any sections seem out of order?

You can print or download this activity at **bedfordresearcher.com**. Click on Activities > Create and Review Your Outline.

> ### QUICK REFERENCE

Developing, Supporting, and Organizing Your Ideas

- ☑ Develop your thesis statement. (p. 180)
- ☑ Identify supporting points for your thesis statement. (p. 185)
- ☑ Choose reasons for your supporting points. (p. 186)
- ☑ Select and organize your evidence. (p. 188)
- ☑ Arrange your argument. (p. 191)
- ☑ Assess the integrity of your argument. (p. 193)
- ☑ Choose an organizational pattern for your document. (p. 196)
- ☑ Develop an informal outline. (p. 198)
- ☑ Create a formal outline. (p. 198)

IV Writing Your Document

14

Drafting

If you're new to research writing, you might be surprised at how long it's taken to get to the chapter about writing your document. If you are an experienced research writer, you know that you've been writing it all along. Research writing isn't so much the act of putting words to paper or screen as it is the process of identifying and learning about an issue, reflecting on what you've learned, and contributing to the conversation about your issue.

14a

How can I use my outline to draft my document?

Your outline provides a framework you can use to draft your document. Your outline likely includes your plans for

- the points you will include in your document
- the order in which you will make your points
- the amount of space you plan to devote to each point

 WHAT'S MY PURPOSE?

Review your purpose and your outline. Check whether you have organized your points in a way that will allow you to achieve your purpose and whether you are addressing the needs, interests, values, and beliefs of your readers.

If you have listed information about the sources you will use to support your points, you can check whether you are

- providing enough evidence to support your points
- relying too heavily on a limited number of sources
- relying too heavily on support from sources that favor one side of the conversation

As you prepare to draft your document, you might find it necessary to reorganize your ideas to achieve your purpose.

If you created an informal outline, it can be the skeleton of your document, and you can now begin fleshing out sections. Translate a bulleted list of items, for instance, into a series of brief sentences, or write paragraphs based on the key points in the outline. If you created a formal outline, such as a topical outline or a sentence outline, you can use each main point in the outline as a topic sentence for a paragraph. For example, you can form supporting sentences from the subpoints under each main point.

If your outline contains references to specific notes or sources, make sure that you use those notes in your draft. Take advantage of the time you spent thinking about which sources are most appropriate for a particular section of your document.

As you work on your document, you might find it necessary to reorganize your ideas. Think of your outline as a flexible guide rather than a rigid blueprint.

TUTORIAL

How do I use an outline to draft my document?

Use your outline as the "skeleton" of the first draft of your document. In this example, Alexis Alvarez expands her outline into a rough draft.

1 Save your outline with a new name, such as Draft1.doc.

2 Turn major headings in your outline into headings and subheadings in your draft.

3 Convert lower-level entries into topic sentences for paragraphs.

4 Use lists of items as sentences in each paragraph.

5 Locate evidence to support your points. Quote, paraphrase, and summarize sources identified in your outline.

---

1. Benefits of Sports for Girls
   a. Physical Health Benefits
      i. Reduces risks of adult-onset coronary disease and some cancers (Kane & Larkin, 1997)
      ii. Enhances immune system, posture, strength, flexibility, and heart-lung endurance (Kane & Larkin, 1997; "Sports in America," 1994)
   b. Mental Health Benefits (Kane & Larkin, 1997; Orozco interview)
      i. Positive body image
      ii. Confidence and self-esteem
      iii. Sense of control
   c. Social benefits (Orozco and Alvarez interviews)
2. Problems Caused by Sports for Girls
   a. Physical side effects

Girls and Sports: The Upside

According to Kane and Larkin (1997), adolescent girls who exercise regularly can lessen their risks for adult-onset coronary disease and certain cancers. Girls' involvement in sports and exercise also tends to improve immune functioning, posture, strength, flexibility, and heart-lung endurance (Kane & Larkin, 1997; "Sports in America," 1994).

In addition, competitive athletics can enhance mental health by offering adolescent girls positive feelings about body image; tangible experiences of competency, control, and success; improved self-esteem and self-confidence; and a way to reduce anxiety (Kane & Larkin, 1997). Juan Orozco, who has coached competitive soccer for nine years at the adolescent female level, confirmed that making a competitive sports team is a privilege that many girls work toward with determination and longing and that being picked to participate encourages these young athletes to believe in themselves and their abilities (personal interview, Sept. 22, 2004).

A final benefit is that sports expand social boundaries and teach many of the personal and social skills girls will need throughout their lives. According to Orozco, through competitive athletics girls learn a crucial lesson in how to

---

Review another example and work on using your outline to draft your document at **bedfordresearcher.com**. Click on Interactive Exercises.

14b

How can I draft effective paragraphs?

Writers use paragraphs to present and develop a central idea. Depending on the complexity of your argument and the type of document you are writing, a single paragraph might be all you need to present a supporting point and its associated reasoning and evidence, or it might play only a small role in conveying your thinking about an issue. You can create effective paragraphs by ensuring that they are focused, organized, and well developed. You can enhance the effectiveness of your document by creating transitions that clearly convey the relationships between paragraphs.

Focus on a Central Idea

Each of your paragraphs should focus on a single idea. Paragraphs often have a topic sentence in which the writer makes an assertion, offers an observation, or asks a question. The rest of the sentences in the paragraph elaborate on the topic. Consider the following paragraph, drawn from Patrick Crossland's research essay:

> Of course, one of the greatest monsters applicants must slay before they can enter college is taking an entrance exam or standardized test, such as the SAT and ACT. These tests are used by many colleges to assess student aptitude and academic capability. According to Joel Levine and Lawrence May, authors of *Getting In*, entrance exams are an extremely important part of a student's college application and carry a great deal of weight. In fact, they claim that a college entrance examination is "one of the two most significant factors" (116) in getting into college (the other, unsurprisingly, being high school grades).

The central idea of the paragraph is provided in the first sentence, following the transitional phrase *of course*.

The second sentence explains the purpose of entrance exams.

The third and fourth sentences use evidence from a source to convey the importance of entrance exams.

Follow an Organizational Pattern

Effective paragraphs follow an organizational pattern, often the same one that the document as a whole follows, such as:

- chronology: identifying the sequence in which events occur over time
- definition: explaining an idea, concept, or event
- description: presenting the distinguishing features of an idea, concept, or event
- categorization: classifying information and ideas
- cause/effect: identifying factors that lead to (cause) an outcome (effect)
- problem/solution: defining a problem and presenting a solution

IV Writing Your Document

- comparison/contrast: exploring similarities and differences
- analogy: suggesting that one thing is like another
- pro/con: presenting reasons and evidence in favor of and against an idea
- costs/benefits: presenting the tradeoffs involved in a choice
- strengths/weaknesses: using a set of criteria to make judgments about an idea, concept, event, or individual
- advantages/disadvantages: contrasting the positive and negative aspects of an idea, concept, event, or individual

These common patterns help readers anticipate what you'll say. (See p. 196 to learn more about organizational patterns.) Readers who recognize a pattern, such as problem/solution, will find it easier to focus on your ideas and argument if they understand how you are organizing your paragraph. Note how the following paragraph, drawn from Alexis Alvarez, uses the problem/solution organizing pattern.

What can we do to help adolescent female athletes avoid illicit drug use? How can we help them avoid the pitfalls of competitive athletics? Parents, coaches, and the athletes themselves all play a crucial role in averting bad choices. First, parents and coaches need to be aware that performance-enhancing drugs are a problem. Some adults believe that steroid use is either minimal or nonexistent among teenagers, but one study concluded that "over half the teens who use steroids start before age 16, sometimes with the encouragement of their parents. . . . Seven percent said they first took 'juice' by age ten" (Dudley, 1994, p. 235).

> The paragraph begins by restating the problem.

> The central idea of the paragraph is provided in the third sentence.

> One part of the solution to the larger problem is provided.

> The fifth sentence provides evidence from a source to illustrate the nature of the problem.

Use Details to Capture Your Readers' Attention

An effective paragraph does more than simply convey information—it provides details that bring an issue to life. Consider the differences between the following paragraphs:

Example 1: Minimal Details:

In fact, pollution from power plants may worsen as the demand for electric power continues to increase. Despite plans to build new power plants fueled by renewable energy and nuclear power, the U.S. Department of Energy projects that use of fossil fuels in power plants will actually increase. Moreover, Clayton (2004) notes that developing nations will also increase their reliance on fossil fuels. All of this is likely to lead to increased air pollution.

Example 2: Extensive, Concrete Details:

In fact, pollution from power plants may worsen as the demand for electric power continues to increase. The U.S. Department of Energy (2005b) predicts that, despite ongoing efforts to build power plants powered by renewable and nuclear energy,

> U.S. demand for power generated by fossil fuels will keep growing. Moreover, demand in developing nations is expected to increase even more dramatically. China and India are poised to build a total of 775 new conventional power plants by 2012 (Clayton, 2004). The addition of so many new plants will almost certainly lead to more global air pollution in the near term.

Both examples, drawn from Pete Jacquez's Web site on wind energy, convey the same main point. The first example, however, does little more than state the facts. The second example provides details from a U.S. Department of Energy report about demand for power in the U.S. and offers statistics about the number of conventional power plants that are projected to be built in China and India in the next few years. These details allow readers to gain a more complete, and more concrete, understanding of the issue.

Integrate Information from Sources Effectively

Information from sources can be used to introduce an important concept, establish the strength of a writer's argument, and elaborate on the central idea of a paragraph. Writers frequently state a point, offer a reason to accept it, and support their reasoning with evidence from a source, typically in the form of quotations, paraphrases, and summaries. In the following example, drawn from Pete Jacquez's Web site, a quotation and a paraphrase are used to support a point introduced in the first sentence of the paragraph:

> In fact, pollution from power plants may worsen as the demand for electric power continues to increase. The U.S. Department of Energy (2005b) notes that "it is likely that the nation's reliance on fossil fuels to power an expanding economy will actually increase over at least the next two decades even with aggressive development and deployment of new renewable and nuclear technologies" (para. 1). Moreover, demand in developing nations is expected to increase even more dramatically. China and India are poised to build a total of 775 new conventional power plants by 2012 (Clayton, 2004). The addition of so many new plants will almost certainly lead to more global air pollution in the near term.

By quoting an authority on the issue, the U.S. Department of Energy, Pete strengthens his argument. The quotation, along with a subsequent paraphrase of a passage from another source, provides evidence to support his point. He follows the quotation and paraphrase with a sentence that restates the main point of the paragraph—and an important supporting point for his argument. (See Chapter 15 for more about intregrating information.)

Create Transitions Within and Between Paragraphs

Transitions are words and phrases, such as *however* and *on the other hand*, that show the relationships between paragraphs and sentences. Transitions help readers understand how one sentence builds on another and how a new paragraph is related to the one that came before it. By signaling these relationships, they help readers anticipate how the information and ideas they are about to read are related to the information and ideas they've just read. Here are some common transitions and their functions.

To Help Readers Follow a Sequence:

Furthermore

In addition

Moreover

Next

First . . . Second . . . Third

To Elaborate or Provide Examples:

For example

For instance

Such as

In fact

Indeed

To illustrate

To Compare:

Similarly

In the same manner

Like

As in

To Contrast:

However

On the other hand

Nevertheless

Nonetheless

Despite

Although

To Signal a Concession:

I admit that

Of course

Granted

To Introduce a Conclusion:

As a result

As a consequence

Therefore

Thus

For this reason

As you create effective transitions, pay attention to the order in which you introduce new information and ideas in your paragraphs. In general, it is best to begin a sentence with a reference to information and ideas that have already been introduced and to introduce new information and ideas at the end of a sentence. For example, consider the following examples, which begin a new paragraph:

Introducing New Information First:

Admissions staff look at the kind of courses students are taking, in addition to looking at grades.

Building on Information that Has Already Been Introduced:

And it's not just grades that matter; admissions staff also look at the kind of courses students are taking.

The second example, by referring to information that has been introduced in the previous paragraph, provides an effective transition to a new paragraph, even as it introduces new information about additional college admissions criteria. In contrast, readers of the first example would not have the benefit of seeing how the new information fits into what they've already read.

14c

How can I draft my introduction?

All readers expect documents to include some sort of introduction. Whether they are reading a home page on a Web site or an opening paragraph in a research report, readers want to learn quickly what a document is about. Drafting an introduction involves framing your main point and choosing a strategy to begin your document.

[**FRAMING MY ARGUMENT**]

Frame the Issue

Your introduction provides a framework within which your readers can understand and interpret your information, ideas, and argument. By calling attention to a specific situation, by asking a particular question, or by conveying a carefully chosen set of details, you can help your readers view your issue in a particular way. Consider, for example, the differences between two introductions to an essay about low turnout among younger voters.

Introduction 1:

Ever since 1972, when 18-year-olds gained the right to vote, voter turnout among America's youth has been significantly lower than that of older Americans. Following an initial turnout of 52 percent of younger registered voters in 1972, the percentage declined to an all-time low of only 32 percent in the 1996 presidential election (Capuano 221). And despite gains in the 2000 and 2004 elections, the youth vote has continued to trail that of older Americans by roughly 20 percentage points (Lopez 2). The causes of this problem are complex and varied: lack of investment in government institutions, lack of attention to issues of concern to younger voters, and the idea that not voting sends a message to government.

Introduction 2:

Americans between the ages of 18 and 24 are in danger of losing the most important privilege granted to U.S. citizens: the right to vote. Since 1972, when 18-year-olds first gained the right to vote, turnout among younger voters significantly lagged behind that of older Americans, with an average gap of roughly 20 percent in presidential elections since 1972 (Capuano 221, Lopez 2). While apologists are quick to point out that low turnout among younger voters results from their lack of knowledge of the importance of voting or their belief that not voting provides an effective protest against politicians who do not recognize them as important members of the populace, younger voters may soon find out that their failure to exercise their right to vote will carry a heavy price. Unless they begin participating in the democratic process, they may lose the right to do so—at least until they reach their early twenties.

The first introduction frames the issue as an explanation of the causes of low turnout among younger voters. The second introduction frames the issue as a warning that the voting age might be raised. While each introduction draws on the same basic information about voting rates, and while both will do a good job of introducing an essay, they ask readers to focus their attention on different aspects of the issue.

The ability to frame your readers' understanding of an issue is a powerful tool. By directing readers' attention to one aspect of an issue, rather than to others, you can influence their beliefs and, potentially, their willingness to take action.

You can frame your discussion by calling attention to specific aspects of a topic, including

- agent: a person, organization, or thing that is acting in a particular way
- action: what is being done by the agent
- goal: why the agent carried out the action
- result: the outcome of the action

Introduction 2:

Americans between the ages of 18 and 24 are in danger of losing the most important privilege granted to U.S. citizens: the right to vote. Since 1972, when 18-year-olds first gained the right to vote, turnout among younger voters significantly lagged that of older Americans, with an average gap of roughly 20 percent in presidential elections since 1972 (Capuano 221, Lopez 2). While apologists are quick to point out that low turnout among younger voters results from their lack of knowledge of the importance of voting or their belief that not voting provides an effective protest against politicians who do not recognize them as important members of the populace, younger voters may soon find out that their failure to exercise their right to vote will carry a heavy price. Unless they begin participating in the democratic process, they may lose the right to do so—at least until they reach their early twenties.

Agent
Action
Goal
Result

Select a Strategy for Your Introduction

You can introduce your document using one of several strategies.

State the Topic.   Tell your readers what your issue is, what conversation you are focusing on, and what your document will tell them about it, as in the following introduction:

> Artists and their artwork do not exist in a vacuum. The images artists create help shape and in turn are shaped by the society and culture in which they are created. The artists and artworks in the Dutch Baroque period are no exception.

Define Your Argument.   If your research document presents an argument, use your introduction to get right to your main point—the point you are trying to persuade your readers to accept. In other words, lead with a thesis statement, as in the following introduction:

> While the private tragedies of its central characters have public implications, William Shakespeare's *Julius Caesar* is more about personal struggles than political

ambition. It is easy to see the play as one whose focus is the political action of public events. The title character, after all, is at the height of political power. However, the interior lives of Julius Caesar, Marcus Brutus, and their wives offer a more engaging storyline. Shakespeare alternates between public and private scenes throughout the play to emphasize the conflict between duties of the Roman citizenry and the feelings and needs of the individual, but it is the "private mind and heart of the individual" (Edwards 105) that the reader is compelled to examine.

Define a Problem.   If your research has led you to propose a solution to a problem, you might begin your document by defining the problem. Alexis Alvarez used this strategy to introduce her essay:

> Almost daily, headlines and newscasters tell us about athletes' use of performance-enhancing drugs. Indeed, stories of such drug use seem to increase each year, with investigations of possible steroid use by college football players, by major league baseball players, and even by Olympic gold medalists. It is easy to gain the impression that many adult athletes, particularly males, may be using drugs in order to improve their performance and physical appearance. What may be surprising and even shocking to most of us, however, is that these drugs, especially anabolic steroids, are increasingly used by adolescent athletes and that girls are just as likely as boys to be users.

> Read Alexis Alvarez's research essay on p. 343.

Ask a Question.   Asking a question invites your readers to become participants in the conversation. At the end of her introduction, Alexis Alvarez encouraged her readers to take an interest in the problem of steroid use by adolescent female athletes by asking a question:

> What role is competitive sports playing in this dangerous trend? Why are some girls feeling the need to ingest performance-enhancing drugs?

Tell a Story.   Everyone loves a story, assuming it's told well and has a point. Patrick Crossland began his research project with a story about his brother, Caleb, a high school student and a star athlete who was applying to colleges and universities:

> Caleb is a junior in high school. Last night his mom attended his varsity wrestling match, cheering him on as he once again defeated his competitors. On the way home, they discussed his busy schedule, in which he balances both schoolwork and a job at his father's company. Caleb manages to get good grades in his classes while at the same time he learns a trade in the woodworking industry. . . .

> Read Patrick Crossland's research essay on p. 373.

Provide a Historical Account.   Historical accounts can help your readers understand the origins of a situation and how the situation has changed over time. A Web site focusing on relations between the People's Republic of China and Taiwan used this historical account:

> On February 21, 2000, the People's Republic of China (PRC) shocked the world with its release of the white paper "The One-China Principle and the Taiwan

Issue." In this 18-page document, the Chinese government outlined its case that, in keeping with the "One China" principle to which the United States and Taiwan had allegedly agreed, Taiwan is the rightful property of the People's Republic of China, and revealed that it intended to use force if Taiwan did not move to reunite with the mainland.

Make a Contrast.   Setting up a contrast asks your readers to begin making a comparison. Elizabeth Leontiev began her essay by contrasting what the word *cocaine* means to U.S. citizens and South American coca farmers:

> To most Americans, the word *cocaine* evokes images of the illegal white powder and those who abuse it, yet the word has a completely different meaning to the coca farmers of South America.

> Read Elizabeth Leontiev's research essay on p. 317.

Lead with a Quotation.   A quotation allows your readers to learn about the issue from someone who knows it well or has been affected by it, as in the following introduction:

> "Without a few lucky breaks, we'd still be bagging groceries at Albertsons," says lead singer Rickie Jackson of the recent Grammy winning band, Soft Affections.

14d

How can I present evidence to support my points?

Using sources to support your points is the essence of research writing. Whether you are making your main point or a supporting point, readers will expect evidence to back it up. Depending on the point you want to make, some types of evidence might be more effective than others. The key is how your readers will react to the evidence you provide. In some cases, for example, statistical evidence might lend better support for a point than a quotation. The following are some of the most effective ways to support your points.

Direct Quotation   Quotations from experts or authorities can lend weight to your argument, and quotations from people who have been affected by an issue can provide concrete evidence of the impact of the issue. Patrick Crossland used a quotation from an admissions expert to support his point about the competitiveness of the college admissions process:

> Duke University Director of Undergraduate Admissions Christoph Guttentag uses a baseball analogy in describing how students advance in the admission process. "Think of it as a baseball game. Everybody gets [his] time at bat. The quality of [students'] academic work that we can measure through test scores and analysis of high school courses gets about 10 percent of the applicants to third base, 50 percent to second base, and about 30 percent to first base. And 10 percent strike out" (qtd. in "College Admissions").

Statistical and Other Numerical Evidence   Much of the support you'll use in your document is textual, typically presented in the form of quotations, paraphrases, and summaries. But your topic may lend itself to numerical evidence. Alexis Alvarez used statistical evidence throughout her essay:

> In May 2004, the Centers for Disease Control and Prevention (CDC) published its latest figures on self-reported drug use among young people in grades 9 through 12. The CDC study, "Youth Risk Surveillance Study—December 2003," found that 6.1% of its survey participants reported using steroids at least once, up from 2.2% in 1993. The report also showed that use of steroids appears to be increasing among younger girls: While only 3.3% of twelfth-grade girls reported using steroids, 7.3% of ninth-grade girls reported using them.

Example   It's often better to *show* with an example than to *tell* with a general description. Examples provide concrete evidence in your document. Kevin Fahey used an example to illustrate a point in his essay about Hemingway's depiction of his character Nick Adams:

> "The End of Something," one of the only stories in which Hemingway depicts Nick alone with a female companion for an extended scene (Flora 55), provides a convincing portrayal of Nick as the Everyman. As the story opens, Nick and his girlfriend row to a beach on Horton's Bay, a once-bustling mill town that is now deserted. Hemingway's description of the town's demise heralds catastrophe for the couple's relationship. While the two fish, Marjorie asks Nick what has been bothering him. Revealing his lack of self-understanding, Nick replies, "'I don't know. . . . It isn't fun any more. . . . I don't know, Marge. I don't know what to say'" (Hemingway 204).

> @ Read Kevin Fahey's research essay at bedfordresearcher.com. Click on Featured Writers.

Definition   Definitions explain what something is, how a process works, or what you mean by a statement. Elizabeth Leontiev used a definition to help her readers understand the uses of the coca plant:

> According to Arthur C. Gibson, an economic botanist at UCLA, *Erythroxylum coca,* or the tropical coca plant, has been grown in the mountainous regions of Colombia, Bolivia, and Peru since 3000 B.C. (Gibson).

Qualification   You can use qualifications to make your meaning more precise and reduce the possibility that your readers might misunderstand your point. Qualifications allow you to narrow the scope of a statement. In the following example, a research writer uses a qualification to clarify the relationship between painting and culture in seventeenth-century Dutch society:

> Because of their faithful depiction of the world and their painstaking attention to detail, seventeenth-century Dutch paintings of domestic scenes can be called realistic. However, it is important to remember that these images do not always simply depict the people and their world exactly as they were. Instead, these works served multiple purposes—to spread and promote ideas about domestic virtue, to instruct viewers about women's roles, and, finally, to entertain viewers (Franits, *Paragons* 9).

Amplification   Amplification expands the scope of your point. Patrick Cross-land used amplification to broaden his discussion of the criteria used in college admissions decisions:

> And it's not just the grades that matter—admissions staff also look at the *kind* of courses students are taking.

Analogy   One of the most common ways to support a point is to describe similarities between one thing and another. You've encountered analogies throughout this book. Here's another: "Drafting a research document is similar to cooking. Without the proper tools, ingredients, and knowledge, the document won't turn out as well as you'd like."

Read Elizabeth Leontiev's research essay on p. 317.

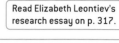 View Chris Norris's multimodal essay at bedfordresearcher.com. Click on Featured Writers.

Association   If you remember the advertising slogan "I want to be like Mike," you're already familiar with association. Through association you can support a point by connecting it with something or someone else. When you support your argument using a quotation from an expert, you're using a form of association. It's as if you're saying, "Look, this intelligent person agrees with me."

Contrast   Contrasts are similar to association, but in reverse. You can use contrasts to show that something is not like something else. You can read more about using information from sources in Chapter 15, Integrating Sources.

Illustration   Visual elements can help your readers understand your points more clearly. In print documents, illustrations are usually photos, drawings, or charts. Elizabeth Leontiev, for example, included a chart tracking the historical impact of the U.S. war on drugs on wholesale and retail cocaine prices.

14e

How can I make sure my document is easy to follow?

In addition to expecting that you'll support your points, readers expect you to organize your document in a sensible way that allows them to understand it easily. Fortunately, you've already spent time organizing your document (see p. 196). It's also likely that you've continued to refine your organization as you've prepared to draft your document.

A well-organized document allows a reader to anticipate—or predict—what will come next, which helps readers understand your goals more easily. The test of good organization is whether your readers can move smoothly through your document without wondering, "Where did that come

Information Literacy
Digital Illustration Electronic documents can also include video, audio, and animations. Chris Norris, for example, included not only images, but also video clips from shows, audio clips of interviews, and full-length songs in mp3 format.

IV Writing Your Document

from?" As you draft, check whether your document is organized consistently and predictably. You might find the following techniques useful.

Provide a Map.   The most direct way of signaling the organization of your document is to provide a map in your introduction. You might write something like "This report will cover three approaches to treating cancer of the bladder: chemotherapy, a combination of chemotherapy and radiation, and surgical removal of the organ."

Use a Table of Contents, a Home Page, or a Menu.   Tables of contents, home pages, and menus are similar to maps. If you are writing a print document, decide whether your document is long enough to justify using a table of contents. While academic essays seldom use a table of contents, a report prepared for a course might use a table of contents if the length runs to 20 or more pages and the report contains several sections. If you are writing an electronic document such as a Web site, you can lay out the key elements of your document on a home page. Similarly, you can add a menu on the side, top, or bottom of your pages that readers can see as they work through your site. Pete Jacquez provided a menu on every page of his site (see Figure 14.1).

Use Headings and Subheadings.   You can help your readers keep their place in your document by using headings and subheadings. Your formatting should distinguish between headings (major sections) and subheadings (subsections).

Provide Forecasts and Cross-References. Forecasts prepare your readers for a shift in your document, such as the boundary between one section and the next. A forecast at the end of a major section might say, "In the next section, you can read about. . . ." Cross-references tell your readers that they can find related information in another section of the document or let them know that a particular issue will be addressed in greater detail elsewhere. On a Web site, forecasts and cross-references might take the form of small images, flags, or statements such as "Continue to next section" or "Follow this link for more information."

Learn More
Fossil Fuel Economics
Fossil Fuel & the Environment
Wind Power Economics
Wind Power & the Environment
Bibliography
Related Links

Take Action
Local Efforts
State-Wide Efforts
National Efforts

About This Site
Written by Pedro Jacquez
References

FIGURE 14.1 Menu on Pete Jacquez's Web Site   The menu helps readers understand the organization of the site and move to pages within it.

14f

How can I make my document more readable?

Even a thoughtful, well-researched document will be ineffective if it's difficult to read. As you draft your document, give attention to paragraphing and paragraph structure, transitions between sentences and paragraphs, tone and style, and economy. These issues are discussed briefly in this section and more fully in Chapter 16, Writing with Style, and Chapter 17, Revising and Editing.

Vary Sentence and Paragraph Structure

Although each of your sentences and paragraphs, when read by itself, might be well written, grammatically correct, and engaging, you run the risk of boring—and even losing—your readers if you fail to vary the structure. To ensure variety in the structure of your paragraphs, use different organizational patterns (see p. 196). Relying on a mix of organizational patterns, such as definition, cause/effect, comparison/contrast, and chronology, for example, can help keep your document lively, interesting, and readable. To ensure variety in the structure of your sentences, use different types of sentences, rely on a mix of independent and dependent clauses, and create a mix of longer and shorter sentences (see p. 245).

Create Effective Transitions

Good writers provide clear directions to their readers in the form of transitions between sections and paragraphs. Effective transitions smooth readers' movement from one idea to another. Some transitions might be sentences, such as "A sudden job loss creates not only a financial burden but a psychological one as well." By referring to an idea already discussed in the document—in this case, the financial burden created by the sudden loss of a job—the author connects what readers have already read with what they are about to read—in this case, the psychological burden associated with the loss of a job. Other types of transitions come in the form of headings and subheadings, which explicitly signal a change in topic. Still others are signal words or phrases, such as *however, on the other hand, in addition,* and *first.*

Use Appropriate and Consistent Tone and Style

In many cases, readers and writers never meet, so your document might be the only point of contact between you and your readers. As a result, your readers will judge you and what you have to say based not only on what you say but on how you say it. Ensure that you are presenting your ideas clearly and effectively by paying attention to the following:

- **Word Choice.** Make sure that your readers understand your words, and use technical language appropriate for your audience. How will your readers react to slang? Also ask yourself whether they will find your words too stiff and formal.

- **Sentence Length and Complexity.** A sentence that is too complex will make your readers work overtime to figure out what it means. Can a complicated concept be more simply stated?

- **Variety.** A steady stream of sentences written in exactly the same way will have the same effect as a lecture delivered in a monotone. Vary your sentence length and structure.

- **Reader Expectations.** Consider not only what you say, but also your readers' expectations about how you should say it. If you are writing a blog entry about the local music scene and you know your readers will expect a casual, down-to-earth report on the show you attended over the weekend, it would be fine to write, "The sound quality was lousy." If, however, you are writing a report about the show for one of your courses, you might want to use a more formal tone, such as "The sound quality was poor," or perhaps "The quality of sound produced by the band's equipment was inadequate."

Strive for Economy

An effective document says enough to meet the writer's goals, and no more. As you draft your document, ask yourself whether you've written enough to make your point. Then ask whether you could make your point more economically without compromising your ability to meet your goals.

Create an Effective Design

As you write your document, pay attention to its design. Using a readable body font that is clearly different from the font used for headings and subheadings, for example, can improve readability significantly. Similarly, breaking out information using bulleted and numbered lists, providing descriptive page headers or footers, and integrating illustrations effectively into your text can greatly enhance readability. You can read more about design in Chapter 18, Designing.

14g

How can I draft my conclusion?

Your conclusion provides an opportunity to reinforce your message. It offers one last chance to achieve your purpose as a writer and to share your final thoughts about the issue with your readers.

You've probably read conclusions that simply summarize the document. These summaries can be effective, especially when the document has presented complex concepts. A conclusion can do more, though, than simply summarize your points. It can also give your readers an incentive to continue thinking about what they've read, to take action about the issue, or to read more about it.

As you draft, think about what you want to accomplish. You can choose from a range of strategies to draft an effective conclusion.

Summarize Your Argument.   Sum up the argument you've made in your document. Elizabeth Leontiev concluded her analysis of the impact of Evo Morales' vision for South American coca farmers by using this technique.

> Through his bold program of "zero cocaine, not zero coca," Morales aims to improve the lives of Andean farmers and the economies of South American countries, while still remaining committed to controlling the illegal drug trade. Morales' example illustrates that it is time to work *with* coca farmers, rather than against them.

Offer Additional Analysis.   Extend your analysis of the issue by supplying additional insights. In his Web site about wind-generated electrical power, Pete Jacquez concluded his discussion of wind power and the environment by linking wind power to the production of hydrogen gas.

> Another promising area—in terms of wind power's contribution to clean energy—is the role it can play in a "hydrogen economy." Because hydrogen gas, when burned, does not produce carbon dioxide (its only emission is water vapor), some legislators and environmentalists are looking to hydrogen as a replacement for fossil fuels. Generating hydrogen gas, however, requires power, and a number of plans to generate it rely on coal-powered plants. Wind-power advocates argue, instead, that wind turbines can supply the power needed to produce hydrogen gas. Recent government studies support this approach ("Wind Power Facts," 2004).

Speculate about the Future.   Reflect on what might happen next. An essay about younger voters, for example, might speculate on the consequences of their historically low turnout and what will be required to increase it.

> While a repeal of voting rights for 18- to 21-year-olds might be unlikely, other effects will certainly be felt: younger people's interests will not be properly evaluated, and the "cycle of mutual neglect" will continue. Clearly, the demographic group of 18- to 24-year-olds in America has shown less of an interest in participating in the political process than everyone else. This will remain true until younger voters feel they have trustworthy sources of information as well as candidates to choose from who they feel listen to them. Finally, they must understand the importance of their vote, and why it is not just a right, but a civic duty.

Close with a Quotation.   Select a quotation that does one of the following:

- sums up the points you've made in your document
- points to the future of the issue
- suggests a solution to a problem

- illustrates what you would like to see happen
- makes a further observation about the issue

Alexis Alvarez used a quotation from a personal interview to underscore her main point about the use of steroids among adolescents girls involved in competitive sports.

> In short, these athletes have not lost sight of the true objective of participating in sports—they know that their success is due to their efforts and not to the effects of a performance-enhancing drug. When asked what she would say to athletes considering steroid use, Melissa Alvarez said:
>
> > If you are training and doing your best, you should not have to use steroids. At the end of the day, it is just a game. You should never put your health at risk for anything, or anyone. It should be your top priority. (personal communication, September 26, 2004)

Close with a Story.   Tell a story about the issue you've discussed in your document. The story might suggest a potential solution to the problem, offer hope about a desired outcome, or illustrate what might happen if a desired outcome isn't realized. Patrick Crossland continued the story he used to introduce his research paper.

> Thus, in the midst of Caleb Crossland's busy schedule, he applies to various colleges he wants to attend. He continues to get good grades, studies for the SAT, and stays involved in extracurricular activities. He researches schools and plans to apply early. And with the support of his family, Caleb should have an edge over the many other students competing against him for a spot at the nation's top colleges.

Link to Your Introduction.   This technique is sometimes called a "bookends" approach because it positions your introduction and conclusion as related ends of your document. The basic idea is to turn your conclusion into an extension of your introduction.

- If your introduction used a quotation, end with a related quotation or respond to the quotation.
- If your introduction used a story, extend that story or retell it with a different ending.
- If your introduction asked a question, answer the question, restate the question, or ask a new question.
- If your introduction defined a problem, provide a solution to the problem, restate the problem, or suggest that readers need to move on to a new problem.

14h

How should I document my sources?

You should document your sources in the body of your document and at the end of it—in a works cited or reference list. Documenting sources acknowledges the contributions of the writers whose work you've used in your project. Documenting sources also helps your readers locate the sources you cited. For a fuller discussion of why you should document sources, see Chapter 19. For guidelines on the MLA, APA, *Chicago,* and CSE documentation systems, see Chapters 20 to 23.

> **QUICK REFERENCE**

Drafting

- ☑ Use your outline to begin drafting your document. (p. 204)
- ☑ Develop effective paragraphs. (p. 206)
- ☑ Draft your introduction. (p. 210)
- ☑ Support your points with evidence. (p. 213)
- ☑ Use an appropriate organizational pattern. (p. 215)
- ☑ Pay attention to paragraph and sentence structure, transitions, tone, style, economy, and design. (p. 217)
- ☑ Draft your conclusion. (p. 218)
- ☑ Document your sources. (p. 221)

IV Writing Your Document

15

Integrating Sources

> **Key Questions**

As you draft your document, remember the range of strategies you can use to support your points, convey your ideas, and illustrate positions taken by other authors. This chapter discusses how you can use source information to meet the needs of your writing situation and addresses the primary techniques for integrating source information into your document: quotation, paraphrase, and summary. It also looks at techniques for working with numeric information, images, audio, and video.

Much of the information in this chapter is based on MLA style, which is commonly used in the humanities. See Chapter 20 for more on MLA style and Chapters 21 to 23 for guidelines on APA, *Chicago,* and CSE styles.

15a

How can I use source information to accomplish my purpose as a writer?

Information from your sources can help you introduce your arguments and ideas, contrast the arguments and ideas of other authors with your own, provide evidence for your arguments, define concepts, illustrate processes, clarify statements, and set a mood.

Introduce an Idea or Argument.   You can use a quotation, paraphrase, or summary to introduce an idea or argument to your readers:

Quotation Used to Introduce an Idea:

"When I came around the corner, a black bear was standing in the middle of the trail," said Joan Gibson, an avid hiker. "We stared at each other for a moment, wondering who would make the first move. Then the bear looked off to the right and shambled up the mountain. I guess I wasn't worth the trouble."

Joan Gibson's story, like those of most hikers who encounter bears in the woods, ends happily. But the growing encroachment of humans on rural areas once left largely to wildlife is causing difficulties not only for people who enjoy spending time in the wide-open spaces, but also for the animals that make those spaces their home.

Paraphrase Used to Introduce an Idea:

A *New York Times* article recently reported that human–bear encounters in Yosemite National Park, which had been on the decline during most of the last decade, had more than doubled in the past year (Spiegel A4). Although no humans have been injured and only one incident resulted in a decision to destroy a bear, park officials point to the uptick in encounters as a warning sign that. . . .

Your choice of a quotation or paraphrase will frame the argument you want to make, calling your readers' attention to a specific aspect of the argument and laying the groundwork for a specific type of response to the issue you are addressing in your document. Think about how the following quotation leads readers to view a public debate about education reform as a battle between reformers and an entrenched teachers union:

"The teachers union has balked at even the most reasonable proposals for school reform," said Mary Sweeney, press secretary for Save Our Schools, which has sponsored a referendum on the November ballot calling for funding for their voucher plan. "We believe the November election will send a wake-up call about the need to rethink their obstructionist behaviors."

If Sweeney and supporters of Referendum D are successful, the educational landscape in. . . .

> Phrases such as "balked at even the most reasonable proposals" and "their obstructionist agenda" place the blame for the problem on the teachers union.

IV Writing Your Document

In contrast, note how the following quotation frames the debate as a question of how best to spend scarce education funds:

> "In the past decade, state and local funding of public education in real dollars has declined by 7.2 percent," said Jeffrey Allister, state chair of the governor's Special Commission on Education Reform. "Referendum D, if passed, would further erode that funding by shifting state dollars to private schools."
>
> As the state considers the merits of Referendum D, which would institute the first statewide voucher program in the United States, opponents of the measure have. . . .

> Phrases such as "funding of public education in real dollars has declined" and "further erode that funding" call attention to the financial challenges faced by schools.

 WHAT'S MY PURPOSE?

As you draft your document, ask how you can use information from your sources to accomplish your purpose as a writer and to address the needs, interests, values, and beliefs of your readers. Consider how quotations, paraphrases, summaries, and various types of illustrations (such as images, tables, charts, and graphs) from your sources can lead your readers to see the issue you are addressing in terms that are most favorable to your purpose. Your careful selection of information from your sources can allow you to present arguments that might be more pointed than you might want to make on your own. Calling opponents of a proposal "balky" and "obstructionists," for example, might signal your biases too strongly. Quoting someone who uses those terms, however, allows you to get the point across without undermining an otherwise even and balanced tone.

Contrast Ideas or Arguments.   When you want to indicate that disagreement exists on an issue, you can use source information to contrast and convey the nature and intensity of the disagreements. The following example uses partial quotations (see p. 227) to highlight differences in proposed solutions to a problem:

> Solutions to the state's higher education funding shortfall range from traditional approaches, such as raising taxes, to more radical solutions, among them privatizing state colleges and universities. Advocates of increased taxes, such as Vincent Richards of the Higher Education Coalition, argue that declines in state funding of higher education "must be reversed immediately or we will find ourselves in a situation where we are closing rural community colleges and only the wealthiest among us will have access to the best education" (A4). Those in favor of privatizing higher education suggest, however, that free market approaches will ultimately bring about "a fairer situation in which the poor, many of whom have no interest in higher education, are no longer asked to subsidize higher and higher faculty salaries and larger football stadiums" (Pieters 23).

Base your choices about how to contrast ideas and arguments on the clarity and conciseness of your sources and on the effects you hope to achieve. If you want to express complex ideas as concisely as possible, you might use paraphrase and summary. If you want to convey the emotional qualities of an author's position on an issue, use quotations.

Provide Evidence for Your Argument. Arguments that consist of a series of unsupported assertions amount to little more than a request for a reader's trust. Even when the writer is eminently trustworthy, most readers find such arguments easy to dismiss. In contrast, providing evidence to support your assertions increases the likelihood that your readers will accept your argument. Note the differences between the following passages:

Unsupported Assertion:

Given a choice between two products of comparable quality, reputation, and cost, American consumers are far more likely to purchase goods that use environmentally friendly packaging. Encouraging the use of such packaging is a good idea for America.

> No evidence is provided to support the writer's assertion.

Supported Assertion:

Given a choice between two products of comparable quality, reputation, and cost, American consumers are far more likely to purchase goods that use environmentally friendly packaging. A recent study by the High Plains Research Institute found that the shelf life of several biodegradable plastics not only exceeded the shelf life of the products they were used to package, but also cost less to produce (Chen and Lohann 33). In addition, a study by the Consumer Products Institute found that, when made aware that products were packaged in environmentally friendly materials, consumers were more likely to buy those products.

> Summaries of the results of two studies provide evidence for the assertion made in the first sentence.

Similarly, visual sources can lend support to an assertion. For example, an assertion about the unintended consequences of military action might be accompanied by a photograph of a war-torn street or a wounded child.

Align Your Argument with an Authority. Aligning an argument with an authority shows your readers that your points are supported by a leader in that area—such as a subject matter expert, a scientist, a politician, or a religious figure—and that you are not alone in your convictions. Essentially, this technique allows you to borrow the credibility and status of someone who has compiled a strong record of accomplishment. Start by making an assertion and follow it with supporting information from a source, such as a quotation, paraphrase, or source summary:

> Although voice recognition appears to be a promising technology, challenges associated with vocabulary, homonyms, and accents have slowed its widespread implementation. "The computer right now can do a very good job of voice recognition," said Bill Gates, co-founder and chairman of Microsoft Corporation. "Demonstrations are good but whenever you get it out and start working with it, it has a hard time, particularly if you are working with a very large vocabulary. It certainly will re-define the way we think of the machines when we have that voice input" (Gates, par. 42).

IV Writing Your Document

Define a Concept, Illustrate a Process, or Clarify a Statement.   Writers commonly turn to information from sources to define concepts, illustrate processes, or clarify statements when the information is clearer and more concise than what they might write themselves. You might define a concept by quoting or paraphrasing a dictionary or encyclopedia, or use an illustration to help readers understand a complex process, such as the steps involved in cellular respiration.

Writers also use information from sources to clarify their statements. A writer might amplify a statement by providing examples from sources or qualify a statement by noting that it applies only to specific situations and then use a quotation or paraphrase from a source to back that up:

> Studies have found connections between weight loss and coffee intake. This doesn't mean that drinking a couple of cups of coffee each day leads to weight loss. However, three recent studies reported that individuals who increased their coffee intake from fewer than three cups to more than eight cups of coffee per day experienced weight losses of up to 7 percent over a two month period (Chang, Johnson and Salazar, Neiman). "It may be that increased caffeine intake led to a higher metabolic level, which in turn led to weight loss," noted John Chang, a senior researcher at the Centers for Disease Control. "Or it might be that drinking so much coffee depressed participants' appetites" (232).

Set a Mood.   You can also choose quotations and illustrations with an eye toward establishing an overall mood for your readers. The emotional impact of images of a celebration at a sporting event, an expression of grief at a funeral, or a calming mountain vista can lead your readers to react in specific ways to your document. Similarly, a striking quote, such as "The screams of pain coming out of that room will stay with me as long as I live," can evoke a specific mood among your readers.

15b

How can I integrate quotations?

A well-chosen quotation can have a powerful impact on your readers' perception of your argument and on the overall quality of your document. Quotations can also add a sense of immediacy by bringing in the voice of someone who has been affected by an issue or lend a sense of authority to your argument by conveying the words of an expert. Quotations can range in form from brief, partial quotations to extended, block quotations. As you integrate quotations into your document, remember to

- choose among partial, complete, or block quotations and blend them smoothly into your text
- acknowledge the sources of quotations in a way that clearly differentiates them from your own ideas
- provide a context for the quotations that demonstrates their relevance

- modify quotations accurately and fairly
- punctuate quotations properly

Use Partial, Complete, and Block Quotations

Quotations can be parts of sentences (partial), whole sentences (complete), or long passages (block). When you choose one type of quotation over another, keep in mind

- the length of the passage
- the complexity of the ideas and information in the passage
- the obligation to convey ideas and information fairly

Partial Quotations Partial quotations can be a single word, phrase, or most of a sentence. They are often used to convey a well-turned phrase or to complete a sentence using important words from a source, as in the following example.

> Nadine K. Maxwell, guidance services coordinator in Fairfax, Virginia, says that students' chances of being admitted can be greater if they apply early, although this varies from school to school and year to year and "may depend upon the applicant pool at the school where they are applying" (32).

> The page number is placed in parentheses before the final period of the sentence.

Complete Quotations Complete quotations are typically one or more complete sentences and are most often used when the meaning of the passage cannot be conveyed adequately by a few well-chosen words, as in the following example.

> Graham pointed out, "In some sports as many as 50 percent of the athletes who are competitive may suffer from what's known as exercise-induced or athletic amenorrhea" (26).

> Since the source of the quotation is identified in an attribution ("Graham pointed out . . ."), only the page number appears in the citation at the end of the sentence.

Block Quotations Block quotations are extended quotations (usually more than four typed lines) that are set off in a block from the rest of the text. In general, use a colon to introduce the quotation, indent the entire quotation one inch (or ten spaces) from the left margin, and include source information according to the documentation system you are using (such as MLA, APA, *Chicago*, or CSE). Since the blocked text indicates to your readers that you are quoting directly, you do not need to include quotation marks.

> In the article "In the Best Interest of America, Affirmative Action in Higher Education Is a Must," William H. Gray III states:

> Quotation marks are not used to surround block quotations.

> High school achievement and test scores are considered to be very important criteria in the admissions process by most of the four-year public degree-granting colleges and universities. Nonetheless, high school grades and test scores are not the only factors

> In block quotations, the citation information is placed after the period.

considered by colleges and universities in the admissions process. Other factors that influence college admissions decisions include high school rank, being an athlete, alumni connections, extracurricular activities, special talents, and other personal characteristics of applicants. (par. 5)

> A paragraph number is provided for an online source.

[**FRAMING MY ARGUMENT**]

Identify the Sources of Your Quotations

You should identify the source of a quotation for three reasons. First, it fulfills your obligation to document your sources. Second, it allows you (and your readers) to distinguish between your ideas and those of your sources. Third, it can help you strengthen your overall argument by calling attention to the qualifications or experiences of the person you are quoting. The following quotation is introduced in a way that clearly indicates who made the statement and what his qualifications are:

> The source of the quotation is identified as an authority.

In *Paragons of Virtue,* art historian Wayne Franits calls attention to this distinction between the ideal and the real, noting "Both art and literature present an exemplary image, a topos that does not necessarily reflect the actual situation of young women in seventeenth-century Dutch culture" (25).

Research writers who use MLA or APA documentation format include citations—or acknowledgments of source information—within the text of their document. These citations, in turn, refer readers to a list of works cited or a list of references at the end of the document. Both systems use a combination of attributions and parenthetical information to refer to sources. Note the following examples:

MLA Style:

Pamela Coke argues, "Education reform is the best solution for fixing our public schools" (22).

"Education reform is the best solution for fixing our public schools" (Coke 22).

> MLA-style in-text citations include the author's name and exact page reference.

APA Style:

Pamela Coke (2008) has argued, "Education reform is the best solution for fixing our public schools" (p. 22).

"Education reform is the best solution for fixing our public schools" (Coke, 2008, p. 22).

> APA-style in-text citations include the author's name, publication date, and exact page reference.

Provide a Context for Your Quotations

Skilled research writers know the importance of providing a context for the quotations they include in their documents. It's not enough to simply put text within two quotation marks and move on. Readers can be confused by "orphan quotations"—quotations that are inserted into a paragraph without any introduction or context.

To introduce a quotation effectively, give sufficient background information about the source of your quotation and use attributions or colons to integrate the quotation into your document. Doing so gives your reader a frame for understanding how you are using the source information.

A description of the debate is given.	Many refute the idea that computer use is as damaging to children as television viewing. According to child development expert Jennifer Doyon, "Even a preschooler can benefit from simple computer activities, which by their very nature promote interactivity in a way that television shows cannot" (qtd. in Reid 89).	**The writer follows MLA style; "qtd. in" indicates the expert's words are quoted in the article by Kathleen Reid.**
An attribution identifies the speaker as an expert.		

To distinguish between your ideas and those obtained through your sources, use attributions—words and phrases, such as *he stated* and *she argued*, that alert your readers to the source of the ideas or information you are using. You should vary your attributions to avoid repetition of the same phrases. In addition, you should remember that attributions can convey important shades of meaning. There is a significant difference, for example, between saying that someone "alleged" something and someone "confirmed" something.

Some Common Attributions:

according to	claimed	expressed	reported
acknowledged	commented	inquired	said
affirmed	confirmed	interpreted	stated
alleged	declared	mused	suggested
asserted	denied	noted	thought
assumed	described	observed	wondered
asked	disputed	pointed out	wrote
believed	emphasized	remarked	

Modify Quotations

You can modify quotations to fit your draft. It is acceptable, for example, to delete unnecessary words or to change the tense of a word in a partial quotation so that it fits your sentence. For example, if you wanted to change the tense of a verb in a partial quotation so that it fits the sentence, you would use brackets to indicate the change.

Original Quotation:

"They treated us like family and refused to accept a tip."

Quotation Modified Using Brackets:

It's a place where the staff treats you "like family and [refuses] to accept a tip," said travel writer Melissa Ancomi.

Brackets indicate a word that has been changed.

Keep in mind, however, that research writers have an obligation to quote sources accurately and fairly. You should indicate when you have added or deleted words, and you should not modify quotations in a way that distorts their meaning.

The most useful strategies you can use to modify quotations include

- using ellipses (. . .) to indicate deleted words (see p. 78)
- using brackets [ ] to clarify meaning (see p. 79)
- using "sic" to note errors in a source (see p. 80)

Punctuate Quotations

The rules for punctuating quotations are as follows:

- Use double quotation marks (" ") around partial or complete quotations. Do not use quotation marks for block quotations.
- Use single quotation marks (' ') to indicate quoted material within a quotation:

  "The hotel manager told us to 'make ourselves at home.'"

- In most cases, place punctuation marks such as commas, periods, question marks, and exclamation points inside quotation marks:

  Dawn Smith asked an important question: "Do college students understand the importance of voting?"

- Place colons and semicolons outside quotation marks:

  Many young voters consider themselves "too busy to vote"; they say that voting takes too much time and effort.

- Do not put a punctuation mark that ends your own sentence inside quotation marks if doing so will alter the meaning of the original text. In the following example, the original quotation is not a question, so the question mark should be placed after the quotation mark:

  But what can be gained from following the committee's recommendation that the state should "avoid, without exceptions, any proposed tax hike"?

- When citation information is provided after a quotation, place the punctuation mark (comma, period, semicolon, colon, or question mark) after the parenthetical citation:

  "Preliminary reports have been consistent," Yates notes. "Without immediate changes to current practices, we will deplete known supplies by mid-century" (335).

- In a block quotation, place the end punctuation before the parenthesis.
- Use three spaced periods (ellipsis) to indicate an omission within a sentence:

  According to critic Joe Robinson, Americans are overworked: "Ask Americans how things are really going and you'll hear stories of . . . fifty- and sixty-hour weeks with no letup in sight" (467).

- Place a period before the ellipsis to indicate an omission at the end of a sentence:

> The most recent information indicates, says Chen, that "we can expect a significant increase in costs by the end of the decade. . . . Those costs, however, should ramp up slowly" (35).

15c

How can I integrate paraphrases?

A paraphrase is a restatement, in your own words, of a passage from a source. Unlike summaries, which are shorter than the text being summarized, paraphrases are about as long as the text on which they are based. Paraphrases can be used to illustrate or support a point you make in your document or to illustrate another author's argument about an issue.

Your notes are likely to include a number of paraphrases of information, ideas, and arguments from your sources. To integrate these paraphrases into your document, remember to

- make sure your paraphrase is an accurate and fair representation of the source. Since most paraphrasing errors occur when writers misread a source, reread the source to double-check the accuracy and fairness of your paraphrase.
- revise the paraphrase so that it fits the context and tone of your document.
- use attributions to ensure a smooth transition from your ideas to the ideas found in the source.
- identify the sources of your paraphrases according to the documentation system you are using.

In the following example, note how Alexis Alvarez lets her readers know where her statement ends and where the support for her statement, in the form of a paraphrase, begins.

> Competitive sports also teach athletes how to cope with failure as well as success. In the best of situations, as Sieghart (2004) noted, athletes are able to assess their achievements realistically, letting neither winning nor losing consume their reality.

Alexis' idea

The source of paraphrase is cited per APA style.

An attribution marks transition from Alexis' idea to source ideas.

TUTORIAL

How do I integrate a quotation into my draft?

After you select a passage to quote, you'll need to acknowledge the source, punctuate the quotation properly, and provide a context for the information. This example uses MLA style; be sure to follow the guidelines for the documentation style you are using.

Original Passage

1 Locate the passage you want to quote and identify the text you want to include in the quotation.

But there is still a black cloud hovering over this seemingly sunny scenario. Wind turbines remain expensive to build — often prohibitively so. On average, it costs about $1 million per megawatt to construct a wind turbine farm, compared to about $600,000 per megawatt for a conventional gas-fired power plant; in the economic calculations of power companies, the fact that wind is free doesn't close this gap. In short, the price of building wind power must come down if it's ever to be more than a niche technology.

Source: Fairley, Peter. "Wind Power for Pennies." *Technology Review* 105.6 (2002): 40–46. Print.

2 Add quotation marks or, if the quotation is long, set the text in a block (see p. 227). If you modify the passage, use ellipses and brackets appropriately (see p. 78).

"Wind turbines remain expensive to build. On average, it costs about $1 million per megawatt to construct a wind turbine farm, compared to about $600,000 per megawatt for a conventional gas-fired power plant"

3 Identify the source of the quotation and the location, such as the page number. Give the author's qualifications in an author tag if you haven't already done so for this source in your document.

In his article "Wind Power for Pennies," Peter Fairley notes, "Wind turbines remain expensive to build. On average, it costs about $1 million per megawatt to construct a wind turbine farm, compared to about $600,000 per megawatt for a conventional gas-fired power plant" (40).

4 Avoid "orphan quotations" by providing a context for your quotation. Introduce the quotation and indicate how it relates to your argument.

At this point, some still argue that the price of wind power is too steep. In his article "Wind Power for Pennies," Peter Fairley notes, "Wind turbines remain expensive to build. On average, it costs about $1 million per megawatt to construct a wind turbine farm, compared to about $600,000 per megawatt for a conventional gas-fired power plant" (40). These differences in cost are then passed on to the consumer in the form of higher energy costs for wind-generated electricity.

Review another example and work on quoting your own sources at **bedfordresearcher.com**. Click on Interactive Exercises.

15d

How can I integrate summaries?

A summary is a concise statement, written in your own words, of information found in a source (see p. 83 to learn about summarizing entire sources and lengthy passages within a source). When you integrate a summary into your draft, remember to

- review the source to make sure your summary is an accurate and fair representation of the ideas in the original source
- properly identify the source

You can summarize an entire source, ideas and information within a particular source, or a group of sources.

Summarize an Entire Source

Research writers frequently summarize an entire work. In some cases, the summary might occupy one or more paragraphs or be integrated into a discussion contained in one or more paragraphs. In other cases, the summary might be as brief as a single sentence.

Alexis Alvarez summarized a report issued by the Centers for Disease Control and Prevention in her research essay about steroid use by adolescent girls involved in competitive sports:

> In May 2004, the Centers for Disease Control and Prevention (CDC) published its latest figures on self-reported drug use among young people in grades 9 through 12. The CDC study, "Youth Risk Behavior Surveillance—December 2003," found that 6.1% of its survey participants reported using steroids at least once, up from 2.2% in 1993. The report also showed that use of steroids appears to be increasing among younger girls: While only 3.3% of 12th-grade girls reported using steroids, 7.3% of 9th-grade girls reported using them. Moreover, girls might be starting to use steroids at a higher rate than boys. The CDC study indicated that 9th-grade girls had reported slightly higher rates of steroid use than boys (7.3% and 6.9% respectively), while 10th-, 11th-, and 12th-grade girls all reported lower use than boys.

The title, publication date, and author are identified in the text, so parenthetical citation is not required for either MLA or APA style.

The main point of the report.

Additional information from the report.

In contrast, Alexis offered a much briefer, "nutshell" summary of a related source:

> A 2003 article in *Drug Week* stated that girls who participate in sports more than eight hours a week are at considerable risk for taking many illicit drugs: The higher the level at which athletes compete, the higher their risk for substance abuse ("Sporting Activities").

Summarize Specific Ideas and Information from a Source

You can also use summaries to convey key information or ideas from a source. In his research essay, Patrick Crossland summarized a section of a book about college admissions. His summary is highlighted in the following passage:

> Bill Paul, author of *Getting In: Inside the College Admissions Process,* a book that tells the stories of several students applying to an elite Ivy League institution, shares three suggestions for students who want to get into a college. Paul bases these suggestions on his discussions with Fred Hargadon, who in 1995 was dean of admissions at Princeton. Hargadon suggested that the best way students can enhance their chances for acceptance into the college of their choice is to read widely, learn to speak a second language, and engage in activities that interest and excite them and that also help them develop their confidence and creativity (238–49).

> The summary is introduced with the author, title, and specific source of the ideas.

> Per MLA style, exact pages are cited.

Summarize a Group of Sources

In addition to summarizing a single source, research writers often summarize groups of sources. It's not unusual, for instance, to encounter in research documents phrases such as "Numerous authors have argued . . ." or "The research in this area seems to indicate that . . ." Such collective summaries allow you to establish a point briefly and with authority. They are effective particularly at the beginning of a document, when you are establishing a foundation for your argument, and can serve as a transitional device when you move from one major section of the document to another.

When you are summarizing a group of sources, separate the citations with a semicolon. MLA guidelines require including author and page information, as in the following example:

> Several critics have argued that the Hemingway code hero is not always male (Graulich 217; Sherman 78; Watters 33).

APA guidelines require including author and date information, as in the following example:

> The benefits of early detection of breast cancer have been well documented (Page, 2007; Richards, 2007; Vincent, 2008).

15e

How can I integrate numerical information?

If it suits the issue you are addressing, you might use numerical information, such as statistics, in your document. You can present this information within sentences, or you might use tables, charts, or graphs, as Pete Jacquez did on his Web site about wind power (see Figure 15.1). Keep in mind that you still need

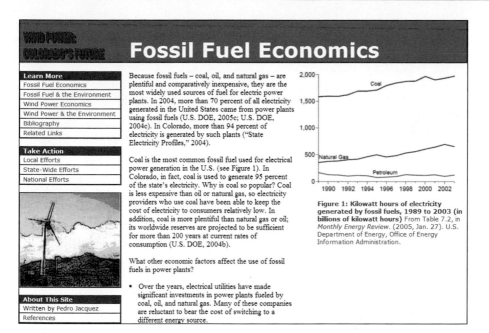

FIGURE 15.1 Chart on Pete Jacquez's Web Site

to accurately and fairly present the numerical information in your document and clearly identify the source of the information, just as you would for textual information. For more information about using tables, charts, and graphs, see p. 271.

15f

How can I integrate images, audio, and video?

Including images in your print document and images, audio, or video files in your electronic document can enhance its effectiveness. Use caution, however, when taking images and audio or video from other sources. Simply copying a photograph into your document might be a form of plagiarism. The same is true of audio and video files. Chris Norris carefully documented the sources of the images, audio clips, and video clips he used in his multimodal research essay. Since he was writing an academic essay—rather than a document intended for publication and wide distribution—he

Information Literacy

The following approach to intregrating digital illustrations into your document is usually best:

- Make a link between your document and a document that contains an image, sound clip, or video clip—rather than simply copying the image and placing it in your document.

- If it isn't possible or appropriate to create a link to another document, you should contact the owner of the image, sound clip, or video clip for permission to use it.

- If you cannot contact the owner, review the fair use guidelines discussed on page 92 for guidance about using the material.

As you've done for the other sources you cite in your document, make sure you fairly present the information and identify its author or creator.

IV Writing Your Document

did not seek permission to use the images, audio, and video that he had found in other sources. (In contrast, the publisher of this book sought and received permission to publish those materials.)

How can I ensure I've avoided plagiarism?

Because plagiarized material will often differ in style, tone, and word choice from the rest of your document, your readers are likely to notice these differences and wonder whether you've plagiarized the material—or, if not, why you've written a document that's so difficult to read. If your readers react negatively, it's unlikely that your document will be successful.

You can avoid plagiarism by

- quoting, paraphrasing, and summarizing accurately and appropriately
- distinguishing between your ideas and ideas in your sources
- identifying sources in your document

Quote, Paraphrase, and Summarize Accurately and Appropriately

Unintentional plagiarism occurs most often when a writer takes poor notes and then uses the information from the note in a document (see p. 88). Notes might contain direct quotations that are not surrounded with quotation marks, paraphrases that differ in only minor ways from the original passage, and summaries that contain original passages from a source. Taking careful notes is the first—and arguably the most important—step in avoiding unintentional plagiarism. For guidance on taking careful notes, see Chapter 6.

Unintentional plagiarism can also occur during drafting. As you draft, keep the following in mind:

- Place quotation marks around any direct quotations, use ellipses and brackets appropriately (see p. 78), and identify the source and the page number (if any) of the quotation.
- Make sure paraphrases differ significantly in word choice and sentence structure from the passage being paraphrased, and identify the source and page number from which you took the information being paraphrased.
- Make sure summaries are not just a series of passages or close paraphrases copied from the source.
- Look for notes that differ from your usual style of writing. More often than not, if a note doesn't sound like your own writing, it isn't.

Distinguish Between Your Ideas and Ideas in Your Sources

Failing to distinguish between your ideas and ideas drawn from your sources can lead readers to think other writers' ideas are yours. Examine how Patrick Crossland might have failed to distinguish his ideas from those of Joel Levine and Lawrence May, authors of a source he used in his essay:

Failing to Credit Ideas to a Source:

According to Joel Levine and Lawrence May, authors of *Getting In*, entrance exams are an extremely important part of a student's college application and carry a great deal of weight. In fact, a college entrance examination is one of the two most significant factors in getting into college. The other, unsurprisingly, is high school grades.

Because the second and third sentences fail to identify Levine and May as the source of the information about the second important factor affecting admissions decisions — high school grades — the passage implies that Patrick is the source of that information.

In contrast, Patrick actually included the following passage in his essay:

Giving Credit to the Source:

According to Joel Levine and Lawrence May, authors of *Getting In*, entrance exams are an extremely important part of a student's college application and carry a great deal of weight. In fact, they claim that a college entrance examination is "one of the two most significant factors" in getting into college (the other, unsurprisingly, being high school grades).

> The attribution, "they claim," credits Levine and May as the source of the information.

> Quotation marks are used to indicate a partial quotation.

To distinguish between your ideas and those obtained through your sources, use attributions — words or phrases that alert your readers to the source of the ideas or information you are using. As you take notes and draft your document, use the name of an author or the title of the source you're drawing from each time you introduce ideas from a source.

Examples of Attribution:

According to Scott McPherson . . .

Jill Bedard writes . . .

Tom Huckin reports . . .

Kate Kiefer observes . . .

Bob Phelps suggests . . .

In the words of Pamela Coke . . .

As Ellen Page tells it . . .

Reid Vincent indicates . . .

Jessica Richards calls our attention to . . .

Check for Unattributed Sources in Your Document

Writers sometimes neglect to identify the sources from which they have drawn their information. You should include a complete citation for each source you refer to in your document. The citation should appear in the text of the document (as an in-text citation, footnote, or endnote) or in a works cited list, reference list, or bibliography.

In the following MLA-style examples, the writer includes parenthetical citations that refer readers to a list of works cited at the end of the document. Note that MLA style allows for a combination of attributions and parenthetical information to refer to sources.

> Reid Vincent argues, "We must explore emerging energy technologies before we reach a peak oil crisis" (322).

> "We must explore emerging energy technologies before we reach a peak oil crisis" (Vincent 322).

> MLA-Style in-text citations include the author's name and exact page reference.

If you are using MLA format, be sure to cite page or paragraph numbers for paraphrased and summarized information as well as for direct quotations. The following paraphrase of Reid Vincent's comments about energy needs includes the page number of the original passage in parentheses.

> Reid Vincent argues that we need to investigate new energy technologies now, instead of while we are facing a critical oil shortage (322).

To learn more about identifying sources in your document, see p. 228 earlier in this chapter. To learn how to document sources using the MLA, APA, *Chicago*, and CSE documentation systems, see Chapters 19 to 23.

> **QUICK REFERENCE**
>
> ### Integrating Sources
>
> ☑ Use source information to accomplish your purpose. (p. 223)
> ☑ Integrate quotations appropriately. (p. 226)
> ☑ Integrate paraphrases appropriately. (p. 231)
> ☑ Integrate summaries appropriately. (p. 233)
> ☑ Integrate numerical information appropriately. (p. 234)
> ☑ Integrate images, audio, and video appropriately. (p. 235)
> ☑ Check for unintentional plagiarism. (p. 236)

16

Writing with Style

> ## Key Questions

It seems as though each writer and every teacher of writing defines *style* differently. It seems equally clear that *appropriate style*—like appropriate behavior—can vary widely. Nonetheless, you'll find that most writers and writing teachers will agree that several aspects of appropriate style can be applied to most writing situations.

16a

How can I begin to write with style?

Good style begins with an understanding of your writing situation. By reading the work of other writers addressing your issue, you can gain insights into the appropriate style for the conversation you've decided to join. For example, if you are involved in an issue that is being addressed by scholars working in the social sciences, you might find that documents written about your issue use long and fairly complex sentences, do not use *I* or other first-person pronouns, and cite sources using the American Psychological Association's documentation system. You might also find that the authors of the documents you have read are cautious about making strong claims—that they hedge their claims through the use of phrases such as "these results appear to suggest" or "it appears that." In contrast, if you are involved in an issue that is being written about in the popular media, such the *Wall Street Journal, TIME Magazine,* or CNN.com, you might find that the sentences are comparatively brief, occasionally refer to the author in first person, cite sources in a general way in the body of the document, and are more likely to make strong claims about the issue.

In addition to understanding your writing situation, you can draw on a number of general principles to develop an appropriate style. Regardless of the issue you are addressing, your readers will appreciate it if you write concisely, use active voice and passive voice effectively, adopt a consistent point of view, vary the structure of your sentences, and choose your words carefully.

Write Concisely

Readers don't want to work any harder than necessary to understand and engage with the information, ideas, and arguments in a document. They get unhappy if they find it hard to read a document—so unhappy, in fact, that they'll often give up on a document that's hard to read.

One of the keys to writing clearly is keeping your words to a minimum. Consider the following examples.

> Please join me, Dr. Watson. I have concluded that I am in a situation in which I require your assistance.

> Come here, Dr. Watson. I need you.

> Help!

The second example, reputed to be the first words ever spoken on a telephone, was spoken by Alexander Graham Bell after he'd spilled acid on his pants. Had he spoken the first sentence instead, he might have wasted crucial time while he waited a few extra seconds for his assistant to figure out what he was being asked to do. It's possible that the simple exclamation of "Help!" might have been even more effective and would certainly have taken less time to utter. Then again, it might have been too vague for his assistant to figure out just how he needed to act and what sort of help was required.

In general, if two sentences provide the same information, you'll find that the briefer sentence is easier to understand. In some cases, however, writing too little will leave your readers wondering what you are trying to get across.

Three techniques can help you write more concisely:

- **Remove Unnecessary Modifiers.** Unnecessary modifiers are words that provide little or no additional information to a reader, such as *fine, many, somewhat, great, quite, sort of, lots, really,* and *very.*

Example Sentence with Unnecessary Modifiers:

The Volvo S80 serves as a really excellent example of a very fine performance sedan.

Revised Example:

The Volvo S80 serves as an excellent example of a performance sedan.

- **Remove Unnecessary Introductory Phrases.** Avoid phrases such as *there are, there is, these have, these are, here are, here is, it has been reported that, it has been said that, it is evident that, it is obvious that,* and so on. Sentences beginning with *There are,* for example, allows you to emphasize a point, but you can often recast such sentences more concisely:

Example Sentence with Unnecessary Introductory Phrase:

There are a number of reasons to oppose the government's new drinking water policy.

Revised Example:

You should oppose the government's new drinking water policy for a number of reasons.

- **Eliminate Stock Phrases.** Search your document for phrases that you can replace with single words, such as the following:

Stock Phrase:	Alternative:
as a matter of fact	in fact
at all times	always
at that point in time	then
at this point in time	now, currently
at the present time	now, currently
because of the fact that	because
by means of	by
due to the fact that	because
in order to	to
in spite of the fact that	although, though
in the event that	if

Example Sentence with Stock Phrase:

Call the security desk in the event that the alarm sounds.

Revised Example:

Call the security desk if the alarm sounds.

TUTORIAL

How can I write concisely?

Write concisely by removing unnecessary modifiers, unnecessary introductory phrases, and stock phrases. In this example, Elizabeth Leontiev revises a wordy, vague sentence into a more concise, specific one.

Original Sentence:
There are many problems that the peasants of South America face due to the fact that America has declared war on drugs.

1 Remove unnecessary introductory phrases such as *there are* and *it is*. Often, these phrases are clues that you are using the passive voice. Rephrase the sentence using the active voice.

The peasants of South America face many problems due to the fact that America has declared war on drugs.

2 Remove unnecessary modifiers — words that provide little or no additional information to a reader — such as *fine, many, somewhat, great, quite, sort of, lots, really,* and *very*. Instead, supply specific information.

The peasants of South America face serious hardship, including poverty and cultural degradation, due to the fact that America has declared war on drugs.

3 Eliminate stock phrases such as *in order to* and *at this point in time*. Often, you can substitute a single strong word for an entire stock phrase. Similarly, use apostrophes to show possession, rather than *of* phrases.

Concise Sentence:
South American peasants face serious hardship, including poverty and cultural degradation, because of America's war on drugs.

Review another example and work on writing concisely at **bedfordresearcher.com**. Click on Interactive Exercises.

Use Active and Passive Voice Effectively

Active and passive voice are used to describe two distinctly different types of sentences. A sentence written in active voice specifies an actor—a person or thing—who carries out an action:

Active Voice:

Juan took an exam.
The tornado leveled the town.

In contrast, a sentence written in passive voice indicates that something was done, but does not specify who did it:

Passive Voice:

The exam was taken.
The town was leveled.

In general, you'll want to emphasize the actor, because sentences written in active voice are easier to understand and provide more information.

Passive voice, however, can be effective when active voice would require the inclusion of unnecessary information. Many scientific experiments, for example, are conducted by large teams of researchers. Few readers would want to know which members of the team carried out every task discussed in an article about the experiment. Rather than using active voice, as in "Janelle Knott, assisted by Jen Lee and Victor Garza, anesthetized the mice, and then Jen Lee and Richard Simpson examined their eyes for lesions," you can use passive voice as in, "The mice were anesthetized and their eyes were examined for lesions." In this case, the sentence written in passive voice is clearer, easier to understand, and does not include unnecessary information.

Passive voice is also useful if you wish to emphasize the recipient of the action, rather than the person or thing carrying out the action. Police reports, for example, often use passive voice, as in "The suspect was apprehended at the corner of Oak and Main Streets."

Adopt a Consistent Point of View

Writers adopt a particular point of view as they write:

- first person: *I, we*
- second person: *you*
- third person: *she, he, it, one, they* or nouns that describe a particular group or individual, such as *doctors, teachers, engineer, lawyer, Mr. Smith,* or *Lee Chen.*

When writers shift their point of view within a sentence, readers notice—and sometimes have to stop and ask themselves what just happened. Consider the following example.

IV Writing Your Document

Shift in Point of View:

After the climbers reached the summit in record time, we burst into song.

The sentence begins with a third-person point of view (*the climbers*) and then shifts to first-person (*we*). The sentence would be easier to understand if it were written in either first- or third-person.

Consistent Point of View:

After the climbers reached the summit in record time, they burst into song.
After we reached the summit in record time, we burst into song.

[**FRAMING MY ARGUMENT**]

Choose Your Words Carefully

Pay attention to level of formality and the extent to which specialized terms are used in the conversation about your issue. Pay attention as well to the variety and specificity of your words.

Formality   Your reading of other documents that contribute to the conversation about your issue will give you insights into the level of formality you should strive for when you draft, revise, and edit your document. Some written conversations, such as those conducted on blogs and Web discussion forums, are relatively informal and can even show evidence of lack of respect for the opinions of other participants in the discussion. Others, such as those conducted through scholarly journals or magazines such as *The Nation* or *Atlantic Monthly*, adopt a formal, restrained tone. Still others, such as those conducted through many popular media outlets, are casual but respectful. As you read about your issue, note the level of formality and the manner in which writers refer to ideas and arguments in other sources.

Informal Writing:

It was awesome to see how great the U.S. soccer team did in the last World Cup.

Formal Writing:

The performance of the U.S. soccer team in the most recent World Cup was gratifying.

Specialized Language   Specialized language, sometimes called jargon, can allow writers and readers to communicate effectively and efficiently — but only if you and your readers are familiar with the terms. If you are contributing to a conversation in which specialized language is used heavily, familiarize yourself with the terms your readers will expect you to use. For example, if you plan to write an article for a Web site that focuses on motorcycle touring, you can write more concisely and with greater accuracy if you use the proper terminology.

Ineffective Use of General Language:

Braking that involves a mechanism that coordinates proportionally the amount of pressure applied to your front and rear brakes during turns that get progressively tighter can be hazardous if you fail to initiate the turn properly.

IV Writing Your Document

Effective Use of Specialized Language:

Linked braking during decreasing-radius turns can be hazardous if you fail to initiate the turn properly.

In contrast, readers who are unfamiliar with specialized language will find it more difficult to understand your point. Most people in the United States, for example, have at least a passing familiarity with basketball, but many would find it difficult to understand the following statement:

Ineffective Use of Specialized Language for a General Audience:

Box-and-one defenses are largely ineffective against well executed pick-and-roll plays that result not in shots, but in skip passes, particularly if the pick-and-rolls are initiated on the baseline.

Variety   Variety is not only the spice of life—it's also the key ingredient in an effective document. Even a well-conceptualized and thoroughly supported argument can fail to impress if it's presented in dull, monotonous language. Consider the differences between the following examples:

Lack of Varied Word Choice:

The U.S. space program has benefited the U.S. in more ways than most U.S. government programs, largely because of the important technologies that have found their way into the U.S. economy.

Varied Word Choice:

NASA has benefited the nation in more ways than most federal programs, largely because of the important technologies that have found their way into the U.S. economy.

16b

How can I polish my style?

You can improve the overall quality of your document by varying your sentence patterns to produce an appealing rhythm, creating effective transitions, varying your source attributions, avoiding sexist language, consulting a handbook, and reading widely.

Vary Your Sentence Structure

On a basic level, there are four types of sentences:

Statements:	Dick runs fast.
Questions:	How fast did Dick run?
Commands:	Run, Dick, run.
Exclamations:	Way to go, Dick!

IV Writing Your Document

There are also four basic sentence structures, distinguished by the types and numbers of *clauses* they contain. A clause—a sequence of words containing a subject and a verb—can be either *independent* or *dependent*. (Sometimes these types of clauses are referred to as *main* and *subordinate*, respectively.) The primary difference between these types of clauses is that independent clauses can function on their own as a complete sentence, while dependent clauses cannot.

Simple (a single independent clause):

Jane runs fast.

Compound (two or more independent clauses):

Jane runs fast, but she doesn't run as fast as Dick.

Complex (an independent clause and a dependent clause):

Although Jane runs fast, Dick is faster.

> Dependent clause   Independent clause

Compound-Complex (two or more independent clauses and at least one dependent clause):

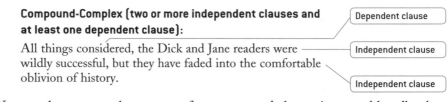

All things considered, the Dick and Jane readers were wildly successful, but they have faded into the comfortable oblivion of history.

> Dependent clause
> Independent clause
> Independent clause

You can learn more about types of sentences and clauses in a good handbook.

If you neglect to vary your sentence structure, your readers are likely to react negatively. They'll find your document monotonous and boring. To keep your readers' interest, vary your sentence structure by attending to sentence type, structure, and length. Consider the following examples.

Similar Sentence Structure and Length:

We decided to spend the morning at El Rastro. El Rastro is a Sunday morning flea market extraordinaire. We decided to take the subway to get there. A man stood quite close as we got on. I found this strange in an uncrowded subway station. Then I felt his hand in my left pocket. I also felt his hand on my back. It's a good thing that I'm ticklish. I instinctively shrugged away from his hands. Then I swore loudly and imaginatively at him. (It's inappropriate to swear on a Sunday in Spain. I wouldn't have done it under normal circumstances.) He had almost gotten away with my sunglasses. This would almost certainly have disappointed him. I know it would have inconvenienced me.

> Each sentence uses the same sentence type (statements) and the same simple sentence structure. Sentence length ranges from seven to nine words.

Varied Sentence Structure and Length:

We decided to spend the morning at El Rastro, a Sunday morning flea market extraordinaire. As we got on the subway to get to El Rastro, I noticed that a man was standing quite close to me—strange, since the subway wasn't crowded. Then I felt his hand in my left pocket and his hand on my back. (Fortunately, I'm ticklish.) "What the heck?" I thought, instinctively shrugging away and swearing at him (an inappropriate thing to do on a Sunday morning in Spain, but I was caught off-guard). He had almost gotten away with my sunglasses, which would have disappointed him and inconvenienced me.

> Sentence types include statements and questions. Sentence structures include simple, compound, and complex. Sentence length ranges from three to twenty-eight words.

Create Effective Transitions

Transitions help readers understand the relationships between sentences, paragraphs, and even sections of a document. Essentially, they smooth the way for readers, helping them understand how information, ideas, and arguments are related to each other. Transitions are most effective when they don't call attention to themselves, but instead move the reader's eye along to the next sentence, paragraph, or section. Consider the following examples of the steps that you should follow after catching a fish:

No Transitions:

Catch the fish. Clean the fish. Filet the fish. Cook the fish. Eat the fish. Catch another fish.

Inconsistent Transitions:

First, catch the fish. Secondly, clean the fish. When you've done that, filet the fish. Next, cook the fish. Fifth, eat the fish. After all is said and done, catch another fish.

Consistent Transitions:

First, catch the fish. Second, clean the fish. Third, filet the fish. Fourth, cook the fish. Fifth, eat the fish. Finally, catch another fish.

Transitions come in many forms: single words, phrases, sentences, and paragraphs. You're probably familiar with words and phrases, such as those used in the previous example, but the idea of transitional sentences and paragraphs might be unfamiliar. Transitional sentences often appear at the end or beginning of paragraphs. They serve to link two paragraphs. Transitional paragraphs are used when you want to call attention to a major shift in focus within a document. Several examples of transitions are found below:

Transitional Words:

First, second, third, . . . finally

However

Nonetheless

Transitional Phrases:

On the one hand, . . . on the other hand

As a result

In turn

Transitional Sentences:

The results of the tests revealed a surprising trend.
Incredibly, the outcome was far better than we could have hoped.

Transitional Paragraphs:

In the next section, we explore the reasons behind this surprising development. We focus first on the event itself. Then we consider the reasons underlying the event. Our goal is to call attention to the unique set of relationships that made this development possible.

Transitions can also be created in the form of headings and subheadings. Section headings serve as transitions by signaling to the reader, through formatting that differs from body text, that a new section is beginning. You can read more about headings and subheadings on p. 265.

[**FRAMING MY ARGUMENT**]

Introduce the Work of Other Authors Effectively

Readers appreciate clear indications of the source of a quotation, paraphrase, or summary. (For more information about these methods of integrating the work of other authors, see Chapter 15.) Far too many writers show little imagination in their decisions about how to introduce that work.

Common Attributions:

The author wrote . . .
The author said . . .
The author stated . . .

Somewhat More Imaginative Attributions:

The author expressed the opinion that . . .
The author denied this, noting . . .
In response, the author observed that . . .

To make your writing stand out, vary the words and phrases you use to identify the sources of the information, ideas, and arguments used in your document. In addition, pay careful attention to the implications of choosing a particular attribution. Remember that there are important differences between using a phrase such as "Stephen Garcia wondered" and "Stephen Garcia acknowledged." You'll find an extensive list of attributions that can be used to acknowledge your sources as well as additional discussion of the implications of choosing particular attributions on p. 229.

Avoid Sexist Language

It is still technically correct to use male pronouns, such as *he, him,* and *his,* when the gender of a noun, such as *doctor* or *nurse,* is unspecified. Most readers, however, object to this assumption—or they are at least sensitive to it. Readers are even more likely to object if you make the mistake of referring to representatives of particular professions using gender specific pronouns.

> When describing your symptoms to a doctor, be sure to tell him everything that's relevant. Similarly, when a nurse is taking your blood pressure, feel free to let her know how you feel.

By implying that all doctors are men and all nurses are female, the writer of this passage plays into common stereotypes. The result is that many readers will form a negative opinion of the writer.

To avoid sexist language, recast your sentences so that generic references, such as *the doctor,* are plural, such as *doctors,* as in the following example.

Sexist Language:

A doctor who pursues an advanced specialization might need to spend as many as 15 years of study before he can go into practice on his own.

Nonsexist Language:

Doctors who pursue advanced specializations might need to spend as many as 15 years of study before they can go into practice on their own.

Consult a Good Handbook

The issues raised in this chapter provide a good starting point for improving your style. Your decisions about style, however, are likely to touch on a far wider range of concerns than are discussed here. As you work to improve your writing, consult a good handbook. You'll find detailed discussions and numerous examples of strategies you can use to polish your style.

Read Widely

The most effective means of improving your style might be the most enjoyable: read as widely and as frequently as you can. Reading widely will expose you to the styles used by published authors—and you'll find that effective style comes in almost as many varieties as there are authors. Reading frequently will keep you engaged with words, and you'll find that you can draw on them more easily as you work on your own writing.

IV Writing Your Document

> **QUICK REFERENCE**

Writing with Style

 Write concisely. (p. 240)

 Use active and passive voice to accomplish your purpose. (p. 243)

 Adopt a consistent point of view. (p. 243)

 Pay attention to word choice. (p. 244)   *(continued)*

QUICK REFERENCE (continued)

- ☑ Use transitions effectively. (p. 247)
- ☑ Introduce the work of other authors effectively. (p. 248)
- ☑ Avoid sexist language. (p. 248)
- ☑ Consult a handbook. (p. 249)
- ☑ Read widely. (p. 249)

IV Writing Your Document

17

Revising and Editing

Key Questions

When writers revise and edit, they evaluate the effectiveness of their drafts and, if necessary, work to improve them. Although the two processes are related, they focus on different aspects of a document. To revise is to assess how well a document responds to a specific writing situation, makes an argument, presents its points, and uses evidence. To edit is to evaluate and improve the expression—at the sentence and word levels—of the argument, ideas, and information in the document.

17a

What should I focus on as I revise my document?

Revising involves rethinking and re-envisioning your document. It focuses on such big-picture issues as whether the document you've drafted is appropriate for your writing situation, whether your argument is sound and well supported, and whether you've organized and presented your information, ideas, and arguments clearly and effectively.

Step 1: Consider Your Writing Situation

As you revise, ask whether your document helps you achieve your purpose.

> **? WHAT'S MY PURPOSE?**
>
> Review your purpose in your research log. If your assignment directed you to inform readers about a particular subject, see whether you've provided appropriate information, whether you've given enough information, and whether that information is presented clearly. If your purpose is to convince or persuade your readers in some way, ask whether you have chosen appropriate reasons and evidence and presented your argument as effectively as you can.

Review as well your readers' needs, interests, values, beliefs, and knowledge of the issue. It's useful during revision to imagine how your readers will react to your document by asking questions such as these:

- Will my readers trust what I have to say? How can I establish my credibility?
- Will my readers have other ideas about how to address this issue? How can I convince them that they should believe what I say?
- Will my readers find my evidence appropriate and accurate? Is my selection of evidence consistent with their values and beliefs?

Finally, identify your requirements, limitations, and opportunities. Ask yourself whether you've met the specific requirements of the assignment, such as length and number of sources. Evaluate your efforts to work around limitations, such as lack of access to information. Think about whether you've taken full advantage of your opportunities and any new ones that have come your way.

Step 2: Consider Your Argument and Ideas

After you've considered your writing situation, focus your attention on the argument you are asserting.

[**FRAMING MY ARGUMENT**]

As you revise, ask how well you are conveying your argument and ideas to your readers. First, check the clarity of your thesis statement. Is it phrased in a way that is compatible with the needs, interests, values, and beliefs of your readers? Second, ask whether the argument and ideas in your document help your readers understand and accept your thesis statement. As you make this assessment, keep in mind your roles—such as advocate, reporter, interpreter, or inquirer (see p. 36):

- If you are writing an argument, ask whether you have made a clear overall point, given supporting points, and provided evidence for your points.
- If you are writing to inform, ensure that the level of detail you've provided is consistent with your readers' knowledge of the issue. If necessary, clearly define key concepts and ideas.
- If you are writing to interpret or analyze, review the clarity and accuracy of your interpretations and check that you've provided appropriate and sufficient background information to help your readers follow your reasoning.
- If you are writing to inquire, ask whether you've clearly explained the issue and your reasons for investigating it. Also reflect on whether you have clearly and accurately conveyed what you learned about the issue.

Step 3: Consider Your Use and Integration of Source Information

Think about how you've used source information in your document. First, review the amount of support you've provided for your points and the appropriateness of that support for your purpose and readers. Then, if you are arguing about an issue, determine whether you've identified and addressed reasonable opposing viewpoints.

It's also important that you integrate your sources effectively into your document and acknowledge them according to the documentation system you are following. Ensure that you have cited all your sources and that you've clearly distinguished between your ideas and those of other writers. Review your works cited or reference list for completeness and accuracy. Remember that improper documentation can reduce your document's effectiveness and your credibility.

Step 4: Consider the Structure and Organization of Your Document

Your readers should be able to locate information and ideas easily. As you read your introduction, ask whether it clearly and concisely conveys your main point and whether it helps your readers anticipate the structure and organization of your document. Reflect on the appropriateness of your organizing pattern (see p. 196) for your purpose and readers. If you've used headings and subheadings, evaluate their effectiveness.

Make sure your document is easy to read. Check for effective paragraphing and paragraph structure. If you have a number of small paragraphs, you might combine paragraphs with similar ideas. If you have a number of long paragraphs, break them up and add transitions. Finally, ask whether your conclusion leaves your readers with something to think about. The most effective conclusions typically provide more than a document summary.

What strategies should I use to revise?

As you revise, you can draw on strategies for reviewing and improving your document. These strategies range from saving multiple drafts of your document to assessing its argument and organization to obtaining feedback from others.

Step 1: Identify and Challenge Your Argument, Ideas, and Evidence

As you use the following strategies, keep track of your ideas for revision by writing comments on sticky notes or in the margins of print documents, by using the Comment tool in word processing documents, or by creating a to-do list in your research log.

Strategies for Identifying Your Argument, Ideas, and Evidence   As you revise, highlight your thesis statement, main points, and evidence. If you are working with a printed document, use a highlighter, colored pens or pencils, or sticky notes. If you are working with your document in a word processing program, use the Highlighting tools to mark the text. You might use different colors to highlight your thesis, main points, and evidence. If you are focusing solely on the evidence in your document, use different colors to highlight evidence from different sources (to help you check whether you are relying too heavily on one or two sources) or to differentiate the type of evidence you are using (such as quotations, paraphrases, summaries, and numerical data).

Strategies for Challenging Your Argument, Ideas, and Evidence   It's easy to agree with an argument that you've developed. Challenge your arguments, ideas, and evidence by using one of the following strategies. Keep track of your challenges by using the Comment tool in your word processor.

- **Put Yourself in the Place of Your Readers.** As you read, pretend that you are one of your readers. Try to imagine a single reader—or, if you're ambitious, a group of readers. Ask questions they might ask. Imagine concerns they might bring to their reading of your document. A reader interested in solving a problem might ask, for example, whether a proposed solution is cost effective, is more

> **Information Literacy**
> **Save Multiple Drafts** You might not be happy with every revision you make. To avoid wishing that you hadn't made extensive revisions to a draft of your document, save a new copy of your draft before every major revising session. Name your drafts by number — as in Draft1, Draft2, and so on — or by date, as in Draft-April6 and Draft-April10. Or come up with a naming system that works for you. What's important is that you save multiple versions of your drafts in case you don't like the changes you've made.

appropriate than alternative solutions, or has unacceptable side effects. As you revise, take these questions and concerns into account.

- **Play Devil's Advocate.** A devil's advocate raises reasonable objections to ideas and arguments. As you review your document, identify your key claims and pose reasonable objections to them. Make note of these potential objections and take them into account as you revise.

- **Play the "So What?" Game.** As you read your document, ask why readers would care about what you are saying. By asking "so what?" questions, you can gain a better understanding of what your readers are likely to care about and how they might respond to your arguments and ideas. Make note of your responses to these questions and consider them as you revise.

Step 2: Scan, Outline, and Map Your Document

Use the following strategies to review the structure and organization of your document.

- **Scan Headings and Subheadings.** If you have used headings and subheadings, they can help you track the overall flow of your argument and ideas. Ask whether the organization they reveal is appropriate for your writing situation and your role as a writer.

- **Scan the First Sentence of Each Paragraph.** A quick reading of the first sentence in each paragraph can reveal points at which your argument shifts. As you note these shifts, think about whether they are appropriate and effective.

As you review the organization and structure of your document, reflect on whether it is appropriate given your purpose, readers, argument, and available information.

Step 3: Ask for Feedback

After spending long hours on a project, you may find it difficult to identify problems your readers might have with your draft. You might read the same paragraph eight times, failing to notice that the evidence you are using to support a point actually contradicts it. Or you might not notice that your document's organization could confuse your readers. You can ask for feedback on your draft from a friend, relative, colleague, or writing center tutor. It's generally a good idea to ask for help from someone who will be frank as well as supportive and to be specific about the kinds of comments you're looking for. Hearing "it's just fine" from a reviewer will not help you to revise.

Information Literacy

- **Outline Your Document.** Create a topical or sentence outline of your document (see p. 197) to assess its structure and organization. This strategy, sometimes called a reverse outline, helps you identify the sequence of your points and amount of space you've devoted to each aspect of your document. If you are viewing your document in a word processor, use the Styles tool to assign levels to headings in your document and then view it in outline view.

- **Map Your Document.** On paper or in a graphics program, draw a map of your document. Like an outline, a map can help you identify the organization of your points and the amount of evidence you've used to support them.

TUTORIAL

How do I strengthen my argument during revision?

By this point in your research writing process, you are probably quite comfortable with your argument. But what would a reader with fresh eyes think? Imagine that you are a reader encountering this essay for the first time, then respond as author.

	Reader's Comments	**Author's Responses**
1 Look for Confusing or Unclear Points. As you read the essay, do any questions form in your mind? Write down your questions, then—wearing your author's hat again—consider how your essay can address them more fully.	— You mention various genres of metal music, but how are they different from each other? — You say that the rise of grunge in the '90s caused the decline of metal's popularity, but then you say there was a thriving underground. Seems contradictory.	— Must distinguish the genres more clearly; define "nu-metal" and "metalcore." Maybe include examples to clarify? — Need to sort out the chronology. Metal *did* decline in popularity during the heyday of grunge, but there were still devoted fans in the "underground" movement.
2 Play Devil's Advocate. Identify your key claims and pose reasonable objections to them. Consider how you could address them in your essay.	— You claim that metal has diversity, but all the song lyrics you include are about the war. Seems like that's the only topic addressed in these songs.	— Need to include different song lyrics about other issues, too — animal rights, the environment, racism, nuclear weapons, etc. Use Cattle Decapitation as an example.
3 Play the "So What?" Game. As a reader, consider why you should care about this topic. Then respond to help readers identify the significance of your issue.	— What if I'm not interested in heavy metal or just don't like the sound? Why should I pay attention?	— Mention recent protests and demonstrations against heavy metal groups to show that it is *still* a controversial issue. — Show bands' MySpace pages to illustrate its popularity and relevance among young fans today.

Review another example and learn more about revising your document at **bedfordresearcher.com**. Click on Interactive Exercises.

> **QUICK REFERENCE**

Revising

☑ **Review your research writing situation.** Ask whether your document helps you achieve your purposes, addresses your readers' needs, interests, values, and beliefs, meets your requirements, effectively works around limitations, and takes advantage of opportunities. (p. 252)

☑ **Evaluate your argument and ideas.** Ask whether your document provides a clear and appropriate thesis statement and whether your argument and ideas support your thesis statement and are consistent with your roles. (p. 252)

☑ **Assess your use and integration of source information.** Ask whether you have offered adequate support for your points, considered reasonable opposing viewpoints, integrated and acknowledged your sources, and distinguished between your work and that of other writers. (p. 253)

☑ **Examine the structure and organization of your document.** Ask whether the introduction is clear and concise, clearly conveys your main point, and helps your readers anticipate the structure of your document. Also think about whether the organizational structure is easy to follow, paragraphs are easy to read, and transitions are effective. Ask whether the conclusion provides more than a summary of the document. (p. 253)

☑ **Use effective revision strategies.** Create multiple drafts to preserve earlier work; review your document to assess its argument and organization; get feedback from other writers. (p. 255)

17c

What should I focus on as I edit my document?

Editing involves assessing the effectiveness, accuracy, and appropriateness of the words and sentences in a document. Editing focuses on issues such as the accurate and concise expression of ideas and information; the balance between consistency and variety; use of nonsexist language; appropriate tone and style; and the proper use of punctuation, spelling, and grammar.

Focus on Accuracy

You'll risk damaging your credibility if you provide inaccurate information in your document. To reduce this risk, do the following:

- **Check Your Facts and Figures.** Your readers might think you're deliberately misleading them if you fail to provide accurate information. As you edit, return to your original sources or your notes to check any facts and figures.

- **Check Every Quotation.** Return to your original sources or consult your notes to ensure that you have quoted each source exactly. Make sure that you have noted any changes to a quotation with an ellipsis or brackets (pp. 78–79), and make sure that those changes haven't altered the original meaning of the passage. Make sure you have cited the source in the text and in a works cited or reference list.

- **Check the Spelling of Every Name.** Don't rely on electronic spelling checkers, which provide the correct spelling for only the most common or prominent names.

Focus on Economy

Editing for economy involves reducing the number of words needed to express an idea or convey information to your readers. Removing unnecessary modifiers and wordy introductory or stock phrases can make your writing more concise and to-the-point (see p. 240). Editing for economy generally makes it easier for your readers to understand your meaning. However, you should use care when you edit for economy; your readers still need to understand the point you are trying to make.

Focus on Consistency

Editing your project document for consistency helps you present information in a uniform way. Use the following techniques to edit for consistency.

- **Treat Concepts Consistently.** Review your document for consistent treatment of concepts, information, ideas, definitions, and anecdotes.

- **Use Numbers Consistently.** Check the documentation system you are using for its guidelines on the treatment of numbers. You might find that you should spell out the numbers zero through ten and use Arabic numerals for numbers larger than ten.

- **Treat Your Sources Consistently.** Avoid referring to some sources using first names and to others using honorifics, such as *Dr., Mr.,* or *Ms.* Also check that you have cited your sources appropriately for the documentation style you are using, such as MLA or APA. Review each reference for consistent presentation of names, page numbers, and publication dates.

- **Format Your Document Consistently.** Avoid any inconsistencies in your use of fonts, headings and subheadings, and tables and figures.

Focus on Avoiding Sexist Language

As you draft your document, avoid using sexist language, language that stereotypes men or women. The simplest way to eliminate sexist language is to revise your sentences so that generic references are plural, as in the following example:

Sexist Language:

Today, the research writer finds at least half of his sources online.

Nonsexist Language:

Today, research writers find at least half of their sources online.

Focus on Tone and Style

Your readers will judge you—and what you have to say   not only on what you say but on how you say it. Use the following techniques as you edit for tone and style.

- **Use Appropriate Words.** Make sure that your language is suitable for your audience. If you are writing a technical report, your language will be much different than if you are writing a feature article for a magazine.

- **Rewrite Complex Sentences.** A sentence can be grammatically correct yet incomprehensible. A sentence that is too complex will make your readers work overtime to figure out what it means.

- **Vary Your Sentence Length and Structure.** A steady stream of sentences written in exactly the same way will have the same effect as a lecture delivered in a monotone. Best bet: add some variety to the length and structure of your sentences.

Focus on Spelling, Grammar, and Punctuation

Poor spelling doesn't necessarily affect your ability to get your point across—in most cases readers will understand even the most atrociously spelled document—but it does affect what your readers think of you. Ignore enough spelling errors in your document and you'll erode their confidence in your ability to present information or make an argument. The same goes for grammar and punctuation. If you haven't made sure that subjects and verbs agree and that sentences end with the appropriate punctuation, a reader might not trust that you have presented your facts correctly.

IV Writing Your Document

17d

What strategies should I use to edit?

Thorough editing involves making several passes through your document to ensure that you've addressed accuracy, economy, and consistency; sexist language; tone and style; and spelling, grammar, and punctuation. Editing strategies include reading, searching, and marking your text; using word processing tools to check spelling and grammar; and obtaining feedback on your document.

Before you begin to edit, remember that editing focuses on the words and sentences in your document, not on its overall structure or ideas. If you're uncertain about whether you've organized your document as effectively as possible or whether you've provided enough support for your argument, deal with those issues first. In the same way that you wouldn't start painting a house until you've finished building the walls, hold off on editing until you're confident that you're finished revising.

Step 1: Read Your Document Carefully

As you've worked on your document, you've become quite familiar with it. As a result, it can be easy to read what you meant to write instead of what you actually wrote. Use the following strategies to read carefully.

- **Set Your Document Aside Before You Edit.** If time permits, allow a day or two to pass before you begin editing your document. Taking time off between revising and editing can help you see your writing with new eyes.

- **Pause Between Sentences for a Quick Check.** Avoid getting caught up in the flow of your document—where the meaning takes precedence over the structure and expression of your sentences—by stopping after each sentence. Slowing down can help you identify problems with your text.

> @ Learn how to use the Highlighting, Search and Replace, and Split Window tools in your word processor at bedfordresearcher.com. Click on Guides > How to Use Your Word Processor.

- **Read Aloud.** Reading your document aloud can help you find problems that might not be apparent when it's read silently.

- **Read in Reverse Order.** To check for problems with individual sentences, start at the end of your document and read the last sentence first, then work backward through the document. To check for problems at the word level, read each word starting with the last one in the document. Disrupting the normal flow of your document can alert you to problems that might not stand out when it is read normally.

Step 2: Mark and Search Your Document

Use the following marking and searching strategies to edit for accuracy, consistency, and use of sexist language.

Mark Your Document. As you read, use a high-lighting pen or the Highlighter tool in your word processor to mark errors or information that should be double-checked. Consider using different colors to highlight specific types of problems, such as sexist language or inconsistent use of formal titles.

> **Information Literacy**
> **Use the Find and Replace Tools.** Use your word processor to edit concepts, names, numbers, and titles for consistency and accuracy. Once you've identified a word or phrase that you'd like to check or change, you can search for it throughout your document. If you are referring to sources using a parenthetical style, such as MLA or APA, use the Find tool to search for an opening parenthesis. If you discover that you've consistently misspelled a word or name, use the Replace tool to correct it throughout your document.
> **Use the Split Window Tool.** Some word processors allow you to split your window so that you can view different parts of your document at the same time. Use this tool to ensure that you are referring to a concept in the same way throughout your document or to check for consistent use of fonts, headings, subheadings, illustrations, and tables.

Step 3: Use Spelling and Grammar Tools

Most word processors provide tools to check spelling, grammar, punctuation, and style. Used with an awareness of their limitations, these tools can significantly reduce the effort required to edit a document. Spelling checkers have two primary limitations. First, they can't identify words that are spelled correctly but misused—such as *to/two/too*, *their/they're/there*, and *advice/advise*. Second, spelling checkers are ineffective when they run into a word they don't recognize, such as proper names, technical and scientific terms, and unusual words. To compound this problem, spelling checkers often suggest replacement words. If you take the advice, you'll end up with a paper full of incorrect words and misspelled names.

Step 4: Ask for Feedback

> Learn how to use the Spelling, Grammar, and Style tools in your word processor at bedfordresearcher.com. Click on Guides > How to Use Your Word Processor.

One of the biggest challenges writers face is reading a draft of their own work as a reader rather than as the writer. Because you know what you're trying to say, you'll find it easy to understand your draft. And because you've read and reread your document so many times, you're likely to overlook errors in spelling, punctuation, and grammar. After you've edited your document, ask a friend, relative, or classmate to proofread it and to make note of any problems.

Information Literacy

The main limitation of spelling checkers and grammar, punctuation, and style checkers is inaccurate advice. Although much of the advice they offer is sound, a significant proportion is not. If you are confident about your knowledge of grammar, punctuation, and style, you can use the grammar and style-checking tools in your word processor to identify potential problem areas in your document. You'll find that these tools can point out problems you might have overlooked, such as a subject-verb disagreement that occurred when you revised a sentence. However, if you don't have a strong knowledge of grammar, punctuation, and style, you can easily be misled by inaccurate advice.

If you have any doubts about advice from your spelling checker, consult an up-to-date dictionary. If you have concerns about the suggestions you receive from your grammar, punctuation, and style checker, consult a good handbook.

> **QUICK REFERENCE**

Editing

☑ **Ensure your document is accurate.** Check facts and figures, quotations, and spelling of names. (p. 257)

☑ **Strive for economy.** Remove unnecessary modifiers, eliminate unnecessary introductory phrases, and avoid use of stock phrases. (p. 258)

☑ **Ensure that your document is consistent.** Use concepts, numbers, and source information consistently. Check your document for consistent use of formatting and design. (p. 258)

☑ **Remove sexist language from your document.** (p. 258)

☑ **Use appropriate tone and style.** Use appropriate words, rewrite overly complex sentences, and vary sentence length and structure. (p. 259)

☑ **Check for correct spelling, grammar, and punctuation.** Use your word processor's spelling, grammar, punctuation, and style tools; consult a handbook and dictionary; and ask someone to proofread your draft. (p. 259)

IV Writing Your Document

18

Designing

> **Key Questions**

The growing sophistication of word processing, Web editing, and presentation programs along with access to high-quality color printers have given writers a great deal of control over the design of their documents. Your design decisions, from choosing fonts to formatting tables to selecting appropriate illustrations, will play a critical role in how your readers understand and react to your document. Those decisions will be shaped by your understanding of design principles and elements as well as the conventions of typical research documents.

18a

How can I use design effectively?

Although the most important factor in the success of your writing project is the ability to express your ideas and arguments clearly, you should also think about how the design of your document can help you achieve your purpose, affect your readers, and meet their expectations.

Understand Design Principles

Before you begin formatting text and inserting illustrations, consider how the document design principles of *balance, emphasis, placement, repetition,* and *consistency* can help you accomplish your goals as a writer.

Balance is the vertical and horizontal alignment of elements on your pages (see Figure 18.1). Symmetrical designs create a sense of rest and stability and tend to lead the reader's eye to focus on a particular part of a document. In contrast, asymmetrical—or unbalanced—designs suggest movement and guide readers' eyes across the page.

Emphasis is the placement and formatting of elements, such as headings and subheadings, so they catch your readers' attention. You can emphasize an element in a document by using a color or font that distinguishes it from other elements, by placing a border around it and adding a shaded background, or by using an illustration, such as a photograph, drawing, or graph.

Placement is the location of elements on your pages. Placing elements next to or near each other suggests that they are related. Illustrations, for example, are usually placed near the passages in which they are mentioned.

Repetition is the use of elements, such as headers and footers, navigation menus, and page numbers, across the pages in your document. As readers move from page to page, they tend to expect navigation elements, such as page numbers, to appear

FIGURE 18.1 Symmetrical (left) and Asymmetrical (right) Layouts

in the same place. In addition, repeated elements, such as a logo or Web navigation menu, help establish a sense of identity across the pages in your document.

Consistency is the extent to which you format and place text and illustrations in the same way throughout your document. Treating each design element—such as illustrations, headings, and footnotes—consistently will help your readers recognize the different roles played by the elements in your document and, by extension, help them locate the information they seek. A consistent design can also convey a sense of competence and professionalism to your readers, increasing their confidence in the quality and credibility of your document.

You should also keep two other principles in mind: moderation and simplicity. An overly complex design can work against the effectiveness of a document by obscuring important ideas and information. Using design elements moderately to create simple yet effective designs is the best approach.

Design for a Purpose

A well-designed document presents your information, ideas, and arguments in a manner that helps you accomplish your purpose. Your purpose, as a result, should inform your design decisions.

 WHAT'S MY PURPOSE?

In your research log, review your purpose to determine if you might use design to achieve the following goals.

- **Setting a Tone.** One of the most powerful tools writers have for accomplishing their purpose is establishing an emotional context for their readers. Drawing on the design principles of balance and placement, you can set a tone by using a particular color scheme, such as bright, cheerful hues, or by selecting photographs or drawings with a strong emotional impact.

- **Helping Readers Understand a Point.** You might use the design principles of emphasis and placement to introduce and help readers understand your points. Headings or pull quotes can call your readers' attention to important ideas and information. To introduce a main point, you might use a contrasting font or color to signal the importance of the information. To highlight a definition or example, you might use borders or place the passage in a pull quote. You can also help readers understand a point by using illustrations.

- **Convincing Readers to Accept a Point.** The key to convincing readers is providing them with appropriate, relevant evidence. Drawing on the principles of emphasis and placement, you can use illustrations, marginal glosses, pull quotes, and bulleted lists to call attention to that evidence.

- **Clarifying Complex Concepts.** Sometimes a picture really is worth a thousand words. Rather than attempting to explain a complex concept using text alone, use an illustration. A well-chosen, well-placed photograph, flow chart, diagram,

Design for Your Readers

A well-designed document helps readers understand the organization of the document, locate information and ideas, and recognize the function of parts of the document. It is also easy on your readers' eyes: Readers working with a well-designed document will not have to strain to read the text or discern illustrations. Use document design to do the following:

Help Readers Understand the Organization of a Document. You can use headings and subheadings to signal the content of each part of the document. If you do, keep in mind the design principles of emphasis and consistency: Format your headings in a consistent manner that helps them stand out from other parts of the document (see Figure 18.2).

Help Readers Locate Information and Ideas. Many longer print documents use tables of contents and indexes to help readers locate information and ideas.

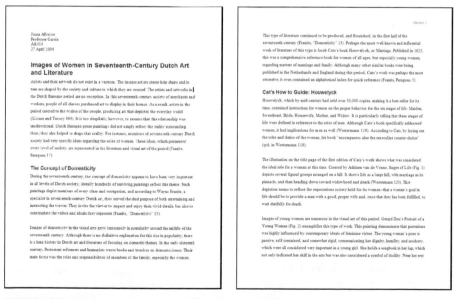

FIGURE 18.2 Headings and Subheadings in a Research Essay
Use of a contrasting font and color helps readers understand the document's organization.

Web sites typically provide a mix of menus and navigation headers and footers to help readers move around the site. When these navigation aids are integrated into pages, they are often distinguished from the surrounding text by the use of bordered or shaded boxes or through the use of contrasting fonts.

Help Readers Recognize the Function of Parts of a Document.   If you include passages that differ from the main text of your document, such as sidebars and "For More Information" sections, help readers understand their function by designing them to stand out visually. Using emphasis, for example, you might format a sidebar in an article with a shaded or colored box. Similarly, you might format a list of related readings or Web links in a contrasting font or color.

Design to Address Genre Conventions

Understanding the design conventions of the type of document you plan to write will help you create a document that meets the expectations of your readers. Genres are characterized not only by distinctive writing styles, types of evidence, and organizational patterns, but also by distinctive types of design. An article in a magazine such as *TIME* or *Newsweek,* for example, is characterized by the use of columns, headings and subheadings, pull quotes, and illustrations, while an academic essay is characterized by wide margins, double-spaced lines, and comparatively restrained use of color and illustrations. Your readers will expect your document to be similar in design to other examples of that genre. This doesn't mean that you can't depart from those conventions should the need arise, but it does mean that you should take their expectations into account as you design your document.

18b

What design elements can I use?

Understanding the range of design elements at your disposal will enable you to decide which of these options to use as you design your document. These elements include fonts, line spacing, and alignment; page layout strategies; color, shading, borders, and rules; and illustrations.

Use Fonts, Line Spacing, and Alignment

Fonts, line spacing, and alignment choices are the most common design decisions made by writers. They are also among the most important, since poor choices can make a document difficult to read. Figure 18.3 provides an overview of the key features of fonts. Figure 18.4, an article from the magazine *Ode,* illustrates the uses of fonts, line spacing, and alignment.

Learn more about formatting fonts, line spacing, and alignment at **bedfordresearcher .com**. Click on Guides > How to Use Your Word Processor or How to Write for the Web.

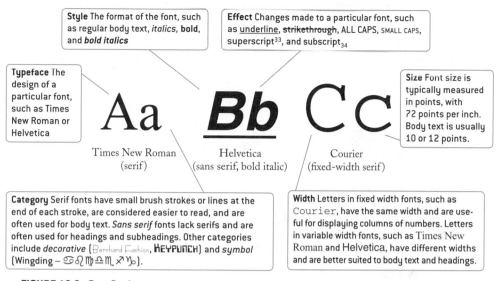

Style The format of the font, such as regular body text, *italics*, **bold**, and ***bold italics***

Effect Changes made to a particular font, such as <u>underline</u>, ~~strikethrough~~, ALL CAPS, SMALL CAPS, superscript[33], and subscript[34]

Typeface The design of a particular font, such as Times New Roman or Helvetica

Size Font size is typically measured in points, with 72 points per inch. Body text is usually 10 or 12 points.

Times New Roman (serif)   Helvetica (sans serif, bold italic)   Courier (fixed-width serif)

Category Serif fonts have small brush strokes or lines at the end of each stroke, are considered easier to read, and are often used for body text. *Sans serif* fonts lack serifs and are often used for headings and subheadings. Other categories include *decorative* (Bernhard Fashion, ΗΕΨΡυΠCΗ) and *symbol* (Wingding – ✋♌︎♏︎♍︎♍ ✗✏︎).

Width Letters in fixed width fonts, such as `Courier`, have the same width and are useful for displaying columns of numbers. Letters in variable width fonts, such as Times New Roman and Helvetica, have different widths and are better suited to body text and headings.

FIGURE 18.3 Font Basics

Use Page Layout Elements

Page layout is the placement of text, illustrations, and other objects on a page or screen. Successful page layout draws on a number of design elements, including white space, margins, columns, headers and footers, page numbers, headings, lists, captions, marginal glosses and pull quotes, and sidebars. Figure 18.5 illustrates these design elements.

@ Learn more about creating effective page layouts at **bedfordresearcher.com**. Click on Guides > How to Use Your Word Processor or How to Write for the Web.

Use Color, Shading, Borders, and Rules

Color, shading, borders, and rules (lines running horizontally or vertically on a page) can increase the overall attractiveness of your document, call attention to important information, help readers understand the organization of your document, help readers recognize the function of specific passages of text, and signal transitions between sections (see Figure 18.6). As you use these design elements, exercise restraint. Avoid using more than three colors on a page unless you are using a photograph or work of art. Be cautious, as well, about using multiple styles of rules or borders in a document.

@ Learn more about formatting color, borders, shading, and rules at **bedfordresearcher .com**. Click on Guides > How to Use Your Word Processor or How to Write for the Web.

IV Writing Your Document

Line spacing refers to the amount of space between lines of text. Larger line spacing appears easier to read, so you'll often find increased line spacing used in introductory paragraphs, executive summaries (which provide an overview of a longer document), and sidebars (see p. 269).

When text is crammed together vertically, it is difficult both to read and to insert written comments. Keep this in mind if you are creating a document such as an essay on which someone else might write comments.

GLOBAL WARMING

"Just give up that car"

DROPPING KNOWLEDGE IS A CITIZENS GROUP that hosts a compelling website enabling you to exchange ideas on contemporary global issues by posting questions, answering others' inquiries and contemplating responses given by leading voices of our time. To the question "What can I do, and tell others to do, to stop global warming?" German-born director Wim Wenders (photo) responds, "Sell your car, ride your bike and use public transportation." So does he follow his own advice?

Says Wenders: "I don't have a car anymore. I tell you, it's a big relief. I ride my bike in Berlin, I take the S-Bahn, the subway, the trains. My life is so much better. I don't get tickets anymore. I don't have the hassle. I can read more. Just give up that car!"—FRAUKE GODAT

FIND OUT MORE: DROPPINGKNOWLEDGE.ORG

Alignment refers to the horizontal arrangement of text and illustrations (such as photos and drawings). You can select four types of alignment:

- **Left,** which has a straight left margin and a "ragged right" margin, is typically the easiest to read.
- **Right,** which has a straight right margin and ragged left.
- **Centered,** which is seldom used for body text.
- **Justified,** with straight alignment on both the left and right. Although it adds a polished look to documents that use columns, justified text produces irregular spacing and results in hyphenated words, which can slow the reading process.

WEALTH

Africa: Richer than you think?

AFRICA IS PORTRAYED BY THE MEDIA AS A BELEAGUERED, poverty-stricken continent, while India and China are cast as economic superpowers. Statistics paint a more nuanced picture. While it's true that some of the world's poorest countries are in Africa, the continent as a whole is wealthier than India, which must divide its gross domestic product among a larger population. Africa's average per capita GDP in 2005 was $954, more than $200 higher than India's. Per capita GDP is higher than India's in a surprising 20 out of 53 countries in Africa. Twelve African nations have a higher per capita GDP than China.

Imagine the investments and business activities lost as a consequence of this biased image, says Vijay Mahajan, a professor with the McCombs School of Business at the University of Texas at Austin. To combat that image problem, Mahajan is writing a book about Africa's potentially powerful consumer market, to be released next summer by Wharton School Publishing.—MARCO VISSCHER

DECEMBER 2007 ODE 25

Fonts are a complete set of type of a particular size and typeface (see Figure 18.3). As you choose fonts, consider the following:

- **Select fonts that are easy to read.** For body text, avoid decorative fonts and avoid the use of italics.
- **Select fonts that complement each other.** A serif body font, such as Times New Roman or Garamond, works well with a sans serif heading font, such as Arial, Helvetica, or Calibri.
- **Use restraint when choosing fonts.** Generally, use no more than four different fonts in a document.

FIGURE 18.4 Using Fonts, Line Spacing, and Alignment

PHOTOGRAPH BY DONATA WENDERS/2005

Numbered and bulleted lists (not shown) display brief passages of related information using numbers or symbols (usually round "bullets"). The surrounding white space draws the eye to the list, highlighting the information for your readers, while the brief content in each entry can make concepts or processes easier to understand.

Sidebars (not shown) are brief discussions of information related to but not a central part of your document. Sidebars simplify the task of integrating supporting information into the body of the article by setting that information off in a clearly defined area.

Case Study

The Marines And MySpace

How the 231-year-old institution got hip with CGC without losing control

BY WENDY MELILLO

L t. Col. Mike Zeliff, a 21-year veteran of the U.S. Marines Corps, is seated in his office in Quantico, Va., surrounded by charts grouping potential recruits into categories like "rural heartlanders" or "disillusioned dreamers." His hair is closely cropped and his uniform neatly pressed to the point of crispness. In his hand is a copy of a *Wall Street Journal* article titled "MySpace, ByeSpace?"

...iling the very buttoned-down Marines with social-networking site ...t. Yet, that is exactly what Zeliff is doing. "On the Internet, you ...clicks away from something bad," says Zeliff, assistant chief of ...ising at the USMC Recruiting Command. "We learned early on ...tise next to any unedited content, we could get caught up in an ...that would not be appropriate for the Marine Corps."

...h digital media may seem like the Wild West, where marketers ...e influx of Web users into their territory and even hand over ...hard-fought—and won—control. Not only have many adver- ...accept the consumer as the new sheriff in town—witness ...ble CEO A.G. Lafley's speech at the annual meeting of the ...National Advertisers in October—but some may forget there ...gotiation, especially within the ...-generated environment. But, ...C began adopting new media ...ng campaigns, it did so cau- ...willing to give up control of ...along the way, the 231-year- ...stitution convinced MySpace ...terms.

...e USMC keep a firm grip on its ...on a popular site that solicits user comments and allows anyone to upload images is a story of risk, selectivity and a clear focus on the mission.

The USMC, which launched its MySpace profile in April, want the page to serve as a ...nterested 17- to 24-year-olds to ...m Web site, where they can get ...tion and request to meet with ...lso knows what it doesn't want: ...ntangled with content it can't ...at might tarnish its image. ...is hardly alone in wanting to ...nd—remember when Chevy ...test after consumer-generated ...7 Tahoe showed how SUVs con-

tributed to global warming? But Zeliff would be the first to admit the USMC is much more persnickety than many about it.

Passing the 'Blues Test'
When New York-based digital shop RMG Connect, which handles the Marines account, first suggested the idea of using MySpace in August 2005, the USMC subjected the site to what they call the "blues test." "Would I be proud to be in that context or at that event in my dress blues," Zeliff says. "We scrub any new advertising idea against whether we think it is an appropriate place to be."

MySpace certainly had the demographic the USMC was looking for. Of the 56 million

unique users in the U.S., 5.9 million are 15-to 24...
minu...
comS...
Bu...
was n...
at the...
parents who were concerned the site wasn't doing enough to protect kids from sexual predators. So, although planning the profile began in '05, it wasn't until after the site hired a child-safety expert in April that Zeliff felt comfortable enough to launch the page.

"As aggressive as we will be when we know it's right, we are very slow to get to the point where we know it's right," he explains.

> 'We learned early on that ... we could get caught up in an association that **would not be appropriate.'** – LT. COL. MIKE ZELIFF

IN CHARGE: Gunnery Sergeant Biggs appears as a drill leader in recent Marine Corps TV spots.

www.adweek.com

Marginal glosses (not shown) are brief notes in a margin that explain or expand on text in the body of the document.

Captions describe or explain an illustration, such as a photograph or chart.

Columns generally appear in newspaper and magazine articles — and, to a growing extent, articles published on the Web. Essays, on the other hand, are typically formatted in a single column. Columns can improve the readability of a document by limiting the physical movement of an eye across the page and by framing other elements.

Pull quotes highlight a passage of text — frequently a quotation — through the use of borders, white space, distinctive fonts, size, and contrasting colors.

Margins are the white space between the edge of the page or screen (top, bottom, right, and left) and text or graphics in your document.

White space — literally, empty space — frames and separates elements on a page.

Headers, footers, and page numbers appear at the top or bottom of the page, set apart from the main text. They help readers find their way through a document; they provide information, such as the title of the document, its publication date, and its author; and they frame a page visually.

Headings and subheadings identify sections and subsections, serve as transitions, and allow readers to locate information more easily.

IV Writing Your Document

FIGURE 18.5   Using Page Layout Elements

Signal the Organization of a Document. In a longer print document, headers, footers, headings, and subheadings might be formatted with a particular color to help readers recognize which section they are reading. On a Web site, pages in each section could share the same background or heading color.

...OF THE YEAR

More great people, ideas, and businesses...

Be Consistent. Use the same colors for top-level headings throughout your document, another color for lower-level headings, and so on. Use the same borders and shading for sidebars. Use rules consistently in pull quotes, headers, and footers. Don't mix and match.

Upstart of the Year

When Whirlpool announced in May 2006 that it would shut down its Maytag division in Newton, Iowa, it offered transfers to a select group of employees. Twenty-year veteran Jordan Bruntz, the manager of the 90-person division, turned down the offer. He wanted to stay in Newton.

An idea sprouted. Bruntz started attending classes on entrepreneurship, and last December he gathered his seven top managers and asked them to be co-owners in a company he was starting. It would be based in Newton, would be called Springboard Engineering, and would do just what their division had done before—industrial design and engineering. The managers agreed, and the notion gained quick support from the other Maytag employees.

Bruntz is starting a company that can thrive in Newton: Corporations are outsourcing extra design and engineering work instead of adding to their head count, and an American company full of trained engineers should be attractive. Bruntz talked the town into offering him tax rebates, then got the state of Iowa to give him both grants and zero-interest loans. (He also financed Springboard with bank loans and cash from each new owner.) He bought a large amount of used equipment from his bosses at Whirlpool and spent $600,000 on a former Kmart for his new headquarters. Fifty onetime Maytag employees will have jobs at Springboard. The new company opens its doors January 7, two weeks after Maytag's Newton office closes for good, and Bruntz has already talked both John Deere and Whirlpool itself into becoming clients. —*Stephanie Clifford*

Signal the Function of Text. A colored or shaded background might indicate that a passage of text is a sidebar or a pull quote. Color and rules can be used to differentiate captions and pull quotes from body text. Rules can also separate columns of text on a page or screen.

Exit Strategists of the Year

Mary and Gary West are probably the richest American couple you've never heard of—and they did it the new-fashioned way. They took their company public, got rich, then took it private again and got richer still. The couple's business, West Corporation, provides large corporations with a variety of services—call centers, teleconferencing, even bill collection—and also runs the technology backbone for the national 911 system. In 2006, the company's top line exceeded $1.8 billion, up from $317 million in 1996, the year of its initial public offering. Timing the private equity bubble adeptly, the Wests closed a deal at the end of 2006 whereby two large funds bought up 66 percent of West Corporation, taking it private. For the founders, it was quite a payday: $1.45 billion plus 23 percent of the company. So how are the Wests spending their newly liquid fortune? First, they plan on funding start-ups in their hometown of Omaha, starting with a payment-processing company called Planet Group, in which the couple recently invested an undisclosed sum. Meanwhile, the Wests continue to indulge their passion for horseracing. Though their Kentucky Derby mounts have run poorly to date, they own several fine horses, including High Limit, Dollar Bill, and a 1999 stakes winner named, yes, Entrepreneur. —*Mike Hofman*

Understand the Effects of Color. Some effects are physical. Bright yellow, for example, can tire your readers' eyes. Other effects are emotional — and are often linked to readers' cultural backgrounds. In many cultures, green is regarded as soothing because it is associated with nature and growth. Red, in contrast, is often associated with danger. As a result, it tends to attract attention.

Call Attention to Important Information. Color, borders, and shading can subtly yet clearly emphasize an illustration, such as a table or chart, or an important passage of text, by distinguishing it from the surrounding body text.

FIGURE 18.6 Using Color, Borders, Shading, and Rules

[**FRAMING MY ARGUMENT**]

Use Illustrations

Illustrations—charts, graphs, tables, photographs and other images, animations, audio clips, and video clips—can expand on or demonstrate points made in the text of your document. They can also reduce the text needed to make a point, help readers better understand your points, and increase the visual appeal of your document.

Photographs and Other Images Photographs and other images, such as drawings, paintings, and sketches, are frequently used to set a mood, emphasize a point, or demonstrate a point more fully than is possible with text alone.

Charts and Graphs Charts and graphs represent information visually. They are used to make a point more succinctly than is possible with text alone or to present complex information in a compact and more accessible form. They frequently rely on numerical information.

Tables Like charts and graphs, tables can present complex information, both textual and numerical, in a compact form.

Other Digital Illustrations Digital publications allow you to include a wider range of illustrations, including audio, video, and animations that bring sound and movement to your document.

> @ Learn more about working with illustrations at bedfordresearcher.com. Click on Guides > How to Use Your Word Processor or How to Write for the Web.

As you work with illustrations, keep the following guidelines in mind.

- **Use an illustration for a purpose.** Illustrations are best used when they serve a clear function in your document. Avoid including illustrations simply because you think they might make your document "look better."

- **Place illustrations near the text they illustrate.** In general, place illustrations as close as possible to the point where they are mentioned in the text. If they are not explicitly mentioned (as is often the case with photographs), place them at a point where they will seem most relevant to the information and ideas being discussed.

- **Include a title or caption that identifies or explains the illustration.** The documentation style you are using, such as MLA or APA, will usually offer advice on the placement and format of titles and captions. In general, documentation systems suggest that you distinguish between tables and figures (which include other illustrations), number tables and figures in the order in which they appear in the document, and use compound numbering of tables and figures in longer documents (for example, the second table in Chapter 5 would be labeled "Table 5.2"). Consult the documentation system you are using for specific guidelines on illustrations.

The following tutorial can help you determine whether to use illustrations in your document.

TUTORIAL

How can I use illustrations in my document?

Illustrations can enhance the effectiveness of your document by supporting your argument, reducing word length, clarifying your argument, and increasing visual appeal. In this example, pages from an essay written by Elizabeth Leontiev show how illustrations can enhance the effectiveness of a document.

Review your draft to determine where you could use illustrations to accomplish the following:

1 **Reduce the text needed to make a point.** Elizabeth found this graph from a reliable source — the United Nations Office on Drugs and Crime. It presents significant data in a concise fashion and illustrates that coca cultivation in Bolivia did not increase after Evo Morales became president.

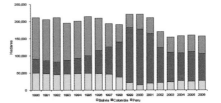

2 **Expand on or demonstrate your argument.** Illustrations can clarify and offer context for the information you provide. The graph Elizabeth uses not only supports her point about Evo Morales's plan, but it also illustrates that Bolivia's coca production is minimal compared with that of other coca-producing countries.

3 **Increase the visual appeal of your document.** Striking and colorful, this photograph of manual coca plant eradication attracts the reader's eye on the page.

4 **Help readers better understand your reasons.** The photograph shows the audience a scene that coca farmers who live in poverty must dread. It creates an emotional appeal by showing exactly how the war on drugs is fought — by soldiers with machetes.

Review another example and learn more about working with images at **bedfordresearcher.com**. Click on Interactive Exercises.

18c

How should I design my document?

Readers familiar with particular genres—or types—of documents, such as academic essays, newspaper columns, informative Web sites, and feature articles, expect documents in a genre to share a particular look and feel. Newspaper articles, for example, are typically laid out in narrow columns of text and are often accompanied by captioned photographs. As you design your document, consider the typical design characteristics associated with the type of document you've chosen. Attending to these conventions will allow you to meet the expectations of your readers. It will also help convey an impression of competence and professionalism.

Understand the Design Conventions of Academic Essays

The design of academic essays is neither flashy nor complex. Their most obvious design features—wide margins, readable fonts, and double-spaced lines—are intended to help their intended audience, typically instructors and classmates, read and review them. These features are influenced by the manuscript preparation guidelines provided by professional organizations such as the Modern Language Association (MLA). The goal of these guidelines is to simplify the task of editing a manuscript and preparing it for its transformation into a book or an article in a scholarly journal. Because the writing assignments given by most college instructors have focused on the written expression of ideas and arguments, academic essays have tended to use images sparingly, if at all, and to make limited use of design elements such as color, shading, borders, and rules. With changes in word processing technology, however, writers of academic essays have begun to take advantage of these design elements. Keep in mind that some instructors prefer that design elements be kept to a minimum in essays. If you are uncertain about your instructor's preferences, ask for guidance.

The pages in Figures 18.7 through 18.10 are from an essay written by college freshman Gaele Lopez for his composition class. They reflect his awareness of his instructor's expectations about line spacing, margins, documentation system, page numbers, and a title page.

For another sample essay formatted in MLA style, see p. 317. For a sample essay formatted in APA style, see p. 343. For a sample essay formatted in *Chicago* style, see p. 373.

IV Writing Your Document

CHECKLIST FOR DESIGNING ACADEMIC ESSAYS

☑ Cover page with title, name, and course information

☑ Readable body font (example: 12-point Times New Roman)

↓

CHECKLIST FOR DESIGNING ACADEMIC ESSAYS (continued)

- ✔ Double-spaced lines
- ✔ Wide margins, one inch or larger
- ✔ Consistent use of assigned documentation system
- ✔ Headers and footers in a readable font distinct from body font
- ✔ If used, headings and subheadings formatted in fonts and colors that distinguish them from the body text and show relative importance of heading levels
- ✔ If used, illustrations labeled and placed either within the text near relevant passages or in an appendix, according to instructor's preferences

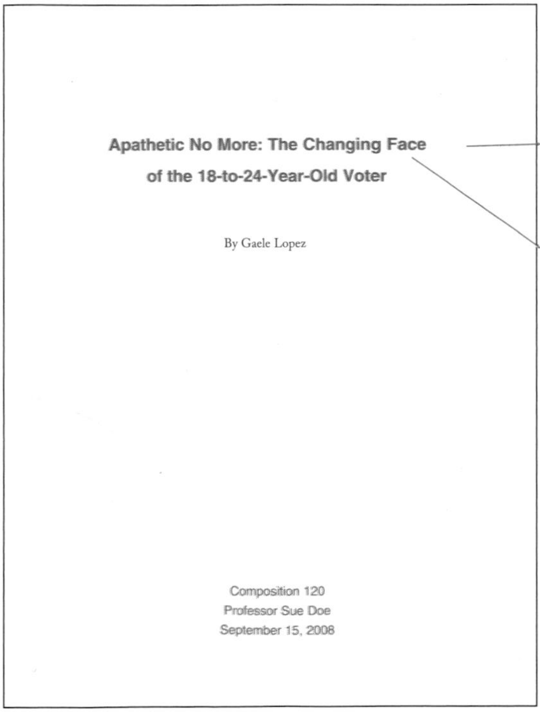

Apathetic No More: The Changing Face

of the 18-to-24-Year-Old Voter

By Gaele Lopez

Composition 120
Professor Sue Doe
September 15, 2008

FIGURE 18.7 Cover Page for an Academic Essay

Cover page provides title, author, information about the course, and date the essay was turned in.

A larger, boldface font distinguishes title from other information on the page.

FIGURE 18.8 First Page of an Academic Essay

A header with writer's last name and page number is repeated at the top of each page.

Title is repeated on first page of essay in a larger, colored, sans serif font that distinguishes it from the body text.

Body text is set in a serif font, which is more readable than most sans serif fonts.

All body text is formatted consistently.

One-inch margins and double-spaced lines provide space for the teacher to write comments.

A graph appears near its mention in the text, supporting claims made there.

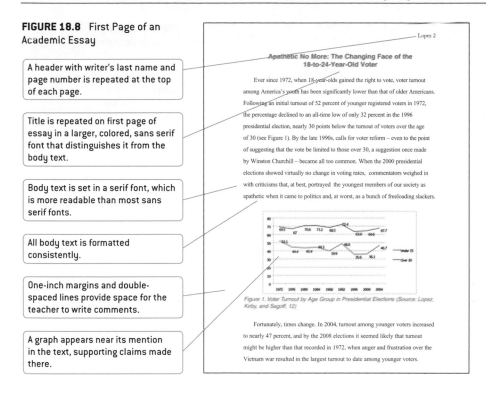

Lopez 2

**Apathetic No More: The Changing Face of the
18-to-24-Year-Old Voter**

Ever since 1972, when 18-year-olds gained the right to vote, voter turnout among America's youth has been significantly lower than that of older Americans. Following an initial turnout of 52 percent of younger registered voters in 1972, the percentage declined to an all-time low of only 32 percent in the 1996 presidential election, nearly 30 points below the turnout of voters over the age of 30 (see Figure 1). By the late 1990s, calls for voter reform – even to the point of suggesting that the vote be limited to those over 30, a suggestion once made by Winston Churchill – became all too common. When the 2000 presidential elections showed virtually no change in voting rates, commentators weighed in with criticisms that, at best, portrayed the youngest members of our society as apathetic when it came to politics and, at worst, as a bunch of freeloading slackers.

Figure 1. Voter Turnout by Age Group in Presidential Elections (Source: Lopez, Kirby, and Sagoff, 12)

Fortunately, times change. In 2004, turnout among younger voters increased to nearly 47 percent, and by the 2008 elections it seemed likely that turnout might be higher than that recorded in 1972, when anger and frustration over the Vietnam war resulted in the largest turnout to date among younger voters.

Lopez 3

In the 2008 primaries, turnouts among younger voters doubled, tripled, and in some case quadrupled the turnouts recorded in any previous primary (Pew Charitable Trust, par. 2). Analysts – even some of those who had suggested raising the voting age – quickly began to investigate why younger voters were turning out in such unprecedented numbers, what impact their votes would have on the upcoming presidential election, and what this change in behavior would have on future elections.

Factors Contributing to the Change in Voting Behaviors

Why the sudden change? Or is it as sudden as it seems? Analysts Mark Hugo Lopez, Emily Kirby, and Jared Sagoff, writing after the 2004 presidential elections, pointed to "the confluence of extensive voter outreach efforts, a close election, and high levels of interest in the 2004 campaign" as factors that drove turnout among younger voters to "levels not seen since 1992" (1). They cautioned, however, that it was unclear whether the 2004 results were indicators of a significant change or simply an aberration.

It would appear, based on patterns seen in the 2006 mid-term elections and in the 2008 presidential primaries, that there really is evidence of a change. In its report on record turnout in the 2008 primaries and caucuses, the Pew Charitable Trust notes,

> The research showed that college students are deeply concerned about issues, involved personally as volunteers and ready to consider voting. But they want political leaders to be positive, to address real problems and to call on all Americans to be constructively involved (par. 5).

As we look toward the fall 2008 elections, it seems clear that young voters will not only play an important role in the election, but might in fact play the deciding role. Voters such as Reid Vincent,

FIGURE 18.9 Interior Page of an Academic Essay

A heading, formatted in blue and using a sans serif font that differs from the serif body font, calls attention to a shift in Gaele's argument.

Block quotation is set off by indenting the margins on both sides. Quotation marks are not needed for block quotations.

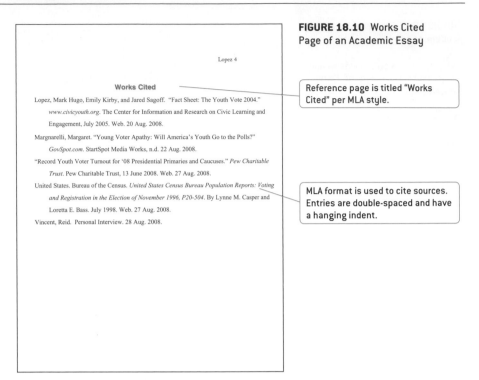

FIGURE 18.10 Works Cited Page of an Academic Essay

Lopez 4

Works Cited

Lopez, Mark Hugo, Emily Kirby, and Jared Sagoff. "Fact Sheet: The Youth Vote 2004."
    www.civicyouth.org. The Center for Information and Research on Civic Learning and
    Engagement, July 2005. Web. 20 Aug. 2008.

Margnarelli, Margaret. "Young Voter Apathy: Will America's Youth Go to the Polls?"
    GovSpot.com. StartSpot Media Works, n.d. 22 Aug. 2008.

"Record Youth Voter Turnout for '08 Presidential Primaries and Caucuses." *Pew Charitable*
    Trust. Pew Charitable Trust, 13 June 2008. Web. 27 Aug. 2008.

United States. Bureau of the Census. *United States Census Bureau Population Reports: Voting*
    and Registration in the Election of November 1996, P20-504. By Lynne M. Casper and
    Loretta E. Bass. July 1998. Web. 27 Aug. 2008.

Vincent, Reid. Personal Interview. 28 Aug. 2008.

> Reference page is titled "Works Cited" per MLA style.

> MLA format is used to cite sources. Entries are double-spaced and have a hanging indent.

Understand the Design Conventions of Multimodal Essays

Multimodal essays are characterized by their essayistic form and their use of multiple types of illustrations. As essays, they present information in a linear sequence, one idea after another. As multimodal documents, they combine text with images, animation, sound, and/or video. Multimodal essays can vary widely not only in form, but also in the software used to create them. For example, one writer might use a word processing program to create a document that contains a wide range of media, another might use multimedia presentation program (such as PowerPoint) to present an essay, and yet another might use a Web development program, such as Dreamweaver, to create an essay. Because multimodal essays rely heavily on digital illustrations, they are usually best viewed on a computer screen.

Figures 18.11 through 18.14 show a selection of slides from the multimodal essay written by Chris Norris. Chris developed his essay with PowerPoint. Note his use of text, illustrations, color, headings and subheadings, sidebars, and lists to clearly convey his argument about the resurgence in the popularity of metal music.

IV Writing Your Document

A table of contents, set in a manner similar to a Web page, allows quick access to pages in the essay.

The title and subtitle are presented in large, readable fonts in colors that contrast with the background.

A photograph draws the reader's eye and sets the tone for the essay.

FIGURE 18.11

Body text is presented in a readable sans-serif font that contrasts with the background.

Photographs illustrate key ideas in the text.

Source information and credits are provided for photographs.

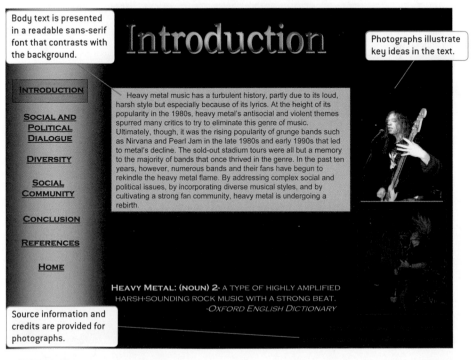

Second Coming
The Resurgence of Heavy Metal in Popular Music

INTRODUCTION

SOCIAL AND POLITICAL DIALOGUE

DIVERSITY

SOCIAL COMMUNITY

CONCLUSION

REFERENCES

HOME

Introduction

INTRODUCTION

SOCIAL AND POLITICAL DIALOGUE

DIVERSITY

SOCIAL COMMUNITY

CONCLUSION

REFERENCES

HOME

Heavy metal music has a turbulent history, partly due to its loud, harsh style but especially because of its lyrics. At the height of its popularity in the 1980s, heavy metal's antisocial and violent themes spurred many critics to try to eliminate this genre of music. Ultimately, though, it was the rising popularity of grunge bands such as Nirvana and Pearl Jam in the late 1980s and early 1990s that led to metal's decline. The sold-out stadium tours were all but a memory to the majority of bands that once thrived in the genre. In the past ten years, however, numerous bands and their fans have begun to rekindle the heavy metal flame. By addressing complex social and political issues, by incorporating diverse musical styles, and by cultivating a strong fan community, heavy metal is undergoing a rebirth.

HEAVY METAL: (NOUN) 2- A TYPE OF HIGHLY AMPLIFIED HARSH-SOUNDING ROCK MUSIC WITH A STRONG BEAT.
-*OXFORD ENGLISH DICTIONARY*

FIGURE 18.12

IV Writing Your Document

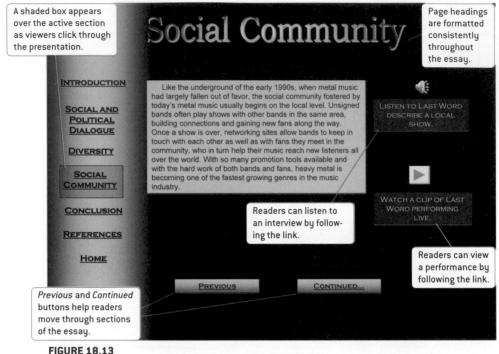

A shaded box appears over the active section as viewers click through the presentation.

Page headings are formatted consistently throughout the essay.

Readers can listen to an interview by following the link.

Readers can view a performance by following the link.

Previous and *Continued* buttons help readers move through sections of the essay.

FIGURE 18.13

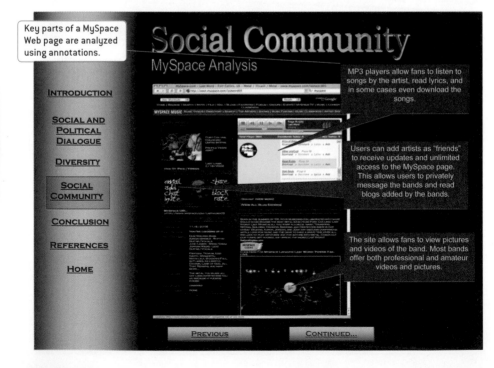

Key parts of a MySpace Web page are analyzed using annotations.

FIGURE 18.14

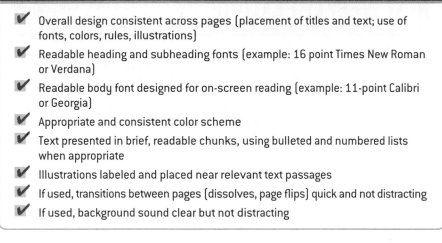

CHECKLIST FOR MULTIMODAL ESSAYS

- ☑ Overall design consistent across pages (placement of titles and text; use of fonts, colors, rules, illustrations)
- ☑ Readable heading and subheading fonts (example: 16 point Times New Roman or Verdana)
- ☑ Readable body font designed for on-screen reading (example: 11-point Calibri or Georgia)
- ☑ Appropriate and consistent color scheme
- ☑ Text presented in brief, readable chunks, using bulleted and numbered lists when appropriate
- ☑ Illustrations labeled and placed near relevant text passages
- ☑ If used, transitions between pages (dissolves, page flips) quick and not distracting
- ☑ If used, background sound clear but not distracting

Understand the Design Conventions of Articles

Articles appear in a wide range of publications, including newspapers, magazines, scholarly and professional journals, and Web sites, among others. Depending on the publication in which they appear, articles might use headings and subheadings, columns, sidebars, pull quotes, and a wide array of illustrations. Writers of articles need to consider several factors that affect design: the overall design of the publication in which they hope to place their article, the audience the publication addresses, the subjects typically written about in the publication, and the style and tone used by other articles in the publication.

The main article in Figure 18.15 was written by Kaitlin Shawgo for Indiana University's student newspaper, the *Indiana Daily Student*. It draws heavily on visual elements to set a mood, call attention to key points, and convey information.

CHECKLIST FOR DESIGNING ARTICLES

- ☑ Column layout appropriate for target publication and target audience
- ☑ Line spacing typically single-space
- ☑ Readable body font (example: 10- or 11-point Century Schoolbook)
- ☑ Color, borders, shading, and rules used appropriately
- ☑ Heading and subheadings formatted in font and colors that distinguish them from body text and show the relative importance of heading levels
- ☑ Illustrations labeled and placed near relevant passages

IV Writing Your Document

FIGURE 18.15 Front Page of a Student Newspaper

Pull quotes in large, sans serif text highlight key quotations from the article.

Large headline in color contrasts with the text and subheading. Subheading summarizes main point of the article, allowing the reader to quickly decide whether to read the article.

Newspaper article is formatted in columns.

Captioned photos add visual interest and information.

Byline is set in bold and sans serif to differentiate it from the main body text.

Understand the Design Conventions of Web Sites

Web sites consist of linked pages, typically organized through a home page and navigational devices such as menus, tables of contents, indexes, and site maps. The main pages of Web sites usually provide broad overviews of the topic, and related pages add detailed information. Designs used for Web sites are growing more similar to those found in magazines, with a heavy use of images and other illustrations. Information is highlighted though colors, borders, shading, rules, fonts, tables, and an expanded range of digital illustrations.

Web sites pose intriguing design challenges to writers. In addition to many of the design elements that are used in print documents, you also must choose from the expanded range of design options for publishing online, such as selecting an organizational structure for a site, selecting navigation tools, and using digital illustrations. Most important, you must have some familiarity with the range of Web sites you can create, such as informative Web sites; articles for Web-based journals, magazines, and newspapers; corporate Web sites; personal home pages; and blogs, to name only a few of the types of sites that can now be found on the Web.

> @ Learn more about creating and designing Web sites at **bedfordresearcher.com**. Click on Guides > How to Write for the Web.

Figures 18.16 through 18.18 show pages from Pete Jacquez's Web site about wind-generated electrical power.

CHECKLIST FOR DESIGNING WEB SITES

✔ Organizational structure consistent with the purpose of the site and the needs and expectations of readers

✔ Home page provides links to main pages on the site

✔ Home page and main pages offer navigation tools appropriate for readers of the site

✔ Overall design consistent across the site (placement of titles, text, and navigation tools; use of fonts, colors, rules, and illustrations)

✔ Information presented in brief, readable chunks, using bulleted and numbered lists whenever possible

✔ Readable body font in font family designed for on-screen reading (examples: 11-point Verdana or Georgia)

✔ Headings and subheadings formatted in fonts and colors that distinguish them from body text and show relative importance of heading levels

✔ Informational flags used to help readers understand links and images

✔ Appropriate use of color

✔ Illustrations placed near the passages to which they refer

✔ Images kept as small (in kilobytes) as possible, while being clear and easy to see

✔ Contact information and other relevant information included and easy to locate

A side menu provides links to pages on the site.

A large heading identifies the issue addressed by the site.

WIND POWER: COLORADO'S FUTURE

Learn More
Fossil Fuel Economics
Fossil Fuel & the Environment
Wind Power Economics
Wind Power & the Environment
Bibliography
Related Links

Take Action
Local Efforts
State-Wide Efforts
National Efforts

About This Site
Written by Pedro Jacquez
References

With the flip of a switch, electricity is there. It powers our lights, televisions, stereos, computers, clothes washers, and refrigerators. Once a luxury, electric power has become a staple of modern life. Yet it is a necessity that Americans consume with little regard for its sources – or its costs.

In Colorado, as in other states, the majority of electricity is produced by power plants that burn fossil fuels, usually coal, oil, or natural gas (U.S. Department of Energy [DOE], 2004c). Unfortunately, the mass production of electricity has significantly reduced supplies of these non-renewable natural resources. It has also increased air pollution and spurred global warming.

What can we do to reduce these negative effects of power plants? One promising approach is to increase our reliance on wind-generated electrical power. Wind power, as it has come to be known, is a cost-effective alternative to power from fossil-fuel-based power plants – and is likely to become even more attractive as the costs of fossil fuels continue to rise. Perhaps more important, wind power generates no air pollution or greenhouse gases.

A new state constitutional amendment (which mandates that clean power be used to generate some electricity) has put Colorado at the forefront of efforts to increase the use of wind power (Gonzalez-Estay, 2004). But more must be done. Coloradoans should lead a national movement to increase the use of wind power. Through this site, you will learn how you can help in that effort. You'll find background information about the environmental and economic issues associated with generating electrical power through fossil fuel and wind. You'll also find an annotated bibliography and a list of links to other sites addressing wind power.

The average visitor to Vail and other upscale ski resorts has come to expect elaborate lighting schemes. Most visitors, however, don't even think about the economic costs and environmental impacts of generating electricity through conventional fossil fuels.

Caption is set off from body text with a different font (Verdana) and contrasting color.

Site information is provided. A list of references cited in the site is available.

A photograph illustrates a key point raised in the body text.

Body text is formatted in a 12-point serif font that is easy to read.

FIGURE 18.16 Web Site Home Page

IV Writing Your Document

> A link to the home page is provided on all other pages.

> Headings are formatted in a large sans-serif font that contrasts with the body text.

> A chart provides information about wind power economics.

WIND POWER: COLORADO'S FUTURE

Wind Power Economics

Learn More
Fossil Fuel Economics
Fossil Fuel & the Environment
Wind Power Economics
Wind Power & the Environment
Bibliography
Related Links

Take Action
Local Efforts
State-Wide Efforts
National Efforts

About This Site
Written by Pedro Jacquez
References

Today, wind power accounts for less than one-tenth of one percent of all electrical power generated in the United States (U. S. General Accounting Office [GAO], 2004). This represents a four-fold increase since 1990, however, and growth is expected to continue for the foreseeable future (U. S. GAO, 2004). The majority of wind power installations are in ten Midwestern and Western states: California, Colorado, Iowa, Minnesota, New Mexico, Oklahoma, Oregon, Texas, Washington, and Wyoming. These states have the natural conditions required for wind power: large open spaces with annual wind speeds of at least 16 miles per hour.

Since the late 1990s, the cost of wind power has become competitive with that of power generated by fossil-fuel power plants. As you can see in Figure 2, the cost of wind power now falls within the same "competitive price bard" as fossil fuels. In large part, this decline in cost can be attributed to improvements in technology, which are likely to continue. Flowers (2005) estimates that the average output of large wind turbines will increase from their current capacity of 1.5 megawatts to 5 megawatts by 2010. In addition, as the number of wind farms increases nationwide, the cost of producing wind turbines has declined (Colorado Green Power, 2005).

Government support of wind power has also helped the industry. The federal government offers a

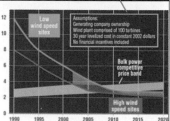

Figure 2: Cost of electricity produced by wind power, 1990 to 2020 (in Year-2002 constant dollars). From U.S. Department of Energy, National Renewable Energy Laboratory. (2004, March). *Wind Power: Today and Tomorrow.*

> The side menu appears in the same place on each page of the site.

> Extra space after each paragraph helps differentiate one from another.

> The figure title is followed by source information.

FIGURE 18.17 Web Site Content Page

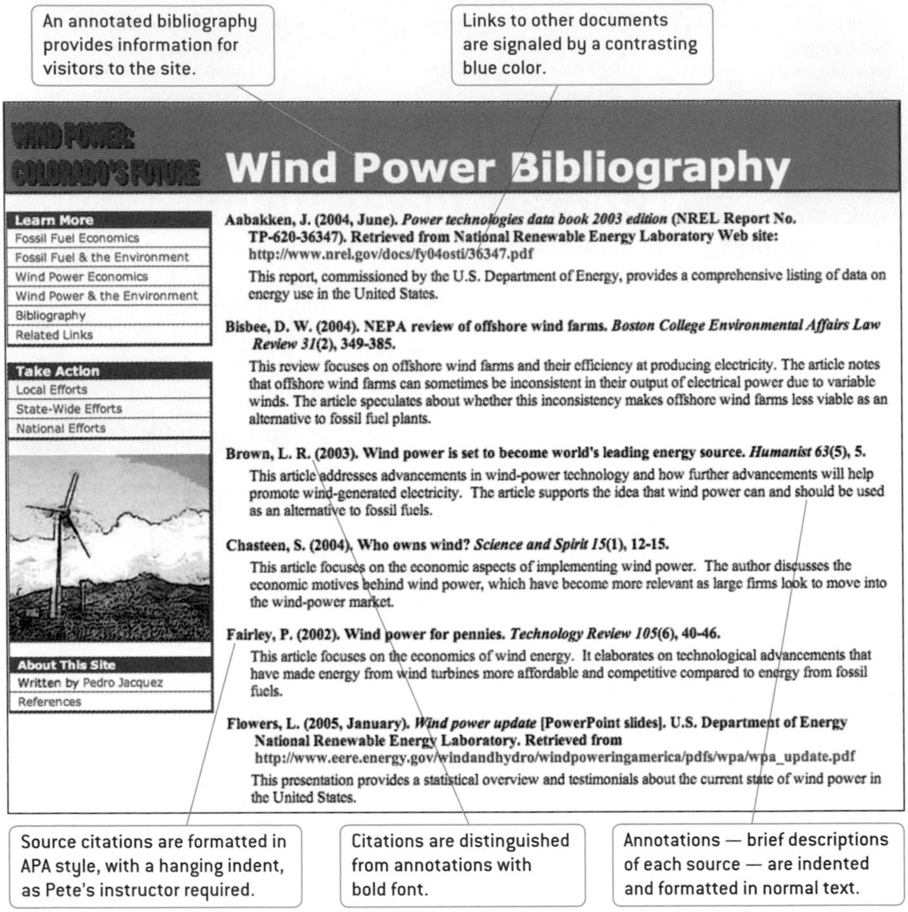

An annotated bibliography provides information for visitors to the site.

Links to other documents are signaled by a contrasting blue color.

Wind Power Bibliography

WIND POWER: COLORADO'S FUTURE

Learn More
Fossil Fuel Economics
Fossil Fuel & the Environment
Wind Power Economics
Wind Power & the Environment
Bibliography
Related Links

Take Action
Local Efforts
State-Wide Efforts
National Efforts

About This Site
Written by Pedro Jacquez
References

Aabakken, J. (2004, June). *Power technologies data book 2003 edition* (NREL Report No. TP-620-36347). Retrieved from National Renewable Energy Laboratory Web site: http://www.nrel.gov/docs/fy04osti/36347.pdf

This report, commissioned by the U.S. Department of Energy, provides a comprehensive listing of data on energy use in the United States.

Bisbee, D. W. (2004). NEPA review of offshore wind farms. *Boston College Environmental Affairs Law Review 31*(2), 349-385.

This review focuses on offshore wind farms and their efficiency at producing electricity. The article notes that offshore wind farms can sometimes be inconsistent in their output of electrical power due to variable winds. The article speculates about whether this inconsistency makes offshore wind farms less viable as an alternative to fossil fuel plants.

Brown, L. R. (2003). Wind power is set to become world's leading energy source. *Humanist 63*(5), 5.

This article addresses advancements in wind-power technology and how further advancements will help promote wind-generated electricity. The article supports the idea that wind power can and should be used as an alternative to fossil fuels.

Chasteen, S. (2004). Who owns wind? *Science and Spirit 15*(1), 12-15.

This article focuses on the economic aspects of implementing wind power. The author discusses the economic motives behind wind power, which have become more relevant as large firms look to move into the wind-power market.

Fairley, P. (2002). Wind power for pennies. *Technology Review 105*(6), 40-46.

This article focuses on the economics of wind energy. It elaborates on technological advancements that have made energy from wind turbines more affordable and competitive compared to energy from fossil fuels.

Flowers, L. (2005, January). *Wind power update* [PowerPoint slides]. U.S. Department of Energy National Renewable Energy Laboratory. Retrieved from http://www.eere.energy.gov/windandhydro/windpoweringamerica/pdfs/wpa/wpa_update.pdf

This presentation provides a statistical overview and testimonials about the current state of wind power in the United States.

Source citations are formatted in APA style, with a hanging indent, as Pete's instructor required.

Citations are distinguished from annotations with bold font.

Annotations — brief descriptions of each source — are indented and formatted in normal text.

FIGURE 18.18 Annotated Bibliography Web Page

> QUICK REFERENCE

Designing

☑ Understand the design principles of balance, emphasis, placement, repetition, and consistency. (p. 263)

☑ Design to achieve your purposes. (p. 264)

☑ Design to address your readers' needs, interests, values, and beliefs. (p. 265)

☑ Design to address genre conventions. (p. 266)

☑ Use design elements — such as, fonts, line spacing, alignment, page layout, color, borders, shading, rules, and illustrations — effectively and appropriately to increase the readability and effectiveness of your document. (p. 266)

☑ Follow the design conventions of the type of document you are creating, such as an academic essay (p. 273), a multimodal essay (p. 274), an article (p. 279), or a Web site (p. 280).

The Bedford Researcher

I	Joining the Conversation
II	Working with Sources
III	Collecting Information
IV	Writing Your Document
V	**Documenting Sources**

PART V

Documenting Sources

As you complete your work on your research project, you can turn your attention fully to the task of citing and documenting your sources. This section discusses reasons to document your sources and describes four major documentation systems: MLA, APA, *Chicago,* and CSE.

19

Understanding Documentation Systems

> **Key Questions**
>
> 19a. What is a documentation system and which one should I use?   287
>
> 19b. How should I document my sources?   289

Research writers document their sources to avoid plagiarism, give credit to others who have written about an issue, and create a record of their work that others can follow and build upon. These reasons illustrate the concept of writing as participation in a community of writers and readers. By documenting your sources, you show that you are aware that other writers have contributed to the conversation about your issue and that you respect them enough to acknowledge their contributions. In turn, you expect that writers who read your document will cite your work.

? WHAT'S MY PURPOSE?

Documenting your sources can help you achieve your purpose as a writer, such as establishing your authority and persuading your readers. If your readers find that you haven't documented your sources, they'll either suspect that you're careless or decide that you're dishonest. In either case, they won't trust what you have to say.

19a

What is a documentation system and which one should I use?

Many professional organizations and publications have developed their own rules for formatting documents and citing sources. As a result, writers in many disciplines know how to cite their sources clearly and consistently, and their readers know what to expect. For example, imagine that a psychologist is writing an article for the *Journal of Counseling Psychology*. The writer is likely to know that submissions to the journal go through a rigorous review for substance and style before being accepted for publication. Among its expectations, the journal requires that writers use the documentation system created by the American Psychological Association (APA). Given the high level of competition for space in the journal, the writer knows that even if the article is substantive and compelling, it will not be accepted for publication if it does not use APA style appropriately. After ensuring the article is clearly written and well argued, the writer double-checks the article to ensure it follows the formatting and source citation guidelines specified by the APA documentation system.

Several of the documentation systems most commonly used in the various academic disciplines are covered in this book.

- **MLA** This style, from the Modern Language Association (MLA), is used primarily in the humanities—English, philosophy, linguistics, world languages, and so on. See Chapter 20.

- **APA** This style, from the American Psychological Association, is used mainly in the social sciences—psychology, sociology, anthropology, political science, economics, education, and so on. See Chapter 21.

- *Chicago* Developed by the University of Chicago Press, this style is used primarily in history, journalism, and the humanities. See Chapter 22.

- **CSE** This style, from the Council of Science Editors (formerly the Council of Biology Editors), is used mainly in the physical and life sciences—chemistry, geology, biology, botany, and so on—and in mathematics. See Chapter 23.

[**FRAMING MY ARGUMENT**]

Your choice of documentation system will be guided by the discipline or field within which you are writing and by any requirements associated with your research writing project. If your project has been assigned to you, ask the person who assigned it or someone who has written a similar document which documentation system you should use. If you are working on a project for a writing class, your instructor will most likely tell you which documentation system to follow.

If you don't have access to advice about which documentation system is best for your project, consider the discipline in which you are writing. In engineering and business, for example, a wide range of documentation styles are used, with most of these specific to scholarly journals or specializations within the discipline. Consider as well the genre you have chosen for your project document. The manner in which sources are cited can vary widely from one type of document to another. For example, while academic essays and articles appearing in scholarly journals typically use a documentation system such as MLA, APA, *Chicago*, or CSE, newspaper and magazine articles often do not and rely instead on identification of sources in the main text of the document rather than in a works cited or reference list.

19b

How should I document my sources?

How you document sources will depend on your writing situation. Most often, you will

1. provide a reference to your source within the text
2. provide a complete set of citations, or formal acknowledgments, for your sources in a works cited or reference list

The specific format of your in-text citations will depend on the documentation system you use. If you use MLA or APA style, you'll cite—or formally acknowledge—information in the text using parentheses and add a list of sources to the end of your document. If you use the *Chicago* notes style, you'll acknowledge your sources in footnotes or endnotes and supply a bibliography at the end of your document. If you use the CSE citation-sequence style, you will number the citations in your text and list your sources in the order in which they are referenced. If you write an electronic document that cites other online sources, you might simply link to your sources.

Table 19.1 presents examples of in-text citations and works cited or reference list entries for each of these major documentation styles. As Table 19.1 shows, although each style differs from the others, especially in the handling of in-text citations, they share a number of similarities.

With the exception of Web style, key publication information is usually provided in a works cited list, reference list, or bibliography. These lists appear at the end of the document and include the following information about each source.

- author(s) and/or editor(s)
- title
- publication date
- publisher and city of publication (for books)
- periodical name, volume, issue, and page numbers (for articles)
- URL and access date (for online publications)

Each documentation system creates an association between citations in the text of a document and the works cited page.

My Research Project

REVIEW YOUR WORKING BIBLIOGRAPHY

Start by reviewing the source citations in your working bibliography. Make sure that you've used the appropriate documentation system and entered sufficient source information to fully document your sources. If you have used the bibliography tools at **bedfordresearcher.com**, you can select from several documentation systems.

TABLE 19.1 EXAMPLES OF IN-TEXT CITATIONS AND BIBLIOGRAPHIC ENTRIES FOR MAJOR DOCUMENTATION STYLES

STYLE	IN-TEXT CITATION	WORKS CITED OR REFERENCE LIST ENTRY
MLA Style	Over the past few years, the Bolivian government has not seen much economic growth (Gordon 16).	Gordon, Gretchen. "The United States, Bolivia, and the Political Economy of Coca." *Multinational Monitor* 27.1 (2006): 15-20. Print.
APA Style	Over the past few years, the Bolivian government has not seen much economic growth (Gordon, 2006, p.16).	Gordon, G. (2006). The United States, Bolivia, and the political economy of coca. *Multinational Monitor 27*(1), 15-20.
Chicago Style: Notes System	Over the past few years, the Bolivian government has not seen much economic growth.[3] 3. Gretchen Gordon, "The United States, Bolivia, and the Political Economy of Coca," *Multinational Monitor 27*, no. 1 (2006): 16.	Gordon, Gretchen. "The United States, Bolivia, and the Political Economy of Coca." *Multinational Monitor 27*, no. 1 (2006): 15-20. *Note: The citation is placed in a footnote or endnote, and again in the bibliography*
CSE Style: Citation-Sequence System	Over the past few years, the Bolivian government has not seen much economic growth.[3]	3. Gordon G. The United States, Bolivia, and the political economy of coca. Multinational Monitor 2006;27(1):15-20. *Note: Numbered citations are placed in the reference list in the order in which they appear in the text.*
Web Style	Gordon notes that, over the past few years, the Bolivian government has not seen much economic growth.	Many Web documents will link directly to a cited work, as shown here. Or they may use a style such as MLA, APA, *Chicago*, or CSE.

> **QUICK REFERENCE**

Understanding Documentation Systems

☑ Choose an appropriate documentation system. (p. 287)

☑ Document your sources in your text and, depending on the documentation system, create a works cited list, reference list, or bibliography. Review your sources for accuracy and completeness. (p. 289)

V Documenting Sources

Part V
Documenting Sources

19 Understanding Documentation
    Systems
20 **Using MLA Style**
21 Using APA Style
22 Using *Chicago* Style
23 Using CSE Style

20

Using MLA Style

> **Key Questions**
>
> **20a. How do I cite sources within the text of my document?** 294
>
> **20b. How do I prepare the list of works cited?** 297

Modern Language Association (MLA) style, used primarily in the humanities, emphasizes the authors of a source and the pages on which information is located in the source. Writers who use the MLA documentation system cite, or formally acknowledge, source information within their text using parentheses, and they provide a list of sources in a works cited list at the end of their document.

For more information about MLA style, consult the *MLA Handbook for Writers of Research Papers,* Sixth Edition. Information about the MLA Handbook can also be found at www.mla.org.

To see featured writer Elizabeth Leontiev's research essay, formatted in MLA style, turn to page 317.

Insert Web Reference: Use the Bedford Bibliographer at **bedfordresearcher. com** to create an MLA-style bibliography.

ENTRIES IN YOUR WORKS CITED LIST

MLA

V Documenting Sources

20a

How do I cite sources within the text of my document?

MLA style uses parentheses for in-text citations to acknowledge the use of another author's words, facts, and ideas. When you refer to a source within your text, place the author's last name and specific page number(s)—if the source is paginated—within parentheses. Your reader then can go to the works cited list at the end of your document and find a full citation there.

1. Basic Format for Direct Quotation   Often you will want to name the author of a source within your sentence rather than in a parenthetical citation. By doing so, you create a context for the material (words, facts, or ideas) that you are including and indicate where the information from the author begins. When you are using a direct quotation from a source and have named the author in your sentence, place only the page number in parentheses after the quotation. The period follows the parentheses.

> Vargas reports that "each year, unintentional drownings kill more than 830 children younger than 14 and cause, on average, 3,600 injuries" (B01).

When you have not mentioned the author in your sentence, you must place the author's name and the page number in parentheses after the quotation. Again, the period follows the parentheses.

> After car accidents, "drowning is the second-leading cause of unintentional deaths" among toddlers (Vargas B01).

When you are using a block (or extended) quotation, the parenthetical citation comes after the final punctuation and a single space.

If you continue to refer to a single source for several sentences in a row within one paragraph—and without intervening references to another source—you may reserve your reference to the end of the paragraph. However, be sure to include all of the relevant page numbers.

2. Basic Format for a Summary or Paraphrase   When you are summarizing or paraphrasing information gained from a source, you are still required to cite the source. If you name the author in your sentence, place only the page number in parentheses after the paraphrase or summary. Punctuation marks follow the parentheses. When you have not mentioned the author in your sentence, you must place the author's name and the page number in parentheses after the quotation.

> Vargas points out that drowning doesn't happen in the manner you might expect; children slip under water quietly, making very little noise to alert unsuspecting parents or guardians (B01).

3. Entire Source   If you are referring to an entire source rather than to a specific page or pages, you will not need a parenthetical citation.

> The explorations of race in ZZ Packer's *Drinking Coffee Elsewhere* can be linked thematically to the treatment of immigrants in Lahiri's work.

4. Corporate or Group Author   Cite the corporation or group as you would an individual author. You may use abbreviations for the source in subsequent references if you add the abbreviation in parentheses at the first mention of the name.

> The Brown University Office of Financial Aid (BUOFA) has adopted a policy that first-year students will not be expected to work as part of their financial aid package (12). BUOFA will award these students a one-time grant to help compensate for the income lost by not working (14).

5. Unknown Author   If you are citing a source that has no known author, such as the book *Through Palestine with the 20th Machine Gun Squadron*, use a brief version of the title in the parenthetical citation.

> The members of the squadron rode horses while the cooks were issued bicycles, requiring the cooks to exert quite a lot of effort pedaling through the desert sand (*Through Palestine* 17).

6. Two or More Works by the Same Author   For references to authors with more than one work in your works cited list, insert a short version of the title between author and page number, separating the author and the title with a comma.

> (Ishiguro, *Unconsoled* 146)

> (Ishiguro, *Remains* 77)

7. Two or More Authors with the Same Last Name   Include the first initial and last name in the parenthetical citations.

> (G. Martin 354)

> (F. Martin 169)

8. Two or Three Authors   Include the last name of each author in your citation.

> Casting physically attractive actors wins points with film audiences: "Primitive as the association between outward strength and moral force may be, it has its undeniable appeal" (Clarke, Johnson, and Evans 228).

9. Four or More Authors   Use only the last name of the first author and the abbreviation "et al." (Latin for "and others"). Note that there is no comma between the author's name and "et al."

> (Barnes et al. 44)

10. Literary Work   Along with the page number(s), give other identifying information, such as a chapter, scene, or line number, that will help readers find the passage.

> The sense of social claustrophobia is never as palpable in *The Age of Innocence* as when Newland realizes that all of New York society has conspired to cover up what it believes to be an affair between him and Madame Olenska (Wharton 339; ch. 33).

11. Work in an Anthology   Cite the author of the work, not the editor of the anthology. (See also #34 on p. 300.)

> In "Beneath the Deep, Slow Motion," Leo says, "The Chinese call anger a weary bird with no place to roost" (Barkley 163).

12. Sacred Text   Give the name of the edition you are using along with the chapter and verse (or their equivalent).

> He should consider that "Where no counsel is, the people fall: but in the multitude of counselors there is safety" (*King James Bible*, Prov. 11.14).

> In the Qu'ran, sinners are said to be blind to their sins ("The Cow" 2.7).

13. Two or More Works   Use a semicolon to separate entries.

> Forethought is key in survival, whether it involves remembering extra water on a safari trail or gathering food for a long winter in ancient times (Wither and Hosking 4; Estes and Otte 2).

14. Source Quoted in Another Source   Ideally, you will be able to find the primary, or original, source for material used in your research project document. If you quote or paraphrase a secondary source—a source that contains information about a primary source—use the abbreviation "qtd. in" (for "quoted in") when you cite the source.

> President Leonid Kuchma insisted that "we cannot in any instance allow the disintegration or division of Ukraine" (qtd. in Lisova A1).

15. Print Source without Page Numbers   If no page numbers are provided, list only the author's name in parentheses.

Although his work has been influenced by many graphic artists, it remains essentially text-based (Fitzgerald).

16. Electronic or Nonprint Source   Give a page, section, paragraph, or screen number, if numbered, in the parenthetical citation.

Teters believes the mascots dehumanize Native Americans, allowing spectators to dismiss the Native Americans' true culture as well as their hardships (Saraceno, par. 20).

20b

How do I prepare the list of works cited?

MLA-style research documents include a reference list titled "Works Cited," which begins on a new page at the end of the document. If you wish to acknowledge sources that you read but did not cite in your text, you may title the list "Works Consulted" and include them. The list is alphabetized by author. If the author's name is unknown, alphabetize the entry using the title of the source. To cite more than one work by the same author, use the author's name in the first entry. Thereafter, use three hyphens followed by a period in place of the author's name; list the entries alphabetically by title. All entries in the list are double-spaced, with no extra space between entries. Entries are formatted with a hanging indent: The first line of an entry is flush with the left margin and subsequent lines are indented one-half inch or five spaces.

In longer documents, a list of works cited may be given at the end of each chapter or section. In electronic documents that use links, such as a Web site, the list of works cited is often a separate page to which other pages are linked. To see a works cited list in MLA style, see p. 317.

> Use the Bedford Bibliographer at bedfordresearcher.com to create an MLA-style bibliography.

Books, Conference Proceedings, and Dissertations

17. One Author

Samet, Elizabeth D. *Soldier's Heart: Reading Literature through Peace and War at West Point*. New York: Farrar, 2007. Print.

18. Two or Three Authors   List all the authors in the same order as on the title page, last name first for only the first author listed. Use commas to separate authors' names.

Cathcart, Thomas, and Daniel Klein. *Plato and a Platypus Walk into a Bar: Understanding Philosophy through Jokes*. New York: Abrams, 2007. Print.

Gastman, Roger, Caleb Neelon, and Anthony Smyrski. *Street World: Urban Culture and Art from Five Continents*. New York: Abrams, 2007. Print.

19. Four or More Authors Provide the first author's name (last name first) followed by a comma, and then the abbreviation "et al." (Latin for *and others*).

Rauschenberg, Christopher, et al. *Paris Changing: Revisiting Eugène Atget's Paris*. Princeton: Princeton Architectural, 2007. Print.

20. Corporate or Group Author Write out the full name of the corporation or group, and cite the name as you would an author. This name is often also the name of the publisher.

National Geographic. *Renaissance and Reformation*. Washington: Natl. Geographic, 2007. Print.

21. Unknown Author When no author is listed on the title or copyright page, begin the entry with the title of the work. Alphabetize the entry by the first word of the title other than *A*, *An*, or *The*.

Through Palestine with the 20th Machine Gun Squadron. MacLean: IndyPublish, 2007. Print.

22. Two or More Books by the Same Author List the entries alphabetically by title.

Chopra, Deepak. *Buddha: A Story of Enlightenment*. New York: HarperCollins, 2007. Print

- - -. *Life after Death: The Burden of Proof*. New York: Three Rivers, 2008. Print.

23. Editor(s) Use the abbreviation "ed." or "eds."

Law-Viljoen, Bronwyn, ed. *William Kentridge Flute*. New York: Krut, 2007. Print.

24. Translated Book List the author first and then the title, followed by the name of the translator and publication information. Use the abbreviation "Trans."

Eco, Umberto. *On Ugliness*. Trans. Alastair McEwen. New York: Rizzoli, 2007. Print.

25. Book in a Language Other Than English You may give a translation of the book's title in brackets.

Márquez, Gabriel García. *Cien años de soledad: Edición conmemorativa* [*One Hundred Years of Solitude: Commemorative Edition*]. Miami: Santillana, 2007. Print.

26. Edition Other Than the First Include the number of the edition and the abbreviation "cd." after the title.

Pitts, Brenda G., and David K. Stotlar. *Fundamentals of Sport Marketing*. 3rd
ed. Morgantown: Fitness, 2007. Print.

27. Multivolume Work   Include the total number of volumes and the abbreviation "vols." after the title.

Taylor, Quintard. *From Timbuktu to Katrina: Sources in African-American
History*. 2 vols. Boston: Wadsworth, 2007. Print.

If you have used only one of the volumes in your document, include the volume number after the title. Then list the total number of volumes after the medium of publication.

Campbell, Gordon. *The Grove Encyclopedia of Classical Art and Architecture*.
Vol. 1. New York: Oxford UP, 2007. Print. 2 vols.

28. Book in a Series   If a series name and/or number appears on the title page, include it at the end of the citation, after the medium. If the word "Series" is part of the series name, use the abbreviation "Ser."

Lamb, Mary E. *The Popular Culture of Shakespeare, Spenser and Jonson*. New
York: Routledge, 2006. Print. Routledge Studies in Renaissance Literature.

29. Republished Book   Indicate the original date of publication after the title.

Melville, Herman. *Moby Dick*. 1851. London: Random, 2007. Print.

30. Book with a Title within the Title

Pitcher, John. *Chaucer's Feminine Subjects: Figures of Desire in* The
Canterbury Tales. New York: Palgrave, 2008. Print.

31. Author with an Editor   Include the name of the editor (first name first) after the title.

Oakley, Gladys. *The Wind Still Whispers*. Ed. Gail P. Main. Charleston:
BookSurge, 2007. Print.

32. Anthology   To cite an anthology of essays, stories, or poems or a collection of articles, list the editor or editors first (as on the title page), followed by the abbreviation "ed." or "eds."

Wise, L. G., ed. *Appalachian Short Fiction Anthology*. Louisville: Greenvue,
2007. Print.

33. Foreword, Introduction, Preface, or Afterword   Begin with the author of the part you are citing and the name of that part. Continue with the title of the work and its author (first name first), following "By." At the end of the entry, list the inclusive page numbers on which the part of the book appears.

Sedaka, Neil. Foreword. *Doo Wop: The Music, the Times, the Era.* By Bruce Morrow and Rich Maloof. New York: Sterling, 2007. 3-12. Print.

If the author of the foreword or other part is also the author of the work, use only the last name after "By."

Lott, John R. Introduction. *Freedomnomics: Why the Free Market Works and Other Half-Baked Theories Don't.* By Lott. Washington: Regnery, 2007. 1-14. Print.

If the foreword or other part has a title, include the title in quotation marks between the author and the name of the part.

Nordhaus, Ted. "From the Nightmare to the Dream. " Introduction. *Break Through: From the Death of Environmentalism to the Politics of Possibility.* By Michael Shellenberger. New York: Houghton, 2007. 1-19. Print.

34. Chapter in an Edited Book or Selection in an Anthology   Begin your citation with the author and the title of the chapter or selection. Follow this with the title of the anthology or collection, the abbreviation "Ed" (meaning "Edited by"), and names of the editors (first name first) as well as publication information. At the end of your entry, give the inclusive page numbers for the selection or chapter.

Voivod, Lani. "Why Aren't You Blogging?" *The New Writer's Handbook 2007: A Practical Anthology of Best Advice for Your Craft and Career.* Ed. Philip Martin. Minneapolis: Scarletta, 2007. 216-18. Print.

35. Two or More Works from One Anthology   To avoid repeating the same information about the anthology several times, include the anthology itself in your list of works cited.

Remnick, David, ed. *Secret Ingredients:* The New Yorker *Book of Food and Drink.* New York: Random, 2007. Print.

In the entries for individual selections or chapters, list the author and title of the selection (in quotations marks) and cross-reference the anthology by giving the editor's name and the page numbers on which the selection appears, with no comma between them. Do not include the medium of publication.

Bourdain, Anthony. "Don't Eat Before Reading This." Remnick 83-89.

36. Screenplay

Reitman, Jason. *Thank You for Smoking: The Shooting Script.* New York: Newmarket, 2007. Print.

37. Published Proceedings of a Conference   Provide information as you would for a book, adding information about the conference after the title: the date, sponsors, and location of the conference. Then add the publication data as for a book. End with the medium.

Becker, Michael, and Andrew McKenzie, eds. *Proceedings of the 3rd*
    Conference on the Semantics of Underrepresented Languages in the
    Americas. 11-13 May 2007, Graduate Linguistics Student Assn., UMass
    Amherst. Amherst: GLSA, 2007. Print.

38. Paper Published in Proceedings of a Conference   Treat a selection from conference proceedings as you would a selection in an edited collection.

Smith, Carlota S., and Ellavina Tsosie Perkins. "Temporal Inference of
    Zero-marked Clause in Navajo." *Proceedings of the 3rd Conference on*
    the Semantics of Underrepresented Languages in the Americas. Eds.
    Michael Becker and Andrew McKenzie. 11-13 May 2007, Graduate
    Linguistics Student Assn., UMass Amherst. Amherst: GLSA, 2007.
    121-34. Print.

39. Sacred Text   Include the title of the version as it appears on the title page. If the title does not identify the version, place that information directly after the title.

The Dhammapada. Trans. Eknath Easwaran. Tomales: Nilgiri, 2007. Print.

40. Published Dissertation or Thesis   Cite as you would a book, with the title in italics, but include information specific to the dissertation, such as the school, the year the dissertation was accepted.

Smith, Thomas B. *Democratic Writing Pedagogy and the Southern Nevada*
    Writing Project. Diss. U of Nevada Las Vegas, 2007. Ann Arbor: UMI,
    2007. Print.

41. Unpublished Dissertation or Thesis   Place the title of the thesis or dissertation in quotation marks and add information about the type of dissertation, the school, and the date.

Adedokun, Olajide. "Future Aspirations of Indiana Rural Education." Diss.
    Purdue U, 2007. Print.

42. Abstract of a Dissertation or Thesis   Treat an abstract as you would an article in a journal. First give the information for the dissertation. Then add the source, abbreviated either *DA* or *DAI* (for *Dissertation Abstracts* or *Dissertation Abstracts International*), volume number, year (in parentheses), and page number.

Kennedy-O'Neill, Joy D. "The Sacred and the Sublime: Caves in American
    Literature." Diss. Indiana U of Pennsylvania, 2007. *DAI* 68.3 (2007):
    3258663. Print.

Sources in Journals, Magazines, and Newspapers

43. Article in a Journal Paginated by Volume Most journals continue pagination for an entire year, beginning again at page 1 only in the first volume of the next year. After the journal title, list the volume number and issue number (if any) with a period between them, the year of publication in parentheses, a colon, and inclusive page numbers. End with the medium.

Yang, Gene. "Graphic Novels in the Classroom." *Language Arts* 85.3 (2008):
    352-64. Print.

44. Article in a Journal Paginated by Issue Some journals begin at page 1 for every issue. After the volume number, add a period and the issue number, with no space.

Nicholls, Richard E. "The Scientist's Fresh Eye. " *American Scholar* 76.2
    (2007): 144. Print.

45. Article That Skips Pages Give only the first page number and a plus sign (+), with no space between.

Steinberg, Jacques. "Don't Worry, Be Students." *New York Times Magazine* 30
    Sept. 2007: 53+. Print.

46. Article with a Quotation in the Title Enclose the quotation in single quotation marks within the article title, which is enclosed in double quotation marks.

Jones, Vanessa E. "'They're Sitting Right next to Us': On College Campuses,
    Students Continue to Struggle with Ethnic Tensions and Racist
    Attitudes." *Boston Globe* 5 Dec. 2007: F1+. Print.

47. Article in a Monthly or Bimonthly Magazine After the author's name and title of the article, list the title of the magazine, the date (use abbreviations for all months except May, June, and July), and the inclusive pages.

Marko, Merrill. "Love for Sale?" *Real Simple* Jan. 2008: 52-57. Print.

48. Article in a Weekly or Biweekly Magazine Give the exact date of publication, inverted.

Rudnick, Paul. "I Hit Hamlet: Behind the Scenes at a Broadway Fiasco." *New
    Yorker* 24 Dec. 2007: 82-90. Print.

49. Article in a Daily Newspaper   If the title of the newspaper begins with *The*, omit the word. If the newspaper is not a national newspaper (such as the *Wall Street Journal, Christian Science Monitor,* or *Chronicle of Higher Education*) or the city of publication is not part of its title, give the name of the city in square brackets [Salem, OR] after the title. List the date in inverted order and, if the masthead indicates that the paper has more than one edition, give this information after the date ("natl. ed.," "late ed."). Follow with a colon and a space, and end with the page numbers (use the section letter before the page number if the newspaper uses letters to designate sections). If the article does not appear on consecutive pages, write only the first page number and a plus sign (+), with no space between.

Sang-Hun, Choe. "Where Boys Were Kings, a Shift toward Baby Girls." *New York Times* 23 Dec. 2007: A1+. Print.

50. Unsigned Article in a Newspaper or Magazine   Begin with the title of the article. Alphabetize by the first word other than *A, An,* or *The.*

"Wick Burning Down on Chance to See Wax Sculpture Exhibit." *Town Crossings* [Boxford, MA] 13 Dec. 2007: 4. Print.

51. Editorial in a Newspaper   Include the word "Editorial" after the title.

"How to Clean Up Baseball's Mess." Editorial. *San Francisco Chronicle* 14 Dec. 2007: B12. Print.

52. Letter to the Editor   Include the word "Letter" after the title.

Simmonds, Scott. "Covered in a Flood or Just Covered in Deep Water?" Letter. *Wall Street Journal* 29 Nov. 2007: A17. Print.

53. Review   After the author and title of the review, include the words "Rev. of," followed by the title of the work under review; a comma; the word "by" (for a book) or "dir." (for a play or film); and the name of the author or director. Continue with publication information for the review.

Thomson, Desson. "'Youth': Coppola's Dizzying Spin on Fleeting Time.'" Rev. of *Youth without Youth,* dir. Francis Ford Coppola. *Washington Post* 11 Jan. 2008: C01. Print.

54. Published Interview   Begin with the person interviewed. If the published interview has a title, give it in quotation marks. If not, write the word "Interview" (no quotation marks or italics). If an interviewer is identified and relevant to your project, give that name next. Then supply the publication data.

Barris, George. "Q & A." Interview by Dave Kinney. *Automobile* Dec. 2007: 20. Print.

MLA

V Documenting Sources

55. Article in a Special Issue   After the author and the title of the article (in quotation marks) include the title of the special issue (in italics), then write the words "Spec. issue of" before the regular title of the periodical.

Feldman, Elliot. "Old Hippy in Hollywood." *View of the Arts 2007*. Spec. issue
    of *Scene 4 Magazine* Jan. 2007: 72-79. Print.

Print Reference Works

56. Encyclopedia, Dictionary, Thesaurus, Handbook, or Almanac   Cite as you would a book (see p. 297).

57. Entry in an Encyclopedia, Dictionary, Thesaurus, Handbook, or Almanac
In many cases, the entries and articles in reference works are unsigned. Therefore, begin your citation with the title of the entry in quotation marks, followed by a period. Give the title of the reference work, italicized, and the edition and year of publication. Include the editor's name if the reference work is not well known. If the entries in the work are arranged alphabetically, you may omit the volume and page numbers.

"Cheese." *McGraw-Hill Encyclopedia of Science and Technology*. 10th ed. 2007.
    Print.

If you cite a specific definition, include that information after the title of the entry, adding the abbreviation "Def." and the number of the definition.

"Heterodox." Def. 1. *The American Heritage College Dictionary*. 4th ed. 2007.
    Print.

If a reference work is not well known (perhaps because it includes highly specialized information), provide all of the bibliographic information.

Schroeder, David. "Aesthetics." *The Cambridge Mozart Encyclopedia*. Ed. Cliff
    Eisen and Simon P. Keefe. Cambridge: Cambridge UP, 2006. Print.

58. Map or Chart   Generally, treat a map or chart as you would a book without authors. Give its title (italicizes), the word "Map" or "Chart," and publication information. For a map in an atlas, give the map title (in quotation marks) followed by publication information for the atlas and page numbers for the map. If the creator of the map or chart is listed, use his or her name as you would an author's name.

Benchmark Road and Recreation: Nevada. Map. Chicago: Rand, 2007. Print.

"Africa: Political." Map. *Oxford Atlas of the World*. 11th ed. London: Oxford
    UP, 2007. 105. Print.

59. Government Publications   In most cases, cite the government agency as the author. If there is a named author, editor, or compiler, provide that name after the title. Use the abbreviations "Dept." for department, "Cong." for Congress, "S." for

Senate, "H." or "HR" for House of Representatives, "Res." for resolution, "Rept." for report, "Doc." for document, and "GPO" for Government Printing Office.

United States. Dept. of Educ. Office of Innovation and Improvement. *Connecting Students to Advanced Courses Online.* Washington: ED Pubs, 2007. Print.

For congressional bills (not reports or resolutions), do not include a period after the abbreviations "S" or "HR".

If you are citing from the *Congressional Record,* the entry is simply *Cong. Rec.* followed by the date, a colon, and the page numbers.

60. Pamphlet   Format the entry as you would for a book (see p. 297).

American Diabetes Association. *Everyday Choices for a Healthier Life.* Alexandria: Amer. Diabetes Assn., 2007. Print.

Field Sources

61. Personal Interview   Place the name of the person interviewed first, words to indicate how the interview was conducted ("Personal interview," "Telephone interview," or "E-mail interview"), and the date.

Templeton, Santo. Personal interview. 26 Feb. 2008.

62. Unpublished Letter   If written to you, give the writer's name, the words "Letter to the author" (no quotation marks or italics), and the date the letter was written. End with the form of the material: use "MS" (for manuscript) for a letter written by hand and "TS" (for typescript) for typed letters.

Wilden, Raquel. Letter to the author. 11 May 2008. TS.

If the letter was written to someone else, give that name rather than "the author."

63. Lecture or Public Address   Give the speaker's name and the title of the lecture (if there is one). If the lecture was part of a meeting or convention, identify that event. Conclude with the event data, including venue, city, and date. End with the appropriate label ("Lecture," "Panel discussion," "Reading").

Anam, Tahmima. Harvard Book Store, Cambridge. 10 Jan. 2008. Reading.

Media Sources

64. Film or Video Recording   Generally begin with the title of the film or recording (italicized). Always supply the name of the director (following the abbreviation "Dir."), the distributor, and the year of original release. You may also insert other relevant information, such as the names of performers or screenplay writers, before the distributor.

Letters from Iwo Jima. Screenplay by Iris Yamashita. Dir. Clint Eastwood. Perf.
Ken Watanabe and Kazunari Ninomiya. Amblin Entertainment, 2007. Film.

If you wish to emphasize an individual's role in the film or movie, such as the
director or screenplay writer, you may list that name first.

Olivier, Laurence, dir. and perf. *Hamlet*. Paramount, 1948. Film.

For media other than film (such as videotape and DVD), cite it as for a film but
identify the medium at the end.

Guess Who's Coming to Dinner. Dir. Stanley Kramer. 1967. Sony Pictures
Home Entertainment, 2008. DVD.

65. Television Program   If the program has named episodes or segments, list
those in quotation marks. Then include the title of the program or series (italicized), the network, the station's call letters and city (if any), and the date on
which you watched the program. If there are relevant persons to name (such as
an author, director, host, narrator, or actor), include that information after the
title. Add the medium at the end.

"A New Day." *The Wire*. HBO. 28 Dec. 2007. Television.

66. Radio Program   Cite as you would a television program.

Fresh Air. Host Terry Gross. Natl. Public Radio. WHYY, Philadelphia. 19 Mar.
2008. Radio.

67. Radio or Television Interview   Provide the name of the person interviewed
and the title of the interview. If there is no title, write "Interview" and, if relevant, the name of the interviewer. Then provide the name of the program, the
network, the call letters of the station, the city, and the date.

Joel, Billy. Interview by Katie Couric. *CBS Evening News*. CBS. KCTV, Kansas
City, MO. 20 Dec. 2007. Television.

68. Sound Recording   Begin with the name of the person whose work you
want to highlight: the composer, the conductor, or the performer. Next list the
title, followed by names of other artists (composer, conductor, performers), with
abbreviations indicating their roles. The recording information includes the
manufacturer and the date. Add the medium of the recording at the end (CD,
LP, Audiocassette, Audiotape, or MP3 file).

Gershwin, George. *Rhapsody in Blue*. Royal Philharmonic Orch. Cond. Leonard
Slatkin. EMI Gold, 2007. CD.

If you wish to cite a particular track on the recording, give its performer and
title (in quotation marks) and then proceed with the information about the

recording. For live recordings, include the date of the performance between the title and the recording data.

Cash, Johnny. "Folsom Prison Blues." *The Great Lost Performance*. Rec. 27 July 1990. Island, 2007. MP3 file.

69. Musical Composition   Give the composer and title. Italicize the title unless it identifies the composition by form ("symphony," "suite"), number ("op. 39," "K. 231"), or key ("E flat").

Berlioz, Hector. Symphonie Fantastique. op. 14.

If you are referring to a published score, provide publication data as you would for a book. Insert the date of composition between the title and the publication information and capitalize the abbreviations *no.* and *op.*

McKinley, Roger. *Jackson Pollock the Musical*. 2007. Manchester: Michael Butterworth, 2007. Print.

70. Live Performance   Generally, begin with the title of the performance (italicized). Then give the author and director; the major performers; and theater, city, and date.

The Importance of Being Earnest. By Oscar Wilde. Dir. Spiro Veloudos. Perf. Hannah Barth and Robert Bonnatto. Lyric Stage, Boston. 9 May 2008. Performance.

71. Work of Art   Give the name of the artist, the title of the work (italicized), the date of composition, the medium of composition, and the name of the collection, museum or owner, and the city. If you are citing artwork published in a book, add the publication information for the book and the medium of publication ("Print") at the end.

Attia, Kader. *Sleeping from Memory*. 2007. Foam and plywood. Inst. of Contemporary Art, Boston.

72. Advertisement   Provide the name of the product, service, or organization being advertised, followed by the word "Advertisement." Then provide the usual publication information.

BlackBerry. Advertisement. *Inc*. Dec. 2007: 13. Print.

73. Cartoon   Treat a cartoon like an article in a newspaper or magazine. Give the cartoonist's name, the title of the cartoon if there is one (in quotation marks), the word "Cartoon," and the publication data for the source.

Chast, Roz. "Philosophers on Strike." Cartoon. *New Yorker* 3 Dec. 2007: 96. Print.

Electronic Sources

74. Article from an Online Database or Subscription Service.   Cite it as you would a print article, then give the name of the database in italics, the medium consulted ("Web"), and the date you accessed the article. (See also p. 315.)

Hergenhan, Laurie. "Beautiful Lies, Ugly Truths. " *Overland* 187 (Winter 2007): 42-46. *Expanded Academic ASAP.* Web. 6 Mar. 2008.

75. Abstract from an Online Database   Provide the publication information for the source, followed by the word "Abstract," the name of the database, the medium ("Web"), and the date you accessed it.

Randall, Kelli. "Depictions of Marriage: Fictions of Race and Gender in the Age of Realism." Diss. Emory U, 2007. *DAI* 68 (2007): 3264. Abstract. *UMI ProQuest.* Web. 11 Feb. 2008.

76. Entire Web Site   Provide the name of the Web site in italics, the sponsor or publisher, the date of publication or last update, the medium, and the date of access.

Skin Deep Cosmetic Safety Database. Environmental Working Group, 2007. Web. 17 Jan. 2008.

77. Work from a Professional or Commercial Web Site   Include the author (if available), the title of the document in quotation marks, and the title of the Web site in italics. Then give the sponsor or publisher, the date of publication or last update, the medium, and the access date. (See also p. 316.)

Thompson, Michael. "Helping America's Boys." *PBS Parents.* PBS, 2008. Web. 8 Feb. 2008.

78. Academic Course or Department Web Site   For a course page, give the name of the instructor, the course title in italics, a description such as "Course home page," the course dates, the department, the institution, the medium, and the access date. For a department page, give the department name, a description such as "Home page," the institution, the date of the last update, the medium, and your access date.

Agatucci, Cora. *WR 123: English Composition III (Research-based Academic Writing).* Course home page. Winter 2008. Humanities Dept., Central Oregon Community Coll. Web. 20 Jan. 2008.

Dept. of English and Technical Communication. Home page. Missouri U of Science and Technology, 2008. Web. 22 Mar. 2009.

79. Work from a Personal Web Site   Include the name of the person who created the site. If the site has no title, give a description such as "Home page." Then follow with the sponsor of the Web site, the date of the last update, the medium ("Web"), and your date of access.

Gaiman, Neil. Home page. Harper Collins, 2009. Web. 5 Jan. 2009.

80. Message Posted to a Newsgroup, Electronic Mailing List, or Online Discussion Forum   Cite the name of the person who posted the message; the title (from the subject line, in quotation marks); if the posting has no title, add the phrase "Online posting"; then add the name of the Web site (italicized), the sponsor or publisher, the date of the message, the medium ("Web"), and the date you accessed the posting.

Kenyon, Rochelle. "New Dyslexia Theory Blames 'Noise.'" *Learning Disabilities
    Discussion List*. Natl. Inst. for Literacy, 10 Jan. 2007. Web. 20 Feb. 2008.

81. Article Posted on a Wiki

"Surrealism." *Wikipedia*. Wikimedia Foundation, 1 Jan. 2008. Web. 3 Jan.
    2008.

82. Entire Blog   To cite an entire Weblog, give the author (if available), the title of the Weblog (italicized), the sponsor or publisher (if none, use "N.p."), the date of publication or last update, the medium ("Web"), and the date of access.

Green, Tyler. *Modern Art Notes*. ArtsJournal.com, 1 Jan. 2008. Web. 1 Jan.
    2008.

83. Entry or Comment Posted on a Blog   To cite an entry or a comment on a Weblog, give the author of the entry or comment (if available), the title of the entry or comment in quotation marks, the title of the blog (italicized), the sponsor or publisher, the date the material was posted, the medium, and the access date.

Ramirez, Cristina. "Tex-Mex Music: Hybridity of Culture and Class."
    Revolutionary Rhetoric: Nuestro Puesto. N.p., 4 Mar. 2007. Web. 17 Jan.
    2008.

84. Email message   Cite the sender of the message; the title (from the subject line, in quotation marks); "Message to" the recipient of the message; the date of the message; and the medium ("E-mail"). (Note that MLA style is to hyphenate "e-mail.")

Willford, Latrisha. "Critique of 'Anna's Ordinary Blues.'" Message to the
    author. 19 Aug. 2008. E-mail.

Pabon, Xavier. "Brainstorming for Essay." Message to Brayden Perry. 24 Apr.
2008. E-mail.

85. Online Book   Cite an online book as you would a print book; then give
title of the database or Web site (italicized), the medium ("Web"), and the access
date (see also #17 on p. 297).

Hughes, Claire. *Dressed in Fiction.* Oxford: Berg, 2006. *Google Book Search.*
Web. 13 Jan. 2008.

86. Article in an Online Periodical   Provide the author, the title of the article
(in quotation marks), and the name of the Web site (in italics). Then add the
publisher or sponsor, the date of publication, the medium, and your date of access (see also #43 on p. 302).

Quirk, Matthew. "Bright Lights, Big Cities." *The Atlantic.com.* Atlantic
Monthly Group, Dec. 2007. Web. 15 Dec. 2007.

87. Online Poem   Cite an online poem as you would a print poem, followed by
the name of the site, the sponsoring organization (if any), the date of publication
or latest update, the medium, and the date of access.

Farrokhzad, Forugh. "In Night's Cold Streets." Trans. Sholeh Wolpé. *Sin.*
Fayetteville: U of Arkansas P, 2007. *Verse Daily.* Verse Daily, 2007. Web.
16 Apr. 2008.

88. Online Editorial or Letter to the Editor   Include "Letter" or "Editorial"
after the title (if any). Follow with the title of the Web site, the sponsor or
publisher, the date of publication, medium, and date of access (see also #51 and
#52 on p. 303).

Spiegel-Coleman, Shelly. "Learning Languages Enriches Children." Letter. *Los
Angeles Times.* Los Angeles Times, 1 Jan. 2008. Web. 12 Jan. 2008.

89. Online Review   (See also #53 on p. 303.)

Emerson, Bo. "90-year-old's Memoir Filled with Ageless Lessons on Race."
Rev. of *When We Were Colored: A Mother's Story* by Eva Rutland. *Atlanta
Journal-Constitution.* Atlanta Journal-Constitution, 21 May 2007. Web.
16 Feb. 2008.

90. Entry in an Online Reference Work   (See also #57 on p. 304.)

"Existentialism. " *Encyclopaedia Britannica Online.* Encyclopaedia Britannica,
2008. Web. 23 Jan. 2008.

91. Online Film or Video Clip   (See also #64 on p. 305.)

Washington, Denzel, dir. *The Great Debaters*. 2007. *Apple Movie Trailers*. Web.
    2 Feb. 2008.

"35th Annual Electric Car Rally!" *YouTube*. YouTube, 26 Aug. 2007. Web. 5
    Feb. 2008.

92. Online Work of Art or Image   Cite like a work of art but omit the medium
of composition, and after the location, add the title of the Web site or database
(italicized), the medium consulted ("Web"), and your date of access. (See also
#71 on p. 307.)

Johns, Jasper. *Perilous Night*. 1982. Natl. Gallery of Art, Washington.
    National Gallery of Art. Web. 10 Mar. 2008.

Haglundc. *Coyote Watching*. 4 Feb. 2008. *Flickr.com*. Web. 26 Mar. 2008.

93. Online Map or Chart   (See also #58 on p. 304.)

"Fareless Square." Map. *TriMet.org*. Tri-County Metropolitan Transportation
    District of Oregon, 2008. Web. 19 Feb. 2008.

94. Online Advertisement   Give the item or organization being advertised
followed by the word "Advertisement." Then add the information about the
Web site. (See also #72 on p. 307.)

Minisode Network. Advertisement. *MySpace*. MySpace.com, 2008. Web. 25
    Jan. 2008.

95. Other Online Sources   For other online sources, adapt the guidelines to
the medium. Include as much information as necessary for your readers to easily
find your source. The examples below are for a radio program available in an
online archive, and an online archive of oral-history interviews.

"Nice Work If You Can Get It." Host Ira Glass. *This American Life*. Chicago
    Public Radio. WBEZ, Chicago. 6 Apr. 2007. MP3 file. 8 June 2008.

Nguni, Mweupe Mfalme. "Recess Came and the Boys Had a Football..."
    StoryCorps. StoryCorps, n.d. Web. 2 Jan. 2008.

96. CD-ROM   Treat a CD-ROM as you would a book, noting "CD-ROM" as
the medium.

Orman, Suze. *Stop Identity Theft Now Kit*. Salt Lake City: TrustID, 2008. CD-
    ROM.

97. Multidisc CD-ROM   Either give the total number of discs or, if you used only one of the discs, give the number of that disc.

Lindley, Philip, and Alex Moseley. *English Parish Churches*. Turnhout, Belg.:
    Brepols, 2007. CD-ROM. Disc 2.

98. Computer Software or Video Game   Cite computer software as you would a book. Provide additional information about the medium on which it is distributed (CD-ROM, Xbox 360, etc.) and the version.

Unchartered: Drake's Fortune. Foster City: Sony Computer Entertainment,
    2007. CD-ROM.

TUTORIAL

How do I cite books using MLA style?

When citing a book, use the information from the title page and the copyright page (on the reverse side of the title page), not from the book's cover or a library catalog.

Consult pp. 297-302 for additional models for citing books.

A **B**

Hajdu, David. *The Ten-Cent Plague: The Great Comic-Book Scare and How It*

C **D** **E** **F**

Changed America. New York: Farrar, Straus and Giroux, 2008. Print.

A **The author.** Give the last name first, followed by a comma, the first name, and the middle initial (if given). Omit titles such as *MD, PhD,* or *Sir;* include suffixes after the name and a comma (O'Driscoll, Gerald P., Jr.). End with a period.

B **The title.** Give the full title; include the subtitle (if any), preceded by a colon. Italicize the title and subtitle; capitalize all major words. End with a period.

C **The city of publication.** If more than one city is given, use the first one listed. For a city that may be unfamiliar to your readers or confused with another city, add an abbreviation of the country or province (Birmingham, Eng.). Insert a colon.

D **The publisher.** Give a shortened version of the publisher's name (*Harper* for HarperCollins Publishers; *Harcourt* for Harcourt Brace; *Oxford UP* for Oxford University Press). Do not include the words *Publisher* or *Inc.* Follow with a comma.

E **The year of publication.** If more than one copyright date is given, use the most recent one. Use "n.d." if no date is given. End with a period.

F **The medium of publication.** Use *Print.* End with a period.

Use the bibliography tools at **bedfordresearcher.com** to create a bibliography formatted in MLA style.

TUTORIAL

How do I cite articles from periodicals using MLA style?

Periodicals include journals, magazines, and newspapers. This page gives an example of a citation for a print journal article. Models for citing articles from magazines and newspapers are on pp. 302-04.

If you need to cite a periodical article you accessed electronically, follow the guidelines below and see also p. 308.

Zachary, G. Paschal. "The Coming Revolution in Africa." *Wilson Quarterly*

D **E**   **F** **G**

32.1 (2008): 50-66. Print.

A **The author.** Give the last name first, followed by a comma, the first name, and the middle initial (if given). Omit titles such as *MD, PhD,* or *Sir;* include suffixes after the name and a comma (O'Driscoll, Gerald P., Jr.). End with a period.

B **The article title.** Give the full title; include the subtitle (if any), preceded by a colon. Enclose the title and subtitle in quotation marks, and capitalize all major words. Place a period inside the closing quotation mark.

C **The periodical title.** Italicize the periodical title; exclude any initial *A, An,* or *The*; capitalize all major words.

D **The volume number and issue number.** For journals, include the volume number; if the journal uses issue numbers, include a period (no space) and then the issue number as well.

E **The date of publication.** For journals, give the year in parentheses followed by a colon. For monthly magazines, don't use parentheses; give the month and year. For weekly magazines and newspapers, don't use parentheses; give the day, month, and year (in that order). Abbreviate the names of all months except May, June, and July.

F **Inclusive page number(s).** For numbers 100 and above, give only the last two digits and any other preceding digits if different from the first number (22-28, 402-10, 1437-45, 592- 603). If an article continues on nonconsecutive pages, include the first page number followed by a plus sign. Include section letters for newspapers, if relevant. End with a period.

G **The medium of publication.** For print publications, use *Print.* End with a period.

Use the bibliography tools at **bedfordresearcher.com** to create a bibliography formatted in MLA style.

TUTORIAL

How do I cite articles from databases using MLA style?

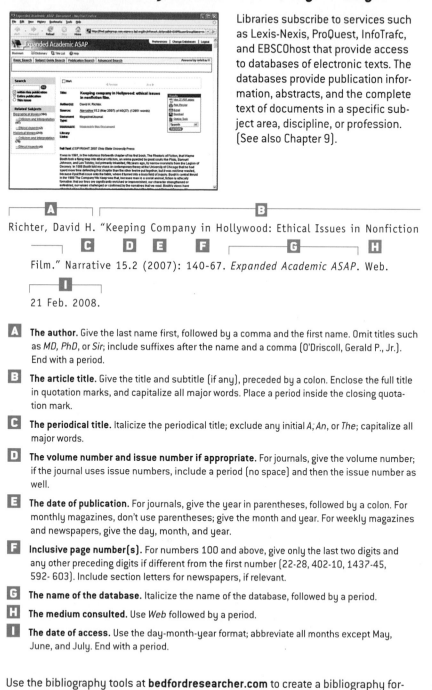

Libraries subscribe to services such as Lexis-Nexis, ProQuest, InfoTrafc, and EBSCOhost that provide access to databases of electronic texts. The databases provide publication information, abstracts, and the complete text of documents in a specific subject area, discipline, or profession. (See also Chapter 9).

A   **B**

Richter, David H. "Keeping Company in Hollywood: Ethical Issues in Nonfiction

C **D** **E** **F** **G** **H**

Film." *Narrative* 15.2 (2007): 140-67. *Expanded Academic ASAP*. Web.

I

21 Feb. 2008.

A **The author.** Give the last name first, followed by a comma and the first name. Omit titles such as *MD, PhD,* or *Sir*; include suffixes after the name and a comma (O'Driscoll, Gerald P., Jr.). End with a period.

B **The article title.** Give the title and subtitle (if any), preceded by a colon. Enclose the full title in quotation marks, and capitalize all major words. Place a period inside the closing quotation mark.

C **The periodical title.** Italicize the periodical title; exclude any initial *A, An,* or *The*; capitalize all major words.

D **The volume number and issue number if appropriate.** For journals, give the volume number; if the journal uses issue numbers, include a period (no space) and then the issue number as well.

E **The date of publication.** For journals, give the year in parentheses, followed by a colon. For monthly magazines, don't use parentheses; give the month and year. For weekly magazines and newspapers, give the day, month, and year.

F **Inclusive page number(s).** For numbers 100 and above, give only the last two digits and any other preceding digits if different from the first number (22-28, 402-10, 1437-45, 592- 603). Include section letters for newspapers, if relevant.

G **The name of the database.** Italicize the name of the database, followed by a period.

H **The medium consulted.** Use *Web* followed by a period.

I **The date of access.** Use the day-month-year format; abbreviate all months except May, June, and July. End with a period.

Use the bibliography tools at **bedfordresearcher.com** to create a bibliography formatted in MLA style.

TUTORIAL

How do I cite works from Web sites using MLA style?

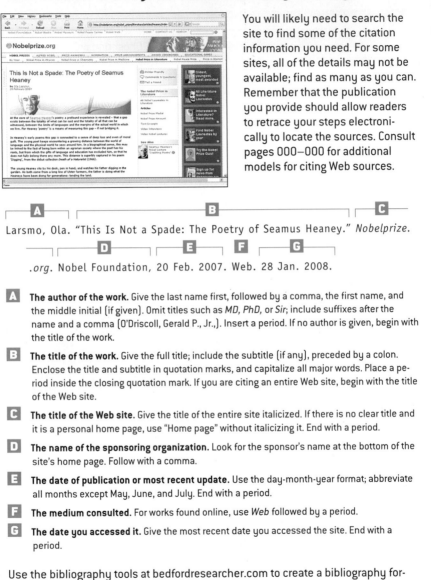

You will likely need to search the site to find some of the citation information you need. For some sites, all of the details may not be available; find as many as you can. Remember that the publication you provide should allow readers to retrace your steps electronically to locate the sources. Consult pages 000–000 for additional models for citing Web sources.

A | **B** | **C**

Larsmo, Ola. "This Is Not a Spade: The Poetry of Seamus Heaney." *Nobelprize.*

D | **E** | **F** | **G**

.org. Nobel Foundation, 20 Feb. 2007. Web. 28 Jan. 2008.

A **The author of the work.** Give the last name first, followed by a comma, the first name, and the middle initial (if given). Omit titles such as *MD, PhD,* or *Sir*; include suffixes after the name and a comma (O'Driscoll, Gerald P., Jr.,). Insert a period. If no author is given, begin with the title of the work.

B **The title of the work.** Give the full title; include the subtitle (if any), preceded by a colon. Enclose the title and subtitle in quotation marks, and capitalize all major words. Place a period inside the closing quotation mark. If you are citing an entire Web site, begin with the title of the Web site.

C **The title of the Web site.** Give the title of the entire site italicized. If there is no clear title and it is a personal home page, use "Home page" without italicizing it. End with a period.

D **The name of the sponsoring organization.** Look for the sponsor's name at the bottom of the site's home page. Follow with a comma.

E **The date of publication or most recent update.** Use the day-month-year format; abbreviate all months except May, June, and July. End with a period.

F **The medium consulted.** For works found online, use *Web* followed by a period.

G **The date you accessed it.** Give the most recent date you accessed the site. End with a period.

Use the bibliography tools at bedfordresearcher.com to create a bibliography formatted in MLA style.

MLA-Style Research Essay

Leontiev   1

Elizabeth Leontiev

Professor Lynda Haas

WR 39C

10 June 2007

Coca Is Not the Enemy

To most Americans, the word *cocaine* evokes images of the illegal white powder and those who abuse it, yet the word has a different meaning to the coca farmers of South America. *Erythroxylum coca*, or the tropical coca plant, has been grown in the mountainous regions of Colombia, Bolivia, and Peru since 3000 BC (Gibson). The coca plant has been valued for centuries by indigenous South American cultures for its ability to alleviate pain and combat fatigue and hunger (Forero, "Bolivia's Knot"). Just as many Americans drink coffee every day, natives of the Andes Mountains chew coca leaves and drink coca tea for a mild stimulant effect. Easy to grow, not addictive, and offering many medicinal benefits, coca is part of the everyday lives of the people in this region.

Aside from its medicinal and cultural value, coca is also important to Andean farmers economically, as a result of a long history of illegal drug trafficking. Dried coca leaves mixed with lime paste or alkaline ashes produce cocaine—a highly addictive substance that delivers euphoric sensations accompanied by hallucinations (Gibson). Supplying the coca for the illegal drug trade accounts for a tremendous portion of the Bolivian, Peruvian, and Colombian economies. In Bolivia, for example, it has been estimated that coca makes up anywhere from one-third to three-quarters of the country's total exports; in 1990 the Bolivian president even asserted that 70% of the Bolivian gross domestic product was due to the coca trade (Kurtz-Phelan 108).

Despite such statistics, for most farmers in the region growing coca is about making a living and supporting their families, not becoming wealthy or furthering the use of cocaine. More than half of Bolivians live in poverty, with a large portion earning less than $2 a day (U.S. Foreign Affairs, Defense, and Trade Div 2). In the words of one coca farmer, "'The U.S. says 'Coca is cocaine, coca is cocaine,' but it isn't,' says Argote. 'Coca is the tree of the poor'" (Schultz and Gordon). Can we reduce cocaine trafficking without eliminating coca? Evo Morales, the current president of Bolivia, believes the answer is "yes" and has advocated a "zero cocaine, not zero coca" policy in his country. This policy would allow native Andeans to maintain their cultural practices, boost South American economies, and channel coca into a new market, away from cocaine traffickers. For all of these reasons, the Morales plan should become a model for other coca-growing countries.

Morales gained recognition for his "zero cocaine, not zero coca" program during his 2005 presidential campaign. His policy aims to legalize the coca crop but not the cocaine that is produced from that crop. He also expressed a desire to get the United Nations to rescind its 1961 convention declaring coca an illegal narcotic. In December 2005, Morales won the election with more than 50% of the vote, and he made history as the first indigenous Bolivian president (Forero, "Coca").

Morales's plan promotes the best interests of the Andean farmers and offers multiple economic and social benefits. First, South American countries would be able to export non-narcotic coca-based products, such as soaps, toothpaste, tea, alcohol, and candies (Logan). Products like these are already being produced for local use in Bolivia, and manufacturers would like to seek an international market for them. These new coca products would stimulate the Bolivian economy and put money in the pockets of coca growers to support their families, rather than in the pockets of the drug lords. Second, if the market for legal coca were to increase, farmers would be able to make a legal living from a crop that has long been a mainstay of their culture. With legal coca products, the indigenous people of the Andes would not have to sacrifice their way of life. Finally, an increase in the demand for legal coca products might also result in less cocaine being trafficked illegally around the world, since more of the raw material for cocaine will be used for new legal coca products. In order to understand the benefits of Morales's plan, we must first investigate the failures of the alternatives. The United States has been waging various "wars on drugs" for decades, spending up to $1 billion trying to control cocaine trafficking from South America (Forero, "Bolivia's Knot"). In the 1990s the United States shifted its efforts from fighting the trafficking of cocaine to eliminating the source of the drug—the coca plants growing in Bolivia, Colombia, and Peru. Coca eradication has taken two main forms. In Bolivia, bands of soldiers move through the countryside using machetes to hack away coca plants (see Fig. 1). This process is slow and dangerous, and there have been reports of human rights abuses and extreme violence against the peasant farmers who grow coca (Gordon 16). In nearby

---

Margin annotations:

A brief title distinguishes two sources by the same author.

Elizabeth addresses counter-arguments and provides support for her assertion.

Reference to a photograph included in the essay

Leontiev   3

Colombia, the United States funded aerial fumigation programs to poison the coca fields; native farmers complain that the herbicide used in the fumigation is causing health problems and environmental pollution ("US Weighs Cost"). By destroying coca plants in Colombia, the United States has "left 500 million people poorer" (Padgett 8). It is unclear whether fumigation results in any benefit, since farmers respond by moving farther and farther into the jungle and replanting their crops there (Otis). Such dense areas are harder to see and therefore harder to fumigate effectively.

FIG. 1. **Manual eradication of a coca field in Chapare, Bolivia. United Nations Office on Drugs and Crime.**

> Caption includes figure number and source information.

Another U.S. effort encouraged farmers to replace coca with other crops, like coffee, bananas, and pineapples. Alternative crop programs seem like a good idea because they will get rid of the coca farms, but they have their own drawbacks. First, as coca grower Leonida Zurita-Vargas noted in her 2003 *New York Times* opinion column, transporting heavy fruits like pineapples from the mountainous coca-growing regions is expensive and difficult. Second, growers are seldom willing to give up coca farming because they can make more money by selling coca than any other crop. Even with government incentives for alternative cropping, coca remains more profitable, a big inducement for poor farmers who can barely support their families and send their children to school. The *Houston Chronicle* reports that even in areas where farmers have planted alternative crops, the farmers are being lured back to the coca plant by larger profits (Otis). One coca farmer asserted that by growing coca,

> The in-text citation provides just the author's name, since the online source did not include page numbers.

he could "make ten times what he would make by growing pineapples or yucca" (Harman). Ultimately, alternative cropping means less coca production overall, which will drive up coca prices and encourage more farmers to abandon their alternative crops and return to coca.

After decades of legislation and various eradication programs, cocaine trafficking remains a major problem. The most recent data show that coca cultivation throughout the region remains steady (see Fig. 2). Contrary to dire predictions, there has been no major spike in Bolivian coca production since Morales was elected at the end of 2005. Furthermore, critics argue that cocaine is no less available in the United States than before eradication began, and street prices remain low (Forero, "Colombia's Coca"). Instead of curbing cocaine trafficking, America's war on drugs has turned out to be a war against the peasants of Colombia, Bolivia, and Peru.

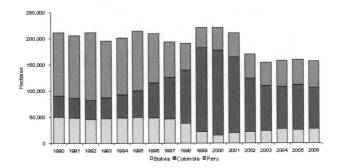

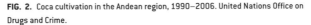

FIG. 2. Coca cultivation in the Andean region, 1990–2006. United Nations Office on Drugs and Crime.

Throughout the years, the various wars on drugs have failed to produce effective results for the United States. The programs of alternative crop-ping and eradication did not succeed due to the legislators' inability to see life through the eyes of the coca farmers—something Evo Morales is able to do. In 2006, Morales addressed the UN General Assembly and waved a coca leaf in the air: "[This] is a green coca leaf, it is not the white of cocaine. [T]his coca leaf represents Andean culture; it is a coca leaf that represents the environment and the hope of our peoples." Through his bold program of "zero cocaine, not zero coca," Morales aims to improve the lives of Andean farmers and the economies of South American countries, while still remaining committed to controlling the illegal drug trade. Morales's example illustrates that it is time to work *with* coca farmers, rather than against them.

The conclusion reinforces Elizabeth's thesis statement.

Leontiev   5

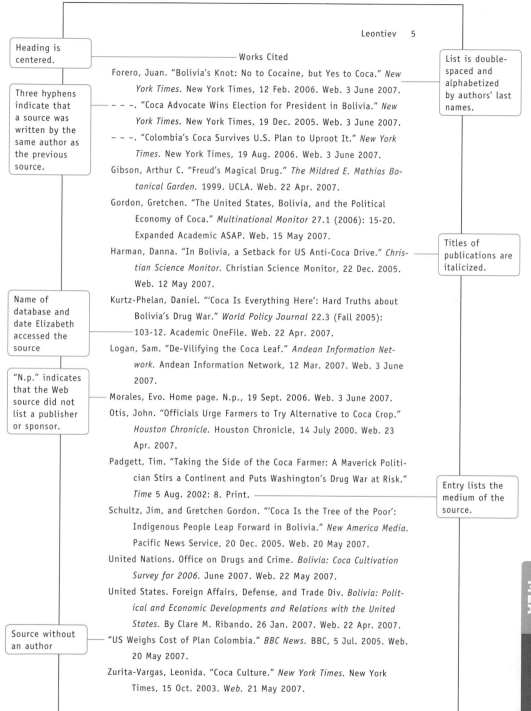

Heading is centered.

Works Cited

List is double-spaced and alphabetized by authors' last names.

Forero, Juan. "Bolivia's Knot: No to Cocaine, but Yes to Coca." *New York Times*. New York Times, 12 Feb. 2006. Web. 3 June 2007.

Three hyphens indicate that a source was written by the same author as the previous source.

– – –. "Coca Advocate Wins Election for President in Bolivia." *New York Times*. New York Times, 19 Dec. 2005. Web. 3 June 2007.

– – –. "Colombia's Coca Survives U.S. Plan to Uproot It." *New York Times*. New York Times, 19 Aug. 2006. Web. 3 June 2007.

Gibson, Arthur C. "Freud's Magical Drug." *The Mildred E. Mathias Botanical Garden*. 1999. UCLA. Web. 22 Apr. 2007.

Gordon, Gretchen. "The United States, Bolivia, and the Political Economy of Coca." *Multinational Monitor* 27.1 (2006): 15-20. Expanded Academic ASAP. Web. 15 May 2007.

Titles of publications are italicized.

Harman, Danna. "In Bolivia, a Setback for US Anti-Coca Drive." *Christian Science Monitor*. Christian Science Monitor, 22 Dec. 2005. Web. 12 May 2007.

Name of database and date Elizabeth accessed the source

Kurtz-Phelan, Daniel. "'Coca Is Everything Here': Hard Truths about Bolivia's Drug War." *World Policy Journal* 22.3 (Fall 2005): 103-12. Academic OneFile. Web. 22 Apr. 2007.

Logan, Sam. "De-Vilifying the Coca Leaf." *Andean Information Network*. Andean Information Network, 12 Mar. 2007. Web. 3 June 2007.

"N.p." indicates that the Web source did not list a publisher or sponsor.

Morales, Evo. Home page. N.p., 19 Sept. 2006. Web. 3 June 2007.

Otis, John. "Officials Urge Farmers to Try Alternative to Coca Crop." *Houston Chronicle*. Houston Chronicle, 14 July 2000. Web. 23 Apr. 2007.

Padgett, Tim. "Taking the Side of the Coca Farmer: A Maverick Politician Stirs a Continent and Puts Washington's Drug War at Risk." *Time* 5 Aug. 2002: 8. Print.

Entry lists the medium of the source.

Schultz, Jim, and Gretchen Gordon. "'Coca Is the Tree of the Poor': Indigenous People Leap Forward in Bolivia." *New America Media*. Pacific News Service, 20 Dec. 2005. Web. 20 May 2007.

United Nations. Office on Drugs and Crime. *Bolivia: Coca Cultivation Survey for 2006*. June 2007. Web. 22 May 2007.

United States. Foreign Affairs, Defense, and Trade Div. *Bolivia: Political and Economic Developments and Relations with the United States*. By Clare M. Ribando. 26 Jan. 2007. Web. 22 Apr. 2007.

Source without an author

"US Weighs Cost of Plan Colombia." *BBC News*. BBC, 5 Jul. 2005. Web. 20 May 2007.

Zurita-Vargas, Leonida. "Coca Culture." *New York Times*. New York Times, 15 Oct. 2003. Web. 21 May 2007.

MLA

∨ Documenting Sources

21

Using APA Style

Key Questions

21a. How do I cite sources within the text of my document? 325

21b. How do I prepare the reference list? 328

American Psychological Association (APA) style, used primarily in the social sciences and in some of the natural sciences, emphasizes the author(s) and publication date of a source. Writers who use the APA documentation system cite, or formally acknowledge, information within their text using parentheses and provide a list of sources, called a reference list, at the end of their document. For more information about APA style, consult the *Publication Manual of the American Psychological Association,* Sixth Edition, and the *APA Style Guide to Electronic References.* Information about these publications can be found on the APA Web site at apa.org. To see Alexis Alvarez's research essay, formatted in APA style, turn to p. 343.

CITATIONS WITHIN YOUR TEXT

1. Basic format for direct quotation   325
2. Basic format for summary or paraphrase   326
3. Two authors   326
4. Three, four, or five authors   326
5. More than five authors   326
6. Corporate or group author   327
7. Unknown author   327
8. Two or more works   327
9. Source quoted in another source   327
10. Source with no page numbers   327
11. Two or more authors with the same last name   328
12. Email and other personal communication   328
13. Document from a Web site   328

ENTRIES IN YOUR REFERENCE LIST

Books, Conference Proceedings, and Dissertations

14. One author   329
15. Two or more authors   329

21a

How do I cite sources within the text of my document?

APA uses an author-date form of in-text citation to acknowledge the use of another writer's words, facts, or ideas. When you refer to a source, insert a parenthetical note that gives the author's last name and the year of the publication, separated by a comma. Even when your reference list includes the day or month of publication, the in-text citation should include only the year. For a quotation, the citation in parentheses also includes the page(s) on which the quotation can be found, if the source has page numbers. Note that APA style requires using the past tense or present perfect tense to introduce the material you are citing: *Renfrew argued* or *Renfrew has argued*.

1. Basic Format for Direct Quotation   When you are using a direct quotation from a source and have named the author in your sentence, place the publication date in parentheses directly after the author's last name. Include the page number (with "p." for page) in parentheses after the quotation.

> Cialdini (2007) noted "a well-known principle of human behavior that says when we ask someone to do us a favor, we will be more successful if we provide a reason" (p. 4).

If you are using a direct quotation from a source and have not mentioned the author's name in your sentence, place the author's last name, the publication date, and the page number in parentheses.

> (Simeon, 2008, p. viii).

APA

V Documenting Sources

2. Basic Format for Summary or Paraphrase   When you are summarizing or paraphrasing, place the author's last name and date either in the sentence or in parentheses at the end of the sentence. Include a page or chapter reference if it would help readers find the original material in a longer work.

> Bray (2007) found that parents, educators, politicians, academics, and agencies worldwide all compare and study educational issues for vastly different reasons (p. 15).

> Parents are unique in that they are solely interested in comparing and studying education issues at various levels only as they pertain to their children's age-appropriate needs (Bray, 2007, p. 16).

3. Two Authors   List the last names of both authors in every mention in the text. If you mention the authors' names in a sentence, use the word "and" to separate the last names, as shown in the first example. If you place the authors' names in the parenthetical citation, use an ampersand (&) to separate the last names, as shown in the second example.

> Dobransky and Stamford (2007) wrote that "the *mammalian brain* (midbrain) is responsible for all things emotional" (p. 3).

> Our midbrain is responsible for our emotional responses to personal events that don't necessarily have anything to do with primal issues like reproduction or survival (Dobransky & Stamford, 2007, p. 3).

4. Three, Four, or Five Authors   In parentheses, name all the authors the first time you cite the source, using an ampersand (&) before the last author's name. In subsequent references to the source, use the last name of the first author followed by the abbreviation "et al." (Latin for *and others*).

> Continued study of the Russian Revolution remains relevant as it is just as important to understand *what* happened as *why* it happened (Petrunkevitch, Harper, Golder, & Kerner, 2007). The modern Yugo-Slav movement cannot be understood outside the context of the world wars (Petrunkevitch et al., 2007)

5. More Than Five Authors   In all references to the source, give the first author's last name followed by "et al."

> Yeomans et al. (2007) noted that borderline personality disorder has a profound effect on family members who never know what to expect except instability and chronic chaos.

6. Corporate or Group Author   In general, cite the full name of the corporation or group the first time it is mentioned in your text. If you add an abbreviation for the group in square brackets the first time you cite the source, you can use the abbreviation in subsequent citations.

> Careful planning is one of the most effective behaviors for dealing with anxiety (American Psychological Association [APA], 2007, p. 1). Anxiety often leads to procrastination or impulsive behavior, in the wake of which success is not likely to result (APA, 2007, p. 1).

7. Unknown Author   Sources with unknown authors are listed by title in the list of references. In your in-text citation, shorten the title as much as possible without introducing confusion. Add quotation marks to article titles, and italicize book titles.

> The debate over evolution and creationism continues in the wake of recent scientific discoveries ("Fossil," 2008).

If a source identifies its author as "Anonymous," use that word to cite the author of the source.

> The rise in water levels along the Missouri River has been referred to as a national crisis (Anonymous, 2008).

8. Two or More Works   List the sources in alphabetical order and separate them with semicolons. If you are referring to two or more sources by the same author, order those sources chronologically.

> Lack of effective communication while trying to exert control makes it difficult to set boundaries and accept the subject's ambitions and exertions (Castillo & Nugent, 2007; Timothy & Igler, 2008).

9. Source Quoted in Another Source   Ideally, you will be able to find the primary, or original, source for material used in your research project document. If you quote or paraphrase a secondary source—a source that contains information about a primary source—mention the primary source and indicate that it was cited in the secondary source. Include the secondary source in your reference list.

> Thieu et al. (2006) has shown that pediatricians should screen all children for autism at their 18- and 24-month checkups (as cited in Delanson, 2008, p. 15).

10. Source with No Page Numbers   Many Web sources lack stable page numbers. If the source has numbered paragraphs, include the paragraph number using the abbreviation "para." If the paragraphs are not numbered, include the section heading and indicate which paragraph in that section you are referring to.

Devaney (2007) suggested that psychotherapy or psychological counseling coupled with careful attention to medical and nutritional needs is the most effective and long-lasting treatment for an eating disorder ("Treatments," para. 3).

11. Two or More Authors with the Same Last Name   Use the authors' initials in each citation.

While C. W. Mills (2006) has advocated viewing these issues as societal ones, not just a personal problem of a particular man or woman, D. Mills (2007) has suggested that issues such as homelessness and hunger can become impersonal and overlooked as a result.

12. Email and Other Personal Communication   Give the first initial(s) and last name of the person with whom you corresponded, the words "personal communication," and the date. Don't include personal communication in your reference list.

(A. L. Chan, personal communication, October 9, 2008)

13. Document from a Web Site   To cite a quotation from a Web site, give the page number or paragraph number, if indicated, and include the source in your reference list.

O'Loughlin (2008) has shown that many students need "direct instruction rather than just unfettered exploration in order to learn" (para. 5).

21b

How do I prepare the reference list?

The reference list contains publication information for all sources that you have cited within your document, with one main exception. Personal communications—such as correspondence, email messages, and interviews—are cited only in the text of the document.

Begin the list on a new page at the end of the document and center the title "References" at the top. Organize the list alphabetically by author; if the source is an organization, alphabetize the source by the name of the organization. All of the entries should be double-spaced with no extra space between entries. Entries are formatted with a hanging indent: The first line of an entry is flush with the left margin and subsequent lines are indented one-half inch or five spaces. In longer documents, a reference list could be given at the end of each chapter or section. In electronic documents that use links, such as Web sites, the reference list is often a separate page to which other pages are linked. For an example of a reference list in APA style, see p. 351.

Books, Conference Proceedings, and Dissertations

14. One Author

Collier, P. (2007). *The bottom billion: Why the poorest countries are failing and what can be done about it*. New York, NY: Oxford University Press.

15. Two or More Authors

List the authors in the same order as the title page does, each with last name first. Use commas to separate authors and use an ampersand (&) before the final author's name. List every author up to seven; for a work with more than seven authors, give the first six names followed by a comma, three ellipsis dots, and the final author's name. (Do not use an ampersand.)

Kraybill, D. B., Nolt, S. M., & Weaver-Zercher, D. L. (2007). *Amish grace: How forgiveness transcended tragedy*. San Francisco, CA: Jossey-Bass.

16. Corporate or Group Author

Write out the full name of a corporate or group author. If the corporation is also the publisher, use "Author" for the publisher's name.

National Geographic. (2007). *Inside China*. Washington, DC: Author.

17. Unknown Author

When there is no author listed on the title or copyright page, begin the entry with the title of the work. Alphabetize the entry by the first significant word of the title (not including *A, An,* or *The*).

On the road of life. (2007). Naperville, IL: Sourcebooks.

18. Two or More Works by the Same Author(s)

Give the author's name in each entry and list the works in chronological order.

Kozol, J. (2006). *The shame of the nation: The restoration of apartheid schooling in America*. New York, NY: Crown.

Kozol, J. (2007). *Letters to a young teacher*. New York, NY: Crown.

19. Translated Book

List the author first followed by the year of publication, the title, and the translator (in parentheses, identified by the abbreviation "Trans."). Place the original date of the work's publication at the end of the entry.

Nietzsche, F. (2007). *Homer and classical philology* (J. M. Kennedy, Trans.). Charleston, SC: BookSurge. (Original work published 1908)

20. Book in a Series

Bourchier, D. (2008). *Illiberal democracy in Indonesia*. Politics in Asia
[Series]. New York, NY: Routledge.

21. Republication

Woolf, V. (2007). *A room of one's own*. Cutchogue, NY: Buccaneer. (Original
work published 1929)

22. Book in an Edition Other Than the First   Note the edition ("2nd ed.," "Rev. ed.") after the title.

Sowell, T. (2007). *Basic economics: A common sense guide to the economy*
(3rd ed.). New York, NY: Basic Books.

23. Multivolume Work   Include the number of volumes in parentheses after the title.

Dickinson, D. K., & Neuman, S. B. (Eds.). (2007). *Handbook of early literacy
research*. (Vols. 1-2). New York, NY: Guilford.

If you have used only one volume in a multivolume work, identify that volume
by number and by title.

Yogananda, P. (2007). *The wisdom of Yogananda: Vol. 2. Karma and
reincarnation*. Nevada City, CA: Crystal Clarity.

24. Editor   Include "Ed." or "Eds." in parentheses.

Tobier, N. (Ed.). (2007). *Voices of Sag Harbor: A village remembered*.
New York, NY: Harbor.

25. Author with an Editor   Include the editor's name and the abbreviation "Ed." in parentheses after the title.

Seay, G. L. (2007). *The art of conversation* (P. J. Bean, Ed.). Washington,
DC: Woodrow Wilson Center Press.

26. Anthology   To cite an entire anthology of essays or collection of articles, list the editor or editors first, followed by the abbreviation "Ed." or "Eds." in parentheses.

Chittick, W. C. (Ed.). (2007). *The inner journey: Views from the Islamic
tradition*. Sandpoint, ID: Morning Light.

27. Chapter in an Edited Book or Selection in an Anthology   Begin the entry with the author, the publication date, and the title of the chapter or selection

(not italicized). Follow this with the names of the editors (initials first) and the abbreviation "Ed." or "Eds." in parentheses, the title of the anthology or collection (italicized), inclusive page numbers for the chapter or selection (in parentheses, with abbreviation "pp."), and place and publisher.

Weil, A. (2007). Why people take drugs. In J. A. Inciardi & K. McElrath (Eds.), *The American drug scene: An anthology* (pp. 4-13). New York, NY: Oxford University Press.

28. Foreword, Introduction, Preface, or Afterword Treat as you would a chapter in a book.

Wilson, E. O. (2007). Foreword. In N. Gingrich and T. L. Maple, *A contract with the earth* (pp. ix-x). Baltimore, MD: Johns Hopkins University Press.

29. Published Proceedings of a Conference Cite information as you would for a book.

Doherty, G. W. (Ed.). (2007). *Proceedings of the 5th Rocky Mountain region disaster mental health conference.* Ann Arbor, MI: Loving Healing Press.

30. Paper Published in the Proceedings of a Conference Treat a conference paper as you would a selection from an edited collection.

Justice, P. (2007). Care for the caretaker. In G. W. Doherty (Ed.), *Proceedings of the 5th Rocky Mountain region disaster mental health conference* (pp. 89-92). Ann Arbor, MI: Loving Healing Press.

31. Sacred Text Treat as you would a book (see p. 329).

The Holy Bible: King James version. (2007). Peabody, MA: Hendrickson.

32. Published Dissertation or Thesis If a published dissertation or thesis is available through a database, give the author, date, title, and a description in parentheses ("Doctoral dissertation" or "Master's thesis"). Then give information about the database and any accession or order number in parentheses.

Smith, J. (2007). Essays on psychology and economics (Doctoral dissertation). Available from ProQuest Dissertations and Theses database. (UMI No. 3247808)

33. Unpublished Dissertation or Thesis Format as you would a book, replacing the publisher information with the phrase "Unpublished doctoral dissertation" or "Unpublished master's thesis," followed by information about the college or university.

Connolly, P. (2007). *A comparison of two forms of spatial ability development treatment* (Unpublished doctoral dissertation). Purdue University, West Lafayette, Indiana.

34. Abstract of a Dissertation or Thesis Treat an abstract as you would an article in a journal. Follow with the *Dissertation Abstracts International* information obtained from UMI.

San Martin, D. (2007). Treatment goals of adult mental health patients: A literature review. *Dissertation Abstracts International, 68*(04). (UMI No. 3264598)

Sources in Journals, Magazines, and Newspapers

35. Article in a Journal Paginated by Volume Most journals continue page numbers throughout an entire annual volume, beginning again at page 1 only in the first volume of the next year. After the author and publication year, provide the article title, the journal title, the volume number (italicized), and the inclusive page numbers.

Malgady, R. G. (2007). How skewed are psychological data? A standardized index of effect size. *The Journal of General Psychology, 134,* 355-359.

36. Article in a Journal Paginated by Issue Some journals begin at page 1 for every issue. Include the issue number (in parentheses, not italicized) after the volume number.

Gravener, J. A., Heedt, A. A., Heatherton, T. F., & Keel, P. K. (2008). Gender and age differences in associations between peer dieting and drive for thinness. *International Journal of Eating Disorders, 41*(1), 57-63.

37. Article in a Magazine The author's name and the publication date are followed by the title of the article, the magazine title (italicized), and the volume number, if any (also italicized). Include all page numbers.

Drury, B. (2007, December). Abandoned on the home front. *Men's Health, 22*(10), 186-192.

38. Article in a Newspaper List the author's name and the complete date (year first). Next give the article title followed by the name of the newspaper (italicized). Include all page numbers, preceded by "p." or "pp."

Egelko, B. (2007, December 14). Mental patients sue governor. *San Francisco Chronicle,* p. B5.

39. Unsigned Article in a Newspaper   Begin with the article title, and alphabetize in the reference list by the first word in the title other than *A, An,* or *The.* Use "p." or "pp." before page numbers.

Lead taints many toys, says health groups' tests. (2007, December 5). *The Boston Globe,* p. C2.

40. Letter to the Editor   Include the words "Letter to the editor" in square brackets after the title of the letter, if any.

Hanks, Steven D. (2007, November 29). E-prescription issues [Letter to the editor]. *The Wall Street Journal,* p. A17.

41. Review   After the title of the review, include the words "Review of the book . . . " or "Review of the film . . . " and so on in brackets, followed by the title of the work reviewed.

Hunter, S. (2007, December 21). "Charlie Wilson": Firing on all cylinders [Review of the film *Charlie Wilson's war*]. *The Washington Post,* p. C01.

When the review is untitled, follow the date with the bracketed information.

Horwitz, J. (2007, December 7). [Review of the film *The golden compass*]. *The Washington Post,* p. WE36.

42. Published Interview   Cite a published interview like a journal article (see p. 332).

Smith, S. (January 2008). Q & A: Jack Pitney. *Automobile, 22*(10), 66.

43. Two or More Works by the Same Author in the Same Year   List the works alphabetically and include lowercase letters (*a, b,* etc.) after the dates.

Travis, J. (2007a). London's super-lab faces hurdles. *Science, 318,* 1704-1705.

Travis, J. (2007b). New animal-rights attacks. *Science, 318,* 1853.

Print Reference Works

44. Encyclopedia, Dictionary, Thesaurus, Handbook, or Almanac   Cite a reference work, such as an encyclopedia or a dictionary, as you would a book (see p. 329).

Ritzer, G. (Ed.). (2007). *The Blackwell encyclopedia of sociology.* Boston, MA: Wiley-Blackwell.

45. Entry in an Encyclopedia, Dictionary, Thesaurus, Handbook, or Almanac   Begin your citation with the name of the author or, if the entry is unsigned, the title of the entry. Proceed with the date, the entry title (if not already given), the title of the reference work, the edition number, and the pages. If the contents of the reference work are arranged alphabetically, omit the volume and page numbers.

Scott, J., & Marshall, G. (2007). Adolescence. In *Dictionary of sociology* (p. 6). New York, NY: Oxford University Press.

46. Government Publication   Give the name of the department (or office, agency, or committee) that issued the report as the author. If the document has a report or special file number, place that in parentheses after the title.

U.S. Department of Health and Human Services. (2007). *Women's health in the U.S.: Research on health issues affecting women* (NIH Publication No. 04-4697). Washington, DC: Government Printing Office.

47. Pamphlet   Format the entry as you would a book (see p. 329).

Rosie's Place. (2007). *Rosie's Place . . . creating community: A directory of programs and happenings.* Boston, MA: Author.

Field Sources

48. Personal Interview   Treat unpublished interviews as personal communications and include them in your text only (see p. 328). Do not cite personal interviews in your reference list.

49. Letter   Cite a personal letter only in the text (see p. 328), not in the reference list.

50. Lecture or Public Address   Cite a lecture or public address the same way you would cite an unpublished paper presented at a conference.

Suarez-Orozco, C., & Suarez-Orozco, M. (2007, December 13). *Learning a new land: Immigrant students in American society.* Lecture presented at Harvard University, Cambridge, MA.

Media Sources

51. Film or Video Recording   List the director and producer (if available), the date of release, the title followed by "Motion picture" in square brackets, the country where the film was made, and the studio or distributor.

Burton, T. (Director). (2007). *Sweeney Todd* [Motion picture]. United States: DreamWorks.

52. Television Program   Cite as you would a chapter in a book. List the director (if available), the broadcast date, the title followed by "Television broadcast" or "Television series episode" in square brackets. Then add information on the series, location, and station.

Gaviria, M. (Writer, Producer & Director), & Cohen, W. (Co-Producer).
     (2008, January 8). The medicated child [Television series episode].
     In D. Fanning (Executive Producer), *Frontline*. Boston, MA: WGBH.

53. Radio Program   List the host, the broadcast date, the title followed by "Radio broadcast," or "Radio series episode," in square brackets.

Lyden, J. (Host). (2007, December 7). The perils of perfectionism [Radio
     series episode]. In W. Stephenson (Senior Producer), *On point*. Boston,
     MA: WBUR.

54. Sound Recording   Name the author of the song; the date; the song title followed by "On" and the recording title in italics; the medium (in square brackets); and the production data.

DiFranco, A. (2007). Subdivision. On *Canon* [MP3]. Buffalo, NY: Righteous
     Babe Records.

Electronic Sources

55. Article with a DOI   A DOI (Digital Object Identifier) is a unique number assigned to specific content, such as a journal article. If a DOI is available, include it; you do not need to provide a database name or URL.

Griffith, L. C. (2008). Neuroscience: Love hangover. *Nature, 451*(7174),
     24-25. doi:10.1038/451024a

56. Article without a DOI   If no DOI (Digital Object Identifier) is provided, give the exact URL for the article or for the home page of the journal, if access requires a subscription.

Abbott, J. M., & Byrd-Bredbenner, C. (2007). The state of the American diet:
     How can we cope? *Topics in Clinical Nutrition, 22*(3), 202-233. Retrieved
     from http://www.topicsinclinicalnutrition.com

If the article comes from a database, give the URL of the home page of the journal.

Pruett, J.M., Nishimura, N.J., & Priest, R. (2007). The role of meditation in
     addiction recovery. *Counseling and Values, 52*(1), 71-84. Retrieved from
     http://www.counseling.org

57. Article in an Online Periodical   Publication information is followed by the URL. Since the article was published online, it is unlikely to have page numbers. Note that the first example is for an online journal, while the second is for online magazine content not found in the print version.

Brunk-Chavez, B., & Miller, S. J. (2007). Decentered, disconnected, and digitized: The importance of shared space. *Kairos, 11*(2). Retrieved from http://kairos .technorhetoric.net/11.2/binder.html?topoi/brunk-miller/index.html

Barrett, J. (2007, December 28). Wealth and waistlines [Online exclusive]. *Newsweek*. Retrieved from http://www.newsweek.com/id/82258

58. Online Book   Cite the electronic version only if a print version is not available or is hard to find.

Shrout, R. N. (n.d.). *True hypnotism*. Retrieved from http://www .onlineoriginals.com/showitem.asp?itemID=253

59. Entry in an Online Reference Work   Give the URL for the home or index page.

Cultural anthropology. (2008). In *Encyclopædia Britannica*. Retrieved from http://www.britannica.com/eb/

60. Nonperiodical Web Document   For a stand-alone Web source, such as a report, an online brochure, or a blog, cite as much of the following information as possible: author, publication date, document title, and the URL. Include a retrieval date before the URL if the material is likely to be changed or updated, or if it lacks a set publication date, edition, or version number. A retrieval date is generally not necessary when citing electronic books and journal articles.

Zamora, D. (2007, December 14). *13 healthy habits to improve your life*. Retrieved from http://www.webmd.com/balance/features/13-healthy- habits-to-improve-your-life

For a chapter or section within a Web document, identify the section as well as the main document.

Søreide, T. (2007). Business corruption: speak out or take part? In *Global corruption report 2007* (chap. 18). Retrieved from http://www .transparency.org/content/download/19093/263155

For a document within a government agency, university, or other complex Web site, include the name of the agency or organization before the URL.

American Psychological Association. (n.d.). *Careers in psychology*. Retrieved from the American Psychological Association website: http://www.apa. org/topics/psychologycareer.html

61. Email Message or Real-Time Communication   Because email messages are difficult or impossible for your readers to retrieve, APA does not recommend including them in your reference list. You should treat them as personal communications and cite them parenthetically in your text (see #12 on p. 328).

62. Article Posted on a Wiki   Since the material on a Wiki is likely to change, include a retrieval date.

Sensory analysis. (2007, June 1). Retrieved January 7, 2008, from The
    Psychology Wiki: http://psychology.wikia.com/wiki/Sensory_analysis

63. Message Posted to a Newsgroup, Electronic Mailing List, or Online Discussion Forum   List the author, posting date, message title, and a description of the message in brackets. Then add the retrieval information, including the name of the list or forum.

Hellebust, L. (2007, August 7). Think tank industry subject of new white
    paper [Electronic mailing list message]. Retrieved from the Political
    Science Research and Teaching List: http://www.h-net.org/~psrt/

64. Entry on a Blog   To cite an entry on a Web log, give the author (or screen name, if available), the date the material was posted, the title of the entry, a description of the entry in brackets, and the URL. To cite a comment on a blog post, use the description "Web log comment" in brackets.

Mankiw, G. (2007, December 5). The limits of egalitarianism [Web log post].
    Retrieved from http://gregmankiw.blogspot.com/2007/12/limits-of-
    egalitarianism.html

65. Video Posted on a Blog   After the title of the video, include the words "Video file" in brackets and then "Video posted to" before the URL. If there is no author's name, list the screen name provided.

Kaufmann, S. (2007, December 26). Bilingual texts and language learning
    [Video file]. Retrieved from http://thelinguist.blogs.com/how_to_learn_
    english_and/2007/12/bilingual-texts.html

Lisajparker. (2007, February 20). How to make an origami boat [Video file].
    Retrieved from http://www.youtube.com/watch?v=iuqVpMdb1NM

66. Image Posted on a Blog

MeetaK. (2007, January 24). Indian spices #1 [Photograph]. Retrieved from
    http://www.whatsforlunchhoney.blogspot.com/2007_01_01_archive.html

67. Presentation Slides

Robbins, S. (2007, March 27). *Immersion and engagement in a virtual
    classroom: Using* Second Life *for higher education* [PowerPoint slides].

APA

V Documenting Sources

Retrieved from http://www.slideshare.net/intellagirl/educause-project-parlor-presentation/

68. Podcast

Leighton, D. C. (2007, October 1). Conceptions of abnormality (Episode 3) [Audio podcast]. *Abnormal Psychology Lectures*. Retrieved from the Portland Community College website: http://spot.pcc.edu/~dleighto/podcasts/psy239

69. Computer Software Sometimes a person is named as having rights to the program, software, or language: in that case, list that person as the author. Otherwise, begin the entry with the name of the program and identify the source in square brackets after the name as "Computer software." Treat the organization that produces the software as the publisher. If you're referring to a specific version that isn't included in the name, put this information immediately after the title in parentheses.

Microsoft Outlook 2007 [Computer software]. Redmond, WA: Microsoft.

Other Sources

70. General Advice about Other Sources For citing other types of sources, APA suggests that you use as a guide a source type listed in their manual that most closely resembles the type of source you want to cite.

TUTORIAL

How do I cite books using APA style?

When citing a book, use the information from the title page and the copyright page (on the reverse side of the title page), not from the book's cover or a library catalog. Consult pp. 325–28 for additional models for citing books.

A   **B**   **C**

Frankel, A. (2007). *Punching in: The unauthorized adventures of a front-line*

              D   **E**

employee. New York, NY: HarperCollins.

A   **The author.** Give the last name first, followed by a comma and initials for first and middle names. Separate initials with a space (Leakey, R. E.). Separate the names of multiple authors with commas; use an ampersand (&) before the final author's name.

B   **The year of publication.** Put the most recent copyright year in parentheses, and end with a period (outside the parentheses).

C   **The title and, if any, the subtitle.** Give the full title; include the subtitle (if any), preceded by a colon. Italicize the title and subtitle, capitalizing only the first word of the title, the first word of the subtitle, and any proper nouns or proper adjectives. End with a period.

D   **The city of publication.** If more than one city is given, use the first one listed. Add the abbreviation of the state, country, or province (Cambridge, Eng.). Insert a colon.

E   **The publisher.** Give the publisher's name. Omit words such as *Inc.* and *Co.* Include and do not abbreviate such terms as *University* and *Press*. End with a period.

Use the bibliography tools at **bedfordresearcher.com** to create a reference list formatted in APA style.

TUTORIAL

How do I cite articles from periodicals using APA style?

Periodicals include journals, magazines, and newspapers. This page gives an example of a citation for a print journal article. Models for citing articles from magazines and newspapers are on pp. 332–33. If you need to cite a periodical article you accessed electronically, follow the guidelines below and see pp. 335–38.

A   B   C   D   E   F

Flora, C. (2007, December). Adieu to all that. *Psychology Today, 40,* 70-78.

A   **The author.** Give the last name first, followed by a comma and initials for first and middle names. Separate the names of multiple authors with commas; use an ampersand (&) before the final author's name.

B   **The year of publication.** Put the year in parentheses and end with a period (outside the parentheses). For magazines and newspapers, include the month and, if relevant, the day (2008, April 13).

C   **The article title.** Give the full title; include subtitle (if any), preceded by a colon. Do not underline, italicize, or put the title in quotes. Capitalize only the first word of the title, the first word of the subtitle, and any proper nouns or proper adjectives. End with a period.

D   **The periodical title.** Italicize the periodical title, and capitalize all major words. Insert a comma.

E   **The volume and issue number, if relevant.** For journals, include the volume number, italicized. If each issue starts with page 1, include the issue number in parentheses, not italicized. Insert a comma.

F   **Inclusive page number(s).** Give all of the numbers in full (248-254, not 248-54). For newspapers, include the abbreviation *p.* for page and section letters, if relevant (p. B12). End with a period.

Use the bibliography tools at **bedfordresearcher.com** to create a reference list formatted in APA style.

TUTORIAL

How do I cite articles from databases using APA style?

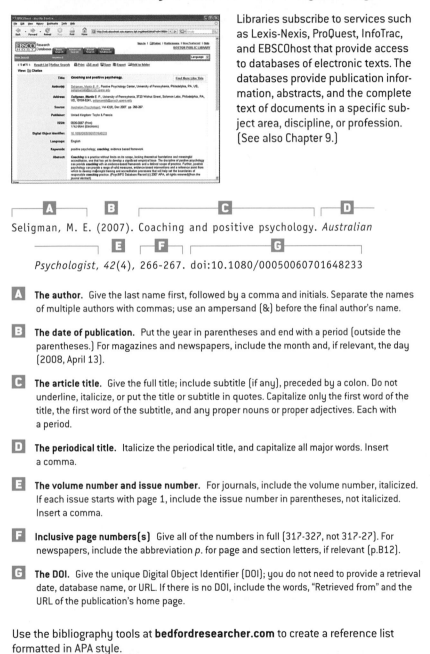

Libraries subscribe to services such as Lexis-Nexis, ProQuest, InfoTrac, and EBSCOhost that provide access to databases of electronic texts. The databases provide publication information, abstracts, and the complete text of documents in a specific subject area, discipline, or profession. (See also Chapter 9.)

A **B** **C** **D**

Seligman, M. E. (2007). Coaching and positive psychology. *Australian*

E **F** **G**

Psychologist, 42(4), 266-267. doi:10.1080/00050060701648233

A **The author.** Give the last name first, followed by a comma and initials. Separate the names of multiple authors with commas; use an ampersand (&) before the final author's name.

B **The date of publication.** Put the year in parentheses and end with a period (outside the parentheses.) For magazines and newspapers, include the month and, if relevant, the day (2008, April 13).

C **The article title.** Give the full title; include subtitle (if any), preceded by a colon. Do not underline, italicize, or put the title or subtitle in quotes. Capitalize only the first word of the title, the first word of the subtitle, and any proper nouns or proper adjectives. Each with a period.

D **The periodical title.** Italicize the periodical title, and capitalize all major words. Insert a comma.

E **The volume number and issue number.** For journals, include the volume number, italicized. If each issue starts with page 1, include the issue number in parentheses, not italicized. Insert a comma.

F **Inclusive page numbers(s)** Give all of the numbers in full (317-327, not 317-27). For newspapers, include the abbreviation *p.* for page and section letters, if relevant (p.B12).

G **The DOI.** Give the unique Digital Object Identifier (DOI); you do not need to provide a retrieval date, database name, or URL. If there is no DOI, include the words, "Retrieved from" and the URL of the publication's home page.

Use the bibliography tools at **bedfordresearcher.com** to create a reference list formatted in APA style.

TUTORIAL

How do I cite works from Web sites using APA style?

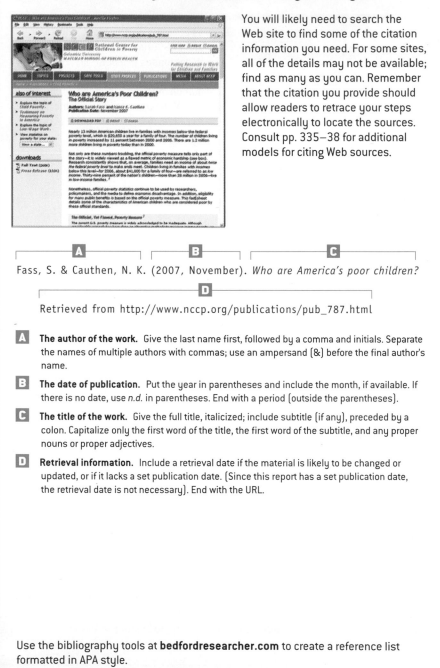

You will likely need to search the Web site to find some of the citation information you need. For some sites, all of the details may not be available; find as many as you can. Remember that the citation you provide should allow readers to retrace your steps electronically to locate the sources. Consult pp. 335–38 for additional models for citing Web sources.

A   B   C

Fass, S. & Cauthen, N. K. (2007, November). *Who are America's poor children?*

D

Retrieved from http://www.nccp.org/publications/pub_787.html

A **The author of the work.** Give the last name first, followed by a comma and initials. Separate the names of multiple authors with commas; use an ampersand (&) before the final author's name.

B **The date of publication.** Put the year in parentheses and include the month, if available. If there is no date, use *n.d.* in parentheses. End with a period (outside the parentheses).

C **The title of the work.** Give the full title, italicized; include subtitle (if any), preceded by a colon. Capitalize only the first word of the title, the first word of the subtitle, and any proper nouns or proper adjectives.

D **Retrieval information.** Include a retrieval date if the material is likely to be changed or updated, or if it lacks a set publication date. (Since this report has a set publication date, the retrieval date is not necessary). End with the URL.

Use the bibliography tools at **bedfordresearcher.com** to create a reference list formatted in APA style.

APA-style Research Essay

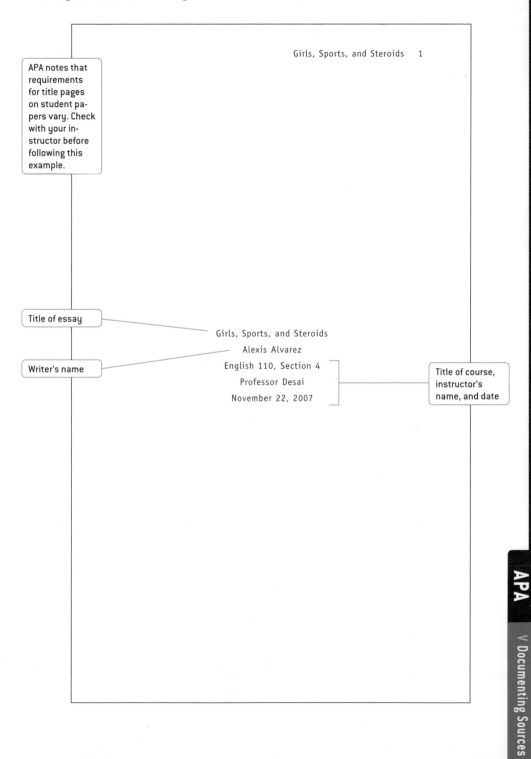

APA notes that requirements for title pages on student papers vary. Check with your instructor before following this example.

Girls, Sports, and Steroids   1

Title of essay

Girls, Sports, and Steroids

Writer's name

Alexis Alvarez

English 110, Section 4

Professor Desai

November 22, 2007

Title of course, instructor's name, and date

Girls, Sports, and Steroids

Title of essay repeated

Almost daily, headlines and newscasters tell us about athletes' use of performance-enhancing drugs. Indeed, stories of such drug use seem to increase each year, with investigations of possible steroid use by college football players, by major league baseball players, and even by Olympic gold medalists. It is easy to gain the impression that many adult athletes, particularly males, may be using drugs in order to improve their performance and physical appearance. What may be surprising and even shocking to most of us, however, is that these drugs, especially anabolic steroids, are increasingly used by adolescent athletes and that girls are just as likely as boys to be users.

Alexis's statement is likely to surprise readers, drawing them into the essay.

In May 2004, the Centers for Disease Control and Prevention (CDC) published its latest figures on self-reported drug use among young people in grades 9 through 12. The CDC study, "Youth Risk Behavior Surveillance — December 2003," found that 6.1% of its survey participants reported using steroids at least once, up from 2.2% in 1993. The report also showed that use of steroids appears to be increasing among younger girls: While only 3.3% of 12th-grade girls reported using steroids, 7.3% of 9th-grade girls reported using them. Moreover, girls might be starting to use steroids at a higher rate than boys. The CDC study indicated that 9th-grade girls had reported slightly higher rates of steroid use than boys (7.3% and 6.9% respectively), while 10th-, 11th–, and 12th-grade girls all reported lower use than boys. Other studies support the conclusion that steroid use is both widespread and rising quickly among adolescent girls. According to Mundell (2004), experts estimate that as many as a million high school students have used steroids — and that a significant percentage of that group are girls. Moreover, since the late 1990s, studies have shown that steroid use is increasing among adolescent girls. In 1998, *Teacher Magazine* reported that steroid use among high school girls had increased 300% since 1991, from 0.4% of all high school girls to 1.4% ("Girls and Steroids," 1998). And Manning (2002) wrote, "A 1999 Youth Risk Behavior Surveillance study by the Centers for Disease Control and the 2001 Monitoring the Future survey both show steady growth in steroid use by 8th- to 12th-graders" ("As Kids Use Steroids," para. 2).

Effective use of statistical evidence shows growth of the problem over time.

Source of paraphrased information acknowledged using APA's parenthetical reference system

A source that does not have an author is identified by shortened title and publication year.

Section heading and paragraph number given for location of material quoted from an online source

What role are competitive sports playing in this dangerous trend? Why are some girls feeling the need to ingest performance-enhancing drugs? Although competitive sports can provide young female athletes with many benefits, they can also have negative effects, the worst of which is increasing drug use. Let's look first at the positives.

Thesis states Alexis's main point

Title of essay, shortened if necessary, followed by page number.

Girls and Sports: The Upside

Headings, boldface and centered throughout, help readers follow the essay's organization.

Millions of girls are now involved in a variety of sports activities, and girls' participation in school athletics and community-based programs continues to increase. As the President's Council on Physical Fitness and Sport (1997) has pointed out, when girls participate in competitive sports, their lives can be affected in a number of positive and interrelated ways. Physical and psychological health, a positive sense of identity, good relationships with friends and family, and improved performance in school all work together to influence a girl's complete growth and development.

According to the President's Council (1997), adolescent girls who exercise regularly can lessen their risks for adult-onset coronary disease and certain cancers. Girls' involvement in sports and exercise also tends to improve immune functioning, posture, strength, flexibility, and heart-lung endurance (President's Council, 1997; Dudley, 1994).

Shortened name of the council; it was introduced by its full name the first time it was cited.

Two sources are cited in one parenthetical citation.

In addition, competitive athletics can enhance mental health by offering adolescent girls positive feelings about body image; tangible experiences of competency, control, and success; improved self-esteem and self-confidence; and a way to reduce anxiety (President's Council, 1997). Juan Orozco, who has coached adolescent females in competitive soccer for nine years, confirmed that making a competitive sports team is a privilege that many girls work toward with determination and longing and that being picked to participate encourages these young athletes to believe in themselves and their abilities (personal communication, September 22, 2007).

Personal communication — an interview — is cited in the text of the document, but not in the reference list.

A final benefit is that sports expand social boundaries and teach many of the personal and social skills girls will need throughout their lives. According to Orozco, through competitive athletics girls learn a crucial lesson in how to interact with, get along with, and depend on athletes from different social and economic groups. In short, they learn to adapt to and enjoy each other's differences. Melissa Alvarez, a 17-year-old athlete who has participated in high school basketball and club soccer, draws a similar conclusion. In an interview, she stated that sports "give you something to work for as an individual and as a team. You learn self-discipline and dedication, which are essential skills to have in life" (personal communication, September 26, 2007). Competitive sports also teach athletes how to cope with failure as well as success. In the best of situations, as Sieghart (2004) noted, athletes are able to assess their achievements realistically, letting neither winning nor losing consume their reality.

An author tag alerts readers that information is taken from a source.

Girls, Sports, and Steroids 4

Girls and Sports: The Downside

In spite of the many positive effects of competitive athletics, sports can have a negative impact on girls' bodies and minds, and some girls falter under the pressure to succeed. Overtraining, eating disorders, and exercise-induced amenorrhea (which may result in osteoporosis) are some of the most common negative physical side effects that young female athletes experience; negative psychological and social side effects include increased stress and anxiety and a loss of self-confidence. Let's look at each of these effects.

Negative Physical Side Effects

Overtraining occurs when your body can no longer adapt to increasing workloads — instead of building up, it breaks down. When a young girl overtrains, her body's balance between training and recovery is lost. Because the athlete's body can't recover, her performance stays flat and she cannot improve. Overtraining also makes a young female athlete prone to a variety of physical and psychological ills, such as unusual fatigue, irritability, feelings of apathy, and menstrual irregularities (Graham, 1999).

Another negative effect is amenorrhea, which refers to an atypical inability to menstruate. Graham (1999) pointed out, "in some sports as many as 50% of the athletes who are competitive may suffer from what's known as exercise-induced or athletic amenorrhea" (p. 26). Furthermore, research has shown that when a woman does not menstruate regularly, she loses bone density and becomes more prone to stress fractures (cracks in bones, especially hands and feet) and osteoporosis later in life. Amenorrhea can be caused by inadequate nutrition as well as by overtraining, both of which cause the athlete to burn more calories than she eats. As a result, her body shuts down its reproductive function to conserve energy (Graham, 1999).

The tendency to develop an eating disorder, such as anorexia or bulimia, is a third possible effect. Although young women may develop eating disorders for a variety of reasons, Graham (1999) noted, "Disordered eating is high among female athletes competing in sports where leanness and/or a specific weight are considered important for either performance or appearance" (p. 74). Being slim and trim may be the goal of many adolescent female athletes, but when they seek that goal by means of an eating disorder, they hinder their athletic performance. A calorie deficit actually decreases immune function, reduces aerobic capacity, decreases muscle mass and strength, and causes low energy and fatigue (Graham).

Page number identifies the location of material quoted from a print source.

Girls, Sports, and Steroids 5

Negative Psychological and Social Effects

Subheadings are set in bold-face and aligned flush left to differentiate them from higher-level headings.

Just as a girl's body and mind often benefit from sports, so too are body and mind linked when it comes to those aspects of sports that are not positive. Often, negative physical effects occur because female athletes feel the need to win at any cost and the pressure to attain an unrealistic ideal. They may resort to extremes such as overtraining in order to have the "ideal" body or be the "best of the best." When they can't meet these expectations, some girl athletes lose self-confidence and become overly stressed and anxious. In fact, they may see their failures as a serious threat to their self-esteem (Davies & Armstrong, 1989).

Pressures at home, at school, among friends, and from coaches can be daunting as well because young athletes tend to worry about the actions and reactions of the people who make up their social circles (Brown & Branta, 1988). In addition, learning to balance the demands of sports, school, family, and fun can be incredibly fatiguing. Juan Orozco recalled that some of the girls he coached were involved in three sports at a time and still had to keep their grades up in order to participate (personal communication, September 22, 2007). Add to these demands the pressure from parents, and real problems can occur. Gary Anderson, a girls' basketball coach for more than two decades, has seen it all: parents who are overly dramatic, teams that serve primarily as stages for a few superstar athletes, and girls who seem "factory-installed with a sense of entitlement simply because they know their way around a ball and a pair of high-tops" (Dexheimer, 2004, para. 15). All of these situations and pressures affect young female athletes and can result in their making some regrettable, if not devastating, choices.

A partial quotation is integrated into the sentence.

Girls' Reactions: Burnout and Steroids

What happens when these young women decide the pressure is too much? What measures will they take to lighten their load? Some of these athletes simply burn out. They stop participating in competitive athletics because the pressure and anxiety make them physically ill. They no longer enjoy competitive sports, but consider them a torment to be endured. In fact, according to Davies and Armstrong (1989), it is not unusual for promising 12-year-olds to abandon the game entirely by the age of 16 and move on to less distressing pastimes. Melissa Alvarez had one such experience while playing high school basketball. The coach put so much pressure on her that her stomach began to ache during games and during practice. The more the coach yelled, the worse she played, but when the coach was absent, her performance improved dramatically and her stomach problems disappeared. Eventually, Melissa quit the basketball team

Girls, Sports, and Steroids 6

because the game had become a burden instead of something she enjoyed (M. Alvarez, personal communication, September 26, 2007).

An alternative much more dangerous than burnout, however, is the use of performance-enhancing drugs such as anabolic steroids. A 2003 article in *Drug Week* stated that girls who participate in sports more than eight hours a week are at considerable risk for taking many illicit drugs: The higher the level at which athletes compete, the higher their risk for substance abuse ("Sporting Activities").

> Since the publication year is given in the sentence, it is not included in the citation.

Teenage girls take steroids for some of the same reasons that professional athletes do — to increase stamina and strength and to acquire a lean, muscular body. However, girls also take steroids to compete for athletic scholarships ("Girls and Steroids," 1998). According to Charles Yesalis, a professor of sports science and senior author of a Penn State report, a lot of young women see steroid use as an investment in their future; athletes can take the hormones for a few months in high school, qualify for a college scholarship, and then stop taking the drugs before sophisticated lab tests can spot them (Faigenbaum, Zaichkowsky, Gardner, & Micheli, 1997). What teenagers don't realize, though, is that even a few months of steroid use can permanently damage the heart, trigger liver failure, stunt physical growth, and put a woman's childbearing ability at risk. Steroids cause muscles to outgrow and injure the tendons and ligaments that attach them to the bone (Faigenbaum et al.). As Farnaz Khadem, spokeswoman for the World Anti-Doping Agency has emphasized, "A lot of these young people have no idea of what this is doing to their bodies. This is a real health danger" (DeNoon, 2004).

> In APA style, the first parenthetical reference to a source with three to five authors lists all authors . . .

> . . . subsequent references to the source use "et al." in place of all but the first author.

Although health is the most important concern in the issue of steroid use, it is not the only one. Possessing or selling steroids without a prescription is a crime, so those who are involved in such activities may also endure criminal penalties (Gorman, 1998). Young women who use steroids are resorting to illegal actions and may eventually be labeled as "criminals," a label that will follow them for the rest of their lives. Doors to coaching jobs, teaching careers, and many other occupations may be shut permanently if one has a criminal past.

How Girl Athletes Can Avoid Steroid Use

What can we do to help adolescent female athletes avoid illicit drug use? How can we help them avoid the pitfalls of competitive athletics? Parents, coaches, and the athletes themselves all play a crucial role in averting bad choices. First, parents and coaches need to be aware that performance-enhancing drugs are a problem. Some adults believe that steroid use is either minimal or nonexistent among teenagers, but one study concluded that "over half the teens

Girls, Sports, and Steroids 7

who use steroids start before age 16, sometimes with the encourage-

ment of their parents. . . . Seven percent said they first took 'juice'

by age ten" (Dudley, 1994, p. 235).

> An ellipsis indicates that words from the source were not included in the quotation.

Parents need to take the time to know their children and know

what their children are doing. Coaches must know their players well

enough to be able to identify a child in trouble. When asked what

parents and coaches could do to help girl athletes remain healthy

and not use drugs or overwork themselves, Juan Orozco offered the

following advice:

> An athlete should be happy in her activity of choice, and
>
> her parents should encourage her desires to do well. Parents
>
> should be involved in her life and let her know that her efforts
>
> are valued highly, but they also need to be on the lookout
>
> for danger signs — such as unusual weight loss or moodiness.
>
> As a coach, I need to know the personalities of my players
>
> and get them to trust me, not only as their coach but as their
>
> friend — someone they can talk to if they have a problem.
>
> (personal communication, September 22, 2007)

> Extended quotation is set off in block style without quotation marks

It is also important for parents and coaches to teach the

athletes how to develop a healthy lifestyle and not focus only

on winning. If an athlete seems to take her sport too seriously,

parents might negotiate with her, encouraging her to balance

sports with other endeavors. Some parents and coaches push kids

too hard, teaching them to win at any cost. In fact, a number of

researchers believe that some parents and coaches are actually

purchasing expensive black-market steroids for their young athletes

(Kendrick, 2004). As University of Massachusetts researcher Avery

Faigenbaum has put it, "I don't know a lot of ten-year-olds who

have a couple of hundred dollars — to spend on drugs or anything

else" (Kendrick, 2004, "Parents as Pushers," para. 1).

Athletes, too, must take responsibility for their own lives. Ado-

lescent girls should try to resist undue pressures imposed by parents,

coaches, and society. They must learn about the damage steroids can

cause and understand that pursuing an "ideal" body type is not only

unrealistic but also unhealthy (Yiannakis & Melnick, 2001). Most of

all, young female athletes need to know that they are more important

than the competition. No scholarship or medal is worth liver failure

or losing the ability to bear children.

The vast majority of excellent athletes do not overtrain, become

bulimic, or wind up using steroids. Clearly, they have learned to

avoid the pitfalls of competitive athletics. They believe in themselves

and their abilities and know how to balance sports and other activi-

ties. They have learned how to sacrifice and work hard, but not at

APA

∨ Documenting Sources

Girls, Sports, and Steroids   8

the expense of their integrity or health. In short, these athletes have
not lost sight of the true objective of participating in sports — they
know that their success is due to their efforts and not to the effects
of a performance-enhancing drug. When asked what she would say to
athletes considering steroid use, Melissa Alvarez said:

> If you are training and doing your best, you should not have
> to use steroids. At the end of the day, it is just a game. You
> should never put your health at risk for anything, or anyone.
> It should be your top priority. (personal communication,
> September 26, 2007)

In the essay's conclusion, Alexis uses a quotation to reinforce her main point.

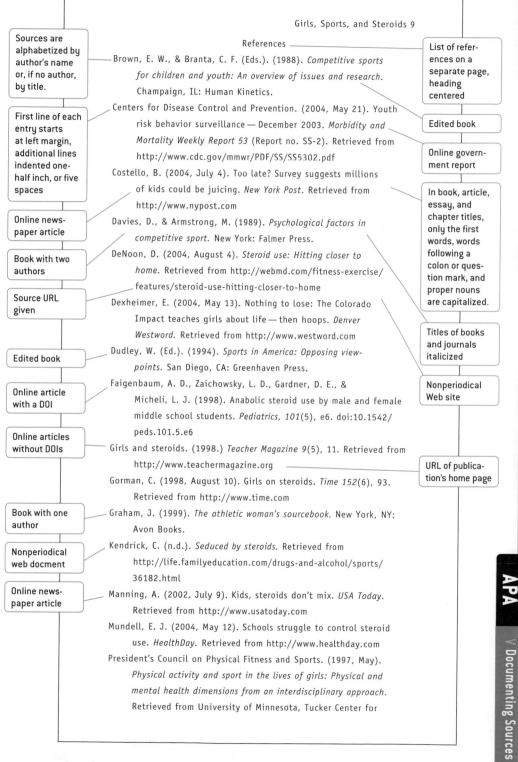

Girls, Sports, and Steroids 9

References

Sources are alphabetized by author's name or, if no author, by title.

First line of each entry starts at left margin, additional lines indented one-half inch, or five spaces

Online newspaper article

Book with two authors

Source URL given

Edited book

Online article with a DOI

Online articles without DOIs

Book with one author

Nonperiodical web docment

Online newspaper article

Brown, E. W., & Branta, C. F. (Eds.). (1988). *Competitive sports for children and youth: An overview of issues and research.* Champaign, IL: Human Kinetics.

Centers for Disease Control and Prevention. (2004, May 21). Youth risk behavior surveillance — December 2003. *Morbidity and Mortality Weekly Report 53* (Report no. SS-2). Retrieved from http://www.cdc.gov/mmwr/PDF/SS/SS5302.pdf

Costello, B. (2004, July 4). Too late? Survey suggests millions of kids could be juicing. *New York Post.* Retrieved from http://www.nypost.com

Davies, D., & Armstrong, M. (1989). *Psychological factors in competitive sport.* New York: Falmer Press.

DeNoon, D. (2004, August 4). *Steroid use: Hitting closer to home.* Retrieved from http://webmd.com/fitness-exercise/features/steroid-use-hitting-closer-to-home

Dexheimer, E. (2004, May 13). Nothing to lose: The Colorado Impact teaches girls about life — then hoops. *Denver Westword.* Retrieved from http://www.westword.com

Dudley, W. (Ed.). (1994). *Sports in America: Opposing viewpoints.* San Diego, CA: Greenhaven Press.

Faigenbaum, A. D., Zaichowsky, L. D., Gardner, D. E., & Micheli, L. J. (1998). Anabolic steroid use by male and female middle school students. *Pediatrics, 101*(5), e6. doi:10.1542/peds.101.5.e6

Girls and steroids. (1998.) *Teacher Magazine 9*(5), 11. Retrieved from http://www.teachermagazine.org

Gorman, C. (1998, August 10). Girls on steroids. *Time 152*(6), 93. Retrieved from http://www.time.com

Graham, J. (1999). *The athletic woman's sourcebook.* New York, NY: Avon Books.

Kendrick, C. (n.d.). *Seduced by steroids.* Retrieved from http://life.familyeducation.com/drugs-and-alcohol/sports/36182.html

Manning, A. (2002, July 9). Kids, steroids don't mix. *USA Today.* Retrieved from http://www.usatoday.com

Mundell, E. J. (2004, May 12). Schools struggle to control steroid use. *HealthDay.* Retrieved from http://www.healthday.com

President's Council on Physical Fitness and Sports. (1997, May). *Physical activity and sport in the lives of girls: Physical and mental health dimensions from an interdisciplinary approach.* Retrieved from University of Minnesota, Tucker Center for

List of references on a separate page, heading centered

Edited book

Online government report

In book, article, essay, and chapter titles, only the first words, words following a colon or question mark, and proper nouns are capitalized.

Titles of books and journals italicized

Nonperiodical Web site

URL of publication's home page

APA

V Documenting Sources

Girls, Sports, and Steroids 10

Research on Girls and Women in Sport Web site: http://cehd.

umn.edu/tuckercenter/projects/PresidentsCouncil/

pcpfs_report.pdf

Online news-paper article

Sieghart, M. A. (2004, August 27). Competitive sport is harsh and

unforgiving: That's why it's good for children. *The Times* of

London. Retrieved from http://www.the-times.co.uk

Sporting activities impact illegal drug use among male and female

teenagers. (2003, September 26). *Drug Week,* pp. 16-17.

Magazine article without a named author

Book editors are identified using (Ed.) or (Eds.)

Yiannakis, A., & Melnick, M. J. (Eds.). (2001). *Contemporary issues in sociology of sport.* Champaign, IL: Human Kinetics.

22

Using *Chicago* Style

 Key Questions

22a. How do I cite sources within the text of my document? 355

22b. How do I format notes and prepare the bibliography? 357

The documentation style described in *The Chicago Manual of Style: The Essential Guide for Writers, Editors, and Publishers*, Fifteenth Edition, is used in the humanities and in some of the social sciences. The *Manual* recommends two systems, an author-date system similar to the APA system (see Chapter 21) and a notes system. This chapter describes and provides models for the notes system.

In the notes system, researchers acknowledge their sources in footnotes or endnotes. Footnotes appear at the bottom of a printed page, whereas endnotes appear at the end of the document. Although a bibliography can be omitted when using the note system (since all relevant publication information is provided in the notes), the manual encourages authors to provide a bibliography or list of works cited in documents where more than a few sources are cited. For more information about this system, consult *The Chicago Manual of Style*. Information about the manual can also be found at chicagomanualof style.org.

To see Patrick Crossland's research essay, formatted in *Chicago* style, turn to p. 373.

CITATIONS WITHIN YOUR TEXT

1. Numbering   355
2. Placement of the note numbers in the text   355
3. Placement of notes   356
4. Including page numbers in a note   356
5. Cross-referencing notes   356
6. Citing the same source in multiple notes   356
7. Citing a source quoted in another source   356

NOTES AND ENTRIES IN YOUR BIBLIOGRAPHY OR LIST OF WORKS CITED

How do I cite sources within the text of my document?

Chicago uses footnotes or endnotes. Notes can also be used to expand on points made in the text — that is, notes can contain both citation information and commentary on the text. For electronic documents such as Web sites that consist of multiple "pages" of text, footnotes can take the form of links to notes at the end of a "page" or to pop-up windows that display the notes.

The first time you refer to a source in a note, provide complete publication information for the source. In subsequent references, you need to cite only the author's last name, a shortened version of the title, and the page numbers (if the source has page numbers) to which you refer. Separate the elements with commas and end with a period. *Chicago* style italicizes titles of books and periodicals.

The following examples illustrate the most common ways of citing sources within the text of your document using *Chicago*'s note system.

1. Numbering   Notes should be numbered consecutively throughout your work, beginning with 1.

2. Placement of the Note Numbers in the Text   Place the number for a note at the end of the sentence containing the reference after punctuation and outside any parentheses. If you are citing the source of material that comes before an em dash (or two hyphens) used to separate parts of a sentence, the note number should precede the dash. Note numbers are set as superscripts.

> Lee and Calandra suggest that the poor organization of online historical documents may impair students' ability to conduct research without guidance.[1]

Tomlinson points out that the erosion of Fiji's culture was accelerated by both British and Indian immigration[2] — though the two immigrant groups inhabited very different roles and social classes.

3. Placement of Notes   You may choose between footnotes, which appear at the bottom of the page containing corresponding note numbers, and endnotes, which appear at the end of the document in a section titled "Notes." Longer works, such as books, typically use endnotes. The choice depends on the expectations of your readers and your preferences. Regardless of placement, notes are numbered consecutively throughout the document. If you use a bibliography, it follows the last page of text or the last page of endnotes. Model notes for various types of sources appear in section 22b, which begins on p. 357.

4. Including Page Numbers in a Note   Use page numbers whenever you refer to a specific page of a source rather than to the source as a whole. The use of page numbers is required for quotations.

4. Tom Brokaw, *Boom! Voices of the Sixties Personal Reflections on the '60s and Today* (New York: Random House, 2007), 77.

5. Cross-Referencing Notes   If you are referring to a source identified in a previous note, you can refer to that note instead of repeating the information.

5. See note 3 above.

6. Citing the Same Source in Multiple Notes   If you refer to the same source in several notes, provide a full citation in the first note. In subsequent notes, provide the author's last name, a brief version of the title, and the page number. If you are referring to the same source cited in the previous note, you can use the Latin abbreviation "ibid." (for *ibidem*, or *in the same place*).

1. Orlando Figes, *The Whisperers: Private Life in Stalin's Russia* (New York: Metropolitan Books, 2007), 26.

2. Ibid., 54.

6. Figes, *Whisperers,* 131.

7. Citing a Source Quoted in Another Source

7. Michael Meyer and Michael Sherman, *The Course of Mexican History* (New York, Oxford University Press, 1990), 361-69, quoted in Daniel Walker Howe, *What Hath God Wrought: The Transformation of America, 1815-1848* (New York: Oxford University Press, 2007), 20.

22b

How do I format notes and prepare the bibliography?

The Chicago Manual of Style provides guidelines for formatting notes and entries in a bibliography of works that are relevant to but not necessarily cited within your document. In print documents and linear documents that are distributed electronically (such as a word processing file or a newsgroup post), the bibliography appears at the end of the document. In longer documents, a bibliography could be given at the end of each chapter or section. In electronic documents that use links, such as a Web site, the bibliography is often a separate page to which other pages are linked. To see a bibliography in *Chicago* style, see p. 372.

For notes, include the number of the note, indented and not superscript, followed by these elements:

- author's name (first name first)
- title (followed by the title of the complete work if the source is an article, chapter, or other short work contained in a larger work)
- publisher (for a book) or publication title (for a journal, magazine, or newspaper)
- date
- page(s) being cited

For entries in the bibliography, include these elements:

- author's name (last name first)
- title (followed by the title of the complete work if the source is an article, chapter, or other short work contained in a larger work)
- publisher (for a book) or publication title (for a journal, magazine, or newspaper)
- date
- page(s) (if the source is a shorter work included in a complete work)

Keep in mind that well-known reference works, such as encyclopedias, and all types of personal communication—personal interviews, letters, surveys, email messages, online discussion groups—are cited in a note only. They are not usually included in the bibliography.

Note: For each type of source, a pair of examples is presented in this section: a model note followed by a model bibliographic entry.

Books, Conference Proceedings, and Dissertations

8. One Author   Use the basic format described on p. 369.

When citing a book, use the information from the title page and the copyright page (on the reverse side of the title page), not from the book's cover or a library catalog.

8. Jeffrey Toobin, *The Nine: Inside the Secret World of the Supreme Court* (New York: Doubleday, 2007), 201.

Toobin, Jeffrey. *The Nine: Inside the Secret World of the Supreme Court.* New York: Doubleday, 2007.

9. Two or Three Authors   List the authors in the order in which they appear on the title page. In a note, list the first name for each author first. In the bibliography, list the first author's last name first and list the first names for each other author first.

9. Bill Cosby and Alvin F. Poussaint, *Come On People: On the Path from Victims to Victors* (Nashville: Thomas Nelson, 2007), 112.

Cosby, Bill, and Alvin F. Poussaint. *Come On People: On the Path from Victims to Victors.* Nashville: Thomas Nelson, 2007.

10. Four or More Authors   In a note, give only the first author's name followed by "et al." or *and others*. In the bibliography, list the authors as they appear on the title page.

10. Burton G. Malkiel and others, *From Wall Street to the Great Wall: How Investors Can Profit from China's Booming Economy* (New York: Norton, 2007), 89.

Malkiel, Burton G., Patricia A. Taylor, Jianping Mei, and Rui Yang. *From Wall Street to the Great Wall: How Investors Can Profit from China's Booming Economy.* New York: Norton, 2007.

11. Corporate or Group Author   Use the corporation or group as the author; it may also be the publisher.

11. National Geographic, *National Geographic Atlas of China* (Washington, DC: National Geographic, 2007), 66.

National Geographic. *National Geographic Atlas of China.* Washington, DC: National Geographic, 2007.

12. Unknown Author   When no author is listed on the title or copyright page, begin the entry with the title of the work. In the bibliography, alphabetize the entry by the first word other than *A, An*, or *The.*

12. *Through Palestine with the 20th Machine Gun Squadron.* (Arlington, VA: IndyPublish, 2007), 63.

Through Palestine with the 20th Machine Gun Squadron. Arlington, VA: IndyPublish, 2007.

13. Translated Book   List the author first and the translator after the title. Use the abbreviation "trans." in a note, but spell out "Translated by" in the bibliography.

13. Yang Sen-Fu, *A History of Nestorian Christianity in China,* trans. Herbert J. Hatcher (Charleston, SC: BookSurge, 2007), 109.

Sen-Fu, Yang. *A History of Nestorian Christianity in China.* Translated by
   Herbert J. Hatcher. Charleston, SC: BookSurge, 2007.

14. Edition Other Than the First   Give edition information after the title.

14. James M. Kouzes and Barry Z. Posner, *The Leadership Challenge,*
4th ed. (San Francisco: Jossey-Bass, 2007), 241.

Kouzes, James M., and Barry Z. Posner. *The Leadership Challenge.* 4th ed.
   San Francisco: Jossey-Bass, 2007.

15. Untitled Volume in a Multivolume Work   In the notes, give the volume number and page number, separated by a colon, for the specific location of the information referred to in your text. In the bibliography, if you have used all the volumes, give the total number of volumes after the title, using the abbreviation "vols." ("2 vols." or "4 vols."). If you have used one volume, give the abbreviation "Vol." and the volume number after the title.

15. Christopher Edgar and Ron Padgett, eds., *Educating the Imagination:*
Essays and Ideas for Teachers and Writers (New York: Teachers & Writers
Collaborative, 2007), 1:84-87.

Edgar, Christopher, and Ron Padgett, eds. *Educating the Imagination: Essays*
   and Ideas for Teachers and Writers. Vol. 1. New York: Teachers & Writers
   Collaborative, 2007.

16. Titled Volume in a Multivolume Work   Give the title of the volume to which you refer, followed by the volume number and the general title for the entire work.

16. Samuel Adams, *The Writings of Samuel Adams 1773-1777,* vol. 3 of
The Writings of Samuel Adams, ed. Harry Alonso Cushing (Charleston, SC:
BiblioBazaar, 2007), 46.

Adams, Samuel. *The Writings of Samuel Adams 1773-1777.* Vol. 3 of *The*
   Writings of Samuel Adams, edited by Harry Alonso Cushing. Charleston,
   SC: BiblioBazaar, 2007.

17. Book in a Series   The series name follows the title and is capitalized as a title but is not italicized. If the series numbers its volumes, include that information as well.

17. Jeffrey A. Hirsch, *Stock Trader's Almanac 2008,* Stock Trader's Almanac Investor Series (Hoboken: Wiley, 2008), 338-40.

Hirsch, Jeffrey A. *Stock Trader's Almanac 2008.* Stock Trader's Almanac
    Investor Series. Hoboken: Wiley, 2008.

18. Republished Book   Place the original publication date before the publication information for the reprint.

18. Joseph Conrad, *Heart of Darkness* (1902; repr., London: Random House, 2007), 224.

Conrad, Joseph. *Heart of Darkness.* 1902. Reprint, London: Random House,
    2007.

19. Author with an Editor   List the author at the beginning of the citation and add the editor's name after the title. In notes, use the abbreviation "ed." before the editor's name. In the bibliography, include the phrase "Edited by" before the editor's name.

19. H. L. Mencken, *Thirty-five Years of Newspaper Work: A Memoir,* ed. Fred Hobson, Vincent Fitzpatrick, and Bradford Jacobs (Baltimore: Johns Hopkins University Press, 2006), 330-32.

Mencken, H. L. *Thirty-five Years of Newspaper Work: A Memoir.* Edited by Fred
    Hobson, Vincent Fitzpatrick, and Bradford Jacobs. Baltimore: Johns
    Hopkins University Press, 2006.

20. Anthology or Collection with an Editor   To cite an entire anthology or collection of articles, give the editor(s) before the title of the collection, adding a comma and the abbreviation "ed." or "eds."

20. Robert S. Miola, ed., *Early Modern Catholicism: An Anthology of Primary Sources* (New York: Oxford University Press, 2007), 465-67.

Miola, Robert S., ed. *Early Modern Catholicism: An Anthology of Primary
    Sources.* New York: Oxford University Press, 2007.

21. Foreword, Introduction, Preface, or Afterword   Give the name of the writer of the foreword, introduction, preface, or afterword followed by the appropriate phrase ("introduction to," "preface to," and so on) before the title of the book. After the title insert the word "by" and the author's name.

21. John McCarter, foreword to *Maps: Finding Our Place in the World,* ed. James R. Akerman Jr. and Robert W. Karrow (Chicago: University of Chicago Press, 2007), vi.

McCarter, John. Foreword to *Maps: Finding Our Place in the World,* edited by
    James R. Akerman Jr. and Robert W. Karrow, v-xii. Chicago: University
    of Chicago Press, 2007.

22. Chapter in a Book or Selection in an Anthology   Give the author and title
(in quotation marks) for the chapter or selection. Then give the title, editor, and
publication data for the book or anthology. In the bibliography, give the inclusive page numbers before the publication data.

   22. Afanasy Nikitin, "West and Central India, 1471-73," in *Visions of
Mughal India: An Anthology of European Travel Writing,* ed. Michael Fisher
(London: I. B. Tauris, 2007), 18.

Nikitin, Afanasy. "West and Central India, 1471-73." In *Visions of Mughal
    India: An Anthology of European Travel Writing,* edited by Michael Fisher,
    15-25. London: I. B. Tauris, 2007.

23. Published Proceedings of a Conference   Cite as for an anthology or collection with an editor (see also #20 on p. 360).

   23. Hein Venter and others, eds., *New Approaches for Security, Privacy
and Trust in Complex Environments* (New York: Springer, 2007), 9-13

Venter, Hein, Mariki Eloff, Les Labuschagne, Jan Eloff, and Rossouw von
    Solms, eds. *New Approaches for Security, Privacy and Trust in Complex
    Environments.* New York: Springer, 2007.

24. Paper Published in the Proceedings of a Conference   Cite as a chapter in
an edited book (see also #22 above).

   24. Paula Thomas and Theodore Tryfonas, "Hard-drive Disposal and
Identity Fraud," in *New Approaches for Security, Privacy and Trust in Complex
Environments* (New York: Springer, 2007), 464.

Thomas, Paula, and Theodore Tryfonas. "Hard-drive Disposal and Identity
    Fraud." In *New Approaches for Security, Privacy and Trust in Complex
    Environments.* 461-66. New York: Springer, 2007.

25. Sacred Text   Cite sacred texts only within the text of your document. A
note should include the book, chapter, and verse, but not a page number.

   25. Qur'an, 2:10 (Cambridge: Gibb Memorial Trust, 2008).

26. Published Dissertation or Thesis   Give the author and title, the phrase
"PhD diss." or "master's thesis," followed by information about the institution

that granted the degree and the year. Include information from *Dissertation Abstracts International* if appropriate.

26. Jennifer E. Smith, *Values and Economic Organization in Brazil and Venezuela* (Ann Arbor: UMI, 2007), 57.

Smith, Jennifer E. *Values and Economic Organization in Brazil and Venezuela.* Ann Arbor: UMI, 2007.

27. Unpublished Dissertation or Thesis   Give the author and title, in quotation marks. Then include the phrase "PhD diss." or "master's thesis," information about the institution that granted the degree, and the date.

27. Jamil Edwin, "Evaluation of a Military Family Support Program: The Case of Operation: Military Kids in Indiana" (PhD diss., Purdue University, 2007), 77-79.

Edwin, Jamil. "Evaluation of a Military Family Support Program: The Case of Operation: Military Kids in Indiana." PhD diss., Purdue University, 2007.

28. Abstract of a Dissertation or Thesis   Provide information as you would for an article in a journal (see also #29 below). Add information about *Dissertation Abstracts International*.

28. Machiko, Inagawa, "Japanese American Experiences in Internment Camps during World War II as Represented by Children's and Adolescent Literature" (PhD diss., University of Arizona, 2007), abstract, *Dissertation Abstracts International* 67 (2007): 122.

Inagawa Machiko. "Japanese American Experiences in Internment Camps during World War II as Represented by Children's and Adolescent Literature." PhD diss., University of Arizona, 2007. Abstract. *Dissertation Abstracts International* 67 (2007): 122.

Sources in Journals, Magazines, and Newspapers

29. Article in a Journal   After the journal title, include the volume number, a comma, and the issue number after the abbreviation "no." Then give the year. In the note, give the specific page number to which you are referring; in the bibliography, give inclusive page numbers of the entire article.

29. Helen McCarthy, "Parties, Voluntary Associations, and Democratic Politics in Interwar Britain," *Historical Journal* 50, no. 4 (2007): 902.

McCarthy, Helen. "Parties, Voluntary Associations, and Democratic Politics in Interwar Britain." *Historical Journal* 50, no. 4 (2007): 891-912.

30. Article in a Monthly Magazine Magazines are cited by their dates rather than by volume and issue.

> 30. Penelope Wang, "How the B.A. Got Cheaper," *Money,* December 2007, 28.

> Wang, Penelope. "How the B.A. Got Cheaper." *Money,* December 2007, 28.

31. Article in a Weekly Magazine Cite like a monthly magazine, but provide the day of publication.

> 31. Richard Preston, "A Death in the Forest: Can the Trees of the Great Smokey Mountains Be Saved?" *New Yorker,* December 10, 2007, 68.

> Preston, Richard. "A Death in the Forest: Can the Trees of the Great Smokey Mountains Be Saved?" *New Yorker,* December 10, 2007, 64-71.

32. Article in a Newspaper If the name of the newspaper does not include the city, insert the city before the name (and italicize it). If an American city is not well known, name the state as well (in parentheses, abbreviated and not italicized). Identify newspapers from other countries with the city in parentheses (not italicized) after the name of the newspaper.

> *Eugene* (OR) *Register-Guard*

> *Sunday Times* (London)

Page numbers may be omitted, since separate editions of the same newspaper may place articles differently. If a paper comes out in more than one edition, identify the edition after the date.

> 32. Troy Anderson, "Urban Waterway Greened and Getting Greener," *San Francisco Chronicle,* December 14, 2007, Bay Area edition.

> Anderson, Troy. "Urban Waterway Greened and Getting Greener." *San Francisco Chronicle,* December 14, 2007, Bay Area edition.

33. Unsigned Article in a Newspaper or Magazine If no author is given, begin with the title of the article.

> 33. "8 States Sue Cigarette Maker over Ad," *Boston Globe,* December 5, 2007.

> "8 States Sue Cigarette Maker over Ad." *Boston Globe,* December 5, 2007.

34. Letter to the Editor Treat as a newspaper article. If no title is provided, place "Letter to the editor" in the title position.

Chicago ∨ Documenting Sources

34. Cécile Alduy, letter to the editor, *New Yorker,* December 10, 2007.

Alduy, Cécile. Letter to the editor. *New Yorker,* December 10, 2007.

35. Review Give the author of the review, the review title, if any, and then the words "review of" followed by the title and author of the work reviewed.

35. Nigel Andrews, "Now You See Him, Now You Don't," review of *Silent Light,* directed by Carlos Reygadas, *Financial Times*, December 6, 2007.

Andrews, Nigel. "Now You See Him, Now You Don't." Review of *Silent Light,* directed by Carlos Reygadas. *Financial Times*, December 6, 2007.

Print Reference Works

36. Entry in an Encyclopedia, Dictionary, Thesaurus, Handbook, or Almanac In notes, provide the title of the work (italicized), the edition, the abbreviation "s.v." (for *sub verbo*, or "under the word"), and the title of the entry.

36. *Encyclopaedia Britannica*, 15th ed., s.v. "Lee, Robert E."

Chicago does not recommend including reference works such as encyclopedias or dictionaries in the bibliography.

37. Government Publication In general, give the issuing body, then the title and any other information (such as report numbers) that would help your readers locate the source. Follow with the publication data and the page numbers if relevant. You may abbreviate "Government Printing Office" as GPO.

37. U.S. Senate, Committee on Homeland Security and Governmental Affairs, *Hurricane Katrina: A Nation Still Unprepared* (Washington, DC: GPO, 2006), 59-63.

U.S. Senate. Committee on Homeland Security and Governmental Affairs. *Hurricane Katrina: A Nation Still Unprepared*. Washington, DC: GPO, 2006.

38. Pamphlet, Report, or Brochure Cite it as you would a book (see p. 357).

38. *WIC: Good Food and a Whole Lot More* (Boston: Massachusetts Department of Public Health, 2007).

WIC: Good Food and a Whole Lot More. Boston: Massachusetts Department of Public Health, 2007.

Field Sources

39. Personal Interview Give the location and date in a note. Do not include unpublished interviews in the bibliography.

39. Rachel Stein, interview by author, Pittsburgh, June 2, 2008.

40. Letter or Other Personal Communication Do not include personal communications such as letters or phone calls in the bibliography. In a note, give the name of the person with whom you communicated, the form of communication, and the date.

40. Megahn McKennan, conversation with author, March 5, 2008.

41. Sangita Thakore, letter to author, November 12, 2007.

41. Survey *Chicago* does not specify how to cite unpublished survey results. Cite them in your text as you would a personal communication (see #40 above).

42. Observation Note *Chicago* does not specify how to cite observation notes. Cite them in your text as you would a personal communication (see #40 above).

43. Lecture or Public Address Provide the title, the nature of the speech (such as lecture or keynote address), the name of the organization sponsoring the meeting or lecture, and the location and date it was given.

43. Vishakha Desai, "India's Role in the World — Then and Now" (lecture, Isabella Stewart Gardner Museum, Boston, April 10, 2008).

Desai, Vishakha. "India's Role in the World — Then and Now." Lecture,
    Isabella Stewart Gardner Museum, Boston, April 10, 2008.

Media Sources

44. Film or Video Recording Provide the title first, the medium (film, videocassette, DVD), the name of the director, the company, and the year it was filmed.

44. *Sicko,* DVD, directed by Michael Moore (New York: Dog Eat Dog Films, 2007).

Sicko. DVD. Directed by Michael Moore. 1 hr. 23 min., Dog Eat Dog Films,
    2007.

45. Television Program *Chicago* does not specify how to cite a television program. Cite as you would a video recording, identifying the medium as "television program" or "television broadcast."

46. Radio Program *Chicago* does not specify how to cite a radio program. Cite as you would a video recording, identifying the medium as "radio program" or "radio broadcast."

47. Sound Recording Give the composer and title of the recording, the performers and conductor, the label, and identifying number.

47. Pyotr Ilyich Tchaikovsky, *Symphony No. 5, Romeo and Juliet Fantasy Overture,* Royal Philharmonic Orchestra, dir. Daniele Gatti, compact disc, Harmonia Mundi, MU907381.

Tchaikovsky, Pyotr Ilyich. *Symphony No. 5, Romeo and Juliet Fantasy Overture.* Royal Philharmonic Orchestra, directed by Daniele Gatti. Compact disc. Harmonia Mundi. MU907381.

Electronic Sources

According to the *Chicago Manual of Style,* 15 ed., access dates for electronic materials are optional. The examples here include them, but you may want to check with your instructor and consider the discipline in which you are writing.

48. Article from a Database

48. Linda K. Wertheimer, "Colleges Struggle over Aid Deals," *Boston Globe,* December 31, 2007, http://www.lexisnexis.com (accessed April 13, 2008).

Wertheimer, Linda K. "Colleges Struggle over Aid Deals." *Boston Globe,* December 31, 2007. http://www.lexisnexis.com (accessed April 13, 2008).

49. Article in an Electronic Journal

49. Robert M. Regoli, Eric Primm, and John D. Hewitt, "Tackled in the Red Zone: The Impact of Race on Football Card Values," *Electronic Journal of Sociology* 10 (2007), http://www.sociology.org/content/2007/_regoli_ tackled.pdf (accessed January 7, 2008).

Regoli, Robert M., Eric Primm, and John D. Hewitt. "Tackled in the Red Zone: The Impact of Race on Football Card Values." *Electronic Journal of Sociology* 10 (2007). http://www.sociology.org/content/2007/_regoli_ tackled.pdf (accessed January 7, 2008).

50. Article in an Online Magazine

50. Taylor Clark, "Don't Fear Starbucks: Why the Franchise Actually Helps Mom and Pop Coffeehouses," *Slate,* December 28, 2007, http://www .slate.com/id/2180301/nav/tap3/ (accessed January 7, 2008).

Clark, Taylor. "Don't Fear Starbucks: Why the Franchise Actually Helps Mom and Pop Coffeehouses." *Slate,* December 28, 2007. http://www.slate .com/id/2180301/nav/tap3/ (accessed January 7, 2008).

51. Nonperiodical Web Site

51. Abdullah Qazi, "The Plight of the Afghan Woman," *Afghanistan Online,* http://www.afghan-web.com/woman/ (accessed November 10, 2007).

Qazi, Abdullah. "The Plight of the Afghan Woman." *Afghanistan Online.* http://www.afghan-web.com/woman/ (accessed November 10, 2007).

52. Online Book

52. Jeane J. Kirkpatrick, *Making War to Keep Peace* (New York: HarperCollins, 2007), http://library.netlibrary.com/BookDetail.aspx?id=193484 (accessed January 9, 2008).

Kirkpatrick, Jeane J. *Making War to Keep Peace.* New York: HarperCollins, 2007. http://library.netlibrary.com/BookDetail.aspx?id=193484 (accessed January 9, 2008).

53. Article Posted on a Wiki   Cite online postings to Wikis in the text, but not in the bibliography.

53. "Labor History," article posted to *Montana History Wiki,* November 16, 2007, http://montanahistorywiki.pbwiki.com/Labor+History (accessed January 5, 2008).

54. Entire Blog

54. Michael Lorenzen and Jennie Weber, *American Presidents Blog,* January 1, 2008, http://www.american-presidents.org/ (accessed January 1, 2008).

Lorenzen, Michael, and Jennie Weber. *American Presidents Blog,* January 1, 2008. http://www.american-presidents.org/ (accessed January 1, 2008).

55. Entry or Comment on a Blog

55. Christopher Allbritton, "Journalism in Iraq Is Very, Very Dangerous," entry on *Back to Iraq* Weblog, November 28, 2007, http://www.back-to-iraq.com/2007/11/journalism-in-iraq-is-very-ver.php (accessed January 15, 2008).

Allbritton, Christopher. "Journalism in Iraq Is Very, Very Dangerous." Entry on *Back to Iraq* Weblog, November 28, 2007. http://www.back-to-iraq .com/2007/11/journalism-in-iraq-is-very-ver.php (accessed January 15, 2008).

56. Email Message   Chicago recommends that personal communication, including email, not be included in the bibliography, although it can be cited in your text.

    56. Brysa H. Levy, e-mail message to author, January 4, 2008.

57. Online Posting to a Discussion Group   Like email, online postings are considered personal communication and are therefore listed in the text only, not the bibliography.

    57. Angela Jancius, online posting to URBANTH-L discussion group, December 7, 2007, http://lists.ysu.edu/pipermail/urbanth-l/ 2007-December/001754.html (accessed January 16, 2008).

TUTORIAL

How do I cite books using Chicago *style?*

When citing a book, use the information from the title page and the copyright page (on the reverse side of the title page), not from the book's cover or a library catalog. This page gives an example of a *Chicago*-style footnote or endnote. An example of the bibliography entry for this source is at the bottom of the page.

Consult pp. 357–62 for additional models for citing books.

Note

```
         ┌────── A ──────┐ ┌────────────────── B ──────────────────┐
```

1. Deborah Rodriguez, *Kabul Beauty School: An American Woman Goes behind*

```
┌──┐ ┌────────────── C ──────────────┐      ┌── D ──┐
```

the Veil (New York: Random House, 2007), 189-90.

A **The author.** In the note, give the first name first. Follow the last name with a comma. Separate the names of multiple authors with commas; use the word *and* before the final author's name.

B **The title.** Give the full title; include the subtitle (if any), preceded by a colon. Italicize the title and subtitle, capitalizing all major words.

C **Publication information.** Enclose the city, publisher, and date in parentheses. If more than one city is given, use the first one listed. For a city that may be unfamiliar to your readers or confused with another city, add an abbreviation of the state, country, or province (Cambridge, MA or Waterloo, ON). Insert a colon.

Give the publisher's name. Omit words such as *Inc.* and *Co.* Include and do not abbreviate such terms as *Books* and *Press.* Insert a comma.

Give the year of publication, using the most recent copyright year. Close the parentheses and insert a comma.

D **Inclusive page number(s).** Give the specific page or pages on which you found the information. For numbers 100 and above, give only the last two digits and any other preceding digits if different from the first number (22-28, 402-10, 1437-45, 599-603).

Bibliography Entry

In the bibliography, give the author's last name first, and separate the elements with periods. Do not enclose the publication information in parentheses.

Rodriguez, Deborah. *Kabul Beauty School: An American Woman Goes behind the Veil.* New York: Random House, 2007.

TUTORIAL

How do I cite articles from periodicals using Chicago style?

Periodicals include journals, magazines, and newspapers. This page gives an example of a *Chicago*-style footnote or endnote for a print magazine article. (An example of the bibliography entry for this source is at the bottom of the page.) Models for citing articles from journals and newspapers are on pp. 362–64. If you need to cite a periodical article you accessed electronically, follow the guidelines below and see p. 366.

Note

A   B   C   D   E

2. Ellen McGirt, "Facebook Opens Up," *Fast Company,* November 2007, 87.

A **The author.** In the note, give the first name first. Follow the last name with a comma. Separate the names of multiple authors with commas; use the word *and* before the final author's name.

B **The article title.** Give the full title; include the subtitle (if any), preceded by a colon. Put the article title and subtitle in quotes, capitalizing all major words.

C **The periodical title.** Italicize the periodical title, and capitalize all major words.

D **The date of publication.** For monthly magazines, give the month and year. For weekly magazines include the day of publication (September 6, 2008). Do not abbreviate the month. Use a comma after the year.

E **Specific page number(s).** Give the specific page or pages on which you found the information, unless you are referring to the article as a whole. For numbers 100 and above, give only the last two digits and any other preceding digits if different from the first number (22-24, 409-10, 1437-45, 599-601).

Bibliography Entry

In the bibliography, give the author's last name first, separate the elements by periods, and give inclusive pages for the entire article.

McGirt, Ellen. "Facebook Opens Up." *Fast Company,* November 2007, 84-89.

TUTORIAL

How do I cite articles from databases using Chicago *style?*

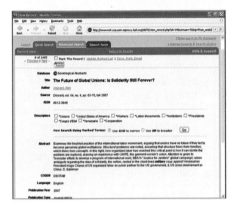

Libraries subscribe to services such as Lexis-Nexis, ProQuest, InfoTrac, and EBSCOhost that provide access to databases of electronic texts. The databases provide publication information, abstracts, and the complete text of documents in a specific subject area, discipline, or profession. (See also Chapter 9.)

This page gives an example of a *Chicago*-style footnote or endnote for a journal article accessed via a database. (An example of the bibliography entry for this source is at the bottom of the page.) To cite magazine and newspaper articles from databases, see also pp. 366–68.

Note

A   **B**

3. Alan Howard, "The Future of Global Unions: Is Solidarity Forever?"

C   **D**   **E**

Dissent 54, no. 4 (2007): 64, http://www-mi4.csa.com.ezproxy.bpl.org/

F

(accessed February 17, 2008).

A **The author.** In the note, give the first name first. Follow the last name with a comma. Separate the names of multiple authors with commas; use the word *and* before the final author's name.

B **The article title.** Give the full title; include the subtitle (if any), preceded by a colon. Put the article title and subtitle in quotes, capitalizing all major words.

C **The journal title.** Italicize the journal title, and capitalize all major words.

D **The publication information.** Insert the volume number followed by a comma, then give the abbreviation *no.*, and the issue number. Include the year in parentheses followed by a colon and the specific page number of the reference. (In the bibliography, give inclusive page numbers.) End with a comma.

E **The main URL for the database.** Give the main URL for the database service; do not use underlining or angle brackets.

F **The access date (optional).** You can include the word *accessed* and the date in parentheses.

Bibliography Entry

Howard, Alan. "The Future of Global Unions: Is Solidarity Forever?" *Dissent* 54, no. 4 (2007): 62-70. http://www-mi4.csa.com.ezproxy.bpl.org/ (accessed February 17, 2008).

Chicago

V Documenting Sources

TUTORIAL

How do I cite documents from Web sites using Chicago style?

You will likely need to search the Web site to find some of the citation information you need. For some sites, all of the details may not be available; find as many as you can. Remember that the citation you provide should allow readers to retrace your steps electronically to locate the sources. Consult pp. 366–68 for additional models for citing Web sources.

Note

3. National Park Service, "Wildland Fire in Yellowstone," National Park Service, http://www.nps.gov/yell/naturescience/wildlandfire.htm (accessed February 27, 2008).

A **The author.** In the note, give the first name first. Follow the last name with a comma. Separate the names of multiple authors with commas; use the word *and* before the final author's name. If no specific author is named, as in this case, give the name of the sponsoring organization.

B **The title of the work.** Give the full title; include the subtitle (if any), preceded by a colon. Put the article title and subtitle in quotes, capitalizing all major words.

C **The name of the sponsoring organization.** If the sponsor's name is not visible on the document page, look at the bottom of the site's home page.

D **The URL.** Give the URL in full; do not use underlining or angle brackets, and be sure not to introduce any new hyphens or slashes.

E **The access date (optional).** If the document is time-sensitive or subject to change, you can include the word *accessed* and the date in parentheses.

Bibliography Entry
National Park Service. "Wildland Fire in Yellowstone." National Park Service. http://www.nps.gov/yell/naturescience/wildlandfire.htm (accessed February 27, 2008).

Use the bibliography tools at **bedfordresearcher.com** to create notes and a bibliography formatted in *Chicago* style.

Chicago-style Research Essay

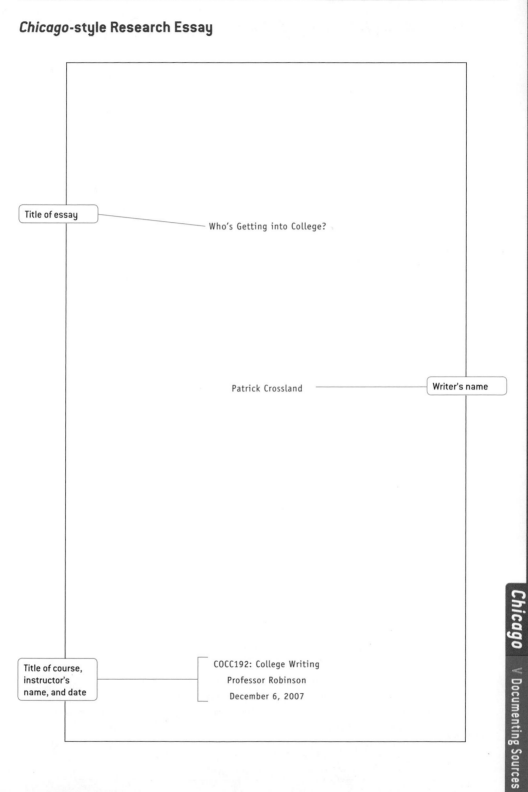

Title of essay

Who's Getting into College?

Patrick Crossland

Writer's name

Title of course, instructor's name, and date

COCC192: College Writing

Professor Robinson

December 6, 2007

Crossland   2

Title of essay repeated

Who's Getting into College?

Caleb Crossland is a junior in high school. Last night his mom attended his varsity wrestling match, cheering him on as he once again defeated his competitors. On the way home, they discussed his busy schedule, in which he balances both schoolwork and a job at his father's company. Caleb manages to get good grades in his classes while at the same time he learns a trade in the woodworking industry. Both of his parents are proud of him and support him as he accomplishes the various feats of yet another busy day.

As his senior year of high school approaches, Caleb is bombarded with information and applications from various colleges he is interested in attending. However, the more he studies the applications and their requirements, the more he is confused. He knows he wants to go to college, he's just not sure how to best position himself to get into his top choices. As he stares at the many essay questions, he wonders what exactly the colleges are looking for and who is getting in.

First two paragraphs offer an anecdote — a brief story — to draw readers into the text.

What many college applicants like Caleb don't realize is that getting into college is much like entering a contest in which each applicant is pitted against thousands of others. The objective of the college contest is to beat out the other competitors by getting good grades and scoring high on standardized tests, participating in academic or extracurricular activities, and having a particular economic background and race.

Thesis states Patrick's main point

Grades and Standardized Test Scores

Headings, centered throughout, help readers follow the essay's organization.

If you ask high school students what they worry most about in terms of getting into the college of their choice, most will answer their grades and standardized test scores. Indeed, experts agree that a student's intellect is an important admissions decision factor, as colleges tend to admit the students they feel have the greatest potential for academic success. Mary Lee Hoganson, college consultant for Homewood-Flossmoor High School in Flossmoor, Illinois, says that many colleges won't make a decision about a student's admittance until they have received his or her first semester senior grades, and many schools' offers of admission are contingent upon a student's continued high performance over the course of their senior year. According to Hoganson: "[Colleges] expect to see a performance that indicates you are ready for college-level work. . . . (Admissions letters often contain [contingency clauses requiring] continued successful performance.) It is not at all rare for a college to withdraw an offer of admission when grades drop significantly over the course of the senior year."[1]

Author tag indicates the source of paraphrased information.

Paraphrased information

Brackets and ellipses indicate the quotation has been modified.

Notes are numbered by order of appearance.

And it's not just grades that matter; admissions staff also look at the kind of courses students are taking. Nadine K. Maxwell, coordinator of guidance services for Fairfax County Public Schools in Fairfax, Virginia, says that college admissions staff are looking to see whether a student's high school academic profile "indicates that [he or she has] the potential for academic success on their campus."[2] Maxwell says admissions staff take into consideration whether the student has taken rigorous courses such as AP or honors courses. In addition, some admissions offices will consider the student's class rank and the quality of the student's high school as they decide whether to admit someone.

> A partial quotation is integrated effectively into the sentence.

Of course, one of the greatest monsters applicants must slay before they can enter college is taking an entrance exam or standardized test, such as the SAT and ACT. These tests are used by many colleges to assess student aptitude and academic capability. According to Joel Levine and Lawrence May, authors of *Getting In*, entrance exams are an extremely important part of a student's college application and carry a great deal of weight. In fact, they claim that a college entrance examination is "one of the two most significant factors" in getting into college (the other, unsurprisingly, being high school grades).[3]

However, in recent years, there has been much debate about the reliance on college entrance exams in assessing student aptitude. Says Derek Bok, professor at the John F. Kennedy School of Government at Harvard, the SAT "tells you very, very little about what [students are] going to contribute to the education of [their] classmates. It tells you very little about what [students are] going to be able to contribute to society, once [they] leave the college and those are very important considerations and have been for more than 100 years to universities."[4] In addition, tests such as the SAT "enhance the performance of those with conventional education and the experiences and values of American middle-class culture."[5] Thus, these tests do not accurately measure intelligence or aptitude because they fail to measure the skills and know-how of students from other cultures.

The good news is that the College Board has addressed the problem and is seeking ways to fix culturally unfair exams, and college admissions staff also have become increasingly aware of these problems; some schools do not even require such tests for admission. Meanwhile, according to howstuffworks.com, most colleges no longer have a set cutoff SAT score.[6] This means that even if an applicant's score is quite low, he or she may still be accepted. As the site notes, however, standardized test scores are all relative: "If your SAT score is under 1,000 and you're trying to get into a highly selective school

> The name of the Web site is used to identify the source.

Writer's name is
followed by the
page number.

that admits less than one-third of its applicants, you'll have to do
some pretty fast talking to qualify."[7] Although a low entrance exam
score won't put a student completely out of contention, those with
higher scores obviously have a greater chance of getting in.

Academic and Extracurricular Activities

Students' high school academic and extracurricular activities
(including their participation in clubs, involvement in sports and
community service, and after-school jobs) also have an impact on
admissions decisions, as colleges view past success as an indication of
future success. By proving that they are at the top of their class in a
certain subject or that they excel at a certain sport, students can el-
evate their chances of being accepted into the college of their choice.

William H. Gray III, president and chief executive officer of
the United Negro College Fund, notes that achievements in high
school play an important role in the admissions decisions made by
most college and universities. According to Gray, factors that affect
admissions decisions include participation in sports, involvement in
extracurricular activities, applicants' personal qualities, and "special
talents" applicants might possess. Duke University director of under-
graduate admissions Christoph Guttentag uses a baseball analogy in
describing how students advance in the admission process: "Think of
it as a baseball game. Everybody gets their time at bat. The quality
of [students'] academic work that we can measure (through test
scores and analysis of high school courses) gets about 10 percent of
the applicants to third base, 50 percent to second base and about
30 percent to first base. And 10 percent strike out."[8] According to
Guttentag, students can get closer to "home base" by participating in
extracurricular activities.

However, critics claim it is difficult to measure achievements,
and so there is no set-in-stone rule regarding how much different
colleges value extracurricular activities. Is earning a varsity letter
in sports worth more than winning a chess championship? Should a
student who has participated in the National Honor Society be rated
higher than a student who has designed Web sites professionally?
Obviously, it is difficult to assess excellence among such a broad
range of activities. However, much of the relevance of an activity
will depend on the particular college a student is applying to. For
example, if a student wants to attend film school, the admissions
department there would most likely value extracurricular activities
relating to film higher than it would those relating to, say, basketball (unless the school has a strong basketball team as well). Most
admissions experts agree that the bottom line is that students with

Crossland   5

extracurricular activities are more likely to get into college, as such activities indicate that the student will be well-rounded and have more to offer the college community.

Economic Background

A student's economic background can also affect his or her likelihood of being accepted into a particular college. Although the majority of colleges have what they call a "need-blind" admission policy, meaning that they do not take into account ability to pay as an admission criteria, there are schools that are "need-conscious," and a student's ability to pay will come into play.

In addition, a student's economic background not only plays a role in predicting who gets admitted into college, it helps determine whether a student is likely to apply to college in the first place. In the article "Getting into the Ivy League: How Family Composition Affects College Choice," Dean Lillard and Jennifer Gerner stress that a student's ability to obtain loans, his or her likelihood of getting financial aid, and family support all affect college admissions choices.[9] Students who grow up in poor neighborhoods or weak school districts are at a disadvantage compared with students from affluent neighborhoods and schools and may not be given the resources they need to help them with the college application process. In fact, many in the field of college education are working to determine what should be done to accommodate the needs of applicants whose backgrounds work against their being admitted to college and succeeding thereafter. They are hoping to improve the system of admittance and yet preserve a standard of excellence, ensuring that students who come from low-income backgrounds are reached and addressed in a manner that provides them the same opportunities afforded to students who come from more affluent backgrounds.

Mary Lee Hoganson, college consultant for Homewood-Flossmoor High School, suggests that students find out before they apply to schools whether they are need-blind or need-conscious. She also advises potential applicants to be aware and discerning: "If you need financial assistance, you wouldn't be well-served at a college that couldn't assist you financially."[10]

Race

Another variable in the realm of student background, and often the most controversial, is race. Affirmative action policies that weight a minority's application higher than a nonminority student's application are practiced frequently in admissions processes to ensure that colleges across the nation have a mixed student body. Although they play an important role in determining who gets into college,

Crossland   6

high school grades, test scores, extracurricular activities, and various other attributes get nowhere near as much attention in public discussions and the news media as does the issue of race-based admissions. In his article "In the Best Interest of America, Affirmative Action in Higher Education Is a Must," William H. Gray III states: "At many colleges it is acceptable to use preferences in admissions based on student characteristics such as special talents, geographic origin, and alumni legacy. The most publicized and debated preference, however, is race."[11]

In fact, Gray observes that ever since John F. Kennedy, "[E]very American President has used an Executive Order to attempt to eliminate discrimination by race, color and gender in the federal government and its agencies." Thus, for years the highest executive powers have attempted to deal with race and equality in college admissions.

Proponents of race-based admissions claim it's important to give minority students an advantage when considering their applications, in part to compensate for disadvantages they normally face and in part because by admitting students of different races, the college prepares all its students for the real world. Says Derek Bok:

> If you understand what the purposes of selective universities are, I think you see very quickly why it's fair to put weight on race. One of the purposes is to educate students for an increasingly diverse society by allowing them to study in an environment where they live and work together with different races. . . . To achieve that purpose, you need to make sure you have a diverse student body. The second thing that we're trying to do is to respond to a need which is proclaimed all the time in the outside society for more minority representation among business executives, doctors, lawyers, other professions and positions of influence in the society. . . .
>
> To do that, you've got to have a pool of well-qualified, well-prepared candidates, so universities are trying to get a student body of people who have a contribution to make as leaders and in the different professions in their communities. . . .
>
> Race becomes a relevant consideration because there are exceptional opportunities for minorities, because they're in such short supply, to move into these professions and positions where they are being asked for by society.[12]

However, there are those who, as Gray puts it, "contend that preferences based upon race are illegal and unfair." Charles Krauthammer, author of "Lies, Damn Lies, and Racial Statistics," claims

> **Extended quotation of eight or more lines is set off in block style without quotation marks.**

> **Source of extended quotation is provided in a note.**

that bright, young minority students who were qualified to attend many schools are "artificially turned into failures by being admitted to high-pressure campuses, where only students with exceptional academic backgrounds can survive."[13] Krauthammer claims that it is important to avoid hurting minorities by sending them into a situation that they are not prepared to deal with.[14]

> Source of paraphrased material is provided in a note.

Although the debate about the fairness of the role of affirmative action in the college admissions process continues, Christoph Guttentag sees the situation in a bit broader terms. He says the most selective schools — those that admit only 30 percent of those who apply — won't admit students "simply to make the school's minority numbers look better. Most schools want students who are going to succeed there. To admit someone who isn't likely to be successful is not good for anybody — not for the university and not for the student."[15] So although race does matter when it comes to admissions, it's not going to guarantee a student a place, nor is it going to necessarily be a factor for exclusion.

> A colon (:) is not used when the quoted text in a quotation is part of the sentence.

Other Factors

Other, somewhat simpler factors affect a student's chance of being accepted into the college of his or her choice. Strong letters of recommendation and a clear, coherent essay can help applicants propel themselves above others. Applying early may also help students get accepted. Nadine K. Maxwell, guidance services coordinator in Fairfax, Virginia, says that students' chances of being admitted can be greater if they apply early, although this varies from school to school and year to year and "may depend upon the applicant pool at the school where [they] are applying."[16] Maxwell advises students to "[d]o your homework first and check to see what percentage of the students in the previous graduating classes at your high school were admitted early decision to a specific college or university. Are you qualified to apply as early decision? If you are, and this is a school you really wish to attend, then apply early decision."[17]

College consultant Mary Lee Hoganson also says that students should let a college know whether it is their first choice, especially if they are placed on the waitlist. She advises further: "Write a letter to the Director of Admission expressing your continuing strong interest and updating the admission office with any new information that reflects well on your ability to contribute to the quality of the freshman class. In addition, you may wish to ask your counselor to make a call on your behalf. Many colleges keep track of these kinds of contacts and students who are enthusiastic and persistent will get

Crossland   8

looked at first. Colleges want to admit students off the waitlist who

they believe will accept the offer of admission."[18]

> **Summarized material from a book follows.**

Bill Paul, author of *Getting In: Inside the College Admissions*

Process, a book that tells the stories of several students applying to

an elite Ivy League institution, shares three suggestions for students

who want to get into college. Paul bases these suggestions on his

discussions with Fred Hargadon, who in 1995 was dean of admissions

at Princeton. Hargadon suggested that the best way students can

> **The original source of the summarized material is identified.**

enhance their chances for acceptance into the college of their choice

is to read widely, learn to speak a second language, and engage

in activities that interest and excite them and that also help them

develop their confidence and creativity.[19] The idea, it seems, is that

being an active learner, someone who is creative and enthusiastic

about what he or she is doing, is more important than what you do.

According to Paul, it might not be important whether you've won a

medal in track or a prize for poetry as long as you are engaged with,

confident about, and committed to the activity.[20]

Finally, just because a student doesn't get into his or her dream

school doesn't mean all hope is lost. Most community colleges have

academic requirements that include only a high school diploma or

GED. If the student earns good grades at the community college level,

he or she may be able to transfer to a more competitive and selective

college or university later.

Conclusion

Harvard professor Derek Bok describes the college

admissions process well: "What you have to ask is [whether] this

student — compared with this student and looked at in the context

of the class as a whole — is going to contribute more to the learning

environment on campus and then has a better chance at making a big

contribution to society than some other student."[21]

> **Patrick returns to the anecdote he used to introduce the essay.**

Thus, in the midst of Caleb Crossland's busy schedule, he ap-

plies to various colleges he wants to attend. He continues to get

good grades, studies for the SAT, and stays involved in extracurricular

activities. He researches schools and plans to apply early. And with

the support of his family, Caleb should have an edge over the many

other students competing against him for a spot at the nation's top

colleges.

Crossland   9

Notes

1. College Board, "Experts Answer Your Application Questions: Get the Inside Scoop on Applying to College," *Collegeboard.com*, http://www.collegeboard.com/article/0,1120,5-26-0-8487,00.html?orig=sec (accessed November 14, 2007).

2. Ibid.

3. Joel Levine and Lawrence May, *Getting In* (New York: Random House, 1972), 116.

4. Derek Bok, interview, *PBS Online,* November 12, 2004, http://www.pbs.org/wgbh/pages/frontline/shows/sats/interviews/bok.html (accessed November 17, 2007).

5. Levine and May, *Getting In,* 118.

6. How Stuff Works, "How College Admission Works," *Howstuffworks.com,* http://people.howstuffworks.com/college-admission.htm (accessed November 20, 2007).

7. Ibid.

8. Ibid.

9. Dean Lillard and Jennifer Gerner, "Getting into the Ivy League: How Family Composition Affects College Choice," *Journal of Higher Education* (November-December 1999): 709.

10. College Board, "Experts Answer."

11. William H. Gray III, "In the Best Interest of America, Affirmative Action in Higher Education Is a Must," *The Black Collegian,* February 1, 1999, 144-146, http://www.elibrary.com/education (accessed November 20, 2007).

12. Bok, interview.

13. Charles Krauthammer, "Lies, Damn Lies, and Racial Statistics: Figures from All the University of California Campuses Paint Another Picture," *Time,* April 20, 1998, 86.

14. Ibid.

15. "How College Admission Works."

16. College Board, "Experts Answer."

17. Ibid.

18. Ibid.

19. Bill Paul, *Getting In: Inside the College Admissions Process* (Reading, MA: Addison-Wesley, 1995), 238-49.

20. Ibid., 249.

21. Bok, interview.

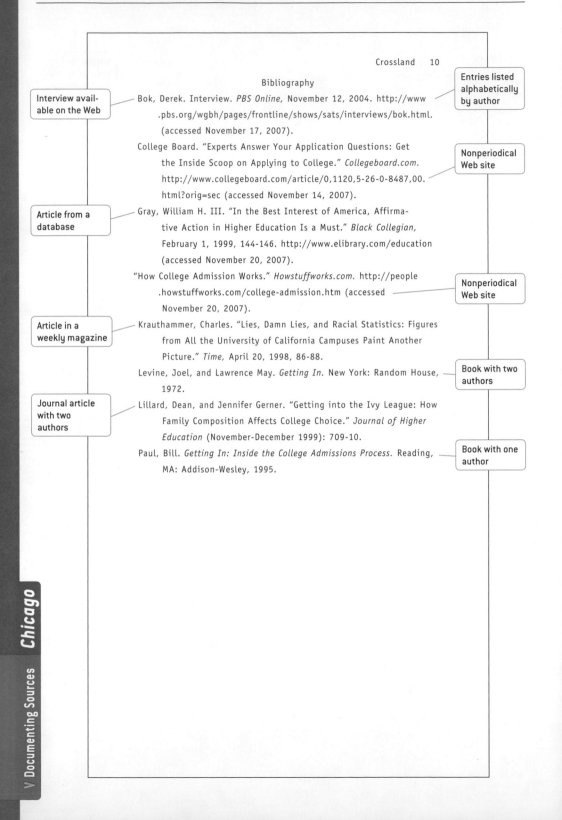

Crossland   10

Entries listed alphabetically by author

Bibliography

Interview available on the Web
Bok, Derek. Interview. *PBS Online,* November 12, 2004. http://www
.pbs.org/wgbh/pages/frontline/shows/sats/interviews/bok.html.
(accessed November 17, 2007).

Nonperiodical Web site
College Board. "Experts Answer Your Application Questions: Get
the Inside Scoop on Applying to College." *Collegeboard.com.*
http://www.collegeboard.com/article/0,1120,5-26-0-8487,00.
html?orig=sec (accessed November 14, 2007).

Article from a database
Gray, William H. III. "In the Best Interest of America, Affirmative Action in Higher Education Is a Must." *Black Collegian,*
February 1, 1999, 144-146. http://www.elibrary.com/education
(accessed November 20, 2007).

Nonperiodical Web site
"How College Admission Works." *Howstuffworks.com.* http://people
.howstuffworks.com/college-admission.htm (accessed
November 20, 2007).

Article in a weekly magazine
Krauthammer, Charles. "Lies, Damn Lies, and Racial Statistics: Figures
from All the University of California Campuses Paint Another
Picture." *Time,* April 20, 1998, 86-88.

Book with two authors
Levine, Joel, and Lawrence May. *Getting In.* New York: Random House,
1972.

Journal article with two authors
Lillard, Dean, and Jennifer Gerner. "Getting into the Ivy League: How
Family Composition Affects College Choice." *Journal of Higher
Education* (November-December 1999): 709-10.

Book with one author
Paul, Bill. *Getting In: Inside the College Admissions Process.* Reading,
MA: Addison-Wesley, 1995.

23

Using CSE Style

 Key Questions

23a. How do I cite sources within the text of my document?   385

23b. How do I prepare the reference list?   385

In 2000, the Council of Biology Editors (CBE) changed its name to the Council of Science Editors (CSE) to more accurately reflect its expanding membership. In this book, CSE style is based on the seventh edition of *Scientific Style and Format: The CSE Manual for Authors, Editors, and Publishers.*

  CSE style, used primarily in the physical sciences, life sciences, and mathematics, recommends two systems:

- a citation-sequence system, which lists sources in the reference list according to the order in which they appear in the document
- a name-year system, which is similar to the author-date system used by the APA (see Chapter 21).

This chapter describes and provides models for the citation-sequence system. For more information on CSE style, visit the Council of Science Editors Web site at councilscienceeditors.org.

CITATIONS WITHIN YOUR TEXT

1. Format and placement of the note   385
2. Citing a previously mentioned source   385
3. Citing a source within a source   385

ENTRIES IN YOUR REFERENCE LIST

Books, Conference Proceedings, and Dissertations

4. One author   386
5. Two or more authors   386
6. Corporate or group author   386
7. Unknown author   387
8. Translated book   387
9. Book in an edition other than the first   387

23a

How do I cite sources within the text of my document?

The CSE citation-sequence system uses sequential numbers to refer to sources within a document. These numbers, in turn, correspond to numbered entries in the reference list. This approach to citing sources reduces distraction to the reader and saves space within a document.

1. Format and Placement of the Note   Sources are cited using superscript numbers or numbers placed in parentheses. Superscript numbers should be formatted in a font one or two points smaller than the body text:

> The anomalies in the data [3] call the study's methods into question.

> The anomalies in the data (3) call the study's methods into question.

2. Citing a Previously Mentioned Source   Use the first number assigned to a source when citing the source for the second time. In the following examples, the author is referring to sources earlier numbered 3, 9, and 22:

> The outlying data points [3,9,22] seem to suggest a bias in the methodology.

> The outlying data points (3,9,22) seem to suggest a bias in the methodology.

3. Citing a Source within a Source   When referring to a source cited in another source, use the phrase "cited in":

> The results [12(cited in 8)] collected in the first month of the study . . .

> The results (12 cited in 8) collected in the first month of the study . . .

23b

How do I prepare the reference list?

CSE style specifies that you should create a list of works that are cited in your document or that contributed to your thinking about the document. Sources cited should be identified in a section titled "References," while sources that contributed to your thinking should be given in a section titled "Additional References."

There are, however, two exceptions: personal communication and oral presentations.

Personal communication, such as correspondence and interviews, is cited only in the text of your document, using the term "unreferenced" to indicate that it is not found in the reference list:

> . . . this disease has proven to be resistant to antibiotics under specific conditions (a 2008 letter from Meissner to me; unreferenced, see "Notes").

Typically, information about personal communication is placed in a "Notes" or "Acknowledgments" section. Similarly, oral presentations at conferences that are not available in any form (such as microform, reference database, conference proceedings, or online) should be cited in the text of your document but not included in your reference list.

The *CSE Manual* does not specify the location of the reference list, deferring instead to the formatting guidelines of individual journals in the sciences. In general, however, the reference list appears at the end of print documents and linear documents that are distributed electronically (such as word processing files or newsgroup posts). In the case of longer documents or documents in which sections of a book (such as chapters) are intended to stand on their own, the reference list might appear at the end of each section or chapter. In electronic documents that use links, such as Web sites, the reference list often is a separate page to which other pages are linked.

To see an example of a CSE-style reference list, turn to p. 398.

Books, Conference Proceedings, and Dissertations

4. One Author   Give the author's last name and first initial with no comma. Next, include the title, capitalizing only the first word and proper nouns, followed by publication information.

4. Lomborg B. Cool it: the skeptical environmentalist's guide to global warming. New York: Knopf; 2007.

5. Two or More Authors   List the authors in the order in which they appear on the title page, each of them last name first. Note that periods are not used after initials. Separate authors with commas.

5. Sawyer GJ, Deak V, Sarmiento E, Miller R. The last human: a guide to twenty-two species of extinct humans. New Haven: Yale University Press; 2007.

6. Corporate or Group Author   Identify the organization as the author.

6. National Geographic. Essential visual history of the world. Washington (DC): National Geographic; 2007.

7. Unknown Author Begin with the title.

7. The first 100,000 prime numbers. Lenox (MA): Hard Press; 2007.

8. Translated Book Identify the translator after the title, giving last name first.

8. Dubuisson D. The western construction of religion: myths, knowledge, and ideology. Sayers W, translator. Baltimore: Johns Hopkins University Press; 2008.

9. Book in an Edition Other Than the First Note the edition (for instance, "2nd ed." or "New rev. ed.") after the title and with a separating period.

9. Lin SD. Water and wastewater calculations manual. 2nd ed. New York: McGraw-Hill; 2007.

10. Multivolume Work Include the total number of volumes if you are making a reference to all volumes in the work, or "Vol." followed by the specific volume number followed by the title of that volume (if that volume is separately titled).

10. Tippler PA, Mosca G. Physics for scientists and engineers. Vol. 2. New York: Freeman; 2007.

11. Authored Book with an Editor Identify the editor before the publication information.

11. Darwin C. Evolution: selected letters 1860-1870. Burkhardt FH, Pearn AM, Evans S, editors. Cambridge (GB): Cambridge University Press; 2008.

12. Book in a Series

12. Nishida T, editor. Conversational informatics: an engineering approach. Hoboken (NJ): Wiley, 2008. (Wiley series in agent technology).

13. Anthology or Collection with an Editor To cite an anthology of essays or a collection of articles, treat the editor's name as you would an author's name. Identify with the word "editor."

13. Naveh Z, editor. Transdisciplinary challenges in landscape ecology and restoration ecology. New York: Springer; 2007.

14. Chapter in an Edited Book or a Work in an Anthology List the author and title of the section; then include the word "In" followed by a colon, the editor's name (last name first followed by initials) and the word "editor." Include the book title, place, and publisher, and note the inclusive pages of the section rather than the total number of pages in the book.

CSE

V Documenting Sources

14. Bader EJ. Thinking green: writing the advocacy essay. In: McEwen C, Statman M, editors. The alphabet of the trees: a guide to nature writing. New York: Teachers & Writers Collective; 2007. p. 49-52.

15. Foreword, Introduction, Preface, or Afterword of a Book If the part is written by someone other than the author of the book, treat it as you would a chapter in an edited book (see #14), but do not identify the author of the book as an "editor."

15. Rhodes R. Introduction. In: Craves G. Power to save the world: the truth about nuclear energy. New York: Knopf; 2007. p. vii-xviii.

16. Chapter of a Book If you wish to refer to a chapter of a book, identify the chapter of the book after the publication information. Identify the inclusive pages of the chapter.

16. Pollan M. The omnivore's dilemma: a natural history of four meals. New York: Penguin; 2006. Chapter 9, Big organic; p. 134-184.

17. Published Proceedings of a Conference List the editors of the proceedings as authors (if there are no editors, write "Anonymous" in square brackets). Give the title of the publication and, if different, the name of the conference that produced it; the date and place of the conference; and the place of publication, publisher, and date.

17. Aslam MJ, Hussain F, Qadir A, Riazuddin R, Saleem H, editors. Mathematical Physics: Proceedings of the 12th Regional Conference; 2006 Mar 28-31; Islamabad. Hackensack (NJ): World Scientific; c2007.

18. Paper Published in the Proceedings of a Conference Format the citation as you would a chapter in an edited book.

18. Leites D, Sachse C. On critical dimensions of string theory. In: Aslam MJ, Hussain F, Qadir A, Riazuddin R, Saleem H, editors. Mathematical Physics: Proceedings of the 12th Regional Conference; 2006 Mar 28-31; Islamabad. Hackensack (NJ): World Scientific; c2007. p. 31-38.

19. Published Dissertation or Thesis Use the general format for a book, adding the word "dissertation" or "thesis" in square brackets after the title. Treat the institution granting the degree as the publisher. Follow with the phrase "Available from" followed by a colon, followed by the *Dissertation Abstracts International* information.

19. Smith-Downey NV. Soil uptake of molecular hydrogen and remote sensing of soil freeze and thaw [dissertation]. Pasadena: California Institute of Technology; 2007. Available from: UMI, Ann Arbor, MI; 3244124.

20. Unpublished Dissertation or Thesis Use the general format for a book, adding the word "dissertation" or "thesis" in square brackets as a final element of the title. Treat the institution granting the degree as the publisher.

20. Seung E. Examining the development of knowledge for teaching a novel introductory physics curriculum [dissertation]. West Lafayette (IN): Purdue University; 2007.

Sources in Journals, Magazines, and Newspapers

21. Article in a Journal Abbreviate and capitalize all of the major words in a journal's title; omit articles, conjunctions, and prepositions. The CSE manual includes specific guidelines for citing journal titles. A semicolon separates the year and volume number. Give the issue number in parentheses, followed by a colon and the page numbers. There are no spaces between the year, volume number, and page numbers.

21. Mayer S. Cape Wind: a public policy debate for the physical sciences. J Coll Sci Teaching. 2007;37(4):24.

22. Article in a Magazine Magazines are not identified by volume. Give only the date (year, month, day for weekly magazines; year and month for monthly magazines).

22. Langreth R. Cancer: the quest for a protective diet. Forbes. 2007 Nov 26:78.

23. Article in a Newspaper Treat newspaper articles as you would magazine articles, identifying their pages by section, page, and column on which they begin (in parentheses).

23. Kay J. Third of kids' jewelry items contained illegal lead levels. San Francisco Chronicle. 2007 Dec 14;Sect. B:3 (col. 1).

24. Unsigned Article in a Newspaper In place of the author's name, write "Anonymous" in square brackets.

24. [Anonymous]. After Annapolis. Wall Street Journal. 2007 Nov 29;Sect. A:18 (col. 1).

Print Reference Works

25. Encyclopedia, Dictionary, Thesaurus, Handbook, or Almanac Begin with the title of the reference work and information about the edition. Identify the editor, if listed. Provide publisher and publication date.

25. Concise encyclopedia of polymer science and technology. 3rd ed. Mark HF, editor. New York: Wiley-Interscience; 2007.

CSE

V Documenting Sources

26. Map or Chart   Use the name of the area in place of an author. Follow with the title, type of map in brackets (such as physical map or demographic map), place of publication and publisher, and a description of the map. If the map is part of a larger document, such as an atlas, provide publication information for the document and the page number(s) of the map.

26. Australia and Oceania. Southwest Pacific [physical and political map].
    In: Oxford atlas of the world. 11th ed. London: Oxford University Press;
    2007. p. 122-123. Color.

27. Pamphlet   Format entries as you would for a book (see also #4 on p. 386).

27. American Academy of Dermatology. Skin cancer. Schaumburg (IL):
    American Academy of Dermatology; 2007.

Media Sources

28. Film or Video Recording   Give the title, then the type of medium identified in square brackets, followed by individuals listed as authors, editors, performers, conductors, and so on. Identify the producer if different from the publisher. Provide publication information.

28. Inside the living body [DVD]. Goodman K, Simon K, directors.
    Washington (DC): National Geographic; 2007.

29. Television Program   CSE style does not provide guidance on citing television programs. Cite as you would a film or video recording.

29. Exposé: the scientific method [television program]. Dewitt M, writer and
    producer. New York: Thirteen/WNET; 2007.

30. Radio Program   CSE style does not provide guidance on citing radio programs. Cite as you would a film or video recording.

30. Talk of the nation: science Friday [radio program]. Flatow I, host.
    New York: National Public Radio; 2008.

31. Sound Recording   Cite as you would a film or video recording.

31. African safari: Madagascar [sound recording]. Quin D, sound recordist.
    Glen Ellen (CA): Wild Sanctuary; 2002.

Field Sources

32. Personal Interview   Treat unpublished interviews as personal communication (see p. 386). Cite them in the text only; do not cite them in the reference list.

33. Personal Letter   Cite personal letters as personal communication (see p. 386). Cite them in the text only; do not cite them in the reference list.

34. Lecture or Public Address   Like an unpublished paper presented at a meeting, lectures or public addresses are treated as personal communication and are cited only in the text (see p. 386).

Electronic Sources

35. Material from an Online Database

35. Koenig R. African penguin populations reported in a puzzling decline. Science. 2007 Mar 2;315(5816):1205. In: Expanded Academic ASAP [database on the Internet]. Farmington Hills (MI): Gale; c2007 [cited 2008 Jan 24]. Available from: http://infotrac.galegroup.com/itw. Article A160713267.

36. Electronic Book (Monograph)

36. Franks S. Dynamics of cancer: incidence, inheritance, and evolution [Internet]. Princeton: Princeton University Press; 2007 [cited 2008 May 1]. Available from: http://www.ncbi.nlm.nih.gov/books/ bv.fcgi?rid=dyncan.TOC

37. Electronic Journal Article

37. Augusteyn RC. Growth of the human eye lens. Mol Vision [Internet]. 2007 Feb 23 [cited 2008 Jun 3];13:252-257. Available from: http://www .molvis.org/molvis/v13/a29/.

38. Electronic Newspaper Article

38. Rosenthal E. Both sides cite science to address altered corn. NY Times on the Web [Internet]. 2007 Dec 26 [cited 2008 Jan 7]. Available from: http://www.nytimes.com/2007/12/26/business/ worldbusiness/26corn.html

39. Web Site

39. Geology & Public Policy [Internet]. Boulder (CO): Geological Society of America; c2005 [updated 2007 Nov 30; cited 2008 Feb 8]. Available from: http://www.geosociety.org/geopolicy/.

CSE

V Documenting Sources

40. Document on a Web Site

40. Centers for Disease Control and Prevention [Internet]. Atlanta: Centers
    for Disease Control and Prevention (US); c2007. Autism spectrum
    disorders overview; 2007 Feb 9 [cited 2008 Jan 16]. Available from:
    http://www.cdc.gov/ncbddd/autism/overview.htm

41. Email Message   Email messages are considered personal communication
(see p. 386). Cite them in the text only; do not cite them in the reference list.

42. Electronic Discussion List Message

42. Matekaire T. Plant leaf nucleus antibody. In: BIONET [discussion list on
    the Internet]. [London; Medical Research Council]; 2007 Nov 12, 4:02
    am [cited 2008 Feb 28]. Available from: http://www.bio.net/bionet/
    mm/plantbio/2007-November/027588.html

43. Article Posted on a Wiki

43. Disease transmission primer. In: Fluwiki [wiki on the Internet]. 2007
    Jun 10 [cited 2008 Jan 8]. Available from: http://www.fluwikie.com/
    pmwiki.php?n=Science.DiseaseTransmissionPrimer

44. Entire Blog

44. Orth JF. Invasive species weblog [blog on the Internet]. 2007
    Dec 31 [cited 2008 Jan 1]. Available from: http://invasivespecies
    .blogspot.com/.

45. Entry or Comment on a Blog

45. Raymo C. Carbon footprints in the sand. Science musings [blog on
    the Internet]. 2008 Jan 5 [cited 2008 Jan 20]. Available from: http://
    www.sciencemusings.com/blog/.

TUTORIAL

How do I cite books using CSE style?

When citing a book, use the information from the title page and the copyright page (on the reverse side of the title page), not from the book's cover or a library catalog. This page gives an example of a citation the CSE citation-sequence system.

Consult pp. 386–89 for additional models for citing books.

A   **B**

1. Hawken P. Blessed unrest: how the largest movement in the world came

C   **D**   **E**

into being and why no one saw it coming. New York: Viking; 2007.

A **The author.** Give the last name first, followed by initials for first and middle names. Separate the last name and initials with only a space, not a comma. Do not separate initials. Separate the names of multiple authors with commas (Cobb C, Fetterolf ML). End with a period.

B **The title.** Give the full title; include the subtitle (if any), preceded by a colon. Capitalize only the first word of the title and proper nouns. Do not underline or italicize the title or subtitle. End with a period.

C **The city of publication.** If more than one city is given, use the first one listed. For a city that may be unfamiliar to your readers or confused with another city, add an abbreviation of the state, country, or province in parentheses: Depew (OK). Insert a colon.

D **The publisher.** Give the publisher's name, omitting *The* at the beginning. Insert a semicolon.

E **The date of publication.** Use the publication date if one is given; otherwise use the copyright date. If a month of publication is given, use that as well (2008 Aug).

Use the bibliography tools at **bedfordresearcher.com** to create a reference list formatted in CSE style.

CSE

∨ Documenting Sources

TUTORIAL

How do I cite articles from periodicals using CSE style?

Periodicals include journals, magazines, and newspapers. This page gives an example of a citation for a print magazine article. Models for citing articles from journals and newspapers are on p. 389. If you need to cite a periodical article you accessed electronically, follow the guidelines below and see p. 391.

A ──────── **B** ──────── **C** ── **D** ── **E**

2. Davies P. Are aliens among us? Sci Am. 2007 Dec: 62-69.

A **The author.** Give the last name first, followed by initials for first and middle names. Separate the last name and initials with only a space, not a comma. Do not separate initials. Separate the names of multiple authors with commas (Cobb C, Fetterolf ML). End with a period.

B **The article title.** Give the full title; include the subtitle (if any), preceded by a colon. Capitalize only the first word of the title and proper nouns. Do not underline or italicize the title or subtitle. End with a period; in this example, the title has its own ending punctuation, a question mark, and therefore does not need a period.

C **The periodical title.** Do not underline or italicize the periodical title; abbreviate and capitalize all major words. Omit articles, conjunctions, and prepositions. The CSE manual includes guidelines for abbreviating journal titles.

D **The date of publication.** For magazines and newspapers, include the month and, if available, the day (2008 Apr 13). Insert a colon.

E **Inclusive page number(s).** Give the page numbers on which the article appears; list the numbers in full (154-177; 1187-1188). End with a period.

Use the bibliography tools at **bedfordresearcher.com** to create a reference list formatted in CSE style.

TUTORIAL

How do I cite articles from databases using CSE style?

Libraries subscribe to services such as Lexis-Nexis, ProQuest, InfoTrac, and EBSCOhost that provide access to databases of electronic texts. The databases provide publication information, abstracts, and the complete text of documents in a specific subject area, discipline, or profession. (See also Chapter 9.) This page gives an example of a reference in CSE citation-sequence style.

A **B**

2. Klieger C, Pollex E, Koren G. Treating the mother–protecting the unborn:

C

the safety of hypoglycemic drugs in pregnancy. J Matern Fetal Neonatal Med.

D **E** **F**

2008 Mar;21(3):191-6. In: PubMed [database on the Internet]. Bethesda

G

(MD): US National Library of Medicine; c2008 [cited 2008 Feb 26].

H

Available from: http://www.ncbi.nlm.nih.gov/pubmed/18297574?

ordinalpos=1&itool=EntrezSystem2.PEntrez.Pubmed.Pubmed_ResultsPanel

.Pubmed_RVDocSum

A **The author.** Give the last name first, followed by initials for first and middle names. Separate the last name and initials with only a space, not a comma. Do not separate initials. Separate the names of multiple authors with commas (Cobb C, Fetterolf ML). End with a period.

B **The article title.** Give the full title; include the subtitle (if any), preceded by a colon. Capitalize only the first word of the title and proper nouns. Do not underline or italicize the title or subtitle. End with a period.

C **The periodical title.** Do not underline or italicize the periodical title; abbreviate and capitalize all major words. Omit articles, conjunctions, and prepositions. The CSE manual includes guidelines for abbreviating journal titles.

D **The date of publication.** For magazines and newspapers, include the month and, if available, the day (2008 Apr 13). Insert a semicolon.

396   CHAPTER 23 • USING CSE STYLE

E **The volume, issue, and inclusive page numbers.** Give the issue number in parentheses; do not insert a space between the volume and issue numbers. Then give the page numbers on which the article appears; list the numbers in full (154-177; 1187-1188). End with a period.

F **Database and publication information.** After the word *In* and a colon, give the name of the database, followed by *database on the Internet* in brackets. Then give the place of publication, the publisher of the database (preceded by a colon), and the copyright year.

G **Date of access.** Give the access date in brackets and end with a period.

H **The URL.** Give the URL, preceded by *Available from* and a colon.

Use the bibliography tools at **bedfordresearcher.com** to create a reference list formatted in CSE style.

CSE

∨ Documenting Sources

TUTORIAL

How do I cite works from Web sites using CSE style?

You will likely need to search the Web site to find some of the citation information you need. For some sites, all of the details may not be available; find as many as you can. Remember that the citation you provide should allow readers to retrace your steps electronically to locate the sources. Consult pp. 391–92 for additional models for citing Web sources.

┌──────────── **A** ────────────┐ ┌──────────── **B** ────────────┐
2. Natural Resources Defense Council [Internet]. Seeking friendlier skies: NRDC

urges U.S. and Canadian airlines to favor renewable energy over dirty fuel.
┌────────── **C** ──────────┐ ┌────────── **D** ──────────┐
New York: Natural Resources Defense Council; c2008 [cited 2008 Feb 27].
┌──────────────── **E** ────────────────┐
Available from: http://beyondoil.nrdc.org/news/friendlyskies

A **The author.** Give the name of the organization or individual author, last name first followed by initials for first and middle names. Separate the last name and initials with only a space, not a comma; separate the names of multiple authors with commas (Cobb C, Fetterolf ML). Include the word *Internet* in brackets. End with a period.

B **The document title.** Give the full title; include the subtitle (if any), preceded by a colon. Capitalize only the first word of the title and proper nouns. Do not underline or italicize the title or subtitle. End with a period.

C **Publisher information.** Give the place of publication followed by a colon, then the publisher or sponsoring organization followed by a semicolon.

D **Publication date and date of access.** Give the date of publication or the copyright date on the Web site; if available, include the date of modification or update in brackets. Then give the date of access in brackets. End with a period.

E **The URL.** Give the URL, preceded by *Available from* and a colon.

Use the bibliography tools at **bedfordresearcher.com** to create a reference list formatted in CSE style.

CSE

V Documenting Sources

A Reference List in CSE Citation-Sequence Style

The reference
list is titled
"References."

REFERENCES

1. Dodds W. Humanity's footprint: momentum, impact, and our global environment. New York: Columbia University Press; 2007.

2. Hall, S. Pandas: still at risk. San Diego zoo: conservation and research for endangered species [blog on the Internet]. 2007 Nov 15 [cited 2008 Jan 22]. Available from: http://www.sandiegozoo.org/wordpress/default/pandas-still-at-risk/

3. Bradshaw C. Having your water and drinking it too: resource limitation modifies density regulation. J Anim Ecol. 2007;77(1):1-4.

4. Skidmore AK, Ferwerda JG. Resource distribution and dynamics: mapping herbivore resources. In: Prins HT, van Langevelde F, editors. Resource ecology: spatial and temporal dynamics of foraging. Dordrecht (NL): Springer; 2008. p. 57-78.

5. Animal Ecology Group [Internet]. c2006. Groningen (NL): University of Groningen [updated 2007 Jun 29; cited 2008 Jan 22]. Available from: http://www.rug.nl/biologie/onderzoek/onderzoekgroepen/dieroecologie/index

The reference list is not alphabetical. Sources are numbered and listed in the order in which they appear in the document.

Titles of books and periodicals are neither underlined nor italicized. All major words in the titles of periodicals are capitalized. For all other sources, only initial words of the main title and proper nouns and adjectives are capitalized.

Acknowledgments (continued from page vi)

Figure 2.7: Birger T. Madsen, "Energy's Wind of Change" Screen shot. Reprinted from *The UNESCO Courier*, March 2000. www.unesco.org/courier. Used with permission of the publisher.

Figure 2.8: CNN.com screenshot. "Farming the Wind Efficiently." © 2008 Cable News Network. Turner Broadcasting System, Inc. All Rights Reserved.

Figure 2.9: Roddy Scheer, excerpt from "A Mighty Wind" from *E/The Environmental Magazine* (September/October 2003). Copyright © 2003. Reprinted with the permission of *E/The Environmental Magazine*.

Figure 4.2: "Getting to the Ivy League: How family composition affects college choice." Highlighted and Annotated by Patrick Crossland, Featured Writer. Article written by Dean Lillard, Jennifer Gerner. First published in *Journal of Higher Education*, 706-70, No. 6 (November/December 1999, pp. 706–730). Copyright Ohio State University Press, Nov/Dec 1999.

Page 58: Chris Norris. "Heavy metal becoming increasingly political." Article marked and annotated by Chris Norris. Published by AP/Associated Press, August 10, 2006. Copyright © 2006 The Associated Press. Used by permission of The YGS Group, on behalf of the publisher.

Figures 4.3: Derek Bok, PBS *Online/Frontline* "Secrets of the SAT" Interview. From Frontline/WGBH Educational Foundation. Copyright © 2008 WGBH/Boston. Full text of interview is located at: www.pbs.org/wgbh/pages/frontline/shows/sats/interviews/bok. Used with permission.

Page 74: UMNnews screenshot. Ann Freeman. "The dope on steroids: why some athletes take the risk." Published online August 21, 2004. www.umn.edu. © 2004–2007 Regents of the University of Minnesota. Used with permission. All rights reserved.

Figure 6.1: Derek Bok. PBS *Online/Frontline* Interview. From Frontline/WGBH Educational Foundation. Copyright © 2008 WGBH/Boston. Full text of interview is located at: www.pbs.org/wgbh/pages/frontline/shows/sats/interviews/bok. Used with permission. Annotations by Patrick Crossland, Featured Writer.

Figure 8.1: "Getting to the Ivy League: How family composition affects college choice" by Dean Lillard, Jennifer Gerner. First published in *Journal of Higher Education*, 706-70, No. 6 (November/December 1999, pp. 706–730). Copyright Ohio State University Press, Nov/Dec 1999.

Figure 9.2: Searching by Keyword in an Online Library Catalog screenshot. © 2008 Innovative Interfaces, Inc. Used by permission.

Figure 9.3: Searching by Keyword in an Online Library Catalog screenshot. © 2008 Innovative Interfaces, Inc. Used by permission.

Figure 9.4: EBSCOHost Research Databases screen site. © EBSCO Publishing, Inc. Reprinted with the permission of EBSCO Industries, Inc. All rights reserved.

Figure 9.5: EBSCOHost Research Databases screen site. © EBSCO Publishing, Inc. Reprinted with the permission of EBSCO Industries, Inc. All rights reserved.

Figure 9.6: OCLC FirstSearch Screen shot, ArticleFirst Advanced Search. FirstSearch® Copyright © 1992–2008 OCLC. Used by permission of OCLC FirstSearch WorldCat Services. All Rights Reserved.

Figure 9.7: EBSCOHost Research Databases screen site. © EBSCO Publishing, Inc. Reprinted with the permission of EBSCO Industries, Inc. All rights reserved.

Figure 9.8: OCLC FirstSearch Screen shot. ArticleFirst Boolean Search in an Advanced Search Form. FirstSearch® Copyright © 1992–2008 OCLC. Used by permission of OCLC FirstSearch WorldCat Services. All Rights Reserved.

Figure 9.9: OCLC FirstSearch Screen shot. ArticleFirst Boolean Search in an Expert Search Form. FirstSearch® Copyright © 1992–2008 OCLC. Used by permission of OCLC FirstSearch WorldCat Services. All Rights Reserved.

Page 121: EBSCOHost Research Databases screen site. © EBSCO Publishing, Inc. Reprinted with the permission of EBSCO Industries, Inc. All rights reserved.

Figure 9.11: EBSCOHost Research Databases screen site. © EBSCO Publishing, Inc. Reprinted with the permission of EBSCO Industries, Inc. All rights reserved.

Figure 9.13a & b: DMOZ "Open directory project" screenshots. © 1998–2008 Netscape. Used with permission. All Rights Reserved.

Figure 9.15: Grokker Selected Sources screen shot. www.groxis.com. © 2008 Groxis, Inc. Used by permission. All Rights Reserved.

Figure 9.16: LyGO Visual Search Screen shot. Copyright © 2008 Lycos, Inc. Used by permission. All rights reserved.

Figure 9.17: ASK.com Screen site. © 2008 Ask.com. Used by permission of IAC/Search & Media. All rights reserved.

Figure 9.18: Google Advanced Search Screenshot. © 2008 Google.

Figure 9.19: Google Searching with Special Symbols screenshot. © 2008 Google.

Figure 10.1d (right): Reprinted by permission of Randy Paul.

Figure 12.3: EBSCOHost Research Databases Screen sites. © EBSCO Publishing, Inc. Reprinted with the permission of EBSCO Industries, Inc. All rights reserved.

Page 146: Example of bibliography use, from *The Humanities: A Selective Guide to Information Sources* by Ron Blazek and Elizabeth Smith Aversa. Published by Libraries Unlimited.

Figure 12.4: CNN.com. future Summit screenshot. Text excerpt by Matthew Knight, for CNN. © 2008 Cable New Network. Turner Broadcasting News, Inc. All Rights Reserved.

Figure 12.5: Google Notebook screenshot. © Google.

Figure 18.4: "Just give up that car" photo of Wim Wenders, taken by Donata Wenders. Published in the December 2007 issue of *Ode,* page 25. © 2007 Donata Wenders. Used by permission of Donata Wenders.

Figure 18.6: Inc. Magazine. "More great People, Ideas, and businesses . . .", page 127, December 2007. Excerpts from "Exit Strategists of the Year" by Mary and Gary West and "Upstart of the Year" by Stephanie Clifford. Copyright © 2007 Goldhirsh Group. Reprinted by permission of the publisher.

Figure 18.15: Reprinted by permission of the *Indiana Daily Student.*

Page 272: United Nations Office on Drugs and Crime.

Page 313: Jacket design by Susan Mitchell from *The Ten-Cent Plague: The Great Comic-Book Scare and How It Changed America* by David Hajdu. Jacket design copyright © 2008 by Susan Mitchell. Jacket illustration by Charles Burns. Reprinted by permission of Farrar, Straus and Giroux, LLC.

Page 314: Reproduced with the permission of *The Wilson Quarterly.*

Page 315: David H. Richter. Excerpt from "Keeping company in Hollywood: ethical issues in nonfiction film." Published in *Narrative* 15.2 (May 2007): p. 140(27). Copyright © 2007 Ohio State University Press. Used by permission of Ohio State University Press.

Page 316: Nobelprize.org Homepage screen site. Excerpt from "This is Not a Spade: The Poetry of Seamus Heaney" by Ola Larsmo, February 20, 2007. © Nobel Web AB 2008. Used by permission of Nobelprize.org.

Page 319: Manual eradication of coca field in Chapare, Bolivia. United Nations Office on Drugs and Crime.

Page 320: Coca cultivation in the Andean Region, 1990–2006. United Nations Office on Drugs and Crime.

Page 339: Reprinted by permission of HarperCollins Publishers.

Page 340: Reproduced with the permission of *Psychology Today.*

Page 341: EBSCOHost Research Databases Screen site. © EBSCO Publishing, Inc. Reprinted with the permission of EBSCO Industries, Inc. All rights reserved. Text excerpt from "Coaching and positive psychology" by Martin E.P. Seligman. From *Australian Psychologist,* vol. 42 (4), December 2007, pp. 266–267. Published by Taylor & Francis, UK.

Page 342: NCCP: National Center for Children in Poverty Homepage Screen site. Excerpt from "Who are America's Poor Children? The Official Story" by Sarah Fass and Nancy K. Cauthen, November 2007. © Trustees of Columbia University in the City of New York for its National Center for Children in Poverty (NCCP). All Rights Reserved. Used by permission.

Page 369: Book cover, copyright © 2007 from *Kabul Beauty School* by Deborah Rodriguez-Turner. Used by permission of Random House, Inc.

Page 370: Reproduced with the permission of *Fast Company*/Monsueto Ventures.

Page 371: Screen shot of excerpt from "The Future of Global Unions: Is Solidarity Still Forever?" by Alan Howard. Published in *Dissent,* Volume 54, No. 4, pp. 62–70. Fall 2007. Copyright © 2007 Dissent Magazine. Used by permission of the publisher.

Page 393: Courtesy Viking/Penguin Group.

Page 394: Reproduced with the permission of *Scientific American, Inc.*

Page 395: NCBI PUBMED Homepage screen site. Excerpt from "Treating the mother–protecting the unborn: The safety of hypoglycemic drugs in pregnancy" by C. Kileger, E. Pollex, G. Koren. Published in *Journal of Maternity Fetal Neonatal Medicine,* March 21 (3): 191–6, 2008. Motherisk Program, Division of Clinical Pharmacology and Toxicology. © 1999–2000 Hospital for Sick Children/University of Toronto. Used by permission.

Page 397: NRDC Homepage screen site. "Move America Beyond Oil, Let's take the road to a clean, secure energy future." © Natural Resources Defense Council. www.beyondoil.nrdc.org. Used by permission.

Index

Illustrations (continued)
mood and, 226
numerical information in, 234–35, 235 (fig.)
readability and, 218
support for points in draft using, 215
Web site design using, 280, 281
Images. *See also* Illustrations; Visual sources
APA style for blog posting of, 331
checking use of, 254
document design and, 271, 273, 274
integrating into a document, 235–36, 254
Web search sites and directories for, 136–37
Web site design using, 280, 281
Indexes, 144–48
to books, 147, 265
of citations, 114, 115, 148
to government documents, 147–48
to pamphlets, 147
to periodicals, 145–47, 147 (fig.)
skimming for information, 27
Web sites with, 280
Influence of writer, 10
Informal outlines
creating, 198, 198 (fig.)
drafting a document using, 204
Information
checking use of sources and, 254
as common knowledge, 91
document design and locating, 265–66
managing, 4–5, 162–76
organizing. *See* Organizing documents;
Organizing sources; Organizing strategies
potential research questions and, 38, 40 (table)
saving and organizing, 162–69
Web site design highlighting of, 280
Information databases, 113–14. *See also*
Databases
Inquirer role, 36, 253
Inquiry, and potential research questions, 38,
40–41 (table)
Integrating source information, 222–38, 248
aligning an argument with an authority and,
225
attributions and, 229, 231, 237, 238, 248
context for quotations in, 228–29
contrasting ideas or arguments and, 224
definitions in, 226
distinguishing own ideas from source's ideas
and, 237
evidence for an argument and, 225
images, audio, and video and, 235–36
introducing an idea or argument and, 223–24
numerical information and, 234–35
paraphrases and, 223, 231
plagiarism avoidance and, 236–38, 236
purpose and, 223–26
quotations and, 223, 226–31, 232, 236
revising a document and, 253
setting a mood in, 226
sources and, 228, 232, 233
summaries and, 223, 233–34, 236
unattributed sources and, 238

Integrity of an argument, 193–95
Intentional plagiarism, 88–90, 94
Interlibrary loans, 114, 141–42
Internet. *See* Electronic mail; Electronic mailing
lists; Newsgroups; Telnet sources; URLs;
Web *headings*
Interpreter role, 12, 36, 197, 253
Interviews
APA style for, 333, 334
CSE style for, 390
checklist for, 153
Chicago style for, 358–59
collecting information using, 151–53
conducting, 153
deciding what to ask, 152
deciding whether to conduct, 151
deciding whom to interview, 152
discussing a topic with others using, 21
evaluating information from, 75
exploring a topic using, 21
MLA style for, 303, 305, 306
note taking during, 153, 77
planning, 151–52
searching, 103, 106
skimming notes from, 26
In-text citations
APA style for, 325–28
Chicago style for, 355–56
CSE style for, 385
MLA style for, 294
similarities between documentation styles
using, 289, 290 (table)
Introduction
APA style for, 331
Chicago style for, 360
CSE style for, 388
conclusion linked to, 220
drafting, 210–13
examples of, 210, 211–13
framing the issue in, 210–11
map to document in, 216
MLA style for, 299–300
readers' expectations and, 210
research proposal with, 45
revising a document and, 253
skimming for information, 64
strategies for, 211–13
Introductory phrases, 241
Investment in project, 4
Issue
choosing, for a topic, 32, 33 (fig.), 33 (table)
conversations about, in sources, 30–32, 103
framing, in an introduction, 210–11
search plan and focus on, 102–03
Italics
document design using, 267 (fig.), 268 (fig.)
skimming for information using, 28 (fig.)

J

Jacquez, Pete (featured writer), 8
Jargon, 244

Directory of Tutorials, Activities, and Checklists

New Features!

Framing My Argument

Students learn to consider their arguments every step of the way and use evidence skillfully.

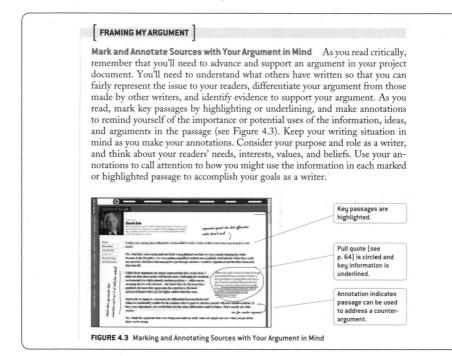

[FRAMING MY ARGUMENT]

Mark and Annotate Sources with Your Argument in Mind   As you read critically, remember that you'll need to advance and support an argument in your project document. You'll need to understand what others have written so that you can fairly represent the issue to your readers, differentiate your argument from those made by other writers, and identify evidence to support your argument. As you read, mark key passages by highlighting or underlining, and make annotations to remind yourself of the importance or potential uses of the information, ideas, and arguments in the passage (see Figure 4.3). Keep your writing situation in mind as you make your annotations. Consider your purpose and role as a writer, and think about your readers' needs, interests, values, and beliefs. Use your annotations to call attention to how you might use the information in each marked or highlighted passage to accomplish your goals as a writer.

Key passages are highlighted.

Pull quote (see p. 64) is circled and key information is underlined.

Annotation indicates passage can be used to address a counter-argument.

FIGURE 4.3 Marking and Annotating Sources with Your Argument in Mind

Information Literacy

This handy sidebar shows how to navigate the complexities of finding, evaluating, and integrating information from print and online sources.

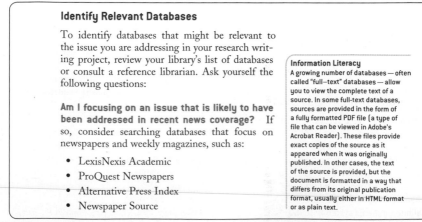

Identify Relevant Databases

To identify databases that might be relevant to the issue you are addressing in your research writing project, review your library's list of databases or consult a reference librarian. Ask yourself the following questions:

Am I focusing on an issue that is likely to have been addressed in recent news coverage?   If so, consider searching databases that focus on newspapers and weekly magazines, such as:

- LexisNexis Academic
- ProQuest Newspapers
- Alternative Press Index
- Newspaper Source

Information Literacy
A growing number of databases — often called "full-text" databases — allow you to view the complete text of a source. In some full-text databases, sources are provided in the form of a fully formatted PDF file (a type of file that can be viewed in Adobe's Acrobat Reader). These files provide exact copies of the source as it appeared when it was originally published. In other cases, the text of the source is provided, but the document is formatted in a way that differs from its original publication format, usually either in HTML format or as plain text.